MANAGING
THE LEARNING
FUNCTION

INFO
LINE

TIPS, TOOLS, AND INTELLIGENCE FOR TRAINERS

AN INFOLINE
COLLECTION

ASTD
PRESS

ASTD Press is an internationally renowned source of insightful and practical information on workplace learning and performance topics, including training basics, evaluation and return-on-investment, instructional systems development, e-learning, leadership, and career development.

Infoline is a real got-a-problem, find-a-solution publication. Concise and practical, *Infoline* is an information lifeline written specifically for trainers and other workplace learning and performance professionals. Whether the subject is a current trend in the field, or tried-and-true training basics, *Infoline* is a complete, reliable trainer's information resource. *Infoline* is available by subscription and single copy purchase.

Ordering information: Books published by ASTD Press, single issues of *Infolines*, and *Infoline* subscriptions can be purchased by visiting our website at store.astd.org or by calling 800.628.2783 or 703.683.8100.

Library of Congress Control Number: 2008927258

ISBN-10: 1-56286-540-4
ISBN-13: 978-1-56286-540-5

ASTD Press Editorial Staff
Deputy Editor: Jennifer K. Mitchell
Senior Associate Editor: Tora Estep
Associate Editor: Justin Brusino
Editorial Assistant: Maureen Soyars
Interior Design and Production: Kathleen Schaner

Printed by Victor Graphics, Inc., Baltimore, Maryland

Managing the Learning Function

An *Infoline* Collection

Editors
Justin Brusino
Jennifer Mitchell

Graphic Production
Kathleen Schaner

Training As a Business Partner

Issue 0307

Training As a Business Partner

AUTHORS

Eric Davis
The Beryl Companies
3600 Harwood Road, Suite A
Bedford TX 76021
Tel: 817.799.3723
Email: ericd_67@yahoo.com

As a 13-year training and development veteran, Eric Davis has held positions at Davis North America, GTE Internetworking, NTT/VERIO, and is currently the Training and Quality Assurance Manager for The Beryl Companies.

Dave McFeely, Ph.D.
The Beryl Companies
3600 Harwood Road, Suite A
Bedford TX 76021
Tel: 817.355.5040, Ext. 4018
Email: dave98@yahoo.com

Dave McFeely has more than 10 years' experience in training, education, and management. He has held positions at The Art Institute of Dallas, Open Medical Systems, NTT/VERIO, and is currently the Senior Training Specialist at The Beryl Companies. McFeely also holds a PhD in Applied Technology, Training and Development from the University of North Texas.

Managing Editor
Mark Morrow

Editor
Tora Estep

Copy Editor
Ann Bruen

Production Design
Kathleen Schaner

Increase Credibility

The recent past has been a difficult time for human resource development professionals. A down economy is cause for concern in any field, but why is training always one of the first areas to be cut? Take a step back and look at your position, your department, and the industry. If you were on the outside looking in, what would you see?

More important, if the chief executive officer or another senior officer in your organization took a walk through your training or human resources development department, what would he or she see? How would management officials describe what you do day to day? If the answer is, "I see them in the training room, but I'm not sure what else they do," or even worse, "I don't know," then you are not a business partner, which is a cause for concern. If you don't think your CEO, division managers, and vice presidents understand what you and your department bring to your organization, then it's time to find ways to make your value known. Companies are reluctant to cut where they perceive value.

Now more than ever, as workplace learning and performance practitioners, you need to increase your sphere of influence and show how training and learning are fundamental to the success of any organization. To do this you need to reposition your department to take on the role of a business partner within the organization.

Practitioners appreciate such a bottom-line approach, but often are resistant to change or unsure how to reposition the training function as a business partner. Risk is another reason to hesitate before taking on the role of business partner. Once you make yourself known in the highest levels of your organization, you are likely to be tied directly to both successes and failures. Staying in the comfort zone of instructional design, delivery, and evaluation is much less risky. Or is it?

The key to increasing your influence is to create a perception of your department as a credible business partner. Credibility is critical for changing your role from reactive to active. Without it, you will always be handed solutions instead of having opportunities to apply your skill and experience to come up with better ones.

To become a business partner, however, you have to develop credibility at the right level. That is what this *Infoline* will help you do by enabling you to evaluate the degree to which your department is a business partner and by providing practical, applicable advice for expanding your sphere of influence. You will learn to build credibility:

- at the classroom level
- at the departmental level
- at the inter-departmental level
- at the executive level.

Note the importance of moving sequentially up through these levels. If you try to move straight to the highest level, bypassing the work you need to do and the relationships you need to build along the way, you run the risk of doing more harm than good. To move on to the next level, you need to be firmly grounded on the level below.

"The path from the training room to the boardroom is not a straight line. It runs through every department"—Eric Davis

To help you move up through the levels, each stage provides a self-assessment tool, two sets of concrete steps to expand and grow your credibility within your organization, and key metrics. To get the most out of this *Infoline,* take the self-assessment at each level. This will give you a good indication of where you are currently.

Steps to help you move forward are broken into two categories: critical transition steps and reinforcing actions. The critical transition step is like a bridge. When you begin it, you are at one stage of credibility; when you complete it, you are at the next highest level. Reinforcing actions further strengthen your credibility at each level. As you engage in these actions, your influence in the organization will grow. And your influence will grow for all the right reasons: You are creating and demonstrating value to the organization while building a broad base of support.

Stage 1 Self-Assessment

Take a moment to assess your current stage. Circle the appropriate response to the following questions. If you answer yes to four or more questions, your department is in Stage 1.

1.	Do you react only to others' requests?	Yes	No
2.	Do your managers feel that training is where you "fix" people?	Yes	No
3.	Is classroom training the only area in which your input is considered?	Yes	No
4.	Are you given solutions, but not presented with the performance issues or goals?	Yes	No
5.	Are you blamed for poor performance because of training?	Yes	No
6.	Are you questioned about what your department does outside of the classroom?	Yes	No
7.	Is classroom training the only solution that you can provide?	Yes	No

The key metrics of each stage focus on the type of reporting you should be doing at each level and the numbers that are important to the people with whom you are seeking to increase your credibility. As you progress through the stages, your reporting metrics should expand to cover your new capacity. This is not to say that you should abandon metrics from preceding stages. Instead, you should continually add new metrics to your expanding foundation.

Stage 1. Classroom Credibility

At this stage, you are credible only within the four walls of your classroom. In the rest of the organization, you are regarded as a necessary evil. The general perception of the work done in the classroom is that it does not really tie into what transpires in the boardroom.

The only people who directly interact with your department while you are engaged in your primary function are class participants. Most managers cannot speak authoritatively about the details of classroom training, so they trust you to run the classes they assign. Once you step outside of the classroom, however, they don't know what you do. To determine if you are in this stage, carry out the self-assessment in the sidebar *Stage 1 Self-Assessment* at left.

Remaining in this reactive state is draining. If you remain in this stage, you risk burnout from too many days in the classroom and the stress of having no control over your workload. The following critical and supplemental steps are designed to help you prepare the groundwork for advancing beyond this stage. Your focus is on expanding your credibility with the managers who request training.

Align With Strategic Goals

The critical transition step in this stage is to align your activities with the strategic goals of your organization. Connect everything you do, every purchase you make, and every class you design and facilitate to your company's strategic goals.

This can be as simple as including on the purchase order the reason for the purchase and what goal it will help the company achieve. What is important is written documentation. This also can be in the form of an email when making the request. When faced with having to create a class, you should ask the requestor, "How does this further the company goals?" The idea of justifying your costs is more about maintaining what you have than increasing your influence. If you cannot cost-justify each activity and each purchase, then you will be understandably nervous when cost cuts are discussed. Be prepared to defend each line item in your budget.

Even if all your training decisions are based on business fundamentals, however, the real world does not go away. You will still have mandated training requests to "fix" a performance problem that you know will not be "fixed" with training, which is why you need to continue to expand your credibility and influence.

Make Your Department Known

To maintain your classroom credibility and make your department known beyond the classroom, you need to increase your department's visibility. Most employees and even upper-level management do not understand what a training department does throughout the day. Building name recognition within the organization is one of the first positive steps you can take to market your training department and its value to the organization. Here are some ways to do that.

1. Ensure that the training department's name conveys the right message. For example, "Widget Learning Center" and "Widget Performance Center" convey very different meanings to your potential customers. Spend some time thinking about what your department does and create a name that reflects that.

2. Ensure that your department's acronym helps your marketing potential. For example, the TYZKQ Center does not sound as good as the PEAK Center. If you have inherited an ill-fitting brand, don't be afraid to change it. You might want to make the change in conjunction with an open house or at the start of a new year. The change is a signal of the great things to come. It's a break with the status quo.

A Word About Corporate "Universities"

Use caution when deciding whether or not to use the term "university" in your departmental name. Depending on the culture and employee backgrounds, it can have negative connotations. Some people might view universities in terms of general education that has little relevance to their current positions.

---

3. Create a logo for your department. Once created, put the logo on the cover of every document you create. Train in logo shirts. Hand out pens with the logo. Do whatever it takes.

4. Create a mission statement that reflects how you support the company's mission. The statement should not be delivered as a mandate.

Instead, get your entire department involved in writing it. Begin by gathering together the company mission statement, values, and strategic goals. Go through your strengths, weaknesses, opportunities, and threats and then use that information as a basis for determining how your department can best support the company's overall mission. Take some time to do this; it does not have to be finished in one day. The process will be more effective if you give these directions to your group in preparation for your meeting.

Once you have determined your mission, follow the same process with the department goals. In many cases, you will have goals set for you, but don't be limited by that. Look at what the company hopes to accomplish and see where your department has the best opportunity to support company goals.

The last step is to tie it together. Create a plaque or sign that lists your mission statement and the goals you hope to accomplish for the coming year. Post the new mission statement in your classrooms.

Key Metrics

Metrics play a part at every stage of the process of increasing departmental credibility. In Stage 1, the metrics of building classroom credibility focus on productivity, the most important of which are:

● number of students trained
● number of days spent in the classroom
● number of classes taught
● reactions as measured in surveys
● occupancy rate of classrooms.

Stage 2. Departmental Credibility

Take the assessment in the sidebar *Stage 2 Self-Assessment* to determine what stage you are in. At the beginning of Stage 2, you are still credible only within the classroom. You are unable to deny a training request, even when you feel that the intervention will not be effective. For example,

Stage 2 Self-Assessment

Take a moment to assess your current stage. Circle the appropriate response to the following questions. If you answer yes to four or more questions, your department is in Stage 2.

1. Do you still consider yourself reactionary?	Yes	No	
2. Is your department still characterized by what happens within the four walls of the classroom?	Yes	No	
3. Are your managers involved in the process of writing training objectives and identifying the observable behaviors that mark the success of the intervention?	Yes	No	
4. Have you given your training requestors some education about the components of a well-written training objective?	Yes	No	
5. Have you introduced the concept of performance evaluation and written up a checklist of observable behaviors?	Yes	No	
6. Will learning retention be measured?	Yes	No	
7. Will the skills required to perform the tasks outlined be observed and signed off by a trainer?	Yes	No	
8. Is the training requestor now invested in the success of the class?	Yes	No	
9. Will the class be screened via pre-test?	Yes	No	

you may receive requests for training that have poor objectives, such as the following:

- "I want them to proactively anticipate our customers' needs."

- "I want them to be more productive."

- "They aren't following the new process; train them again."

These are requests that you may not be able to fulfill. However, an outright refusal to train could be fatal. You are not a stop sign. You are not there to say no. Continually saying no to training requests is as counterproductive and damaging to building credibility as continually saying yes. You want to be a speed bump. The key is to alter the perception and expectations of training.

To expand your credibility, you must take steps to educate your customers about training and what it can and cannot do. In Stage 2, you will draw your managers/training requestors into the classroom to share responsibility for classroom outcomes. The critical transition step is to engage your managers in writing training objectives. You are educating the people who request training as to what is achievable and what is specific, measurable, and realistic. They now begin to have a context for requesting training.

Write Objectives With Managers

Educate your managers as to what a well-written training objective contains. Ensure that each objective ties back to a departmental goal. Agree to how you will measure achievement of the objectives and have the manager sign the agreement. This will help you to eliminate the fluff and focus on measured outcomes.

Training objectives are stated in measurable and observable terminology. Good objectives should always include the performance you expect the learner to achieve, under what conditions, and the level at which the learner should be able to perform. Saying that the learner will be able to "understand how to write a letter" is vague and not measurable. A better way to say this would be: "Given a template, the learner will be able to write a business letter three paragraphs in length with no grammatical errors."

You also should discriminate between performance objectives and training objectives. A performance objective is the change in behavior that you want the learner to exhibit on the job. Because a classroom environment cannot be an exact copy of "real life," a training objective should state what is reasonably expected of the learner after completing the training. For instance, a performance objective might be: "Learners will be able to recall the definitions of medical terms most frequently used in their jobs." On the other hand, a training objective might be: "Given a list of medical terms, the learners will be able to identify the correct definition from a list with 90 percent accuracy." There is a subtle but significant difference between the two objectives. Refer to the references and resources at the end of this *Infoline* for help in learning to write good objectives.

After applying this process to a training intervention, one of two outcomes will occur: The performance issue will be resolved, or it will not. If the intervention is successful, you get to claim some of the credit because you were involved in developing the objectives, which can set a precedent for future classes. However, if the participants don't exhibit the desired behaviors after the training intervention, new possibilities open up. This is where the second piece of education comes in. Get back together with the manager. Explain that skills and knowledge are just two components of performance. Step through the other factors, such as tools, processes, motivation, capability, standards, and measurement. You can now quantify that skills and knowledge are not the issue and can propose an alternative solution by performing a needs analysis. Up to this point, you had no data to support your assertions. Now you do.

Show Your Value

To embed and expand your newfound credibility, try some of the following activities:

■ *Create Your Own Metrics*

Most training departments track the numbers of students they train, how many passed, and data from reaction surveys, but little else. None of these measures will elevate you to the level of business partner. It's up to you to put into place additional metrics that show value. Utilize pre- and post-test outcomes to show knowledge gain. Quantify your

---

How to Handle the Phrase "Train Because I Said So"

Sometimes, even our best efforts fail to convince. When faced with a situation in which you must provide training against your better judgment, follow these steps to help you gain credibility:

1. Set clear, achievable goals.

2. Offer alternatives in writing. If training is ineffective, you have forecasted it and already have your suggestions on record.

---

time spent in and out of the classroom. How many classes did you develop? Process documents? Job aids? Performance checklists?

■ *Map Key Processes*

Often, a manager's perception of how the work gets done is significantly different from the reality. Capturing work-arounds and tacit knowledge will help managers develop a better idea of their territory and increase understanding of the true work function.

■ *Highlight Department's Intellectual Capital*

What does it take to become a trainer? The paths are as varied as the subjects taught. (See the sidebar *Professional Development: The Road to Success.*) Whether you are a former subject matter expert who has learned the profession or someone coming in with a degree in training and development, let everyone know. If you are a subject matter expert, make the number of years of experience with the subject you have known around the organization. Indicate your degree, certification, and experience if you are an old pro.

The important thing is to make sure that the rest of the company recognizes that you have a significant amount of intellectual capital within your department. An effective way to highlight this information is to post staff bios on your company intranet and in the classroom. If your staff has any certifications, you could put them on display as well. Let people around the organization know about your department's extensive skill set—a meeting, hallway conversations, any time is a good time to promote your people.

Professional Development: The Road to Success

As you show the credibility and worth of your department through the steps you have undertaken to become a strategic business partner, it is important not to neglect your own professional development and that of your team. What are you putting into your educational suitcase? As budgets get leaner and the dollars for professional development are harder to come by, some initiatives may be more within reach than others. Here are some ideas to offer professional development.

Articles

Assign different members of your training staff articles from industry publications such as *T+D*. They could prepare a 10-minute presentation to be given at a weekly staff meeting.

Mentoring

Ask a member of your team to help prepare an annual report, be the point person on a project, or help review and write strategic departmental goals. If you are the person who would like a mentor, seek out your boss and ask him or her about the possibility of being mentored.

Training Certification

Gaining certifications in this field is important, not only because of the leverage it can bring to you, but also to build credibility for the professional field of training and development. There are several well-known professional train-the-trainer organizations and certification providers. ASTD also offers professional development certification through its HPI Certificate Program.

Colleges

Depending on your desire and professional aspirations, a graduate degree in training and development might be something to consider. More and more of these programs are springing up across the country and are found under different names such as adult education, career and technology, training and development, and human resources development. Many offer evening courses and online courses, making it more convenient for the busy professional.

Professional Meetings

ASTD has local chapters all over the country. Attending a monthly meeting will allow you to rub shoulders with other professionals in your field. Meetings usually consist of a dinner and a guest speaker, who often talks about the latest and greatest in training. The annual meeting is the crème-de-la-crème of professional development. Nowhere else will you have access to so much intensive, cutting-edge material to absorb and apply in your career.

Books

Some prefer utilizing their discretionary time for professional development. Books are the best portable solution for accomplishing this. But where should you begin? Find out what other people are reading. For starters, go look at what is on your CEO's bookshelf. Also, check the references and resources section at the end of this *Infoline*.

■ *Market Your Department*

The outstanding work of training and development leaders often goes unnoticed by the larger organization. It is necessary to raise the level of consciousness within your organization. Co-workers might understand that you exist and at a high level what you do, but unless they attend a class, they don't know what to expect from you. As a knowledge broker, you need to sell your product. You have already begun to market your department by creating a name and logo.

■ *Celebrate Your Successes*

If no one knows you trained, did it really happen? Celebrate classes in session by taking a group photo and let each participant create a short bio. This is especially effective for new hire training. It's a chance to get to know the newest team members. Celebrate graduations. Invite other managers. Give out certificates and serve cake. It's a nice reward for the attendees and helps to induct them into the company culture while raising the awareness of your activities. Management meetings are another good opportunity to celebrate your successes. Talk about progress toward goals, courses created, analysis, and staff achievements—anything that will give insight to what you do when you are out of the classroom.

■ *Use Your Company's Intranet*

The company intranet can be a great marketing tool, as it helps raise awareness of your department. Create a separate webpage for training. Instead of placing learning documents in various places on the intranet (such as on another department's webpage), make sure that any and all content that you provide to the company is directed through your branded webpage. As owners of the content and the center of learning for the company, your intranet Webpage becomes the knowledge portal for the entire company.

Possible content for your intranet includes:

- course listings
- staff bios
- research links
- library
- job aids
- training request form
- department policies and procedures
- department news
- success stories
- online courses
- classroom schedules.

Key Metrics

At Stage 2, the key metrics to add to your expanding basis include:

- knowledge gain
- passing rate
- average class scores
- success against co-defined objectives
- month-to-month and class-to-class trends.

Stage 3. Inter-Departmental Credibility

To discover what at what stage you are, take the assessment presented in the sidebar *Stage 3 Self-Assessment* at right. In this stage, you have shifted from being reactive to having some control over training content and outcomes. Managers who request training should view you as a credible

---

Stage 3 Self-Assessment

Take a moment to assess your current stage. Circle the appropriate response to the following questions. If you answer yes to four or more questions, your department is in Stage 3.

1.	Are you recognized for more than classroom training?	Yes	No
2.	Have you begun to be considered for non-classroom interventions?	Yes	No
3.	Have you demonstrated your worth and the worth of your department outside of the classroom?	Yes	No
4.	Are you, as a performance consultant, freely engaged to look at tools, processes, incentive programs, and so on to boost productivity and reduce errors?	Yes	No
5.	Are you viewed as a free internal consultant?	Yes	No
6.	Are your opinion and the opinions of your staff valued and sought?	Yes	No

---

department head. These co-workers now understand that you have performance and productivity goals to meet, just as they do. Before, they may not have known how (or if) you were measured. Now they realize that you have finite resources and must prioritize your workload.

By focusing on the knowledge and skill that support department goals, you have altered the perception of your value and utility. You have brought training requestors into the classroom and made them your partners in creating successful outcomes. Your managers have learned something new, and they know how to request training. This stage ends with the opportunity to look into performance issues that traditionally fall outside of training. In Stage 3, you will bring other managers into contact with you through needs analyses and process mapping.

Needs Analysis Planning

Unfortunately, many companies lose time, effort, and funds on unsuccessful needs studies, and all too often their failures can be traced to poor planning. Sound decisions at the beginning guarantee a strong foundation throughout the analysis. Start making wise choices by thinking through the following checklist, which was adapted from *Infoline* No. 8502, "Be a Better Needs Analyst."

☐ Who is being trained? What is their job function? Are they from the same department or a variety of areas in the organization?

☐ What are their deficiencies? Why are they deficient?

☐ What are the objectives of the needs analysis?

☐ How will a needs analysis assist in solving problems and benefit the organization?

☐ What are the expected outcomes? Will they have a pervasive effect on many organizational levels (departmental, divisional, regional, and corporate)?

☐ Will assessment instruments (questionnaires, surveys, tests, and so forth), interviews, or a combination be most appropriate? Who will administer these, in-house personnel or external consultants?

☐ Will the analysis interrupt the work process? What effect will this have on the workforce and productivity?

☐ Will there be a confidentiality policy for handling information? Will the individuals working with the information honor this policy?

Perform a Needs Analysis

By getting the training requestor involved in writing training objectives, you have increased your credibility with the requestor, who is often a line manager or department head. Because the training requestor has agreed on outcomes for the training, and how they are to be measured, he or she cannot place the blame for ongoing performance issues on the training. However, as a performance specialist, you should be prepared to further assist the manager by conducting a needs analysis to identify the other performance factors.

By looking at the process chain under the auspices of process re-engineering, you come into contact with other departments or organizations that either supply the department in question or are recipients of the department in question's work. Use your existing relationship with the training requestor as an entry point into the other departments in the process chain. Let them understand that your focus is to help everyone involved perform better, enabling them to achieve the goals they are being measured against. This procedure widens your sphere of influence, but it does not elevate it on the organization chart. For help in getting started with needs analysis, refer to the sidebar *Needs Analysis Planning* at left.

Extend Influence

Trainers can be change catalysts and are often best positioned to ensure that there is no distortion between the vision and the execution of organizational vision, goals, and strategies. Here are some ways to help you extend both the influence and power of the training function in your organization:

- hold an open house
- focus on performance
- get out of your office
- be a knowledge broker
- create account managers
- volunteer to be a meeting facilitator.

Hold an Open House

If you want to start with a splash, consider holding an open house. Create a course catalog to hand out, talk to management from other departments, and show off your wares. Raise awareness about the types of professional development activities that are available. Explain that the internal training department is the most cost-effective way to approach professional development.

Invite people from all levels of the organization. Be prepared to give them your value statement, for example, "We link learning and performance." Identify your products. They include needs analysis, task analysis, meeting facilitation, classroom training, internal consulting, and so forth. What can you offer line workers in terms of professional development? How can you help them get the promotion they desire?

Focus on Performance

Business partners do more than increase the skill and knowledge of their participants. As a strategic partner, analyze every facet of employee performance. Discover the standard for success in various positions. You want to know how people are measured and what incentives are offered to them. Are you dealing with a training issue, a management issue, a process issue, a tool issue, or an accountability issue? The sidebar *Non-Training Case Study* at right demonstrates how training is not always the answer to performance problems.

Here are some questions to start asking as a performance consultant.

1. What does success look like? Clearly defined, achievable objectives have to be the basis of every training initiative.

2. If you held a gun to their head, could they do the job? If the answer is yes, then this is not about skills and knowledge; there is a larger issue involved. Your next task is to find out what is causing a lack of motivation or find out if anything is available to them in training that is not available in their work environment.

3. Have they ever been able to do it? If the answer is no, then perhaps the standard is too high.

4. Do the systems and tools support the tasks? As Geary Rummler mentioned in a recent *T+D* article, "If you pit a good performer against a bad system, the system wins every time."

5. Does this require classroom training? Can the goal be accomplished by a job aid, computer-based training, a change in process, and so on?

What is important about this process is that at no time are you saying yes or no. A decision is impossible until you get a better understanding of the situation.

Non-Training Case Study

Don't just throw training stones at performance monsters. Not all performance issues in a company require training as the solution. Being a strategic business partner means educating your managers on what is needed to solve a performance problem. Many performance issues can be corrected without spending one minute in the classroom.

For instance, one technology company had several different billing computer systems that were a result of acquisitions and mergers. A billing research department manager was requesting "refresher training" on one of the billing systems because few people in his department were actually working with a particular system.

Before agreeing to providing the training, the training department suggested doing some research into the matter to see where the knowledge or skill gaps were so that training could designed to address those gaps. After talking with a couple of billing agents, however, it became clear that it wasn't a knowledge or skill gap that was causing the problem. In fact, the issue turned out to be that this particular billing system was a lot more complex than the other systems. Subsequently, it took longer for billing tickets related to this system to be worked than tickets related to the other systems.

Furthermore, built into the billing department employees' daily expectations was the requirement to finish a certain *number* of tickets each day. Once they had met their quota, they had some free time. At the same time, the employees had the ability to select any ticket they wanted. Guess which tickets the employees were not selecting? You guessed it—the most difficult ones to do.

Thus it wouldn't have mattered how many hours billing department employees spent in the classroom learning, reviewing, and applying knowledge on this system. They would never have transferred it back to their job. The training department recommended that the manager assign daily tickets. After this change was implemented, this performance gap was eliminated without the need for training. Why didn't the manager see it? That is difficult to tell, but if you do not approach every training request from the standpoint of an internal consultant, then you will likely be spending time in the classroom on efforts that are not worthwhile, which diminishes your credibility as a problem solver.

Get Out of Your Office

To get involved with other departments, it is imperative to study them while they are on the job instead of during an interview. You will have better information if you can see how a department works firsthand. Let them see you when they are working on their problems.

It's all too easy to get into the routine of train-evaluate-update-train. It is vital to be visible in the organization. Walk the floor, attend departmental meetings, and follow up with colleagues after meetings. Find out what is happening in other departments. This can be a great source of leads, but you won't find it in your office. Never underestimate management by walking around.

Be a Knowledge Broker

As trainers, you are the systems thinkers because you understand how all departments interact. If you don't know, you know where to find out. By capturing knowledge, you are in a position to improve efficiency. You should be the single source for training. Any request should be filtered through training before a department turns to the outside. When requests can be filled within the department, you add a direct cost savings to your ROI. If the best solution lies outside the company, you can make the arrangements. This also helps to achieve buying power when you speak for the company.

More and more is being written about capturing, archiving, and transferring the tacit knowledge collectively gained by employees. One inexpensive way to implement this is to set up a threaded discussion board to be used by co-workers at all levels in the organization. It can be a great source of information about improving efficiency within work teams or departments and can be invaluable in helping you identify potential knowledge or skill gaps that need to be addressed through training.

Many mini-training sessions happen right under your nose that you may not be aware of; for example, when a new product is introduced to the sales department, a new application is installed, or a business process is re-engineered. Even if you are not responsible for providing training, a knowledge broker is aware of their existence and what impact that might have on another part of the organization.

Create Account Managers

Establishing an account manager program will improve both your information gathering and systems view. Assign members of your department to your primary training audience. The departments who generate the most training requests will benefit from increased representation from training. The training account manager can sit in on staff meetings and represent your department.

These account managers then come back to you to discuss issues, concerns, and changes. This is a key information-sharing session. Often, changes made to policy or procedure in one department have a ripple effect throughout an organization. By catching these changes early, the training department can then forewarn other department managers who will be affected by the change. Often, trainers' counsel as to the repercussions for the proposed change can forestall an ill-advised change.

Volunteer to Be a Meeting Facilitator

Facilitating meetings is a great way to get involved with other departments. Facilitating critical or contentious meetings is a way to expand your reach within your organization. Often during these meetings, having an impartial third party act as moderator will help increase the likelihood of a successful outcome. Allowing other departments to see you in this new capacity will enhance your credibility outside of the classroom.

Another way to get involved is to act as a meeting scribe. The advantage is twofold. First, you gain access to the information generated. This allows you to see how decisions are made and other critical factors. Second, by summarizing information and distributing the results, you have an opening to discuss the meeting with each meeting member and ask questions about the content.

Key Metrics

Your success in this stage is tied to the job performance of your training participants and your ability to help your "training partners" achieve their goals. Note that in enabling other departments to reach their goals, you may need to work in concert with quality assurance.

Training ensures that workers have the skills and knowledge needed to be successful in their jobs, while quality assurance monitors job performance and identifies knowledge gaps. The functional areas can lead to disagreements between the two departments. To create and maintain a healthy relationship: 1) attend calibration meetings between quality assurance and supervisors to identify knowledge gaps or performance issues; and 2) work in concert with quality assurance to avoid morale issues and reduced effectiveness.

What you choose to measure is important. You can't take credit for the entire department, nor should you set yourself up to take the blame if you fall short. Focus on those performance metrics that support the goals you can most directly affect, such as reduced cycle time, reduced scrap, increased productivity, increased sales, reduced re-work, increased customer satisfaction, and reduced customer churn.

After performing outcome-based actions such as those presented in this stage, you will gain credibility as a performance consultant across the organization. Through the needs analysis and supporting actions, you have moved out of a reactionary role into a proactive one. Managers are now aware of alternatives to classroom training. With a respect for your abilities, managers are more open to non-classroom interventions.

Stage 4. Executive Credibility

Stage 4 is characterized by a deepening of your credibility. You now move up the organizational chart to the executive level. Credibility at this level is tied to your ability to affect strategic goals and demonstrate your value to the company as a whole. To determine where you are in your pursuit of becoming a strategic business partner with your organization, take the assessment presented in the sidebar *Stage 4 Self-Assessment* at right.

Stage 4 Self-Assessment

Take a moment to assess your current stage. Circle the appropriate response to the following questions. If you answer yes to four or more questions, your department is in Stage 4.

1.	Do executives recognize that you are trying to achieve the company's migration to their vision?	Yes	No
2.	Are you viewed as a change catalyst?	Yes	No
3.	Do you have the most accurate map of the organization?	Yes	No
4.	Are you brought in during the initial phase of projects?	Yes	No
5.	Are you asked to attend meetings just for your input?	Yes	No
6.	Do you speak to prospective clients as part of the sales process?	Yes	No
7.	Are you asked to present your annual report to other departments?	Yes	No
8.	Do people bring you problems instead of solutions?	Yes	No
9.	Do you have a defined product to sell to external clients?	Yes	No
10.	Do you generate revenue?	Yes	No
11.	Are you asked to facilitate meetings over contested issues?	Yes	No
12.	Are you unaffected by budget cutting?	Yes	No
13.	Are you brought in to help resolve non-training performance issues?	Yes	No
14.	Are you brought in to a project in lieu of an external consultant?	Yes	No

Prepare an Annual Report

The critical transition step at this stage is to prepare an annual report that documents departmental ROI. This document is the culmination of your efforts and where you state your case as a strategic partner. For suggestions on what to include in your annual report, see the Job Aid.

Maintain Your Position

Once you have achieved the status of a strategic partner, you need to focus on maintaining your position and establishing a reinforcing cycle. Some activities that could help you do this include:

- becoming an internal consultant

- making training a product

- using training as an employee benefit and retention tool.

Become an Internal Consultant

As you have progressed through the first stages, hopefully your counterparts in other departments have come to see you in a new light. Now is the time to capitalize on this change in attitude. As budgets shrink, the ability to go outside the organization to hire consulting expertise wanes. As a performance consultant, and one with a systems view of the company, you are available for identifying and eliminating performance barriers. Managers understand that they need to qualify and quantify what they want to accomplish before they come to you. They know they won't be rejected outright, because you are not there to be a stop sign. They have your attention when it comes to changing people's behavior.

You begin this process as a natural extension of your visibility. Casual water cooler conversations are a good opportunity to offer insight into performance issues. At first, you may have to reassure your counterpart that just talking through the issue can help in problem identification. Ask questions. Clarify to get a full understanding. Bring in similar issues that you may be aware of in other departments. This is where good listening skills are critical. Don't jump to solve the problem. Continue to peel away layers until you can present the issue yourself. Remember your training and performance perspective can cast a new light on the issue.

Find out what keeps department heads up at night. There is no better way to determine what the major issues are for your counterparts than to ask. Many issues are common to a number of departments. For example, recruitment and retention are always a concern for human resources.

Training As a Product

Re-evaluate how you view training. You have shown what the tools of the training professional can do for the organization. You can apply the same industry standard processes as other organizations. Create a training product. Find a way to get in front of the paying client. This elevates the role of training, placing it right alongside other company products. Training can be used as a product differentiator, an addition to the value proposition.

When training is a product, it also can be used as negotiating leverage. Even if you end up throwing the training in for free, there is a perceived value. If you throw in training instead of lowering another product's price, you save the company money. You now generate revenue, instead of just being a cost center.

Make Training an Employee Benefit

With companies scaling back financial incentives more and more, one way to attract and keep quality employees is to include training and development as part of the employee benefit package. Having a training benefit package says that the company values people so much that it is willing to invest time and resources to make them even better employees. A few years back, ASTD's *T+D* magazine ran a series of articles on free agent learners called "It's a Free Agent World." These individuals seek out learning opportunities on their own in order to stay competitive in their careers. Companies run the risk of losing such employees to competition if they train them, but they also run the risk of losing them if they do not train them. Free agent learners are more likely to be loyal to a company if they feel that they are being enriched through various development and training programs. The sidebar *Recruiting and Retention* at right discusses some ways to make training more valuable as a recruiting and retention tool.

Key Metrics

The key metric for this stage is departmental ROI. By moving into the role of strategic business partner, you not only solidify your value to your organization, you also adopt a position that is much more challenging, rewarding, and exciting. You are able to grow as a professional, learning new skills and honing existing ones. Just as you have educated your managers on training, you have now learned more about their roles. Most important, you have developed a track record of success that any employer would desire.

Recruiting and Retention

So you understand the need and value of using training as a recruiting and retention tool. But what does that look like? Here are some suggestions to help make it happen.

1. Make training a selling point in job advertisements. Describe it as a benefit, along with health insurance and other traditional benefits.

2. Utilize a learning management system and employee bulletin boards to highlight employee successes such as courses taken, certifications obtained, e-learning classes completed, and degrees earned.

3. Show off training right up front with potential employees on a tour. Show them the classrooms, the bulletin boards, the learning management system, anything that says that your company cares about their development.

4. If you don't have one already, develop a succession plan for all employees. Highlight the classes needed or other learning that has to take place before being considered for a promotion. This not only will allow you to identify qualified candidates for open positions, it also will allow you to know what to look for if you need to go outside the company to fill them.

5. Keep a library of relevant books and materials available for employees to check out. Many people prefer to read at home or are more comfortable utilizing a textbook in addition to e-learning initiatives.

6. Get feedback from line-level employees through surveys and informal interviews as to what training they would like to have offered by way of professional development.

7. Cross-train employees on other jobs. The benefits of this are two-fold. First, it will allow that person to gain new skills and knowledge. Second, it will make that person better at the job they currently do because they will be able to see how their job fits into the larger system of the organization.

References & Resources

Articles

"The Business of Training: How Halliburton's 'I-Learn' Strategy Links to Its Business Mission." *IOMA's Report on Managing Training & Development,* February 2002, pp. 1, 7, 10.

"Cost Control: Exclusive IOMA Study Reveals the 5 Best Ways to Control Training Costs." *IOMA's Report on Managing Training & Development,* February 2002, pp. 1, 11, 13.

Eugenio, V. "Implementing Learning Technologies: Start with a Strategic Plan." *Corporate University Review,* March/April 1998, pp. 33-39.

Gay, D.L., and T.J. LaBonte. "Demystifying Performance: A Roadmap." *T+D Magazine,* May 2003, pp. 64-75.

Rummler, G. "What Lies Ahead." *T+D Magazine,* January 2003, pp. 32-43.

Short, D., and R. Opengart. "It's a Free Agent World." *T+D Magazine,* September 2000, pp. 60-66.

"Training Strategy: 7 Steps to Turn Your Department into a 'Business Training Unit.'" *IOMA's Report on Managing Training & Development,* March 2002, pp. 1, 12-14.

Willmore, J. "How to Give "Em Performance When They Insist on Training." *T+D Magazine,* May 2002, pp. 54-59.

Books

Barksdale, S., and T. Lund. *Rapid Strategic Planning.* Alexandria, VA: ASTD, 2002.

Mager, R. *Preparing Instructional Objectives: A Critical Tool in the Development of Effective Instruction.* Atlanta: The Center for Effective Performance, 1997.

Mager, R., and P. Pipe. *Analyzing Performance Problems: Or You Really Oughta Wanna.* 3rd Edition. Atlanta: The Center for Effective Performance, 1997.

Robinson, D., and J. Robinson. *Performance Consulting: Moving Beyond Training.* San Francisco: Berrett-Koehler, 1996.

Infolines

Larsen, N.G. "Implementing Strategic Learning." No. 0210.

Sharpe, C., ed. "Be a Better Needs Analyst." No. 8502.

Spitzer, D. "Link Training to Your Bottom Line." No. 0201.

Web Resources

International Society for Performance Improvement. Available at http://www.ispi.org.

Langevin Learning Services. Available at http://207.107.10.214.

Annual Report Template

Below are suggestions for the layout and content for writing an annual report.

Content

☐ Table of Contents

☐ Executive Summary

- This is your three-minute elevator pitch. It should contain the information most relevant to your executive team; ROI, cost savings, and strategic initiatives affected are all good examples.

- The goal is to have your executives want to read the rest of the report after reading the summary.

☐ Customer Base

- What groups did you provide work for? Be sure to list not only classroom interventions, but also any internal consulting, meeting facilitation, or analysis work.

- The goal is to show how broad your impact is on the organization.

☐ Classroom Utilization

- Break this down by classroom. Be sure to count not only the number of days used for training, but also any time you have an event. For example, include meetings, video- or teleconferences, and so on.

- The goal is to show that you are using what you have. This is the first step for justifying additional resources.

☐ Website and Learning Management System (LMS)

- Report on number of participants registered, hits by month, and trends in usage.

- The goal is to show this as a tool that you use. Both an LMS and a website require funding. Showing that these tools are used throughout the organization will aid you in justifying their continued or expanded cost.

☐ Instructor Utilization

- The goal is to show utilization of people. Include days in the classroom (note 120 days/year is an average benchmark for preventing burnout), days of instructional design, days of class prep, and days of meeting facilitation or internal consulting.

☐ Training Metrics

- Level 1: Reaction sheets. It is helpful to break the questions into sub-categories if you don't already do this. For example, include instructor, materials, test or simulations, environment, and so on. Make sure you have a goal and indicate by what percentage you exceeded it or came up short.

- Level 2: Test averages, performance checklists, and pre- and post-test knowledge gain are good methods for showing the increase in knowledge. Be sure to indicate any standard. For example, the score for passing might be 85 percent minimum.

- Level 3: Look where you can have an impact: Reduced cycle time, reduced scrap, reduced error rate, increased customer satisfaction, and quality assurance scores are all good places to start. Ask yourself, "How will this intervention affect the employee in their position?"

- Level 4: Try looking at ROI from the departmental level instead of the individual course level. Ask yourself, "What is the cost to the organization if the training department is not in place?" In terms of cost savings vs. cost avoidance, take the course that was developed internally and compare that to the cost of bringing in a consultant. In terms of revenue, if you were able to provide services for external recipients, that revenue can be used to offset your budget impact. If training is included in a sale, determine what the perceived value is and include that as an offset to your budget.

(continued on next page)

Job Aid

☐ Financial Summary

- This is generally a table showing the various components of your cost savings, revenue, and cost avoidance measures. This is where the bottom line ROI figure will reside.

- The goal is to summarize all of your financial information onto one page.

☐ Last Year's Milestones

- Major accomplishments, goals completed, and major changes should all be included.

☐ Next Year's Goals

- These goals should all tie into strategic goals.

- The goal of this section is to demonstrate to the executives how you will help their strategic vision come about.

Style and Format

☐ This is not a time to be stingy.

☐ Use color throughout the document.

☐ Coil bind the report.

☐ Use a clear cover and a vinyl back.

☐ Use heavy paper. You don't want the pages to be translucent.

☐ Pull quotes:

- Take the most provocative numbers and add them as a pull quote to the bottom of each page. For example, cite ROI, number of students trained, knowledge gain, and so on. Another good source of pull quotes can come from your reaction surveys. Think of it as a product testimonial.

☐ Use white space and graphs:

- Leave plenty of white space in your document. Use charts and graphs to quickly visualize data. Be sure to add the underlying data.

☐ Analyze your findings:

- At the bottom of each page of data, leave enough room for a short paragraph of analysis. This is where you want to emphasize particular numbers or trends.

Developing and Administering Training: A Practical Approach

Issue 9201

Developing and Administering Training: A Practical Approach

AUTHOR:

Karen Overfield, EdD
Education Management
    Corporation
300 6th Avenue, Suite 800
Pittsburgh, PA 15222-2598
Tel.: 412.562.0900

As assistant vice president, faculty development, Karen Overfield works with The Art Institutes International, the National Center for Professional Training, and New York Restaurant School. In her role, she creates and provides support opportunities to ensure quality faculty performance.

Editorial Staff for 9201

Editor
Barbara Darraugh

ASTD Internal Consultant
Catherine Fisk

Revised 1997

Editor
Cat Sharpe

Designer
Steven M. Blackwood

Copy Editor
Leanne Eline

Program Life Cycles: Tinker, Tailor...

Training programs, like other products, have life cycles. They are designed to teach a specific skill or knowledge that a needs analysis has determined is both necessary and missing from the workforce. The needs analyst turns his or her findings over to an instructional designer to design and develop an appropriate training intervention. A practitioner then conducts the course and collects and analyzes results of the intervention.

You may recognize the instructional systems development model in the above paragraph: analyze, design, develop, implement, and evaluate. The model, however, doesn't speak to ongoing, cyclical programs and what activities occur in those programs as they adapt to changing business needs: These programs are repeated—often with "tinkering and tailoring"—to address business needs. Ask yourself the following questions to determine whether your training programs require constant "tinkering" to update content:

● What are the administrative details?

● How do day-to-day operating procedures fit in?

● When do you schedule people for classes, pay invoices, and order supplies?

● Who conducts program maintenance, handles recommendations, and makes necessary revisions to the program to tailor it to a particular audience or update its content?

The classic instructional systems development (ISD) model does not directly address these issues, most of which involve implementation and maintenance. For an ongoing program, the implementation stage of the training program may well take a number of years to complete. A single question raised by a trainee during a class may "throw" the program from "implementation" into "design," which may call into question "evaluation" or "analysis." In other words, practitioners may find themselves repeating or skipping some steps in the ISD model; later having to backtrack to pick up a particular step. They "loop" through the model, instead of traversing a strict, straight-ahead path through it.

As practitioners "loop" through the model, they play many different roles. It is important to remember that roles are not job titles; they are functional groupings of outputs. A job title may match a role title, but often a job encompasses more than one role. For example, an individual with the title "program designer" may perform both the role of "program designer" and that of a "program materials developer." Roles played in the various ISD process steps are discussed at the end of each section.

This *Infoline* will discuss one approach that allows for such "looping," emphasizing program administration and its effect on a program's life cycle. Recognizing the potential for confusion, we will refer to the roles being carried out, while acknowledging that these different roles may be performed by the same individual.

Program Development Process

Program development represents a synergistic process. In other words, the sum is equal to more than the parts—it consists of a system made up of several subsystems. The ISD model identifies the following phases for program development:

1. Research and analysis.

2. Design.

3. Development.

4. Implementation.

5. Monitoring and evaluation.

Additionally, practitioners need to deal with ongoing program administration, maintenance, and revision. These administrative activities are time consuming, often cause the biggest headaches, and are absolutely necessary for successful ongoing programs.

When should practitioners handle the administrative functions and details? Where do the day-to-day operating procedures fit in? When should practitioners schedule people for classes, pay invoices, or order supplies? Administration and monitoring activities, such as site selection, attendance record keeping, and bill paying, continue throughout the life of the program. They do not end with implementation. In fact, they really only begin with implementation.

The role of an instructional designer is to establish systems for ongoing program evaluation. But, what about program maintenance? Revisions, updates, modifications, and enhancements represent reality.

In some situations, a "begin at the beginning and work to the end" approach is not practical. The designer needs a way to jump in at the middle and work both ways. Practitioners need methods by which they can work on two or more phases of the project simultaneously, and they also need the means to cut revision and maintenance time. See the Circular Design box at left for a visual depiction of the circuitous route revisions often take.

Systems Defined

The instructional systems development approach involves five basic systems. Each includes inputs, processes, and outcomes. Ongoing program practitioners often find themselves involved in appended and mutated systems. Needs analysis becomes research, design and development blend together, and evaluation becomes monitoring. Analysis is involved in each system. Administration is needed for ongoing programs.

These elements compose the systems model and the model relates to process as opposed to function. Inputs represent conditions that exist before the developers start to work. During the process, developers complete activities to effect the desired outcomes. Developers pick and choose which activities to do and how much time to spend working on each system. Each system affects the others and the program as a whole.

The following provides an explanation of the processes and roles in each system.

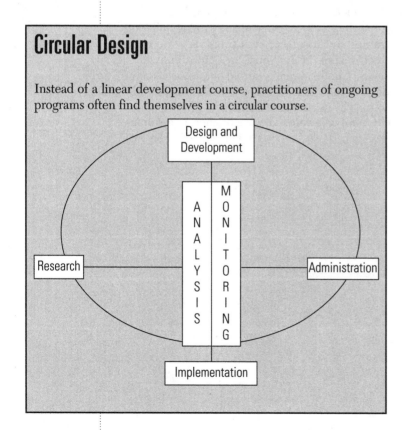

Circular Design

Instead of a linear development course, practitioners of ongoing programs often find themselves in a circular course.

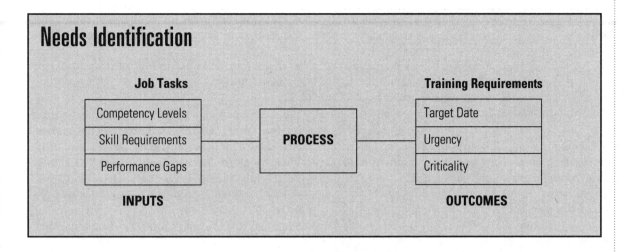

Research

During this phase, the practitioners—wearing their "researcher" hats—gather information about resources and about optimal and actual performance and audiences. They identify tasks, skills, and competency levels needed for the job. Then they carefully define whether a training problem exists before going for a training solution.

Needs identification. During this step in the research phase, researchers collect and analyze information on job tasks, competency or skill levels, performance gaps, and the employees who are actually doing the work. From this information, researchers can determine the training requirements, target audience, target date, and criticality of the training intervention.

Practitioners can use this formula to identify training requirements:

Required Skills – Current Skills = Training Requirements

The box above illustrates this process.

The researcher's role. During this phase, practitioners act as researchers. In this role, they identify, develop, or test new information and translate it into possible improvements in individual and organizational performance. Researchers produce the following:

- research designs and instruments
- findings, conclusions, and recommendations
- data on current and future needs.

Analysis

Analysis is a central activity that takes place after all the material is collected. The analysis step takes the requirements identified in each system and incorporates options for the intervention and other criteria. Outputs of this step include the following:

- deliverables
- measurables
- service levels.

The "Analysis" box illustrates the this process.

The analyst's role. The practitioner, in assuming the role of analyst, makes judgment calls. The analyst relies on problem-solving skills to process data and identify outcomes. This takes place in conjunction with each step of the life cycle—it is not an isolated step, but rather, central and integrated with the program. The outputs of needs a analysts include the following:

- analyses of individual or group behavior

- measurement tools for individual, group, or organizational performance gaps

Research Tools

One of the best sources of information during the needs analysis phase is the individual currently working in the position. This particular person (it could even be more than one person) knows what the job entails, the skills needed, and the competency levels required. If the practitioners are not involved in the needs analysis, trainers may face two often insurmountable hurdles—training will not meet the requirements, and the program will be delivered to "prisoners" instead of willing participants.

Among the tools trainers use to gather information and involve the participants are the following:

Task analysis. This process is performed to identify the tasks associated with a job function. The objective is to identify skills needed, knowledge required, difficulty, frequency of use, and criticality associated with each of the tasks.

Needs analysis. This process identifies the areas, topics, and skills in which people need training. Techniques used to identify requirements include questionnaires, one-on-one or group interviews, and observation.

Self-assessment. This is the process in which individuals compare their skills with standards established for the job. The purpose is to identify performance gaps.

Feedback from performance appraisals. This includes information from the dialogue that takes place between employee and supervisor during a performance appraisal. Feedback identifies areas in which the employee needs improvement. Information is obtained from the supervisor, employee, or personnel representative.

Feedback from review of performance objectives. This comprises information obtained from discussions between supervisor and employee as relates to the completed or future objectives. Information identifies areas in which objectives were not met and specific skill gaps. This material can identify future objectives that require new skills or may identify new areas for development.

Management discussion. This includes information on the planned implementation of new procedures, systems, or programs; or the acquisition of new equipment. For the latter, training is required for the entire work group.

- recommendations for changes in individual, group, or organizational performance

- definitions and descriptions of desired performance levels.

For more information on research and analysis, see *Infolines* No. 8502, "Be a Better Needs Analyst"; No. 8503, "Be a Better Task Analyst"; No. 8612, "Surveys From Start to Finish"; No. 8903, "Be a Better Job Analyst"; No. 9008, "How to Collect Data"; No. 9408, "Strategic Needs Analysis"; No. 9401, "Needs Assessment by Focus Group"; and No. 9411, "Conducting a Mini Needs Assessment."

Design and Development

The design and development phases are overlapping rather than isolated stages. As program designers, practitioners identify what the course will cover and how to best present information. Training needs identified in the research phase become the training events and curricula, and training objectives are transformed into instructional materials.

During this phase, the design and development practitioners, wearing their "program developer" hats, face many decisions; some involve taking risks. During this phase, developers use their creativity.

Following are some of the questions practitioners should ask themselves:

- Should I develop a program or purchase one off the shelf?

- Should I use on-the-job training (OJT) or conduct a formal event?

- What are the costs, benefits, and value added?

- How can I make the program cost-effective?

- What techniques can I apply to increase retention, shorten the learning curve, and make learning a pleasure, not a drudgery?

The program design and development phase occurs as depicted in the Design and Development box on the next page.

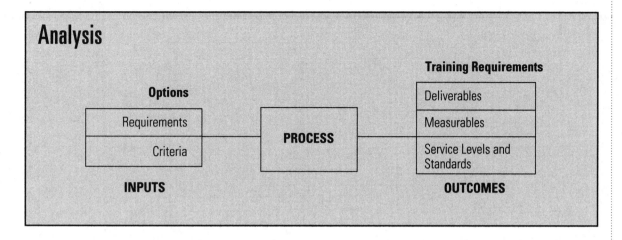

This phase has three inputs:

■ *Participants*

Research on human behavior and learning indicates that people may have different learning styles, learning curves, abilities, levels of retention, and frames of reference. These affect program design and development.

■ *Resources*

Time, money, and other resources play important parts in the decision to buy or build. Should the developer design a program, buy one off the shelf, or do a little of both?

■ *Training Requirements*

In addition to the best learning transfer approach and the resources committed to the design and development of a program. The nature of the skills to be taught will impose requirements on the training program. The method used to teach a course in time management, for example, may be very different from that used to teach a course in machine maintenance.

Outcomes from the program design and development phase include course materials, training objectives, delivery media, budget, and logistical requirements.

The designer's and developer's role. Course or program designers prepare objectives, define content, and select and sequence program activities. Designer outputs include program objectives and program designs.

Course developers, on the other hand, produce course materials, such as:

- graphics
- audio and visual materials
- job aids
- instructor guides
- participant manuals.

For more information on design and development, see *Infolines* No. 9707, "High Performance Training Manuals"; No. 8905, "Course Design and

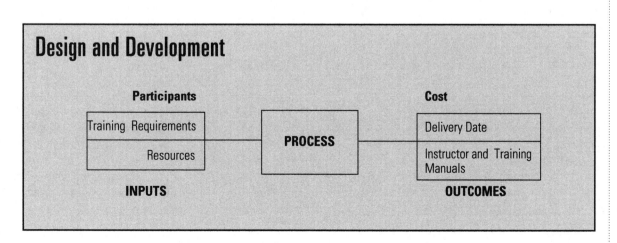

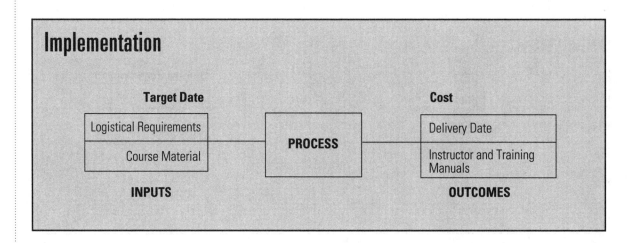

Implementation

	Target Date			Cost	
	Logistical Requirements		**PROCESS**	Delivery Date	
	Course Material			Instructor and Training Manuals	
	INPUTS			**OUTCOMES**	

Development"; No. 8906, "Lesson Design and Development"; No. 9706, "Basics of Instructional Systems Development"; No. 9104, "Using Mapping for Course Development"; and No. 9711, "Create Effective Job Aids."

Implementation

During the program implementation phase of a classroom training program, practitioners manage and teach the course. The phrase encompasses several distinct steps. Although the course material is ready and the logistical requirements are set, there's much for a trainer to do before beginning the actual class. Program implementation includes program management and teaching.

The instructor's role. During the implementation of a stand-up training program, practitioners function in the following capacities:

- present course materials
- facilitate discussions and media use
- provide individual and group feedback
- oversee testing.

Administration

Administration involves delivery of individual events; day-to-day, ongoing working procedures for the program; and maintenance of statistics related to program standards, guidelines, deliverables, and measurements. Inputs to this step include costs, delivery dates, participants, delivery guidelines or leader manuals, and locations. Outputs include course roster and schedule, invoices

Alternatives to Training

Developers need to determine in the analysis stage whether training is the right solution to the performance problem. If the performance problem cannot be solved with training, the designer should explore other options. Training professionals should use training as a solution only when observable skill gaps exist in performance.

One way to identify a skill gap is to ask the question, "If the person's life depended on it, could he or she perform the task?" If the answer is yes, it's not a training problem.

If training is not the solution, the training professional can suggest the following types of solutions:

- develop job aids

- redesign the task

- change the procedures

- automate the task

- designate a coach

- assign someone else to do the task

- don't do the task.

Administration

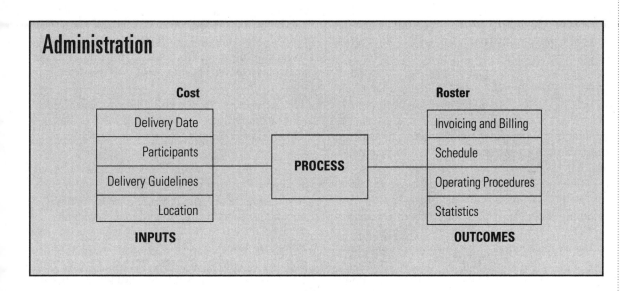

Cost

| Delivery Date |
| Participants |
| Delivery Guidelines |
| Location |

INPUTS

PROCESS

Roster

| Invoicing and Billing |
| Schedule |
| Operating Procedures |
| Statistics |

OUTCOMES

Media Comparison

During the design phase, trainers consider which delivery medium will best serve their training program. The delivery media that developers select directly affects the design of their programs. This chart compares some of the costs associated with various decisions made during the design and development phase.

Delivery Medium	Development Costs	Delivery Costs	Costs
Multimedia	Medium	Low	Low
Instructor-led	Low	High	High
Mainframe CBT	High	Low	Medium
PC-based CBT	Medium	Low	Medium
PC-based IBT	Low	Low	Low
CD-ROM	High	Medium	Medium
Self-paced manuals	Medium	Low	Medium
Web-based	Low	Low	Low

and billing, operating procedures, and statistics. The box on Administration (page 27) illustrates this process.

Operating procedures include guidelines on when to notify people of training, how to enroll people in courses, who to bill, who to designate to handle payments, and so forth. These activities eat up time, require attention to many details, demand accuracy, constitute routine tasks, and tend to be repetitive. If someone does not pay close attention to them, however, the program won't run smoothly. They also represent targets to automate.

In the administration phase, practitioners look for ways to work smarter. They should look for ways to streamline administrative procedures as much as possible. They should eliminate duplicate effort and rework. They need to make sure they know the purpose behind what they do: if they don't, they should not do it. They need to make sure they do not do things just because things have always been done that particular way in the past.

One effective technique for this phase requires working backwards. First, come up with a mental picture of what a successful program will look like. Then brainstorm about the details that will need to be accomplished to create that successful program. Group the items into categories or key areas, and sort all the details into a logical sequence to be followed.

After doing this, it is helpful to pull out a calendar and set target dates to complete each item on the list. To help coordinate everything, make a checklist that identifies the activity, who is responsible for it, target completion date, actual completion date, and any comments related to the activity. This checklist becomes your memory for the project. You can depend on the checklist to make sure things get done, and accomplished on time. This especially helps if you need to enlist several other people to help you.

The next time you deliver the program, simply pull out the checklist. It saves a lot of time and "reinventing the wheel." The checklist provides documentation on the program: It gives a working "to-do" list, audit trail, and reminder of problem areas.

All that you need to do is to change the dates. See the "Administrative Worksheet" on page 33 to give you a starting point from which to work. You can customize this checklist to meet your needs.

The administrator's role. During the implementation process, practitioners act as course administrators. In this role, they do the following:

- select and schedule facilities and equipment
- keep records on programs and trainees
- offer logistical support and service to trainees
- render program support and management.

For more information on program implementation, see *Infoline*s No. 8410, "How to Prepare and Use Effective Visual Aids"; No. 8611, "Be a Better Writer"; No. 8606, "Make Every Presentation a Winner"; No. 8808, "Basic Training for Trainers"; No. 9102, "How to Make a Large Group Presentation"; No. 9409, "Improve Your Communication and Speaking Skills"; and No. 9411, "Theater-Based Training."

Monitoring and Evaluation

The program monitoring phase is a continual process. When done in conjunction with the design and development phase, it denotes formative evaluation. When done in conjunction with the implementation subsystem, it exemplifies summary evaluation. The box on the next page illustrates this phase.

During this phase, developers collect, compile, and correlate the statistics that relate to program standards or service levels, deliverables, and measurements. These statistics are vital because they provide the means to measure the success of the program. Outcomes of the monitoring and evaluation process include the following:

- reports
- revisions
- measurements.

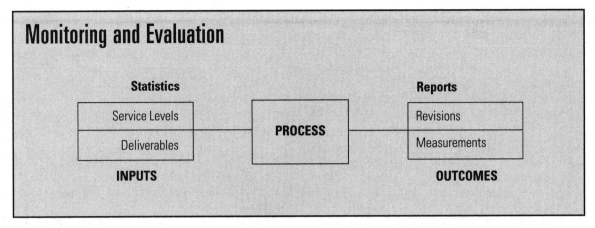

Monitoring and Evaluation

Statistics

Service Levels
Deliverables

PROCESS

Reports

Revisions
Measurements

INPUTS

OUTCOMES

Developers should document events as they occur. After several weeks pass, everyone forgets exactly what happened, and without something to refer back to, people may lose track of their decisions and the reasons that certain decisions were made.

Typical ways to monitor the program include survey forms, informal interviews, and follow-up phone calls. These often act as "smile sheets"; they don't give much information on how well participants actually perform once they are back on the job. Developers should involve the employees' supervisors as much as possible in the monitoring effort—supervisors are the ones who see changes in behavior that are related to training. Ask the supervisors to cite specific instances of performance improvement.

One way to help involve supervisors in the monitoring of the program once the student returns to the workplace is to include "back home" action plans in the program. Students develop the action plan, by specifying objectives to accomplish, setting target dates for completion, and defining a way to measure success. The supervisor should know about the plan, discuss it with the student, and offer support in its completion.

When practitioners talk with a trainee's supervisor, they can refer to the success of this action plan (whether the student completed it, how well the student completed it, and if the student's work behavior continued after completing the action plan).

Trainers, in turn, can use this type of information to continuously improve their product. It provides specific instances where changes did or did not occur and where training needs to be modified. When they make revisions, they reenter the instructional design phases as needed.

The evaluator's role. Practitioners often identify the impact of a course on individual or organizational effectiveness. In this role, they monitor the following:

● designs and plans
● instruments
● processes.

In their role as evaluators, practitioners do the following:

● Provide coaching and feedback.

● Develop findings and conclusions on the success of a training program.

● Make recommendations for change.

For more information on monitoring and evaluation, see *Infolines* No. 9705, "Essentials of Evaluation"; No. 9110, "Measuring Affective and Behaviorial Change"; No. 9112, "Tracking Operational Results"; No. 9801, "Benchmarking"; No. 9605, "How to Focus an Evaluation"; and No. 9709, "Evaluating Technical Training: A Functional Approach."

An Information Systems Case Study

Several years ago, we were charged with developing a training program for the application systems group of an information systems department. Because the department was large, diversified, and divided into work groups, we chose to implement the training program in stages, training one work group at a time.

The first group served as a pilot. Techniques were developed and refined, and then they were applied with the next work group. This approach was selected for several reasons:

- Management had established a career path.

- Job descriptions existed for various positions.

- Past training programs could serve as a reference point.

- The people wanted or needed training, or both.

- Management was committed to providing the training.

Position/Skills Matrix

In the application systems group, the career ladder consisted of different levels and career alter-

Position/Skills Matrix

SKILL DESCRIPTION	Programmer Analyst	Programmer Analyst I	Programmer Analyst II	Programmer Analyst III	Senior Programmer Analyst
Manages projects	N	A	C	C	P
Develops systems	N	A	C	P	P
Uses problem-solving process	A	C	C	C	P
Plans use of time	N	A	C	C	P
Applies ways to reduce stress	N	A	C	C	P
Uses spreadsheet software	A	C	C	C	C
Uses word-processing software	A	C	C	C	C
Identifies PC concepts	A	C	C	C	C
Uses email	A	C	C	C	C
Uses voicemail system	A	A	A	C	C
Does cost/benefit analysis	N	A	C	C	P
Uses performance management process	C	C	C	C	P
Recognizes terminology	A	A	C	C	P
Recognizes basic concepts	A	A	C	C	P

N–Not needed (skill not required for job)   A–Aware (should know about skill)
C–Confident (able to use skill on job)   P–Proficient (able to perform at an advanced level)

Position/Skills Matrix

Name_____ No._____

Supervisor _____ Date_____

SKILL DESCRIPTION	Programmer Analyst	Current Skill Level	Training Priority Needed	Time Frame
Manages projects	N	_____	_____	_____
Develops systems	N	_____	_____	_____
Uses problem-solving process	A	_____	_____	_____
Plans use of time	N	_____	_____	_____
Applies ways to reduce stress	N	_____	_____	_____
Uses spreadsheet software	A	_____	_____	_____
Uses word-processing software	A	_____	_____	_____
Identifies PC concepts	A	_____	_____	_____
Uses email	A	_____	_____	_____
Uses voicemail system	A	_____	_____	_____
Does cost/benefit analysis	N	_____	_____	_____
Uses performance management process	C	_____	_____	_____
Recognizes terminology	A	_____	_____	_____
Recognizes basic concepts	A	_____	_____	_____

N–Not needed (skill not required for job)
C–Confident (able to use skill on job)

A–Aware (should know about skill)
P–Proficient (able to perform at an advanced level)

natives. For instance, when people reached the Programmer Analyst III level, they had to make a career choice: They could follow a technical route leading to a senior programmer analyst position, or follow a management route leading to a senior systems analyst position. Differences involved skill levels, internal and external relationships, accountability, and degrees of supervision.

Managers selected three people from each position to serve on the training design task force. Before the task force met, a skills inventory was drafted; it was based on job descriptions, research-based information, examples from other organizations, personal experience, as well as the previous training program.

The skills inventory served solely as a starting point. The people on the task force identified the actual skills needed and defined their competency level requirements. To identify skills and competency levels, I set up a series of two-hour meetings with members of the task force and the manager. We met separately with members of the task force for each position.

Before the first group met, copies of the initial skills inventory were distributed. At the meeting, people in the group contributed their ideas, suggestions, and shared their knowledge. This process allowed the profile to be revised, and defined the competencies of the "ideal" person for each position.

continued on next page

At the end of each meeting, the task group was asked to give input and to rate the competency levels of the positions both above and below theirs. This served as a starting point for the discussion with the next group. The profile was revised and distributed to the people in the next group to review before their meeting with us. This procedure continued until we had met with all the people in each position.

After meeting with each group separately, a joint meeting with one representative from each position was held. At that meeting, we finalized the position/skills profile and identified where training, if needed, should begin.

Once everyone was comfortable with the position/skills matrix, it was presented to management for approval. The accompanying chart (see next page) shows a section of the matrix. We agreed to handle individual job differences on an exceptional basis later, during individual training-needs interviews.

Using the position/skills matrix, existing courses that met the specified objectives were researched. This activity falls under the category of "design/development."

Needs Identification

To conduct the needs identification, we gathered data from the position/skills matrix and created forms that listed the skills and competency levels for each position. Included was space for the trainees to indicate their current competency levels, their perceived need for training, and their priority for the training. There was also space for me to fill in the time frame. The second matrix chart (see page 193) shows a section of the needs identification form for the programmer analyst position.

After an "all-hands" meeting to discuss the training development process, individual meetings with each person in the application systems group were scheduled. Before each interview, a copy of the position/skills matrix, the appropriate needs analysis form for the position, and definitions of the skill level identifiers were sent to each person.

Before the meeting, each person was to fill in the column of the form that identified his or her current competency levels for each skill listed. During the interview, individual and job differences in required skills, and training and development needs were discussed. As the interviews progressed, patterns in the trainees' needs became evident and we began conducting research to determine alternatives for meeting these needs.

After the initial interviews, a learning contract for each trainee was prepared and given to his or her manager. During the second interview, the managers went over the contracts with the trainees and made any necessary changes. Both the manager and the trainee signed the contract. This procedure was used because an outside consultant represented an unbiased, neutral third party. Trainees rated their competency levels and identified their skills gaps. The consultant accepted them without judgment. Any differences between the individual's evaluation and his or her manager's evaluations were handled during the second interview. This system allowed the consultant to gain the trust of the managers and trainees since no past history existed around the consultant nor the approach used to develop the training.

Adapted from "Program Development for the Real World," by Karen Overfield. Training & Development Journal, *November 1989.*

Administrative Worksheet

Activity	Responsible Party	Target Date	Completed	Comments
I. Training Facility				
Room checked out				
Requirements identified				
Confirmation				
Rooms set up				
Folders distributed				
Audiovisual equipment in place				
Trainee manuals distributed				
Markers in room				
Refreshments delivered				
II. Coordination				
Dates confirmed				
Letter of indemnity				
Maps/hotels/class location				
Manuals received				
Pre-work distributed				
Cost determined				
Students notified				
Go/no-go decision made				
Invoices paid				
Cost centers charged				
III. Class				
Welcome				
Instructor ready to teach				
Instructor objectives				
Manuals in place				
Folders in place				
Meeting with instructor				
Students in seats				
Monitor class/students				
IV. Administration				
Room scheduled				
Confirmation memo, maps				
Refreshments ordered				
Folders assembled				
Roster				
Sign-in sheet				

References & Resources

Articles

Aloian, Dena, C., and William R. Fowler. "How to Create a High-Performance Training Plan." *Training & Development,* November 1995, pp. 43-44.

Dixon, Nancy M. "New Routes to Evaluation." *Training & Development,* May 1996, pp. 82-85.

Gramiak, Lori H. "Maintenance: The Sixth Step." *Training & Development,* March 1995, pp. 13-14.

Holton, Elwood F.III, and Curt Bailey. "Top-to-Bottom Curriculum Redesign." *Training & Development,* March 1995, pp. 40-44.

Jedrziewski, David R. "Putting Methods to the Madness of Evaluation Training Effectiveness." *Performance & Instruction,* January 1995, pp. 23-31.

Kaufman, Roger. "Auditing Your Needs Assessments." *Training & Development,* February 1994, pp. 22-23.

Madhumita, Kumar K.L. "Twenty-one Guidelines for Effective Instructional Design." *Educational Technology,* May/June 1995, pp. 58-61.

McClelland, Sam. "A Systems Approach to Needs Assessment." *Training & Development,* August 1992, pp. 51-53.

Overfield, Karen. "Program Development for the Real World." *Training & Development Journal,* October 1989, pp. 32-42.

Phillips, Jack J. "How Much Is the Training Worth?" *Training & Development,* April 1996, pp. 20-24.

———. "Measuring ROI: The Fifth Level of Evaluation." *Training & Development,* April 1996, pp. 10-13.

———. "ROI: The Search for Best Practices." *Training & Development,* February 1996, pp. 42-47.

———. "Was It the Training?" *Training & Development,* March 1996, pp. 28-32.

Robinson, Dana Gaines, and James C. Robinson. "Training for Impact." *Training & Development Journal,* August 1989, pp. 34-42

Rogers, James L. "Helping Clients Make Training Decisions." *Performance & Instruction,* vol. 35, no. 6, pp. 24-27.

Schultz, Fred, and Rick Sullivan. "A Model for Designing Training." *Technical & Skills Training,* January 1995, pp. 22-26.

Scott, Parry B. "Measuring Training's ROI." *Training & Development,* May 1996, pp. 72-77.

Books

International Board of Standards for Training, Performance, and Instruction. *Instructional Design Competencies: The Standards.* Batavia, Illinois: International Board of Standards for Training, Performance, and Instruction, 1994.

McClelland, Samuel B. *Organizational Needs Assessments: Design, Facilitation, and Analysis.* Westport, Connecticut: Quorum Books, 1995.

Rothwell, William J. and H.C. Kazanas. *Mastering the Instructional Design Process: A Systematic Approach.* San Francisco: Jossey-Bass, 1992.

Wilcox, John (ed.). *ASTD Trainer's Toolkit: More Needs Assessment Instruments.* Alexandria, Virginia: American Society for Training & Development, 1994.

Infolines

Austin, Mary. "Needs Assessment by Focus Group." No. 9401 (revised 1998).

Callahan, Madelyn, (ed.). "Be a Better Needs Analyst."No. 8502.

———. "Be a Better Task Analyst." No. 8503.

Gupta, Kavita. "Conducting a Mini Needs Assessment." No. 9611.

Long, Lori. "Surveys From Start To Finish." No. 8612.

O'Neill, Mary. "How To Focus a Training Evaluation." No. 9605.

Sparhawk, Sally and Marian Schickling. "Strategic Needs Analysis." No. 9408.

Waagen, Allice. "Essentials for Evaluation." No. 8601.

Wircenski, Jerry L, and Richard L. Sullivan. "Make Every Presentation a Winner." No. 8606 (revised 1998).

Systems Program Development Checklist

Systems program development divides the design and development process into six concurrent phases. The following checklist gives you an overview of the phases and their activities.

I. Needs Identification

Inputs:

☐ Job Tasks

☐ Competency Levels

☐ Skill Requirements

☐ Doers

☐ Performance Gaps

Outcomes:

☐ Training Requirements

☐ Participants

☐ Target Dates

☐ Urgency

☐ Criticality

II. Analysis

Inputs:

☐ Options

☐ Requirements

☐ Criteria

Outcomes:

☐ Deliverables

☐ Measurables

☐ Service Levels

III. Design and Development

Inputs:

☐ Participants

☐ Training Requirements

☐ Resources

Outcomes:

☐ Course Materials

☐ Training Objectives

☐ Delivery Media

☐ Budget

☐ Logistical Requirements

IV. Implementation

Inputs:

☐ Target Date

☐ Logistical Requirements

☐ Course Material

Outcomes:

☐ Delivery Guidelines

☐ Cost

☐ Delivery Date

☐ Manuals

IV. Administration

Inputs:

☐ Cost

☐ Delivery Data

☐ Participants

☐ Delivery Guidelines

☐ Location

Outcomes:

☐ Roster

☐ Invoicing/Billing

☐ Schedule

☐ Operating Procedures

☐ Statistics

VI. Evaluation and Monitoring

Inputs:

☐ Statistics

☐ Service Levels

☐ Deliverables

Outcomes:

☐ Reports

☐ Revisions

☐ Measurements

■INFO LINE■

Managing Training Projects

Issue 0512

AUTHORS

Lisa Toenniges

Innovative Learning Group
514 East Fourth Street
Royal Oak, MI 48067
Tel: 248.895.7693
Email: lisa.toenniges@
innovativeLG.com

Lisa Toenniges is owner and president of Innovative Learning Group (ILG), which provides learning and performance support services. She has nearly 20 years of experience in the performance improvement industry and has consulted with many *Fortune* 500 companies.

Karyn Patterson

Innovative Learning Group
514 East Fourth Street
Royal Oak, MI 48067
Tel: 248.894.4275
Email: karyn.patterson@
innovativeLG.com

Karyn Patterson is a project manager and performance consultant at ILG. With more than 10 years' experience in the learning field, she specializes in leading project teams for training and performance improvement initiatives.

Managing Editor
Tora Estep
testep@astd.org

Editor
Sabrina E. Hicks

Copy Editor
Ann Bruen

Editorial Consultant
Bill Shackelford

Production Design
Kathleen Schaner

Manager, Acquisitions and Development, ASTD Press
Mark Morrow

Reprinted 2006

Managing Training Projects

Training Projects

Strong project management must be an element of any mission-critical organizational change. The implementation of Six Sigma or an enterprise resource planning (ERP) system, the launch of a new product, a merger, or an acquisition—these are all monumental corporate events. If there are learning initiatives that support these high-level corporate directives (and there should be), they warrant excellent project management.

On any training project, the project manager is the person ultimately accountable for the success of the project. That means that if you are in the role of project manager, you are responsible for

- clarifying roles and responsibilities by answering questions such as, "Who's sponsoring this?" "Who's on the team?" "What are his or her skills?"

- defining the project goal clearly by answering questions such as, "What exactly are we developing?" "How will we measure success?"

- conducting a solid project kick-off meeting

- coordinating development activities

- tracking the budget

- maintaining and driving the schedule

- ensuring that the intended results are achieved.

Most complex learning initiatives involve working with multiple learning methods, multiple audiences, multiple sponsors, and multiple locations. You must contend with unclear job roles; fuzzy performance requirements; countless subject matter experts (SMEs); and, quite often, not enough time or budget to get it all done. As project manager, you need to make sense of all that and manage the quality, schedule, and budget effectively.

As training professionals strive to highlight the value of learning to the bottom line, a trainer's project management skills become more important. If your training doesn't increase sales, improve productivity, increase customer satisfaction, reduce expenses, or have some similar positive effect, the training has failed.

Good project management is a combination of two things: one, following a proven, sequential process and two, doing all the right things, every day, throughout the project. Once you've studied the project management process described below, you should be able to apply it to your next training project.

The Project Management Process

The process for managing training projects is simply an overlay on the instructional systems development (ISD) process. So, let's begin with a review of a standard ISD process.

The most widely known ISD process is the ADDIE model: *a*nalysis, *d*esign, *d*evelopment, *i*mplementation, and *e*valuation. Because it's a proven approach to accomplishing typical training goals, most organizations use some form of this standard process when developing training programs. As authors Harold Stolovitch and Erica Keeps write in *Handbook of Human Performance Technology*, "Today many operational ISD models exist in practice, but most either can trace their roots to ADDIE or accept the ADDIE concept as a foundation." The ADDIE model is illustrated in the sidebar.

With this general understanding of a standard ISD process, let's look at how the project management process aligns with it. In project management, there are tasks that must take place at a specific point during the project (such as "conduct the kick-off meeting"), and there are other tasks that you must continue to perform, again and again, throughout the project (such as "prepare project status reports" or "update the project schedule"). You'll also encounter tasks ("validate the implementation plan") that are a mix of ISD and project management. The diagram in the sidebar *Project Management Within the ISD Process* provides an illustration of the project management process and how it overlaps with the ADDIE model.

The ADDIE Model

The main elements of a commonly used ISD model are *a*nalysis, *d*esign, *d*evelopment, *i*mplementation, and *e*valuation; thus, it is often referred to as the ADDIE model. This version of the model includes key ISD steps as well as the outcome or milestone for each of the five phases. You will use these steps and outcomes to organize your project plan.

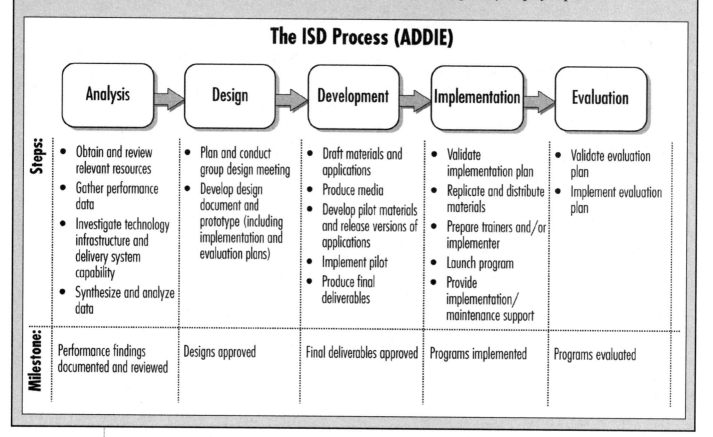

The ISD Process (ADDIE)

	Analysis	Design	Development	Implementation	Evaluation
Steps:	• Obtain and review relevant resources • Gather performance data • Investigate technology infrastructure and delivery system capability • Synthesize and analyze data	• Plan and conduct group design meeting • Develop design document and prototype (including implementation and evaluation plans)	• Draft materials and applications • Produce media • Develop pilot materials and release versions of applications • Implement pilot • Produce final deliverables	• Validate implementation plan • Replicate and distribute materials • Prepare trainers and/or implementer • Launch program • Provide implementation/ maintenance support	• Validate evaluation plan • Implement evaluation plan
Milestone:	Performance findings documented and reviewed	Designs approved	Final deliverables approved	Programs implemented	Programs evaluated

In addition to the tasks noted in the diagram, you—as project manager—will conduct the following activities repeatedly throughout the project—from the kick-off meeting through the final project closing activities:

- monitoring the budget

- taking action to remedy out-of-scope situations

- monitoring the schedule

- updating the schedule to reflect changes and revise project approach, if necessary

- creating methods of communication

- creating and distributing status reports

- coaching team members

- keeping stakeholders informed

- monitoring quality and taking action as needed

- preparing and conducting ongoing team meetings.

The remainder of this *Infoline* will closely investigate project management for training initiatives, focusing on these critical parts of the process:

- defining the project
- planning the project
- kicking off the project
- managing the project to completion
- wrapping up the project.

Project Management Within the ISD Process

The diagram below shows the project management process, now with the ISD steps grayed out and some new project management steps in bold. You'll notice that two phases are added up front: project definition and project planning. Note also the expanded text included in some of the milestones to detail specific project management outcomes.

	Project Definition	Project Planning	Analysis	Design	Development	Implementation	Evaluation
Steps:	• Identify background information needed • Gather background information	• **Identify and secure resources needed** • **Determine project tasks** • **Establish schedule** • **Establish budget** • **Draft project plan**	• **Plan kick-off meeting** • **Conduct kick-off meeting** • **Finalize project plan** • Obtain and review relevant resources • Gather performance data • Investigate technology infrastructure and delivery system capability • Synthesize and analyze data	• Plan and conduct group design meeting • Develop design document and prototype (including implementation and evaluation plans) • **Validate project scope**	• **Plan development** • Draft materials and applications • Produce media • Develop pilot materials and release versions of applications • Implement pilot • Produce final deliverables	• Validate implementation plan • Replicate and distribute materials • Prepare trainers and/or implementer • Launch program • Provide implementation/maintenance support	• Validate evaluation plan • Implement evaluation plan • **Complete project close activities**
Milestone:	Project defined	Project plan drafted	Performance findings documented and reviewed	Designs approved and **project plan revised**	Final deliverables approved	Programs implemented	Programs evaluated and **project closed**

Defining the Project

Generally, the training project manager does not conceive of training projects. That responsibility is held, usually, by stakeholders higher in the organization or by management in the department requesting the training solution and counting on it to improve employee performance. That being the case, you have a duty to gather as much background information as you can about the decisions that were made before you were given control of the project.

You can obtain that information in a number of ways. Below are three ideas that may be helpful to you:

1. Ask for all written documentation that may exist about the project:

   - meeting minutes
   - white papers
   - business planning documents
   - request for proposal/request for cost estimate
   - statement of work.

2. Conduct interviews with people, such as those listed below, who have been involved in the project to date:

   - your manager

   - the head of your department

   - the internal customer

   - the beneficiary of the training

   - the department head for whom the solution is being developed

   - people in departments with whom you will partner on the project.

3. Conduct any independent research on the topic that may provide helpful background information. Areas to investigate include

   - the content that will be discussed

   - the technology that will be used

- the delivery method(s) that will be employed and the infrastructure needed to support those delivery methods

- partner companies that will be involved

- previous projects or efforts that are relevant (including the individuals involved in these efforts)

- the current state of the training audience members' work environment.

As you complete some of the tasks listed above, you'll likely develop more questions. You might need to cycle back to earlier documents or people to ask follow-up questions. (It's a good idea to keep a running list of open questions and issues.) But at some point, even if you still have unanswered background questions, you'll need to begin the project.

Although starting a project when you still have unanswered questions is frustrating, it's also the reality of the role of the project manager. You'll want to keep your running list of questions close at hand and continue to get your questions answered as the project progresses. Eventually, you may realize that some issues are no longer relevant.

The checklist in the sidebar *Project Definition Checklist* at right provides some insight into the kind of background information you may find helpful.

Planning the Project

Once you've uncovered as much background information as you can, it's time to plan the project. Tasks involved include securing your resources, establishing the systems necessary to manage the project, and drafting the project plan.

Identify and Secure Resources

You'll need several different types of resources to achieve the project goals. The project stakeholders may have already identified some resources, but there are others that a project manager will need to request. (See the job aid at the end of this issue for a list of key resources and some considerations for each.)

Determine the Project Tasks

Determining the detailed process you will follow is another important project set-up task. The ADDIE model is the foundation for the development process. But that model provides only the major phases and milestones. The more detailed exercise is to determine the discrete tasks within each phase, which will vary depending on the solution you've chosen and the project resources, budget, and schedule. As the project manager, you'll need to answer the following questions:

Analysis

- What are the deliverables for this phase? What are the specifications for the deliverables (format, software used, estimated number of pages, and so forth)?

- Will steps be taken to quantify and document current performance?

- Is it clear what the desired performance looks like?

- How many people will need to be interviewed? How much time should you allow for each interview?

- Will existing training need to be reviewed or obtained?

- Are there documents or other research results that must be reviewed? About how much time will that take?

- If technology is involved in the training solution, are there steps needed to understand the specifications, requirements, and limitations of the technology?

- Must the deliverables be approved before continuing to the next phase? If so, obtain and document approvals for this phase before proceeding to the next phase.

Project Definition Checklist

Use this checklist to help you gather the background information to define the key elements of your project.

- ☐ To whom are you accountable?

- ☐ Why is this project being undertaken?

- ☐ What business results should be affected by this solution?

- ☐ What are the goals of the project?

- ☐ Who are the stakeholders and what is their role?

- ☐ How does each stakeholder define success?

- ☐ How does each stakeholder define quality?

- ☐ What resources have been secured for the project?
  - people
  - money
  - facilities
  - equipment
  - intellectual property

- ☐ Who is the target audience of the project solution?

- ☐ What are the project deliverables?

- ☐ What is the budget? What is included in the budget? (For example, travel costs, training room costs, hosting fees?)

- ☐ Is there a hard deadline when you must complete the project? Are there milestones that you must achieve?

- ☐ Are there points in the project with "go/no go" decisions?

- ☐ Have there been previous attempts to complete portions of the project that have been unsuccessful?

- ☐ Are there other organizations, companies, or individuals with whom you'll partner?

- ☐ Is your training project part of a larger corporate initiative that you must link into?

- ☐ Are there any standards that have been set for the larger initiative that you should be aware of (status reports, meeting schedules, quality standards)?

- ☐ What tasks have already been completed?

Design

- What are the deliverables for this phase? What are the specifications for the deliverables?

- Will a group design meeting be conducted?

- How many drafts of the design document will be developed?

- Will there be a review meeting of the design document, or will team members simply forward their feedback to the project manager?

- Must the deliverables be approved before continuing to the next phase? If so, obtain and document approvals for this phase before proceeding to the next phase.

- Has the scope of the project changed now that the design is complete? And does that affect the project resources or the schedule? If so, have the project sponsors and stakeholders been informed so the team can make decisions on how to address these changes in scope? If yes, modify the project plan as needed before proceeding to the next phase.

Development

- What are the deliverables for this phase? What are the specifications for the deliverables?

- How many drafts of the materials or applications will be developed?

- Will there be a review meeting of the materials or applications, or will team members simply forward their feedback to the project manager?

- Will a pilot be conducted? If yes, what is the pilot strategy?

- Who will see to it that all materials are thoroughly edited? When and how?

- Must the deliverables be approved before continuing to the next phase? If so, obtain and document approvals for this phase before proceeding to the next phase.

Implementation

- What are the deliverables for this phase? What are the specifications for the deliverables?

- Will a train-the-trainer be necessary? If yes, what is the strategy?

- Must materials be reproduced or duplicated?

- Will facilities and equipment need to be reserved to implement the training?

- Must materials be shipped?

- Will the applications need to be loaded and tested?

- How much time is needed for all learners to complete the training? (In other words, calculate the time necessary for all learners to complete synchronous or asynchronous training. For example, it may take six months for all 100 learners to complete the process.)

- Must the deliverables be approved before continuing to the next phase? If so, obtain and document approvals for this phase before proceeding to the next phase.

Evaluation

- What are the deliverables for this phase? What are the specifications for the deliverables?

- Will evaluation data be collected, tabulated, and reported?

- Is the target audience available to participate in the evaluation?

- How many drafts of the evaluation report will be developed?

- Must the deliverables be approved before completing the project? If so, obtain and document approvals for this phase before completing the project.

Once you've answered these questions, you should document the development process that you'll follow and make it available to your team and the stakeholders. When documenting the process, treat the tasks as if they are actions: Start with a verb. For example, a few common tasks include *conduct* group design meeting, *write* first draft of facilitator guide, and *program* beta version of courseware. Once you've documented your detailed development process, you've essentially completed the first step in creating your project schedule.

Establish the Schedule

The development process, which provides the detailed list of tasks, is the basis for the project schedule. To complete the project schedule, establish dates and determine accountabilities. A first-time project manager might be surprised by the intricacies of this process. You have to consider many variables before picking dates on the calendar:

- Can tasks be completed simultaneously, or must one task be completed before the next can start?

- Are there dates when certain project team members are unavailable and, therefore, the schedule must be adjusted around the constraints?

- Will materials and equipment be available when needed, or must the schedule be adjusted around any constraints? (For example, is the new computer available to test the steps in the training?)

- Is content available, or must the schedule be adjusted around any constraints? (For example, have stakeholders approved the new process that is the subject of the training?)

- Is it possible to complete the tasks by the agreed-upon milestones and deadlines?

- Will any tasks need to be shortchanged or skipped?

In building a schedule, it's important to include the following:

- phases and tasks (phases may map to the ADDIE model, while tasks are the activities carried out in each phase)

- the identity of the person who will complete each task

- task start date and end date.

When creating a project schedule, you have a number of different tools from which to choose; however, the logic built into the schedule is more important than the specific tool. Be careful not to get too distracted by creating lengthy, complicated project schedules that forecast out for months. Inevitably, items will shift, and you'll spend a great deal of time continually tracking and updating the project schedule. It makes sense for the near term to have a detailed schedule; but for the later project dates, don't get too deep into the details.

Below are some examples of tools that you can use to create project schedules:

- Microsoft Word table
- Microsoft Excel Gantt chart
- Microsoft Project
- flipchart, white board, or other visual tool.

Whatever method you choose, don't be a slave to the tool. It should make your job easier, not harder. In the sidebar *Sample Project Schedule* at right is a partial example of a project schedule for an e-learning project.

Establish the Budget

Another important task when setting up your project is establishing the baseline budget. Different organizations track different types of costs and at different levels of detail. So, your first action is to make sure that you understand how your organization requires you to track the budget. Ideally, you have already learned this in the project definition phase.

Below are the key tasks involved in preparing the budget. Your organization may provide you with a specific project management software application that you can use to complete these tasks. If not, Microsoft Excel is an excellent tool.

■ *Estimate Project Costs*
You may need to identify both labor and nonlabor costs. To estimate labor costs, review the tasks from the project schedule and determine the amount of time needed for each. Assign a dollar figure per hour of labor and calculate the total. If your organization adds standard hourly overhead amounts for internal labor, add that as well. That calculation will give you a budget based on money rather than time. Next, identify additional costs for nonlabor items (such as materials, travel, equipment, facilities, and audio or video production costs). After completing the estimate, document any assumptions you've made to generate your estimate. (For example, the instructional designer will interview no more than five SMEs for a total of 10 hours of research time.)

■ *Set Up the Budget*
Your baseline budget should include a line item for each role (for example, instructional designer, graphic designer, and so forth) and type of cost (for example, audio recording). In your estimate, you detailed every task. In the budget, you only need the total for each type of cost. If you developed your estimate using a column format, it is simply the total dollars (or hours) for each column. The budget should also enable you to enter actual costs and then compare those actual costs with budgeted costs to determine if you are on, under, or over budget.

■ *Inform the Team*
Once you've established the budget, inform your team members of the portions of the budget that are relevant to them. They need to know your expectations of the time (or dollars) allotted for them to complete tasks. You also need to determine how you will obtain actual budget data. If you have a project management software application, team members simply complete a time report, and the data is reflected in a project status report. If your organization does not use a software application, you'll still need to ask team members to report their data to you at regular intervals.

In the sidebar *Estimates and Budgets* is a sample of an estimate template that allows you to enter the estimated hours for several roles for discrete tasks in the project. You can enter the appropriate hourly rates for each team member, add any other projected costs, and calculate a total project estimate.

That sidebar also presents a sample budget report that you can use to track actual expenses throughout the project and compare them with the original budget.

Draft the Project Plan

The purpose of the project plan, also called a project charter or statement of work, is to document your understanding of the project and obtain approval to proceed. That document serves as the basis for the kick-off meeting, and you can share it with stakeholders as well. You may, however, choose to wait until after the kick-off meeting to share the document, if you still have significant questions that need to be answered. But it's important that you get this document started, as it will help you identify any open issues that need to be discussed at the kick-off meeting before the project can move forward.

Again, you can use Microsoft Word to create the document, with the following sections:

- project purpose
- deliverables
- process and schedule
- contact information
- budget
- assumptions
- approvals.

Sample Project Schedule

The project schedule is an important tool that helps you and your team stay on track for a successful project. But sometimes just starting the schedule can seem overwhelming. Use the sample below from an e-learning project to help you get started.

Portion of a Sample Project Schedule

XYZ Project Schedule

Phase, Tasks	Who	Start Date	End Date
Development Phase			
Write first draft storyboards	Instructional designer	4/14	4/28
Review first draft storyboards	Team	4/29	5/3
Conduct first draft review meeting	Team	5/4	5/4
Write second draft storyboards	Instructional designer	5/4	5/8
Edit storyboards	Editor	5/9	5/9
Review and input edits	Instructional designer	5/10 (8:00 a.m.)	5/10 (12:00 p.m.)
Create graphics	Graphic designer	5/9	5/10 (12:00 p.m.)
Program alpha version	Programmer	5/10 (12:00 p.m.)	5/17

Estimates and Budgets

Use the following template as a guide when establishing your estimate. Be sure to include tasks, roles, and the estimated hours of work for each task.

Sample Project Estimate Template

Labor | **Project Team**

Phase, Tasks	[Role]	[Role]	[Role]	[Role]
Total Hours				
Cost/Hour				
Total Labor Cost				

Below is a sample budget report. Use it to help you track actual expenses throughout your project—and compare those expenses with your original budget.

Sample Budget Report

Date: _____

Role	Budgeted	Actual	Balance
Total			

Kicking Off the Project

After the project planning is completed, you're ready to get the project underway with the kick-off meeting. Plan this event carefully, as it is one of the most important steps in your project.

The purpose of this meeting is to gather all of your team members together to ensure that everyone has a shared understanding of both the project and what is expected of him or her. Be sure you have all the right people involved in this meeting. Because you will be discussing and agreeing on some fundamental aspects of the project, attendance by your project sponsors and stakeholders is critical, as well as your team members, your manager (if appropriate), and any other individuals who may play a key role in the project.

A typical agenda for a kick-off meeting includes the following topics:

- project purpose and scope
- team roles and responsibilities
- deliverables
- process
- schedule
- next steps.

At the completion of the kick-off meeting, you should finalize the project plan by incorporating any revisions or new information that was discussed during the meeting. You should capture your current understanding (as best you can) and not worry about minor open issues. Then, distribute the project plan to all team members and stakeholders.

As the project progresses, some of your assumptions or other project information may change. You'll need to decide whether you want to maintain the project plan at this point. You may decide to pull certain sections out of the project plan to continually update throughout the project, such as the schedule and budget.

You may also want to create other kinds of communication to keep your project team and stakeholders updated on your progress. The use of these types of communications is often easier than continually going back and updating the project plan. (For communication ideas, see the section called "Maintain Communications" below.)

Managing the Project to Completion

Now that you've had a successful kick-off meeting, your project is off and running. But your job as a project manager is far from over. Many of the tasks from this point forward become ongoing or maintenance-type tasks. But, there's one more point-in-time task that you must complete: validating the project scope at the completion of the design phase. To do this, you need to look at the project deliverables, specifications, and approach and see if anything has changed since you first planned the work. Based on what you learn during the analysis phase and the solution you end up designing, the project scope could be measurably different than when you first started. If this is the case, you may need to adjust the project budget or schedule accordingly. Therefore be sure to validate the project scope at the completion of the design phase.

When it comes to managing the project on a daily basis, you need to continually focus on the following:

- quality
- schedule
- budget.

You also need to focus on the interdependence of those items. Generally, when a change occurs in one, one or both of the others are affected.

Your communication strategy will command your attention throughout the project. Keeping your project team and stakeholders informed and aware of any issues that arise is a major task, and you need to establish your communication strategy early in the project and share it with your team members.

Monitor the Quality

During the project planning phase, you determined how quality is defined on your initiative. So, throughout the project, you need to ensure that the actual project deliverables are meeting the defined standards and level of quality. To do that, you need to either review the deliverables yourself or receive updates from the team member assigned to that role (perhaps the lead instructional designer). It's always good, however, to have some familiarity with the deliverables yourself, so you can converse knowledgeably with your client.

Ideally, your defined development process includes one or more edit cycles at the appropriate places. Presenting deliverables that contain typos, formatting problems, or careless errors undermines your credibility.

Monitor the Schedule

Your role as project manager is to drive the schedule forward. You must be the leader, the person who is always one step ahead. You cannot wait until the day a task is due to check on its progress. You need to look ahead to the coming week and month and ask yourself the following:

- Is person X prepared to start the next task? Does he or she have what is needed?

- Does the original schedule still make sense or does the logic need to change?

- Should the schedule be modified now to include a deeper level of detail for the next sequence of tasks? (For example, rather than simply indicating that a task will take a week, should you define what needs to happen each day to meet the deadline?)

- Has the deadline changed? If so, the schedule needs to be reworked.

- Have you completed steps early? If so, you can make modifications to the balance of the schedule.

- Have milestones been missed and now you have to play catch-up? If so, you may need to change the logic (for example, allowing tasks to overlap rather than be end-to-end) or add additional resources.

One of the most important tasks when managing the schedule is to monitor the handoffs. For example, team member Jane completes a task (her output); completion of that task triggers the next team member, John, to take that output (which is now his input) and begin his task. You'll need to ensure that Jane communicates to John that she has completed the task and shares any issues that should be passed along. You'll also want to make sure that John knows he can begin his task, has what he needs, and doesn't have unanswered questions. These simple handoffs, if not handled well, can add days to a project—not to mention a great deal of frustration.

Monitor the Budget

Along with monitoring the schedule, you must monitor the budget. No stakeholder likes to be informed late in the project that you just realized the project is over budget. Depending on the pace and nature of the project, you should monitor the budget on a weekly or monthly basis. You need to ask yourself the questions noted in the sidebar *How to Monitor Your Budget* at right and be prepared to take action to get your project back on track.

Your team members are your best resources to help you answer those questions. Often, they are the first to note any gap between the original budget and the actual budget. You should remind team members to update you, as required, and ask them for input throughout the project.

Maintain Communications

Communication can make or break your project. Your strategy should address these items:

- With whom do you need to communicate? What type of information do you need to share with each audience? What level of detail does each audience need?

- Will the team meet face-to-face (or via conference call) on a periodic basis? If yes, how frequently? Will you (or someone on the team) create meeting minutes?

- Will there be some type of ongoing project status report? If yes, how frequently? Is there a template? To whom will it be distributed?

Regular project status reports can be a simple and effective way to keep all team members and stakeholders informed of the project's progress. If you create status reports, be sure to do it on a regular basis and include such information as recent accomplishments and decisions, open and planned tasks, and any open issues or concerns.

You might also consider including a quick status symbol at the top of the report, such as a red-yellow-green indicator, to give your audience an immediate update on the project. Green means that everything is going according to plan; yellow means that you are off plan, but you have identified a way to get back on track; red means that you arc off plan, and you have not identified a way to get back on track. Using a symbol system makes it easy for stakeholders to quickly determine what needs their attention.

In addition to establishing a formal communication structure, a project manager must also spend a lot of time holding everyday conversations:

- "How are you doing with setting up the interviews? Are you able to reach everyone?"

- "Will you be able to complete the design document by noon so I can review it before we send it out at the end of the day?"

- "I learned in the meeting yesterday that the director will want more detail, rather than less, on the benefits content."

How to Monitor Your Budget

Monitoring the budget is a task that you must perform throughout a project. Ask the following questions to ensure that you don't encounter any surprises when the project is complete:

Is the overall project on budget? In other words, if you have used 20 percent of the budget, have you completed 20 percent of the work?

If you are over budget, ask the following:

- Do you see a way that you will recover by the end of the project? (Be brutally honest with yourself and with your stakeholders and team on this one; it's best to address cost overruns *now* rather than later.)

- Has a scope problem caused you to be over budget? If so, should you go back to your stakeholders?

- Does a team member have a performance problem that is causing too much time to be spent on a task?

- Was the original estimate not accurate, causing the tasks to take longer than anticipated?

If you are under budget, ask the following:

- Are tasks being shortchanged? Is the quality suffering as a result?

- Is the scope different than you believed at the beginning of the project and should you confirm this with stakeholders?

- Can you complete the project sooner?

- Should you give back some of the budget, or allow it to be better spent on a different aspect of the project?

Project Close-Out Checklist

When closing out your project, use this checklist to tie up all loose ends and, more important, to ensure that you've recognized your team for its hard work.

☐ Determine what will happen with electronic files:

- Move to another server.
- Burn to CD and store.
- Leave as-is.

☐ Delete electronic files that are no longer needed.

☐ Determine what will happen to all hard-copy documents:

- Throw away or recycle.
- Shred.
- Return to SMEs or clients.
- Move to different location.

☐ Prepare and store samples of the project deliverables.

☐ Obtain final budget figures and prepare the final budget. Distribute as appropriate.

☐ Prepare for and conduct a lessons-learned activity or meeting with stakeholders and team members. (This may be one or multiple meetings.)

☐ Share the business results of the project with the organization, as appropriate.

☐ Prepare for and conduct a project celebration event with your team:

- Thank your team members.
- Provide a token of the organization's appreciation.
- Showcase the project deliverables and other artifacts.
- Share business results and success stories.
- Enjoy refreshments.
- Have fun and celebrate!

- "Joe is out sick, so we should get prepared to jump in and complete his tasks if he is not back by Wednesday."

- "I heard from the program manager that the executive team is very pleased with the prototype. Thanks for your great work!"

With this kind of regular communication, you can stay on top of emerging issues, keep everyone informed, motivate your team, and drive the project forward. It's a critical part of your job as a project manager.

Wrapping Up the Project

Just when it seems the project is over and you're thinking about that long overdue vacation to Mexico, take a deep breath and think about finishing a few last tasks. You owe it to the organization and your team to lead these efforts.

The sidebar *Project Close-Out Checklist* at left can guide you in these important activities.

Because your organization has invested a great deal of time and energy on this project, it's vital that you bring some closure to the project to satisfy stakeholders, recognize your team, and tie up all the loose ends.

Managing a successful project—especially a training project—can be a richly rewarding professional experience. As you prepare for your next big training initiative, make sure you arm yourself with some of the project management tools and tips described here. Relentlessly drive the project forward. Pay excruciating attention to the details. Encourage and reward your team. And, oh yes—be sure to have fun along the way.

Articles

Toenniges, L.A. "How to Manage a Large-Scale Learning Initiative: Tools and Templates Based on 20 Years of Award-Winning Programs." Available at http://www.brandonhall.com /public/publications/pm2004/index .htm, 2004.

———. "Not Just Good Project Management—*The Best* Project Management." *ASTD Links.* Available at http://www.astd.org/astd /Publications/ASTD_Links/2005/Marc h2005/Links_home, March 2005.

Books

Buckingham, M. *First, Break All the Rules: What the World's Greatest Managers Do Differently.* New York: Simon & Schuster, 1999.

———. *Now, Discover Your Strengths.* New York: Free Press, 2001.

De Bono, E. *Six Thinking Hats.* Toronto: MICA Management Resources, 1985.

Nelson, B. *1001 Ways to Reward Employees.* New York: Workman Publishing, 1994.

Mager, R.F. *The New Mager Six-Pack.* Atlanta, GA: CEP Press, 1997.

Russell, Lou. *Project Management for Trainers: Stop Winging It and Get Control of Your Training Projects.* Alexandria, VA: ASTD Press, 2000.

Shackelford, Bill. *Project Managing E-Learning.* Alexandria, VA: ASTD Press, 2002.

———. *Project Management Training.* Alexandria, VA: ASTD Press, 2004.

Stolovitch, H., and E. Keeps. *Handbook of Human Performance Technology: Improving Individual and Organizational Performance Worldwide.* 2nd Edition. San Francisco: Jossey-Bass Pfeiffer, 1999.

Infolines

Thompson, C. "Project Management: A Guide." No. 259004 (revised 1998).

Job Aid

Key Resource Considerations

To achieve your project goals, you must rely on several different types of resources. The following table presents a list of key resources—and some considerations for each.

Resource	Considerations
■ People Description: The human capital you need to complete the work. This includes the employees who create the project deliverables as well as the people who must provide input and those who must provide approval.	● What skills do you need? ● If any team members have already been identified, what skills do they have? ● What skills are you missing? ● How many hours per week of each skill set will you need? ● If team members have already been identified, what constraints do they have (for example, not in your department, part-time schedule, flexible hours, planned vacation or business trip, ability to travel)? ● Are SMEs needed? ● If so, do the SMEs have the necessary availability? Or do they have other constraints? ● Who will review and approve the project deliverables? ● Will the review team members be available? Or do they have other constraints?
■ Budget Description: The financial capital needed to do the work.	● Has a budget already been established? ● What is not covered by the existing budget? ● What is the process for requesting additional funds if necessary? ● Are you required to track the budget and report regularly? If yes, at what level of detail?
■ Facilities Description: The physical spaces and locations needed to complete the project. Examples include ● war room for the project team to work ● office space for team members to co-locate ● storage space for materials and equipment ● training rooms for instructor-led training ● conference facility for any large gathering.	● Do team members need to be co-located? ● Does the team need to work in a shared war room, so they can leave items posted around the room? ● Do team members need meeting rooms for work sessions and team discussions? ● Will there be training materials and equipment that must be stored? ● If the training is instructor-led, how large will the audience be? What dates will the facility be needed? Will refreshments be provided? Is access to a business center necessary? What equipment is needed to conduct the training? ● Will there be some type of opening session that will require conference space larger than a typical training room?
■ Equipment Description: The tangible items needed to complete the project.	● Do team members have appropriate computers and compatible software? ● Do team members have access to the product if this is the content of the training? ● Do team members have appropriate communication tools like email, voicemail, File Transfer Protocol (FTP) sites, cell phones, and web conferencing?
■ Intellectual Property Description: The subject matter or content needed to create the training. This may include electronic files, databases, and so forth.	● Does the project team have access to the content needed to create the training? Does content need to be purchased, or do licenses need to be obtained? ● Is special security needed to obtain or access certain documents or files? ● Is any training required before team members can access the intellectual property? ● Will you need to procure a system for sharing files, such as web portal software?

The material appearing on this page is not covered by copyright and may be reproduced at will.

How to Budget Training

Issue 0007

AUTHOR

Alice K. Waagen, PhD
President
Workforce Learning
1557 Hiddenbrook Drive
Herndon, VA 20170-2817
Tel: 703.834.7580
Email: worklearn@aol.com
Web:
www.workforcelearning.com

Alice Waagen is president and
founder of Workforce Learning, a full-service training and
development company. She
has more than 18 years of
experience in all facets of
training program development
and evaluation. Dr. Waagen
holds MS and PhD degrees in
education.

Editor
Cat Sharpe Russo

Managing Editor
Sabrina E. Hicks

Production Design
Leah Cohen

How to Budget Training

Fear of the Training Budget

Few words strike as much fear in the heart as the word "budget." Whether in business, volunteer work, or at home, few people enjoy the combination of financial rigor, forward planning, and accountability associated with the budget process. Yet, as disliked as budget planning may be, it is critical to running a business, organization, or home. Budgets force us to weigh the costs and make choices about what we plan to accomplish in the upcoming year.

What is a budget? According to the *American Heritage Dictionary,* 2nd edition, a budget is "an itemized summary of probable expenditures and income for a given period, or a systematic plan for meeting expenses in a given period." Thus, a budget has a dual purpose. First, it is a plan by which you balance planned expenditures against expected income; second, it is the working plan to ensure that you spend the appropriate levels of funds on initiatives, programs, and projects.

The budget process is especially critical to training and development functions. No matter where it is positioned in an organization, training serves as an organization support function—providing your workforce with the skills and knowledge it needs for business success. As a support function, you need to organize and run training like a business itself, demonstrating as much planning and fiscal responsibility as your parent organization. By running your training function like a viable business enterprise, you gain credibility with business leaders and will be able to command greater responsibility in the organization.

Talking with veterans of budget processes, one hears terms like "budget wars" and "battling for funds." If budgets are no more than our plans and their associated costs, why then is the budget process so feared and loathed? Like many activities in organizations, budgeting combines both the logical, objective world of numbers with the subjective arena of relationships and politics. Rarely do organizations have sufficient funds for all their desired plans.

A good budget is much more than an annual event designed to document spending; it is a working plan that guides fiscal decisions. And if soundly designed and executed, a good budget forms the foundation for developing the next year's budget.

Regardless of budget process details, you will find it useful to think about the implications of budgets for training. Budgets are important to training because they show the costs and benefits of investing in the future of the organization. Whether training is intended to correct past inadequacies or bring new expertise into the organization, understanding the value of the training investment requires the financial data a budget provides.

In addition, assessing training goals in terms of cost emphasizes the linkage between training and the strategic plan for the overall enterprise. The decision making that goes into planning a clearly budgeted training program helps management understand exactly how training can enable the organization to realize its vision. As the organization commits resources to training, it also makes a commitment to creative growth. So while the numerical boundaries of a budget may seem like constraints, the budget itself delineates the opportunities for training to contribute to the business and its success.

You will not find a magic solution to help you design the perfect, ultimately defensible budget. But you can adhere to certain principles that will greatly increase the probability that your budget will be funded to the levels you require. These principles help us to go beyond our own area of expertise and seek support and partnerships with others in the organization that can help us.

The purpose of this *Infoline* is to present the fundamentals of the budget process. It covers general principles and guidelines for developing good budgets. While each organization may have its own accounting practices, the theoretical underpinnings of how you account for income and revenue remain the same. This *Infoline* focuses on these general principles rather than on the details of accounting or bookkeeping that are specific to every organization.

Budget Process Overview

Although we refer to budgeting as a process, in reality it is part of a larger accounting system. A typical accounting system includes the following elements:

A. Budget design and development.

B. Budget execution.

- expense tracking and record keeping
- program monitoring
- project management

C. Reporting and reconciliation.

This process is circular. You execute your budget within a specific window of time, normally a calendar year, and just before the yearly cycle closes, you again begin at step one: design and develop a new budget for the next fiscal year.

The accounting system is a subset of the overall business management process, which actually begins with the planning process. Management develops both long-term strategic and year-long tactical plans for the organization, then it designs the accounting systems to ensure that it specifies adequate funds to each plan. In the optimal business planning process, you design budgets based on the business plan, not on other factors like available revenue to fund the plan or prior year spending levels. The assumption here is that the business goals will justify the expenditures.

A good training budget must follow the same planning rigor. Training managers can develop a strategic and annual training budget plan, designed to support the overall goals of the business. They can then prioritize training programs, services, and projects based on the overall impact each has on organizational business goals.

In many organizations, the budget process begins with a series of memos or a visit from someone in the financial department. The training manager receives information about the budget process, usually a timeline of submission deadlines, as well as guidance on how to submit the figures and printouts of the past year's chart of accounts with proposed and actual expenditures. This informa-

tion is often accompanied by spending target requirements for the next year, usually stated as percentage reductions.

Once the budget is drafted, it typically goes through various rounds of submissions and approvals, from the training manager's immediate supervisor up to various senior levels, depending upon the size of the organization. No matter how critical the funding need, unless you present your proposed budget in a logical, concise manner that documents how projects and programs directly link to the success of the business, it will be subject to revisions and budget cuts.

Preparing and managing budgets involves three major steps:

1. Pre-work research.

2. Training plan processes.

3. Budget management.

Use these steps to design a realistic, defensible, and manageable budget.

Step 1: Pre-Work Research

Whether you are the training manager of an existing training function or building the training function from scratch, what sources can you use to gather information about your next budget? Spreadsheets listing account codes can be daunting if you do not know what to put in them. Along with your training plan, use the following sources to gather pertinent information:

■ *Historical Records*
The past can (sometimes) predict the future. If you have records of prior years' budgets, examine them to discern any trends. Some of the more stable accounts like audio/video (A/V) or travel may have a regular percentage increase every year. This will give you a quick indication of how much to fund those accounts.

■ *Baseline Funds*
Likewise, prior years' training activity records can give you good information about funding amounts for your baseline programs. If you have offered 12 "Introduction to Supervision" programs each year

Glossary

Accounting: the process of recording, classifying, and reporting the financial data of an organization.

Accounting period: the time period for which accounting reports are related to, typically one year.

Accounts receivable: amounts owed to an organization from its customer for goods or services it has provided.

Accrual: revenue earned or expense incurred by an organization that has not yet been received or paid.

Amortization: the periodic decline in value of an intangible asset that is charged to an expense account.

Asset: an economic resource of an organization that may be expressed in monetary terms.

Budget: a summary of expected future cash inflows and outflows for a given period.

Chart of accounts: the listing of account lines maintained in the general ledger.

Cost-benefit analysis: a comparison to weigh the costs of a training activity against the outcomes achieved. A cost-benefit analysis is done to determine ROI.

Cost center: a unit within an organization that contributes costs without offsetting these costs with revenue.

Expenses: costs that an entity incurs in the process of earning revenues and conducting business.

Financial statements: the four statements that present the end result of an organization's financial condition: the balance sheet, the income statement, the statement of cash flows, and the statement of owner's equity.

Incurred expense: an expense in which the obligation has been fulfilled, however, not paid.

Operating expense: an expense that relates directly to business operations, not product or service production.

Overhead: costs within an organization that are not directly attributable to the operations of a business and, therefore, occur regardless of business volume fluctuations.

Profit center: a unit within an organization whereby the attributable revenues are greater than the expenses, and, therefore, the unit is said to have a net income.

Revenue: money an organization earns by providing goods or services to its customers.

ROI: an acronym for "return-on-investment," meaning the amount (expressed as a percentage) earned on an organization's invested capital. This percentage is a useful way of measuring an organization's efficiency as well as the viability of their product lines. A "return" can be dollar or non-dollar amounts.

SWOT: an acronym used to refer to the identification of organizational strengths, weaknesses, opportunities, and threats. A SWOT analysis presents a realistic view of an organization's current framework based on those four factors.

Budget Research Checklist

Gather the following items before you start designing your budget:

☐ A copy of prior year's budget.

☐ A copy of prior year's actual expenses (for example, general ledger reports and budget tracking reports or worksheets).

☐ Any guidelines or procedures from your finance department.

☐ A copy of your budget process timeline, including deadlines and deliverables.

☐ Needs assessment data and reports.

☐ Any client program and service requests.

☐ A copy of the guidelines from your unit management on budget targets and reductions.

☐ A copy of your organization's vision statement.

☐ A copy of your organization's mission statement.

☐ A copy of your organization's strategic plan.

☐ A copy of your organization's annual report.

☐ Your organization's prior year reports to its board of directors.

☐ Prior year's performance reports on accomplishments to goals.

for the past three years and plan to do the same the next year, expenses for these programs will be a matter of record and easy to pull together.

■ *Budget Accuracy*
Examine prior years' actual data to verify the accuracy of prior budgets. If you budget $10,000 every year for travel, yet you never get approval to spend more than $5,000, the actual data will tell you a more accurate figure for next year's budget.

■ *Benchmark Data*
If your training department is new, you may not have historic data. If this is the case, look at external benchmark data for funding information. ASTD has extensive benchmark data that is cross-referenced by industry, size of organization, and other factors. Network with other training managers and use them as another source of information about program costs and expenses.

■ *Postmortems*
Conduct project postmortems to determine why projects succeed or fail. Especially in program development projects, failure or success may hinge on adequate funding. A development project inadequately funded may have lacked resources for proper instructional evaluation, adequate instructors, or other factors. This information can help you more accurately budget for new development in the next year.

Finally, remember that training never drives the budget process, finance does. Thoroughly research successful budgets from outside your functional area. Perhaps even ask someone on the financial staff of your organization the following questions:

● Has anyone ever submitted a budget that was approved with minimal revision?

● What made the process work well for that manager?

● What tips can he or she give you to help you help the financial staff?

Ask this person to share some of his or her budget "horror stories." Use your colleagues in finance as strategic partners in the budget process rather than as adversaries.

Step 2: Training Plan Processes

You already know the importance of starting the budget process with a good training plan. A sound, realistic plan, based on the business, makes developing a budget a fairly simple task. Without a plan, you may be reduced to guesswork on how to fund the various budget accounts. Without a solid plan that is tied to the business, the amount of funds you request will be subject to potential reduction and elimination. So how do you come up with a good plan? In most planning processes, you will obtain information from two directions:

1. Top-down.

2. Bottom-up.

Top-Down Process

Business organizations determine direction and priorities based on their stated vision, mission, and strategic plan. Often these planning documents are supplemented with core value statements. Some organizations also specify core competencies required to meet business goals and objectives.

When starting the planning process, you need to gather all documents describing strategic, long-term business goals as well as annual operational objectives. These documents specify the results the business leaders need to achieve in the next 12 to 18 months. The question you need to answer in your training plan is this: What training programs or services does the training department need to provide to ensure that the workforce meets these goals? Include these programs as part of the offerings listed in your training plan for the upcoming year.

Top-down planning can sometimes be "organizational detective work" depending on how much access you have to this high-level organizational information. Many organizations will restrict the distribution of strategic plans or future forecasts for fear that they will end up in the hands of competitors. But as difficult as it may be to find out strategic information, it is critical for the future success of your development efforts.

Building the training plan based on the "words from the top" would seem like a foolproof way to build a defensible budget. But there are some inherent flaws with relying only on top-down input:

- Often organizational planning information may be vague or generalized and not specific enough to determine training needs from this information alone.

- Top-down information often overlooks what you need to run the day-to-day operations of the organization.

- The skill and knowledge needed to develop new products or explore new markets, as indicated by the long-term goals, may not be the same as those needed to support existing customers or maintain existing products. For this information, you need to look at the bottom-up information.

Bottom-Up Process

Bottom-up information is the needs assessment data and participant feedback information gathered from your clients. Because these requests frequently are in reaction to current situations or crises, the focus of the training programs in response to these needs tends to be more operational than strategic. But there are advantages to using the bottom-up process:

- Frontline management and employees usually generate training requests based on a critical current need.

- If you deliver to these needs in a timely way, you gain real advocacy for your programs.

- This advocacy, in the form of satisfied customers, can be a genuine asset in budget defense.

Measurement, Metrics, and Budget Data

Measurement and metrics are key to managing any business function. When you talk about training, you need to prepare the facts and figures in a language familiar to all managers. As in other business functions, financial data is an essential component of many human resource (HR) metric systems. If you do not have good financial data for your training function, you will not be able to accurately determine the following business measures:

- return-on-investment (ROI)

- cost of training (per employee, organizational unit, initiative, company, and so forth)

- training costs as a percent of operating costs

- training investment as a percent of other business investments

- cost-benefit analyses.

Not only does good financial data help you measure and manage the training function, training cost data is also a key component of many HR measurement systems such as the following:

- cost of employee turnover (the training investment is lost once employees leave the company)

- cost of hires (new hire training)

- cost of employee benefit programs (if training is defined as an employee benefit)

- individual project or program costing (to acquire skills for specific tasks).

One cautionary note: You must research what you define as a training "cost" and track it uniformly for all programs and services. Consistently tracking costs for all programs should include both internally and externally sourced training (in-house and outsourced training). Estimating costs for programs using internal resources can be essential to decisions about who should perform the training. This seems like a simple thing to do, but organizations can vary considerably in what they include in costing the training efforts. Consider the following factors as you begin your research.

■ *Black and White Factors*
These factors are almost always included in costing training and are referred to as "hard" or "fixed" costs:

- course materials
- instructor fees
- facility rental fees
- catering or food
- travel (participants or instructors)
- equipment purchase or rental
- audiovisual rental, purchases, or lease.

■ *Gray Factors*
You may or may not include gray factors in cost tracking. They are "soft" or variable costs such as the following:

- lost opportunity costs for employees absent from their jobs while attending training

- overhead costs on a facility owned by the organization

- instructor costs when the instructor is an employee

- participants' pay or salaries while attending training.

These lists are by no means exclusive. Cost variables can exist in all organizations. Your financial department is a good source for information when determining the costs for training. Ask someone on the staff to provide you with what he or she would include in costing training based on the organization's policies or philosophies on budget management.

One final note: The variability of training costs makes benchmarking these costs a challenge. If you are comparing what your organization spends on training with that of a competitor, you need to make sure that the competitor's financial data is drawn from the same costing model as yours or your comparisons will be invalid. The ASTD Benchmarking Forum has done extensive research in defining a standard model for costing training and in collecting costing data across different organizations. The Forum reports can provide you with a great place to start researching your own costing model.

Like the top-down planning information, bottom-up data is essential because it anchors the training to perceived real business needs. Sources for this information include:

- end-of-course appraisal forms (with responses to questions like "Would you recommend this training to others in the organization?" and "What other training programs do you need?")

- line manager surveys

- other feedback devices (for example, email suggestion boxes)

- analysis of current operational plan objectives for indicated training needs

- introduction of new product or programs that might require training of internal staff.

Although valuable, bottom-up data, like top-down data, should never be the sole source of information for your training plan. Not only does it tend to lack the "long view," but it is also frequently in response to current crises. Developing and delivering training programs in response to crises can result in a plethora of unrelated topics or skill offerings that give the impression of "flavor of the month" offerings as opposed to a well thought-out plan.

Components of a Training Plan

Include the following elements in your training plan:

Organizational elements. Each of these items illustrates the link between your training plan and the organizational strategic plan:

☐ organization's vision statement

☐ organization's mission statement

☐ strategic goals

☐ annual goals or objectives

☐ value statements

☐ organization's core competencies.

Training plan elements. Link these items to organizational elements:

☐ training program title

☐ knowledge, skills, and abilities (KSAs)

☐ program objective

☐ competencies taught.

Training data needed for costing programs. Include the training data you require to cost programs, such as the following:

☐ duration (in days or hours)

☐ frequency (how many times taught per year)

☐ number of participants per class

☐ instructor costs

☐ travel expenses (instructor and participants)

☐ facility costs (room rental, equipment rental)

☐ A/V (video rental, purchase)

☐ materials (workbooks, handouts)

☐ equipment (purchase or rental).

Step 3: Budget Management

When you put a budget together, you need to document accounts and amounts. Although you may need reams of backup documentation, the actual budget itself is a simple total of line-item accounts and dollars. But once your budget is approved, you need to track some additional information to manage those approved funds.

Expense Logs

There may be considerable lag between the date that you purchase goods or services and the date that expense is recorded in your organization's general ledger (GL) system. If you have many purchases, the delay in debiting the accounts could cause you to overspend, thinking you have more funds in the account than you actually have. Following is an example of how budget problems can occur:

Sam, a training manager for ABC Electronics, has $2,000 in his A/V account to purchase training videos. In February, he purchased a new safety video for $995.00. The video arrived mid-March with an invoice, payment due in 30 days. Sam sent the invoice with a payment approval form to accounts payable on March 30. Accounts payable sent the check to the vendor mid-April, noting the expense in the GL system. Sam receives his GL reports from accounting the last week of every month. Thus, from the day he purchased the video to the day that his budget reports reflected the debited amount was a span of nearly three months, from February to April.

Thus, the first tracking system you need to establish is one that logs in all expenses the day that you incur them. These logs give you an indication of expenses that are currently in "the pipeline" and not reflected on your GL reports. This tracking log functions much like your check register in your personal checkbook, noting expenses when they occur, not necessarily when the bank deducts the funds from your account. Once the expense is actually debited from your budget, you can remove it from this tracking system.

Variances

By keeping an accurate expense log, you can report with great accuracy the actual funds spent and remaining per account. You need this information to explain variances. A variance is any deviation from budget. You may need to justify variance on a monthly, quarterly, or biannual basis. The example below illustrates how variances affect your budget:

Assume that you budget $12,000 in your travel account. The finance department in your organization assumes that you spend funds evenly throughout the year and allocates $1,000 per month in your monthly budget breakdown. But in February, you and three of your staff attend a conference, totaling $3,000 in travel expenses. Your February

budget report shows a negative variance for the year of $1,000 even though there were adequate funds in the year to cover these expenses.

Organizations differ in how they deal with variances. Some require written justification of any negative variance. Some require documentation on both negative and positive variances. Others want variance explained monthly, quarterly, or not at all. The degree of accurate detail you need to track on your budget will vary depending on the accounting standards for your organization. Check with your finance department on variance tracking to learn its standards.

Budget Reviews and Outlooks

Another accounting standard that can vary across organizations is whether or not they perform periodic budget reviews and outlooks. Most frequently, organizations conduct a mid-year review in June. At mid-year budget review, GL reports are examined for any positive variances in accounts. If you cannot explain these positive variances with evidence of planned spending in the second half of the year, management will remove the funds and reallocate them to other budgets:

Pat had budgeted $5,000 to purchase workbooks for the Forklift Training Program this year. In March, she was told that the shipping department was retiring the current forklifts and replacing them with a new model from a different vendor, due to be delivered in July. The manager of operations requested that Pat suspend all forklift training until the fourth quarter of the year. In June, at mid-year budget reset, the finance department notified Pat that it was taking $2,500 from her supplies account unless she could document that she had plans to spend that money before year end. Pat immediately prepared a memo to finance documenting that the training had been postponed and requesting that they not remove these funds from her budget.

Once again, a well-researched budget, tied to an approved training plan, allows a manager to determine whether losing funds is an appropriate or inappropriate action.

Cost vs. Revenue Centers

Overhead. This is the one word ascribed to a training function that can spell doom to requests for additional dollars or resources. "Overhead" refers to those functions and activities in organizations that do not directly contribute revenue to the organization. If you do not contribute revenue, you are called a "cost center" or an organizational element that contributes costs without offsetting these costs with revenue.

In every organization, the goal is to have costs centers that are as lean and efficient as possible. Because all costs need to be outweighed by revenue to have a profitable business, organizations have two paths to follow to be successful: reduce costs and increase revenue.

Thus, upper management often challenges training functions to curtail expenses as much as possible. But can training pursue the other path and generate revenue? Some training organizations have been successful at converting themselves from cost centers to revenue centers by selling some form of product or service to external customers. Often the product or service sold is one that you develop for internal clients but find that it also has external value.

Finding the value in the external market can take some time. As you begin to sell training, you develop an understanding of what you can market and what resources you require. Training organizations usually have three products they can sell externally: training programs, training facilities, and training expertise.

You can sell or license programs; you can sublease training classroom space; and you can contract out experienced training staff to external clients. Although turning internal resources into revenue is very tempting, you have to recognize that you are converting a support organization into its own business enterprise. A training revenue center needs careful planning and business management to succeed, especially in the area of financial management. Consider the following when planning to generate revenue out of your training unit:

- Develop a business plan that researches all aspects of marketing and selling your product. This plan gives you the information you need to judge the feasibility of the entire operation.

- Define revenue and costs carefully, and build them into a model that you use consistently across all programs (see the sidebar *Measurement, Metrics, and Budget Data*). Is all revenue booked to the training accounts or will you have to share part of it with other business centers that support your business? Remember, you use resources such as marketing, information systems, and finance to support your training function.

- Work with your finance department to define your revenue chart of accounts. Will you have one account ("training revenue") or separate ones for each product or service sold?

- Determine your organization's rules for booking revenue: Is it on invoice date or receipt of payment?

- Know who will process invoices. Do you have an accounts receivable department that manages this for you or does management expect you to process your own invoices?

- If you are billing and receiving payment, document your policy on how you will deal with past due bills or customers delinquent in payments.

- Determine who will sell your training services and products and how they will be compensated. This issue is not insignificant in these days when services are often the most profitable part of the business.

These issues are just a few that you need to think about before you attempt to offset your training costs with revenue. Many training managers, tempted by the prospect of bringing income into their organizations, find that the levels of profit they expected are soon diminished by the additional expenses they incur supporting the production, sales, and customer support needed in running a complete revenue generating business enterprise. But, if you have a product or service you feel is marketable externally, do your research. The training organization that is managed as a profitable revenue center commands greater credibility in any organization as a productive business partner rather than as simple overhead.

Managing Your Account and Developing a Training Plan

Keeping a chart of accounts is a simple and easy way to track and manage your budget. On this chart, you should list your account codes and titles and track the expenditures for each.

Sample Chart of Accounts

Account Code	Description	Prior Year	Proposed	Variance Percentage	Variance Amount
1000	Salaries				
2000	Benefits				
3000	Professional Services				
4000	Supplies				
5000	Transportation				
6000	Conferences and Seminars				

Sample Training Plan

To develop a good, defensible budget, you will find it helpful to plan out your programs, projects, and events for the upcoming year. To do this, you need to create a training plan. Your annual training plan should combine those existing programs and services you intend to continue providing along with proposed new programs. The following example is typical of annual plans.

Program	Link to Business Plan	Length	Amount Frequency
HR Policy Overview	Supports organizational objective of reducing costs associated with employee turnover, lawsuits, and so forth.	1/2 day	3 classes of 25, offered monthly
Performance Management	Supports organizational objective of measuring and managing workflow, productivity, and business results.	1/2 day	10 classes of 15 offered during third quarter only
Workplace Harassment	Supports organizational value of fair and equitable treatment of all employees.	2 hours	2 classes of 20, offered monthly

Budget Types and Techniques

Generally, every organization prepares two types of budgets on an annual basis: operating budgets and capital budgets. Operating budgets contain those general and administrative expenses needed to run the business day-by-day: salaries, supplies, travel, and so forth. Capital expenses cover the purchase of equipment and property. You need to consider both of these budgets to effectively manage your fiscal responsibilities.

Operating Budgets

If you approach developing a budget from a financial analyst's point of view, you start with a chart of accounts. This chart lists account codes and account titles used to track expenditures and typically looks something like the sidebar at left.

The norm for most accounting systems is to store and manage the chart of accounts, in summary and detail, on spreadsheets. As a tracking and management tool for a budget, it is the simplest and easiest to use.

But to design a good, defensible budget, you need to put aside the account system and go directly to your plan for projects and programs for the upcoming year. Your annual training plan should be a combination of existing programs and services that you will continue to offer along with proposed new programs. Training plans take many shapes and forms. You should design yours to fit the format required by your planning department. A typical annual plan looks something like the sample training plan on the previous page.

Once you have determined the training program, its frequency, class size, and duration, you can then project the expenses associated with each program. Existing baseline programs will incur the typical expenses shown in Part 1 of the sidebar on the following page. New program development and implementation will have some of the expenses outlined in Part 1, but may also incur the additional expenditures detailed in Part 2.

Once you determine the costs per program, you can determine total costs based on the number of times you plan to teach the program in the upcoming year or the number of participants. Combine these totals and transfer these figures to the chart of accounts spreadsheets required by your finance department for budget submission.

Why start the process at the program or project level? Because by building your budget up from the actual deliverables to the account level, you have the basis for truly defending the spending amounts. If you are then asked to reduce certain accounts by a fixed percent or amount, you can specify the impact of that cost on the particular program or service affected. By presenting decision makers with the program impact, you give them the information required to balance competing priorities to make the right decisions for the organization.

The finance department was asking all managers to reduce their budget submission by 25 percent. Evan clicked on the sheet that sorted all expenses by project and initiative. In a meeting with his boss and the finance managers, he demonstrated, line item by line item, what program the expenses were supporting. "In conclusion," Evan remarked, "What do you want to cut? If we eliminate the OSHA training, we are at risk for accidents or fines. If we eliminate the leadership training, we won't deliver programs specifically requested by the CEO. And if we eliminate the New Hire Program, it will put the responsibility for company acclimation on the hiring managers. You tell me which of these negative business impacts you want to have." After some deliberation, Evan's training budget was approved as submitted.

Capital Budgets

Capital expenses, those expenses used to purchase equipment or property, generally are handled as a separate budget because they require separate accounting procedures. And because capital accounts tend to be quite large in today's technology-driven business world, capital funds can be difficult to defend. Early in the budget process, find out how your organization handles capital budgeting. Find answers to the following questions:

- What is the budgeting procedure for capital expenses? Is it a separate set of deadlines and procedures?

- What constitutes a capital expense? Is it by dollar limit or type of purchase? For instance, does your organization consider desktop personal computers a capital expense? What about calculators? Data projection devices? Overhead projectors?

Projecting Training Expenses

Part 1. Typical Expenses of Baseline Programs

After developing a training plan that identifies your training programs and their corresponding frequency, class size, and duration, you can extrapolate the expenses associated with each program. Your existing baseline programs will incur the following typical expenses:

Account Code	Description	Item	Costs	Total
3000	Professional Services	Instructor fees	$1,500 per diem (class 2 days long)	$3,000
4000	Supplies	Participant materials	$100/participant (20 participants per class)	$2,000
5000	Audio/Video	Video rental	$195 per class	$195
			Total Per Class	$5,195

Part 2. Additional Expenses for New Programs

Any new programs you decide to develop and implement will have some of the above expenses. New programs may also cause you to incur some of the following additional expenditures:

Account Code	Description	Item	Costs	Total
1000	Salaries	Course developer	300 hours @ $150/hour	$45,000
5000	Audio/Video	Video development	Studio costs for development of one five-minute video	$5,000
7000	Facilities	Room rental	Rent for 3 days for offsite dry run @ $450/day	$1,350
			Program Total	$51,350

Tips for Defending Your Budget

In many organizations, you must present and get approval of your training budget from various layers of management—from the direct manager of the training function up to the senior leaders. Use the following tips to help preserve your plan and budget:

☐ Be able to tie every expense back to an organizational goal or objective, demonstrating the impact of any cost reduction.

☐ Ascertain how management likes to receive information before you design your presentation. Following are some options:

- ultimate detail—short text papers on major proposed projects, listing plan, costs, and estimate impact on the business

- moderate detail—overhead presentation with side notes on major initiatives and expenses

- minimal detail—short talking points in outline format.

☐ Present some either/or options in your budget (for example, make or buy and insource or outsource). This demonstrates flexibility on your part.

☐ Don't sweat the small stuff. Line expenses like audio/video and printing can pale in comparison to the big items. Below are the largest budget items (and thus the items most put to scrutiny):

- salaries
- travel
- professional fees (consulting, outside resources).

Make sure you can fully justify every dollar in these accounts first.

☐ Be creative on staffing options:

- Use contract trainers and developers on a per project basis. They may command a higher hourly rate than salaried staff, but you can "pay as you go" and not use them in the training slow periods like summer and year-end.

- Look at using temporary help for administrative work rather than salaried support.

☐ Check and re-check everything. One typo or error can ruin the credibility of your entire presentation.

Early in the budget process, review your plans and highlight any expenses for capital equipment or facilities. Check with your financial staff for their procedures. Careful research saves rework and frustration. Capital budgets often require different documentation and defense. If you put capital items into your operating budget in error, you may miss the timetable to later resubmit them under your capital budget process.

Building in Flexibility

Building a budget can be as much art as science. As you work from your plan to the budget, always keep in mind what you can do to reduce expenses if needed. Essentially, you must build in strategies to reduce the size of your budget that will have minimal impact on your overall training plan:

Eliminate entire programs or services. This obviously reduces the various accounts associated with the eliminated program.

Reduce costs within a specific account by doing things differently. For instance, if you budget dollars for vendor-provided course development but later find that your professional services account exceeds targeted levels, you may decide to purchase an existing program and modify it rather than develop custom training.

Negotiate lower rates, if you are using outside resources for services, by giving more work to fewer vendors. Many vendors will discount the price of their service for a larger contract.

Be wary of large travel accounts that may indicate haphazard organization. You can achieve overall expense reduction with better planning. Advanced bookings on flights and incentives for travelers to stay over a Saturday are some of the ways to trim travel expenses.

Look into virtual meetings using email, teleconferencing, and video conferences to limit travel expenses.

Research local training providers rather than pay instructor travel expenses to deliver equivalent training.

Obtain bids from both small and large companies when outsourcing training. Often the smaller provider will be more flexible on price and can discount for volume commitments. Also, the smaller vendor will often have lower overhead costs and can react more quickly to last-minute requests.

How much flexibility you build in from the beginning really depends on your organization's whole approach to the budget process. Some organizations expect two to three versions of the budget from each manager, gradually reducing costs with each version. Other organizations expect a manager to develop a lean budget with the first draft and will be suspicious if a manager can continually reduce costs with every version. Research the cultural practices in your organization to determine how much flexibility you may need to include.

No More (Budget) War

If fear is based on facing the unknown, hopefully you see by now that there is little to fear in designing and managing a training budget. Successful budget design is nothing more than documenting the financial side of a good plan. If you build your training plan to support the needs of the organization, defending it is no more than ask-

ing the client to verify that he or she still requires the services stated in the plan.

But it would be shortsighted not to acknowledge that business decisions are not always based on clear, sound logic. Instead, interpersonal relations or office politics can carry as much weight in determining program funding as logic and a clear plan. Many managers have done their homework, developed sound plans and reasonable budgets, but have still seen dollars and headcount cut to fund other programs.

So, here is one final caution in this process of budgeting: keep a balance between the fact-based activities of planning and budgeting and relationship building and alliance formation. It is often the combination of activities in these two realms that determines management success.

References & Resources

Articles

Allerton, Haidee. "What Things Cost." *Training & Development,* June 1996, pp. 20-23.

Anon. "Training Budgets." *Training,* October 1999, pp. 43-50.

———. "Training Budgets." *Training,* October 1998, pp. 47-52.

Barron, Tom. "A New Wave in Training Funding." *Training & Development,* August 1996, pp. 28-33.

Callahan, Madelyn. "Training on a Shoestring." *Training & Development,* December 1995, pp. 18-23.

Cohen, Sacha. "Big Ideas for Trainers in Small Companies." *Training & Development,* April 1998, pp. 26-30.

Filipczak, Bob. "Training on the Cheap." *Training,* May 1996, pp. 28-34.

Flynn, Gillian. "Training Budgets 101." *Workforce,* November 1998, pp. 91-92.

Geber, B. "Budgets Barely Budge." *Training,* October 1990, pp. 39-47.

Jossi, Frank. "The Outsiders." *Human Resource Executive,* October 20, 1997, pp. 15-20.

Kuhn, Nancy. "Training from Scratch." *Training & Development,* October 1998, pp. 44-49.

Schriver, Rob, and Steve Giles. "Where Have All the $$$ Gone?" *Technical Training,* July/August 1998, pp. 22-25.

Books

Brookson, Stephen. *Essential Managers Handbooks: Managing Budgets.* London: Dorling Kindersley, 2000.

Costales, S.B., and Geza Szurovy. *The Guide to Understanding Financial Statements.* New York: McGraw Hill, 1993.

Ittelson, Thomas R. *Financial Statements: A Step-By-Step Guide to Understanding and Creating Financial Reports.* Franklin Lakes, NJ: Career Press, 1998.

Moore, Norman. *Forecasting Budgets: 25 Keys to Successful Planning (The New York Times Pocket MBA Series).* New York: Lebhar-Friedman, 1999.

Nilson, Carolyn. *How to Start a Training Program: Training is a Strategic Business Tool in Any Organization.* Alexandria, VA: ASTD, 1999.

Rumble, Greville. *The Costs and Economics of Open and Distance Learning."* London: Kogan Page, 1997.

Singh Gill, Indermit, et al. *Vocational Education and Training Reform: Matching Markets and Budgets.* Oxford University Press, 2000.

Thorne, Kaye, and Alex Machray. *Training on a Shoestring: Getting the Most from Your Time, Your Budgets, and Your Staff.* London: Kogan Page, 1998.

Tracy, John A. *How to Read a Financial Report: Writing Vital Signs Out of the Numbers.* 5th edition. New York: John Wiley & Sons, 1999.

Project Expense Worksheet

Need to calculate the costs of a curriculum development project but do not know how to get started? Begin by using this worksheet to identify the particulars of your project. This collected data will help you calculate the costs.

Research				Total
Purchase books, articles, CDs, and so forth	Item	Number	Amount	
Purchase materials and equipment	Item	Number	Amount	
Travel for onsite research	Item	Cost Per Trip	No. of Trips	
Researcher expenses	Item	No. of Hours	Hourly Rate	
Subject matter expert (SME) expenses	Item	No. of Hours	Hourly Rate	
Other research expense				
Curriculum Development				
Developer/writer	Number	Hourly Rate	Hours	
SMEs	Number	Hourly Rate	Hours	
Other development expense				
Marketing				
Copy development	Item	Cost		
Printing	Item	Cost		
Postage/shipping	Item	Cost		
Other marketing expense				
Implementation				
Copying/printing	Rate	Amount		
Materials purchase (videos and so forth)	Rate	Amount		
Facility rental/lease	Rate	Amount		
Audio/video rental/lease	Rate	Amount		
Catering	Rate	Amount		
Instructor expense	Number	Hourly Rate	Hours	
Travel	Item	Cost Per Trip	No. of Trips	
Participant expense	Number	Hourly Rate	Hours	
Travel	Item	Cost Per Trip	No. of Trips	
Other implementation expense				
Grand Total				

Build Credibility for the Training Function

Issue 0709

AUTHORS

Kate Domenick, EdD
Principal
Training and Communications Group, Inc.

David Gallup, EdD
Principal
Training and Communications Group, Inc.

Marge Gillis, RN, MSN
Vice President, Business Development
Training and Communications Group, Inc.

The Training and Communications Group, Inc. is a full-service training and consulting firm involved in training design, production, and evaluation. Founded in 1981, the company has served *Fortune* 500 organizations globally and in the United States and is committed to ensuring training receives the recognition it deserves as a valued business partner.

Build Credibility for the Training Function

***Infoline* Associate Editor**
Justin Brusino

Copy Editor
Ann Bruen

Production Design
Kathleen Schaner

Generating Credibility

Training is a business that exceeds $5 billion in the United States alone, where more than 2.2 percent of payroll is devoted to training and more than 22,000 full-time trainers are at work. With numbers like these the business of training demands a far more strategic approach than it commonly receives.

It's important not only to deliver the highest-quality training but also to ensure that the organization credits the training for its positive impact. As a trainer, you need to make your organization, from supervisors to the CEO, understand what the training department is bringing to the table.

All successful and respected training functions share three commonalities:

1. The most effective training and development occurs at organizations where training is valued as a strategic corporate investment.

2. The training function must be firmly aligned with the organization's corporate goals.

3. The training function must make sure the organization is aware of its contribution toward advancing those goals through a well-developed communication plan.

This *Infoline* will show you how to

- use an inventory to rate the value, impact, and perception of training throughout your organization

- increase the perception of your training department's credibility and value

- establish your training as a business-critical function at your organization.

Evaluate Your Organization

Before you begin, it is important to know how training is viewed by your organization. To do this, you need to answer the following questions:

- Given the forces driving and restraining training, how is your training function performing in its role?

- How is training perceived by the entire organization?

- In what areas is the training department viewed as excelling? In what areas is the training department lacking?

Surprisingly, many training professionals respond to these questions with only a "gut" feeling about the way in which their organization perceives training's contribution. This is because no data exist to assess how the organization views the training function.

A simple but powerful approach to compiling this information is to use a VIP (value, impact, and perception) survey. This assessment is designed to measure critical areas with regard to training. If the value, impact, and perception score of a training organization is high, you can be reasonably sure that your training is aligned with organizational and departmental goals and is satisfying the needs of your customers. If your score is low, training needs to be more closely tied to the goals and objectives valued by your organization. In any case, it's important to begin with a baseline score to diagnose how training is viewed throughout the organization.

■ *Value*

Value describes the worth placed on training by the organization as a whole. Is training considered critical to achieving organizational and departmental goals? Is it seen as a key function in the organization? If not, in what areas does your training need to improve to raise its value? The VIP survey provides insight into the way in which your training department is perceived, and offers a starting point for delving into areas that need attention.

■ *Impact*

Is your training having an effect on the entire organization and on the individuals it serves? Is training viewed as a vital component in ensuring that your organization meets its objectives? A proactive, vibrant training function that actively collaborates with other departments to develop training that helps meet goals and objectives is likely to score high on impact rating.

■ *Perception*

Perception is inextricably tied to value and impact; in fact, value and impact are aspects of perception. The overall perception of training, like value and impact, is a subjective measurement; still, it is critical to understanding how your organization views training.

Before you begin implementing any changes, see the job aid *Value, Impact, Perception Survey,* to rate your organization and get a baseline score by which to measure your improvement.

A Picture of Success

What does a successful training function look like? Let's consider an organization in which training is valued as a strategic investment rather than just a cost of doing business.

All successful training functions have a few things in common. Successful training functions

- measure their progress against goals that are clearly aligned with those of the organization

- communicate their progress regularly to customers and stakeholders

- evaluate and revise their direction as needed in response to goal achievement

- become part of the ongoing executive-level conversation about organizational goals and strategies.

In a successful training department, members have a high regard for their department's contribution to the organization. Because they understand their company's business and can articulate the value of their contribution, training professionals take a proactive role in recommending, reviewing, and refining proposed training initiatives with customers.

Take a moment to think about what your training department is doing right. Training can be considered successful when it

- aligns with corporate goals

- is viewed as a business-critical function

- measures its progress against goals

- is proactive in approaching initiatives

- communicates systematically

- revises direction as needed

- is part of the ongoing dialogue about organizational goals.

To find more information about what other factors could be driving and impeding your training, see the sidebar *Training Drivers and Constraints.*

Saying "No" to Training

It's important to note that not all requests for training should be fulfilled after training professionals and their customers have identified their needs. There are times when training is an inappropriate or ineffective answer to a problem. Don't get your training program involved where it is doomed to do little good.

Still, it can be counterproductive to repeatedly deny training requests. If you find yourself faced with a situation where you must provide training where you deem it inappropriate, take measures to protect the training department from blame.

Step 1. Educate your customers on what training can and cannot do. Let them know the reasons why you think that training is likely to be unsuccessful.

Step 2. Set clear, achievable goals. Even if you think your training is likely to have little or no impact, it's still important to set goals, by which to measure the results.

Step 3. Offer alternatives in writing. Then if your training is ineffective, you will have a record that you suggested other options.

Get Training Respect

No matter how successful your training programs, chances are you would like them to be better received. By following this six-step iterative process, you can ensure that your organization is giving training the respect and support it deserves.

Step 1. Set goals.

Step 2. Identify success factors.

Step 3. Support specific goals.

Step 4. Develop an evaluation plan.

Step 5. Anticipate change.

Step 6. Foster continuous improvement.

Training Drivers and Constraints

What drivers are pushing training to the foreground in many organizations? What constraints interfere with its success? Use this list to find out what is assisting and what is impeding training in your organization.

Drivers

- Focus on individual productivity
- Focus on employee retention and succession planning
- New technology
- New products
- Lack of skilled workers
- Global competition
- Increasing regulation and compliance issues
- Professionalizing of training
- Recognition of training as a business-critical core function.

Constraints

- Training is viewed as a cost of doing business.
- Training is not accountable for results.
- Training does not speak the language of business.
- Training budget is insufficient to handle increased training needs.
- Trainers lack instructional design competency.
- Training does not hold itself in high regard.
- Training does not view itself as a business-critical function.

Set Goals

Step 1 will build recognition and work to establish training as a strategic corporate investment. Get your training department involved in organizational goal- and direction-setting conversations.

■ *Self-Promotion*

How can training achieve a seat at the table? One of the most important tactics successful training organizations use is self-promotion. Establishing the value of training is an ongoing requirement for training leadership. Take these actions:

- Start a dialogue with stakeholders and customers to learn about employee development in relation to achieving goals. Also, talk to managers about departments achieving organizational goals. Ask what role training can take in this.

- Listen to and integrate feedback into your goals.

- Disseminate training results strategically throughout the organization.

These small steps can help you get your training noticed. Integrating participant feedback gets others involved and invested. By posting training results, you allow employees and their managers to track improvement.

Another useful tool for marketing your training department is your company's intranet. Create a separate webpage for training items. Instead of placing learning documents in various places on the intranet, make sure that any and all content that you provide to the company is directed through your training webpage. As owners of the content and the center of learning for the company, your intranet page will become the knowledge portal for the entire organization.

Possible content to include on your intranet includes

- course listings

- staff bios

- research links

- job aids

- training request forms

- a change control policy, which allows others to suggest changes or updates to current training

- success stories

- online courses

- classroom schedules.

■ *Hierarchy of Learning*

A hierarchy of learning means that each person in the organization takes responsibility for his or her continuous improvement. For management, this means taking an active role in the improvement of corporate reports as well. This responsibility begins at the highest level of the corporate ladder and flows down the organization.

In an organization that has a true hierarchy of learning, managers and supervisors recognize the development of human resources as critical to the organization's ability to thrive in an increasingly competitive world. Alignment between training and the organization as a whole is easier to achieve in organizations with a fully-developed hierarchy of learning. In these organizations training is included in the highest levels of planning.

At the same time, each level in the hierarchy sees coaching and developing people as a critical job function. Organizational leaders know that training will provide a strategic advantage in building and maintaining a competitive workforce. In a hierarchy of learning, training is an integrated and integral function because it ensures the flow of knowledge and the coalescence of corporate wisdom and competence up and down the ranks of the organization. For more information, see the sidebar *Hierarchy of Learning Case Study*.

Hierarchy of Learning Case Study

This case study shows how a hierarchy of learning was developed with the help of an attentive manager.

One organization was charged at the highest level with developing its field management in the area of personnel development. This mandate cascaded down to the training department, which was not included in the original discussion, as a demand to "develop training for our field managers to make them better at coaching."

The training department translated this mandate into a plan to develop expensive classroom-based training for field managers, taking them out of territory for 40 hours to "develop better coaching skills." But one training manager new to the organization balked at the plan. She asked two critical questions: "What are we really trying to do, and how does it support corporate goals?"

This manager called a halt to the classroom training effort until she could assess the situation strategically. She surveyed field managers to learn what their needs were and interviewed top management to delve more deeply into what they truly wanted. Her month-long analysis suggested a training intervention very different from that originally proposed. The surveys and interviews confirmed that managers needed more on-the-job coaching experiences conducted by their own managers, more "real-world" case studies, and more distance learning.

The results of the findings were compelling, and the training manager got the go-ahead to develop field training. She established an advisory board composed of high-level management and new and tenured field managers to review training programs and establish metrics for success. These metrics were aligned with those of the entire organization—for instance, increases in bonus compensation and market share as measures of district and territory success.

Equally important, this experience constituted the first step in establishing a hierarchy of learning at the company. Because the initiative encouraged field management to take responsibility for developing its managerial ranks, ownership of training resided with field leadership, where it belonged. And executive leadership began to view training as a valuable partner in employee development.

A hierarchy of learning can begin just about anywhere in the organization in which a champion exists. Start at the level most receptive to the idea and work up and down from there to establish buy-in. Let one success story be a model for others.

Recruiting and Retention

Opportunities for continual growth and improvement are very important to today's employees. Here are some ways to use training as a tool for recruiting and retaining employees.

- Present training as a selling point in job advertisements. Describe it as a benefit, along with health insurance and other traditional benefits.

- Use the learning management system, employee bulletin board, and company intranet to emphasize employee successes, including classes completed and certificates obtained.

- Develop a succession plan for all employees. Highlight the classes or other learning needed to be considered for a promotion. This not only will allow you to identify qualified candidates for open positions, it will allow you to know what to look for if you need to go outside the company to fill them.

- Get feedback from employees through surveys and informal interviews as to what training they would like to have offered for professional development.

- Cross-train employees on other jobs. The benefits of this are two-fold. It will allow the person to gain new skills and knowledge. Also, it will make that person better at the job they currently do because they will be able to see how their job fits into the larger system of the organization.

■ *A Business-Critical Function*

One of the most compelling cases that can be made for the value of training is that it is instrumental in ensuring that the organization achieve its goals. The idea that training is an active partner in developing the people who make goal achievement possible is central to positioning training as a business-critical function.

Ironically, now that the value of training is being recognized as a key to organizational success, more and more organizations are outsourcing their training. This is due to a number of factors, one of which is training's historic reluctance to link its results to organizational metrics so it can position itself as a business-critical function. No wonder corporate cost-cutters view training as low-hanging fruit when it comes time to pare the organizational tree.

Establishing training as a business-critical function can be accomplished by any number of means. For example:

- conducting and disseminating results of customer satisfaction surveys, interviews, and evaluations

- dashboarding—visually presenting important data, the correlation between training and the enhancement of key performance indicators in an ongoing graphic representation

- using the learning management system to promote business results by providing evidence of advancement on a competency continuum

- measuring training outcomes versus the cost of training

- collecting and disseminating anecdotal information, testimonials, and feedback to support specific initiatives.

Training is also critical to your business in that it is a vital part of both recruitment and retention. With today's highly motivated employees, it's important to let them know that your organization is committed to their personal and professional development. To learn more about using training as a recruiting and retention tool, see the sidebar *Recruiting and Retention.*

Identify Success Factors

It seems logical that training be aimed at enhancing critical success factors, but in fact, training is frequently disconnected from what the rest of the organization values most. A common mistake many training functions make is measuring the training's impact in terms of the number of people trained and through a Level 1, or reaction, evaluation score. If you want your training results to be valued, you must present results in terms that management can appreciate. Focus your results on what the organization values, such as

- sales numbers
- market share
- quality
- efficiency.

When training uses a language of success different from that of the rest of the organization, it tends to become alienated from the rest of the organization. By speaking the language of business, training results can be more fully understood.

Establish Metrics

Traditionally training has been reluctant to establish hard-and-fast metrics to measure success because of the many variables that can affect the training effort. As one training manager put it, "Product training for a new drug may be excellent, but if the drug is recalled, or if a new competitor comes on the market, the impact of the training is nil. I don't want to be responsible for that."

Remember, other functions throughout the organization are measured by standards that are also likely to be affected by uncontrolled variables. Technology, marketing, sales, and research and development are all subject to forces beyond their direct control. Unlike the functions that are routinely measured in terms of organizational success factors, training has shown undue caution in avoiding measurements that demonstrate the impact training has on business.

Another argument raised against measuring the effect of training is that training cannot be isolated from other factors. For example, how do we know training is responsible for an increase in quality when we also deployed new equipment in the factory?

Training is often one of a number of initiatives aimed at goal achievement—just as advertising, new technology, and new product development are frequently accompanied by other efforts aimed at reaching a certain target. When the goal is met, training professionals are likely to assume that the role of training is intuited by those involved in the effort. This is a dangerous assumption that can leave the training out in the cold.

Depending on what type of training is involved you can create specific metrics to measure the success of your training. For example, if you wanted to create metrics for your training initiative on Global Regulatory Compliance, you could focus on the reduction of incidents of non-compliance. This could be measured by

- auditing investigational reports

- reviewing benchmarking surveys

- measuring the costs associated with non-compliance

- judging the increased market share through better application of compliance principles.

It's important that you measure the continued impact of your training. Between one and two years after your initial evaluation, perform a further review to judge the training's effect. You can look at changes in

- number of compliance violations
- number of penalties
- percentage of market share.

The important thing to remember is to speak the business language. Make sure that the impact of your training programs is understood in concrete metrics that management both understands and values. For more information, see the sidebar *Metrics Case Study*.

Metrics Case Study

This case study demonstrates the importance of establishing clear, relevant metrics by which to measure your training results.

A pharmaceutical organization decided that it would change the way in which new-hire training was conducted. Rather than bring new hires into corporate headquarters for a full week of training, the company decided to deliver the first week of training in a self-study format to be completed at the new hires' homes. Topics such as expense reporting, compensation, and car allowance were presented in the form of interactive readings and discussions with the new hires' managers.

Before the shift in training method took place, the training organization worked with senior management to ensure that critical measures were evaluated before and after the training. Because this was a sales organization, the highest value was placed on sales results. At the same time, those involved in the new initiative recognized that factors other than training would affect sales outcomes. For example, new hires were to be provided with new, state-of-the-art computers and immediate access to product information not previously available.

Training proposed measuring sales results for new hires at three, six, and 12 months. They would then compare those results with those of representatives trained in the classroom at the same tenure points, keeping in mind the other factors that could influence results. The outcomes were impressive. Representatives who had been trained in the new method reached peak performance sooner than those trained in the classroom. Even allowing for new technology and access to product information, training was rightfully credited with playing a key role in producing the improved results.

Support Organizational Goals

Another important step in gaining value for training is tying training to organizational goals. Link your specific training initiatives to departmental or business unit objectives.

For example, an organization's goal could be to reduce non-manufacturing conformances related to errors in reading written instructions. Training's response could be to design a program for engineers, teaching them strategies for eliminating the need for written instructions through use of icons, graphs, and color-coding. The result would be reduced non-conformance through a new competency gained by engineers.

This also means that you must take increased care in evaluating training requests against the goals of the organization. In some cases this means justifying training in terms of strategic goals with the requirement that training clearly demonstrate how it supports a specific organizational goal. This is often done by drafting a project charter.

Develop a Project Charter

Your project charter should describe the project's objectives and deliverables against the organizational objectives it supports. It sets the standards for project management and should include

- mission and customers
- scope and approach
- objectives and evaluation
- resource requirements.

Example: An organizational goal is to improve output in the factory area by five percent this year. One area of opportunity in this effort is to train operators in the standard operating procedures for maintenance of the equipment. Managers have identified this as an area of opportunity in improving results on the floor. Right now maintenance is taking an estimated 10 to 20 percent longer than it should due to lack of training.

■ *Mission and Customers*

This section identifies the mission of the project and the targeted customers, both internal (division, subsidiary, department) and external (trade, consumer). It also describes the benefits of the project outputs to these customers. This section of the charter identifies what the customer needs and how the project output will respond to the need.

Example: This objective is aimed at operators who require training in maintenance and benefits external customers with improved quality of product. Financial benefits to the organization will be realized in improved output.

■ *Scope and Approach*

This section provides a description of work, how the project objectives will be accomplished, and the functions to be performed. This includes

● outputs/deliverables

● constraints, including the availability of special resources or funds that may affect project results.

Example: Training will be developed for lead supervisors who will train other supervisors in proper equipment maintenance procedures. This will involve a train-the-trainer program for supervisors that will take eight hours of classroom time. Deliverables will be a train-the-trainer manual, a leader's guide for supervisors who will train their operators in equipment maintenance, a videotape on proper maintenance procedures, and a guide for trainers in certifying supervisors.

One constraint is in releasing supervisors for time off in the classroom. We suggest a rotational schedule that will take up to five days to ensure that at least three supervisors are present on the floor during training.

■ *Objectives and Evaluation*

Here the project's goals and objectives are outlined with the criteria by which the results will be evaluated in areas such as

● cost
● schedule
● performance
● quality
● customer satisfaction.

Example: The ultimate goal of the training is to ensure supervisors can train their operators in proper equipment maintenance. We expect supervisors to be fully trained and ready to lead their operators through maintenance training in four weeks.

Supervisors' training will be evaluated at eight weeks and again at four months to assess the results of the training. Supervisors will keep records of maintenance logs pre- and post-training. Post-training evaluations will focus on the time it takes operators to perform maintenance as well as supervisors' observations.

■ *Resource Requirements*

This section determines the resources needed, including personnel, time, money, equipment, materials, and so on, both for the short and long term. This objective focuses on overall financial impact, including budget, anticipated sales, profit margins, and return on project investment.

Example: The personnel needed includes one trainer to develop the training and evaluations over a 16-week period, then spend approximately two weeks on site facilitating training with supervisors. Additional requirements are

● three lead supervisors to serve as subject matter experts to review training documents, checklists, and evaluations; approximately 40 hours of review and one four-hour run-through of the training

● one lead supervisor to lead the training over a one-week period

● four hours of training per operator

● approximately four hours of supervisors' evaluation to measure change before and after the training.

Financial impact will be based on numbers related to maintenance today versus post-training. Financial impact includes an estimated savings of between $750,000 and $1 million per year in improved productivity. This estimate is based on supervisors' assessments.

Develop an Evaluation Plan

This is where you have an opportunity to showcase the critical role your training plays in assisting the organization in meeting its goals. For this to be successful, your training function needs to broadcast its results if it is to assert its role as a key player in the organization.

Creating an evaluation strategy involves tactics that have to do with the resources and specific initiatives that will be involved in designing and delivering the training—for example, classroom versus e-learning, resources available, and materials to be developed. A variety of models exist for ensuring the soundness of training program design, and many professional trainers are good at identifying tactics related to training. They are frequently less successful at linking tactics to strategy and ensuring that the evaluation plan is developed and agreed upon up front.

The evaluation strategy should be built on the critical success factors identified early on in the process. Again these factors should be tied directly to concrete business results like increased sales numbers, improved efficiency, and decreased non-compliance. This can be accomplished by looking at hard data around the metrics that training is designed to affect and—even more important—collecting anecdotal information before and after training.

Conduct a Level 3 Evaluation

Training functions often do not routinely conduct Level 4 (results) and Level 5 (return-on-investment) evaluations. Level 4 and 5 evaluations can be powerful if they have the buy-in of the organization concerning their value, but most training functions are reluctant to commit the resources to do them. Even when they are done, these evaluations are likely to be met with at least some skepticism by managers outside of training.

Instead, focus your attention on a Level 3, or behavior evaluation. Nothing is more effective in establishing the value of training than testimonials from high-visibility people who can attest to training impact. As you might expect, the most convincing testimonials are combined with hard, quantitative data, so include numbers and statistics whenever possible. "My department experienced a reduction in defects..." or, "We experienced a sales increase of..."

This kind of information can be mined by conducting Level 3 evaluations with managers and speaking with learners themselves about the impact of training. Almost any training organization can gather information on the success of training from learners, their managers, and stakeholders.

This is not to discount the value of Level 4 and 5 evaluations. If your organization allocates you the time and resources to conduct one, do it. There are few things organizational leaders value more than seeing bottom-line results.

Anticipate Change

How many training programs are lost through a failure to keep them current—and how much money is lost in the process? For your training to stay relevant and useful, it must go through periodic changes. If the customer-stakeholder advisory panel is in place, change control should become a natural part of its responsibilities.

Who Is Responsible?

In some organizations, the ultimate responsibility for change resides with the program owner, who is responsible for modifying training when changes occur. In other organizations, training takes the lead in managing change control by gathering changes from the program owner and stakeholders who have input into the program.

Regardless of your organization's view on who is responsible for change, your training function should keep its eyes and ears open at all times. Organizational goals and initiatives change and your training should adjust to reflect those changes. By anticipating change and driving your insights back to the organization, you make your training function a more valuable business partner.

Whoever is responsible, a change control policy should specify who is in charge of developing, initiating, and overseeing changes to all training programs to ensure they consistently reflect the organization's needs. See the sidebar *Create a Change Control Policy* for more information.

Create a Change Control Policy

Your change control policy will keep your training updated and significant. Get employees at every level in the organization involved by making them aware that they can propose changes to training. Not all proposed changes need to be implemented, but they should be reviewed and commented upon to make employees feel that their opinion matters. This sidebar outlines what information should be contained in your change policy and the various people involved in making change happen.

Person Responsible	Tasks
Change Initiator: can be anyone in the organization who feels the training needs to be changed or updated.	**Change Request Initiation:** Complete a proposed change form and note whether the requested change is ● content ● format ● out of cycle review. Attach the current version of any affected training materials along with the proposed version or change as applicable. Forward to Change Management Liaison.
Change Management Liaison: can be anyone in the training department.	**Review:** Create the plan for implementing proposed changes and forward plan to the Program Administrator; then the changes can be approved or denied.
Program Administrator: typically the person who has taken ownership of the training program.	**Development and Implementation:** Review changes. If the changes are approved, a change package is created according to the implementation plan. Take the necessary action to complete implementation of the change. Review all related training materials to determine if other documents are affected by the proposed change. If so, notify the Change Management Liaison for review and approval. Update all appropriate document histories to ensure master copies reflect implementation of the change. Then file the change package in a folder that is maintained for each training document.

(continued on next page)

Create a Change Control Policy (continued)

Person Responsible	Tasks
	Periodic Update Cycle:
Program Administrator: typically the person who has taken ownership of the training program.	Conduct interviews or surveys of program stakeholders, program audience, and executive management to determine current trends that may affect training materials.
	Ensure training materials undergo a general review on a periodic basis. The periodic cycle will not be more frequent than four months or less frequent than six months.
	Issue a memo to all Initiators as to when the end of the next update cycle will occur. This notice will include a cut-off date as to when requests for changes must be received by the Program Administrator so as to allow sufficient time for review to ensure inclusion in the next periodic update.
Initiator: may be program stakeholders, program audience, management, or other interested parties.	Submit requests for change as they occur during the update cycle. On a periodic basis, Initiators may forward early change packages prior to the end of the update cycle. The change package issued at the end of the update cycle will include all early changes along with those received on or about the cycle cut-off date.
	Out of Cycle Changes: Any changes implemented during the update cycle will not be included in the update cycle change package. Document history will be updated as these changes are implemented.
	Maintain a complete set of all up-to-date training materials as well as a folder containing all distributed change packages along with all appropriate documentation that supports each change.

Improvement Through Change

The continuous improvement process takes into account change management. It can be structured this way for a single training program or for the entire training department. Use this chart to help guide your training through change and tailor your training to the needs of the business.

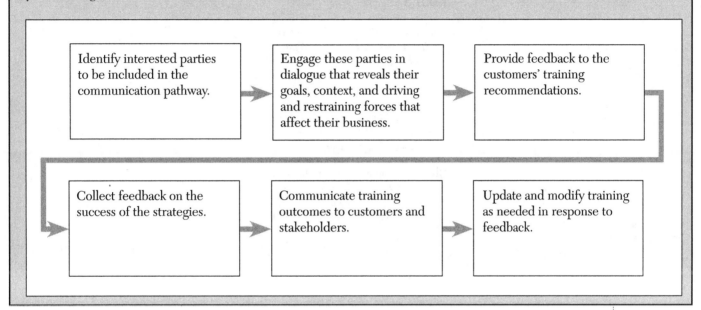

Foster Continuous Improvement

The continuous improvement process drives the business forward by ensuring an ongoing dialogue with customers, stakeholders, and other interested parties. To maintain a top-rated training department, you must

- communicate regularly to stakeholders and customers

- conduct surveys and broadcast your results

- hold advisory board meetings about specific initiatives

- develop and implement a continuous improvement plan that ensures training is up-to-date and responsive to business needs.

For more information, see the sidebar *Improvement Through Change.*

Strive for Success

Successful training functions view themselves as key contributors to the goals of the organization. In turn, the organization values the role training plays in goal achievement. A tool such as the VIP survey can tell you whether the organization values training and areas in which training needs to dig deeper to identify and resolve issues related to perception of training.

To be a successful training leader you must position your training as a critical business function and engage in an ongoing dialogue with customers and stakeholders. Your training should speak the language of the larger organization, and measure its success against metrics valued by the organization rather than the typical metrics training tends to focus on.

It's time for training professionals to get serious about engaging customers in ongoing dialogues about their needs and emphasizing training's role in achieving the goals of the organization. Training functions that have succeeded in doing this find themselves taking a seat at the table at the highest levels of the organization.

References & Resources

External Consultant

Donna Steffey
President
Vital Signs Training

Articles

Willmore, Joe. "How to Give 'Em Performance When They Insist on Training." *T+D*, May 2002, pp. 54-59.

Books

Buckingham, Marcus, and Curt Coffman. *First Break All the Rules: What the World's Greatest Managers Do Differently.* New York: Simon & Shuster, 1999.

Hale, Judith. *Outsourcing Training & Development: Factors for Success.* Hoboken, NJ: Pfeiffer, 2005.

Oberstein, Sophie, and Jan Alleman. *Beyond Free Coffee and Donuts: Marketing Training and Development.* Alexandria, VA: ASTD Press, 2003.

Tichy, Noel. *Leadership Engine.* New York: Harper Collins, 2002.

Tichy, Noel, and Stratford Sherman. *Control Your Destiny or Someone Else Will.* New York: Harper Collins, 2005.

Infolines

Davenport, Theresa. "Marketing Training Programs." No. 250102.

Davis, Eric, and Dave McFeely. "Training as a Business Partner." No. 250307.

Kirkpatrick, Donald L. "The Four Levels of Evaluation." No. 250701.

Spitzer, Dean, and Malcolm Conway. "Link Training to Your Bottom Line." No. 250201.

Thomas, Susan J. "Developing Thought Leaders." No. 250410.

Value, Impact, Perception Survey

The sample questions below are designed to give training departments quantified information about how training is valued in their organization. This sample survey is looking for information about how training affects users, especially with regard to achieving departmental and corporate goals. Use this information to benchmark training's position within the organization. You can also use the results to help training functions target continuous improvement strategies and tactics to increase the effectiveness in supporting long- and short-term corporate objectives.

You can develop specific questions based on those shown here to learn the value, impact, and overall perception of training in your organization.

Ask respondents to rate statements on a scale of 1 to 5. 5 = strongly agree; 4 = agree to a some extent; 3 = neither agree nor disagree; 2 = disagree to some extent; 1 = strongly disagree.

---

1. Our training function supports the development of critical competencies in my workforce.

       1   2   3   4   5

   Please explain:

2. The training function supports a culture of continuous learning.

       1   2   3   4   5

   Please explain:

3. Our training function takes appropriate responsibility for the success of our workforce in ensuring that our external customers are satisfied.

       1   2   3   4   5

   Please explain:

4. The training department understands and responds effectively to business-wide goals and initiatives.

       1   2   3   4   5

   Please explain:

5. Our training function plays an important role in achieving organizational goals—that is, building shareholder value, customer loyalty, and revenue.

       1   2   3   4   5

   Please explain:

6. The training function is critical to my success in my job.

       1   2   3   4   5

   Please explain:

7. The business impact of existing training is a good investment of the time and resources required.

       1   2   3   4   5

   Please explain:

8. The current training and development programs are key to attracting and hiring top talent.

       1   2   3   4   5

   Please explain:

(continued on next page)

Job Aid

Value, Impact, Perception Survey (continued)

9. The current training and development are key to reducing turnover.

1   2   3   4   5

Please explain:

10. Our training function is appropriately responsive to changing performance needs.

1   2   3   4   5

Please explain:

11. I am able to measure the impact of training against specific business metrics—for example, employee retention, sales, customer satisfaction and loyalty, time to market, share value, market share, and incentive compensation.

1   2   3   4   5

Please describe those metrics:

12. I seek out training for assistance in performance, gap, and needs analysis that will help us achieve our business objectives.

1   2   3   4   5

Please explain:

13. Our training department is excellent in:

A. *Analysis*

1   2   3   4   5

Please explain:

B. *Planning*

1   2   3   4   5

Please explain:

C. *Responsiveness*

1   2   3   4   5

Please explain:

D. *Keeping commitments*

1   2   3   4   5

Please explain:

E. *Communication with stakeholders and customers*

1   2   3   4   5

Please explain:

F. *Serving as a leadership pipeline*

1   2   3   4   5

Please explain:

When completed, total the participant's score and compare it to the ratings below.

80-100: Your training function is doing a good job with its customers and stakeholders.

60-79: Your training organization can benefit from building stronger links to customer and stakeholder goals.

Less than 59: Your training organization needs to establish stronger ties to customers and their goals.

Outsourcing Training

Issue 0002

AUTHOR

Stella Louise Cowan, M. Ed.
Plante & Moran, LLP
505 N. Woodward Avenue
Suite 2000
Bloomfield Hills, MI 48304
Tel: 248.644.0300
Fax: 248.644.2990
E-mail: Indybridge@msn.com

Stella Cowan is a Senior Consultant with Plante & Moran, LLP and an adjunct professor in management at Baker College. Her areas of expertise include instructional design, organizational behavior, and change management. She has worked in training and organizational development for 15 years.

Editor
Cat Sharpe Russo

Managing Editor
Sabrina E. Hicks

Production Design
Leah Cohen

Internal Consultant
Phil Anderson

Outsourcing Training

What is Outsourcing?

To outsource or not to outsource? It is a question frequently asked by training, performance improvement, human resources, and organizational development managers. But what is it? Outsourcing is the idea of using external resources or products to meet business needs. This idea is gaining a new kind of momentum on several fronts to accommodate today's fast-evolving, competitive world:

- as a viable strategic planning option
- as a targeted cost-saving tool
- as an avenue for greater flexibility

This trend toward external help is the norm in light of the tremendous pressure on organizations to, among other challenging feats achieve the following:

- meet changing, and sometimes unpredictable, customer demands

- respond to increasing technology advancements

- stay one step ahead of marketplace shifts

Organizations must be skillful and nimble to survive competitive waters. Training managers, trainers, instructional designers, and organizational development professionals have a great opportunity to benefit from partnering with high-caliber, results-focused vendors. This applies whether you outsource to internal organizational experts or external resources and consultants.

This *Info-line* discusses two aspects of outsourcing: First, how to use outsourcing as a strategic advantage and second, how to proactively address potential challenges. In addition, essential areas including cost, contracting, and locating vendors are discussed within the context of these themes. The job aid, located on the last two pages of this issue, will help you assess how well a vendor matches or meets your outsourcing requirements.

Types of Outsourcing

The decision to outsource is not an easy one to make. It depends on a number of factors, including the following:

- cost
- internal capability

- program or project objectives
- content

These components are key in the decision-making equation. And the quality of the decision making affects the overall success of the outsourcing endeavor. So it is important to identify the appropriate type of outsourcing for the specific need. Keep in mind that outsourcing can take many forms. A number of those forms are described in the glossary.

Strategic Advantage

The decision to engage in any type of outsourcing is a serious business decision; thus, you should view it strategically. Every aspect of the outsourcing process, from identifying the need for services to writing the contract, presents an avenue for advancing your organization's strategic position. The Four Quadrants of Opportunity, detailed in the following sections, illustrate this perspective (see diagram that follows).

These four quadrants provide a framework for the following:

- assessing the value of outsourcing in your particular situation

- developing criteria for evaluating potential vendors

- creating a plan for long-term benefit

I. Time, Resources, and Budget

Often, you do not have the time or resources to research and develop new processes, services, or products. Outsourcing frees up your staff to perform the more critical tasks. It also provides another benefit: helping you acquire needed knowledge and expertise for the duration of a project. Learn from vendors by tapping into their knowledge bank. Where feasible, ensure that they leave your department with information, products, or processes that continue to support your business goals.

The Four Quadrants of Opportunity

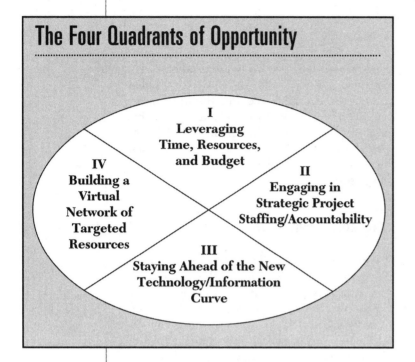

Equally important to time and resource constraints are issues involving budget dollars. When you find that budget dollars allocated to maintaining a full-time training and development staff are shrinking, outsourcing may provide an escape. Contract, as-needed trainers, and off-the-shelf programs can be very inviting from a budget-sensitive perspective. Of course, calculating cost-savings is not a simple exercise. The sidebar on the following page provides more detail on costs.

There are a number of ways you can leverage time, resources, and budget—including the following:

1. Outsourcing allows you to use validated programs, interventions, and instruments that have a proven track record. Potentially, you can verify the success of the product.

2. Outsourcing allows you to save budget dollars on start-up costs for new research or product ventures. In theory, you share or shift part of the cost to your outsourcing partners. A program like "Partnership Has Its Perx," highlighted in a following sidebar, is an example of this.

The bottom line is that outsourcing can serve as a quasi-strategic option in your effort to change quickly and timely in an unforgiving market. Three primary drivers precipitate outsourcing: staffing, money, and time.

II. Strategic Project Staffing/Accountability

Your primary goals when using outsourcing as a strategic option are as follows:

1. Identify how best to use your internal resources.

2. Identify how best to leverage external resources.

You must think through critical issues and questions as you create your outsourcing strategy:

- Can your department or organization put internal resources into other areas and use outsourcing to fill the vacancies?

- Does your staff have the expertise, intellectual clout, or status to influence a particular customer?

Let us say, for example, that the senior leadership group is your customer. In this scenario, all senior leaders are going through an executive assessment process. Who is the best resource for administering the process? Who is the best resource for giving the feedback? Perhaps an outside vendor with no political ties to the organization or who can relate to senior leaders (in terms of gender, perceived intellectual stature, or perceived status) is the best candidate for providing accurate assessment.

Remember, to use outsourcing strategically means that you identify its potential impact from several key angles, such as the following:

flexibility—just in time, just enough training delivery

targeted expertise—access to high-level, specialized talent for a specified, budget-driven period of time

III. The Technology/Information Curve

The new technology/information curve is fast moving. The fact that technology is in such an explosive state makes this especially true. Innovative design and delivery methods for creating solutions to performance needs (for example, customer service immersion training, virtual performance coaching, and Web-based training) are continuously bursting forth. That is why trying to keep abreast of the cutting-edge in high quality, effective performance products and services can be daunting.

The use of outsourcing partners provides some of the answer. External vendors can infuse new knowledge and perspective into your culture. In some cases, they have a broader information and technology base than your organization. They often incorporate the review of new materials and technologies as a standard part of their operation.

Equally significant, they typically have a library or reference center of current and classic resources. You can tap into their knowledge regarding, for example, the latest or best team development simulations. The vendor or external resource could easily assess the degree to which the simulation meets your specific needs. In addition, it is possible that the vendor could provide the staff to administer the simulation.

In some instances, interventions or assessment instruments and processes require certified individuals to deliver the training. If so, you should ensure that the vendor you select has certified staff or is willing to share responsibility for the

---

Generally Accepted Contract Costs

The table below lists some generally accepted costs included in various types of products and services.

Category	Costs
Presenters/facilitators	<ul><li>speaker's fee</li><li>transportation, lodging, and food</li><li>handouts and participant materials</li><li>media needs</li><li>special room arrangements</li></ul>
Courses/seminars	<ul><li>enrollment fees</li><li>participant's travel, lodging, and food</li><li>participant's materials, books, and texts</li><li>on-site costs if held at the organization's facility</li><li>additional training the organization may need to provide</li></ul>
Packaged programs	<ul><li>basic costs, including participant materials, instructor guides, films, videos, and shipping</li><li>pilot programs conducted by the resources</li><li>outside instructors (for example, salaries and expenses)</li><li>instructor training or certification</li><li>AV equipment</li><li>on-site costs</li><li>licensing or copyright costs</li></ul>
Tailored or custom programs (in addition to cost listed in the previous sections)	<ul><li>analyzing the organization's needs</li><li>designing the training or process</li><li>developing the product</li><li>evaluating the results</li></ul>

Trainer's Outsourcing Glossary

Contractors: Training and development experts who are not employees of the organization. Contractors can perform assignments on-site or on their premises.

Generic (off-the-shelf): An existing product, program, or process (for example, a training course or curriculum, team intervention, or performance coaching system) that meets the criteria for a specific need (in terms of content, format, accessibility, and so forth) without adaptation or modification.

Customized: A product, program, or process designed from concept to end-product to meet the criteria for a specific need.

Tailored: An existing product, program, or process adapted or modified to meet the criteria for a specific need. This saves time and cost over an original design.

Resource leasing: Training and development staff are hired through human resources leasing agency. This agency handles the screening, hiring, and benefit administration costs. The leasing arrangement covers a specified period of time.

Resource pool: An internal database or file of prescreened individuals with specific skills, who can meet a designated need (such as training delivery, performance coaching, or curriculum design). Use of the individuals depends on the organization's cycle of need and the individual's availability. The organization can monitor the internal success records of individuals and use this information to determine which individuals to use on a repeat basis. This concept can be beneficial when the organization is involved in a multiphase hiring blitz (such as the staffing ramp-up during the launch of a new operation or the addition of a new location). Having information on file can cut down on the time it takes to locate and screen resources.

Trainer "in a box": A relatively new concept that involves contracting, at a fixed fee, for the range of training delivery and development services for use as/when needed. Vendors provide products and services at wholesale prices in return for up-front payment of a total package fee. The vendor does not take over the training function, but it provides a "box," if you will, of people, products, and services that the organization can access when needed. This concept can provide a unique, mutually beneficial, long-term business relationship between the organization and the vendor.

certification. (You can negotiate these types of details in the contract discussions. See the sidebar *Developing a Contract* for highlights on contract development.) Furthermore, large training vendors typically have a development arm of their operations and create their own content, process, or technologically advanced products. This can translate into an advantage for your organization.

IV. Virtual Network of Resources

If you manage or direct the training and development function without a full staff, building a virtual network of resources can help you succeed. Create your own database of vendors categorized by expertise and abilities—whether your projects are short-term and narrowly focused or long-term and multi-faceted. (See the job aid for suggested database elements.)

Identify each vendor's capabilities by assessing its products based on qualitative and quantitative metrics. Find internal customers with whom the vendors have worked and collect information. Use a simple checklist or conduct a quick telephone interview (asking three or four key questions) to track each vendor's capabilities. You should schedule periodic formal and informal vendor evaluations, and solicit feedback from customers at the end of every project. This effort takes time, but in the long run you will benefit greatly. Do not forget to look at their interpersonal abilities (influencing customers, handling difficult situations, and so forth).

You should also evaluate the project management ability. Regardless of the nature or extent of the outsourcing project, skillful management of deliverables, deadlines, resources, and people is a requisite for success. In some instances, creativity or out-of-the-box thinking might be appropriate. Time, location, or audience challenges can result in a need for greater creativity in the design of training or organizational development solutions. Here are some examples of such challenges:

● An organization wants an interactive mentoring program for participants who are geographically dispersed.

● A virtual organization wants training in group decision making.

Partnership Has Its Perx

"Partnership Has Its Perx" is the name of a "trainer/developer/needs assessor in a box" concept used successfully by one manager at the Kmart Resource Center in Troy, Michigan. Partnership Has Its Perx provides a broad range of training and organizational development-related services (for example, instructional design, team interventions, change management, and career development) delivered by high-caliber professionals. It also provides an opportunity to build a mutually beneficial, long-term business relationship. This package delivers impressive value "in a box" in a number of ways, including the following:

- site licensing for an entire library of first-class training programs

- monthly support for the partner organization's ongoing customization, design, research, and train-the-trainer needs

- ongoing updates and new programs added to the partner organization's library at no additional cost

- significant discounts on shelf products from acclaimed publishers

Determining up front what value and quality look like in your specific organization and situation is paramount to successful outsourcing. *Value* as well as *quality* are key outcomes organizations want to realize from their relationships with external resources.

Finding the Right "Outside Partner"

Hope Hoffman, Manager of Learning and Development at the Kmart Resource Center, has experienced the advantages of Partnership Has Its Perx first hand. Faced with multiple, high visible projects requiring high-end design, facilitation, and assessment skills, and working in an environment where head count is hard to get, Ms. Hoffman sought an effective solution. She explored various options by interviewing a number of individual contractors (instructors and course developers) and training vendors. She realized that she might have to work with more than one vendor but still wanted a focal point (that is, a single vendor to handle the majority of the project components).

She was looking for an "outside partner" as she described it. She believed it was not advantageous to find separate resources for each project. Ms. Hoffman had specific criteria in mind, which is key to locating the right resource and assessing that resource's ability to meet your needs. Also, she sought to understand her internal customer's needs, as well as comprehend the operational and cultural-fit of the various projects she was assigned.

Identifying Primary Selection Criteria

The primary selection criteria should guide your search. Ms. Hoffman's primary selection criteria included an outside partner who could perform the following:

- offer systemic solutions that incorporated all the support systems essential to making a culture change

- understand culture and all of the steps in the process to make a change

- demonstrate versatility and knowledge depth in organizational development tools and techniques (theory and application)

- provide designers and instructors with high-end skills for developing *and* managing projects

Through situation/example-based interviews with various vendors, Ms. Hoffman determined that Partnership Has Its Perx could satisfy these criteria. Specifically, she has used Partnership Has Its Perx for the following:

- team development
- career coaching workshop facilitation
- instructional design for customer service training
- professional skills presentations

Developing a Contract

This chart describes the typical elements of a contract. The chart is not intended to be a definitive description of vendor contract components. Rather, it is a guide or reference for your contract development efforts. In addition, depending on the protocol established in your organization, human resources, legal, or purchasing departments usually handle writing vendor contracts.

Contract Section	Description/What to Include
Parties engaging in the contract or agreement	• Legal name and address of the parties engaging in the agreement (the organization and the vendor).
Scope of services	• Specific services or products the vendor will deliver. • Anticipated outcomes or benefits of the services or products. • Name of the contract administrator (that is, the person in your organization who acts as the vendor's primary client or is responsible for coordinating the vendor's activities).
Terms of agreement	• Effective date for the contract. • End date for the contract.
Payment	• Amount vendor will be paid (for example, hourly rate, lump-sum amount, or payment schedule amount). • How vendor will be paid (for example, within 30 days of receipt of invoices). • Purchase order number (if applicable). • Extent to which costs not directly related to the scope of services will be paid, such as travel, meals, and lodging (for example, reimbursement for travel beyond 40 miles at a rate of 30.5 cents per mile).
Termination	• Conditions under which the contract can be terminated (for example, specification that the organization can exercise the right to cancel the contract in whole or part with a 60-day written notice to do so).
Compliance with law	• Specification that both parties will comply with all federal, state, and local laws, ordinances, rules, and regulations applicable to the activities and obligations under the contract.
Professional standards	• Specification that the vendor must perform the work delivered under the contract with the degree of skill and care required by current, good, and sound professional procedures and practices. • Expectations for correction of work that does not meet professional standards. • Consequences for failure to meet professional standards (for example, cancellation of contract or withholding of payment).
Right to audit	• Indication that the organization has the right (upon reasonable notice and at reasonable times) to audit the vendor's business records and invoices directly related to fulfillment of the contract. • Specification of timeframe that the organization expects the vendor to maintain records of all matters related to fulfillment of the contract (for example, three years after the expiration of the contract).

Confidentiality	• Conditions of confidentiality relative to written, electronic, or oral information (for example, specification that all files must be returned to the organization at the end of the contract, or specification that the obligations of confidentiality survive the term of the contract).
Original works	• Indication that all original works developed by the vendor under the contract will be "works for hire" under the United States Copyright Laws and remain the sole and exclusive right of the organization.
Non-solicitation of employees	• Specification of conduct (that is, what is acceptable and what is not) related to soliciting the services or employing persons of the other party.
Non-competition and conflicts of interest	• Specification of what constitutes conflict of interest relative to fulfilling the contract.
Arbitration	• Description of the process for handling any controversy or claim arising out of or related to the contract (for example, indicating that such situations shall be settled exclusively by final and binding arbitration in accordance with the rules of the American Arbitration Association).
Insurance	• Description of insurance coverage and limits the vendor is expected to maintain (for example, liability or Worker's Compensation).
Signatures	• Signatures of both parties to indicate agreement with the contract.

- An organization is quickly ramping-up with a large number of additional staff for a new operation and needs a training curriculum delivered in a quick-strike manner.

- A newly merged organization is bringing together several cultures across the globe and seeks a teambuilding strategy.

- An organization is downsizing and seeks a systematic process for job transition support for displaced workers.

Addressing Challenges

Coupled with adopting a strategic approach to outsourcing is the commitment to proactivity. In other words, you must be vigilant in your efforts to anticipate and address potential roadblocks to success. This vigilance should start from the moment you entertain the idea of outsourcing. Tactics like combating culture resistance, influencing decision makers, and finding the best fit vendor require forethought and pre-planning.

Outsourcing Process

The Four Quadrants of Opportunity previously detailed represent only part of the picture for outsourcing success. Proactively addressing potential challenges is equally critical. Such proactivity is applicable at any point along the process spectrum provided on the following page.

Combating Resistance

When selecting vendors, make sure they fit with your culture in terms of diversity (that is, organizational attitudes, ideas, and approaches) and what you are attempting to achieve. You should also assess the effectiveness of vendors. Do this by using a quick, user-friendly assessment tool to periodically evaluate their effectiveness on a "how" (for example, achieving goals or behaviors) and "what" (achieving products or outcomes) perspective. Because vendors have to interact with employees and leadership, you want a partnership or collaboration not a "great divide."

Outsourcing Process Spectrum

Although the steps along this spectrum are basic, they still illustrate a good framework for the outsourcing endeavor. The feedback arrow denotes the importance of monitoring and assessing the vendor's performance outcomes. Through these actions, you identify behaviors and results that are synchronous with your expectations and those that require modification.

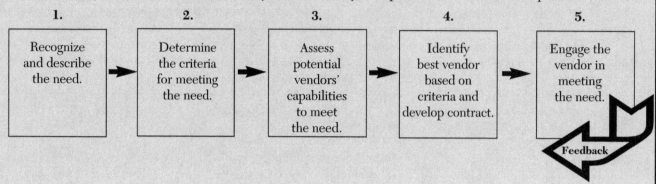

1.	2.	3.	4.	5.
Recognize and describe the need.	Determine the criteria for meeting the need.	Assess potential vendors' capabilities to meet the need.	Identify best vendor based on criteria and develop contract.	Engage the vendor in meeting the need.

Feedback

Beware of vendors who are more interested in acquiring additional business in your organization than tending to their existing contract with you. A vendor's behavior may be subtle, but the impact is the same. It can affect your ability to reduce culture resistance because it redirects your energy and focus. You need a true partner.

If you notice that a vendor is acting in a self-serving manner, you must discuss this behavior in a formal performance feedback setting. Provide specific behavioral examples, and give the feedback as soon after the incident as possible. This is especially important if the project or function outsourced to a vendor is relatively long-term.

Besides vendor assessment, another way to combat culture resistance is to *prime the pump*—that is, let everyone involved know what is happening. This act is important in situations where you outsource needs assessment or you outsource only part of the project.

Talk with the vendor to ensure that he or she understands organizational sensitivities. For example, if the organization does not use the term "consultant" or "contractor," makes sure the vendor knows. If there are other cultural sensitivities, such as chain-of-command or protocol issues, make sure the vendor if aware of that information as well. Brief the consultant before he or she starts the project. Advise him or her about significant or distinctive qualities of the culture.

Decision Makers

You will not always be the primary decision maker. Sometimes you have internal clients who are the ultimate decision makers; sometimes, the individual you report to or individuals in upper management are the ultimate decision makers. Regardless of the scenario, it is cost and value that influence decision makers. Your job is twofold:

1. Determine to what degree the cost and value assumption is true. Survey or interview decision makers about their expectations of the external resource relative to the bottom-line value of its service.

2. Identify what cost and value "looks like" to the individual decision makers. Because you need to know what decision makers are willing to pay for, try to both quantify (for example, how many, how much, how soon, and how often) and qualify (for example, what kind and to what degree) expectations. Take note, any number of items can represent value currency. Examples of such currency include the following:

   - staff with doctorate degrees

   - experience in a particular industry

   - client list containing prestigious organizations

Value currency could also be how quickly vendors can design and deliver the work. If possible, find out what the "make it or break it" decision elements are for the individual decision makers. Structure your presentation or sales campaign around addressing those elements. Also inherent in cost and value are the intrinsic factors that influence the individual decision makers. For example, decision makers might look for consultants who embody the same values or approach to business as they do. (See the chart on the following page.)

Find a Best Fit Vendor

Design a quick, straightforward assessment tool or process for evaluating vendors. Consider a variety of elements, then assign an appropriate weight to each element. The weight should depend on your needs and your expectations about the quality of the product or service. Here are some elements you might include in your process:

- credentials of the staff

- feedback from previous clients

- your organization's previous experience with the vendor

- degree of cohesion between the organizational philosophies of the vendor and your organization

- depth of the vendor's related experiences

- vendor's staffing capabilities

- quality of vendor's products

The objectives of the service or product considered must reflect your organization's objectives. It is not enough for a vendor to submit a flawless proposal or deliver an impeccable presentation. If the vendor does not meet your organization's specific needs and objectives, you waste your money. More important, you waste the precious time of internal staff and training participants. And you may compromise your credibility.

Fit also refers to the "relationship factor." You should not underestimate the power and importance of a good vendor relationship. The advantages in terms of the ease of getting things done and the synergy from collaboration is invigorating.

Although the key elements for relationship success are basic, they still warrant attention:

Mutual respect. Understand and respect each other's values and perspectives.

Role clarity. Ensure roles and accountabilities (for example, the quality standards or delivery date for a product) are clear and understood. The written contract as well as an in-person review of the project deliverable support achieving role clarity.

Role responsibility or accountability. Accept responsibility for the project and the relationship.

Trust. Establish and maintain a high degree of trust around the work, internal politics, interpersonal interactions, and contract issues. Confidentiality is also an aspect of trust. Both parties must feel comfortable with the other's regard for confidential matters.

Feedback. Create frequent contact and feedback opportunities. You should schedule regular (two-way) feedback sessions. Frequent, quality feedback can help avert problems before they occur as well as promote consistency and quality.

In contrast, relationships breakdown for the following reasons:

- Money is the sole reason for the relationship.

- Internal support for the project is nonexistent or disappears during the execution of the project.

- Accountabilities are confused.

- Communication breaks down.

- Trust is low or lacking.

Determining Decision Maker's Cost and Value Currency

This grid is helpful whether you are working with several decision makers or you are solely responsible for making decisions. Putting on the hat of each decision maker, assign each factor a number between one and seven (with one being most critical; seven being least critical). In the last column, jot down notes that will help you promote or compensate for that factor. This exercise will help you understand the priorities of each decision maker.

Factors	Priority of Factor for Decision Maker (1 = most critical/7 = least critical)	Influence or Sales Strategy (Depending on the situation, how you will promote or compensate for the factor.)
Staff credentials		
Technology capabilities		
Track record		
Client list		
Geographic range of resources		
Depth of experience in a specific industry		
Reputation or perceived ranking in the training and performance industry		
Range and reputation of products and programs in the marketplace		
Consulting style		
Existing business relationship		
Past personal experience		

Evaluating Outputs

Finding the best fit vendor establishes the foundation for creating a successful partnership. Evaluating the quality of the vendor's outputs as the work unfolds adds depth to that foundation. In essence, giving feedback on product quality or methods helps you manage expectations and deadlines. Include a process in the contract for periodic feedback. For long-term projects that you outsource, this is especially important. Ensure that feedback focuses on performance and is based on the criteria you established for success.

If something occurs that affects production, quality, or interpersonal relations, give feedback immediately (or as close to the time of the occurrence as possible). Your feedback mechanism can be as simple as a checklist of productivity and quality criteria. Think about the appropriate mechanism and criteria ahead of time. You do not want to spend money to later realize that you did not get what you wanted or expected.

One good idea is to stipulate in the contract that if the vendor does not improve the product or service after specific feedback, this constitutes a breach of contract and reason to cancel the contract. Be specific in your contract about quality, quantity, and deadlines.

Costs

While finding the best fit and evaluating outputs as the project unfold form a critical foundation for success, managing cost is perhaps the linchpin. You must account for *all* costs incurred with outsourcing. While vendors do not hide costs intentionally, most assume that the individual representing the organization knows about extra costs inherent in the purchase of the product or service. To avoid unnecessary hassles, get it in writing.

Where appropriate, consider a sliding fee scale for varying levels of experience and expertise among the external resource's staff used on your project. Beware of the vendor that uses your organization as a training ground for its new crop of consultants. Typically, this is more of an issue on long-term projects with multiple components. Managing who is doing what on these projects can be more difficult. For this reason, it is critical to establish specific quality checkpoints and scheduled performance feedback opportunities. You need to establish criteria for success. What does it look like? It is essential that you answer this question before you engage the vendor.

Contracting

You can negotiate for several different types of contracts:

Firm fixed price. The product or service can be clearly defined (for example, a presentation, video, or generic program).

Cost plus fixed price. Analysis and development are involved and a negotiated percentage of the overall cost is identified as profit. Government procurement offices often use this procedure.

Cost plus incentive fee. When time is critical, the resource gets a bonus if the contract is completed ahead of schedule. The reverse is also possible, in which the contract imposes a penalty for missed deadlines.

Performance contracts. A certain percentage of the fixed fee is added based on the successful performance of individuals on the job. This works only where desired performance can be specifically described and measured.

Often the legal or financial management departments of an organization negotiate the terms of the contract and Human Resources supports (or leads) negotiating the content. You may, however, find that you alone are responsible for developing the contract. Refer to the *Developing a Contract* sidebar for an overview of contract parts.

Reproduction Rights

Presenting text in a downloadable format has inspired new concern about reproduction rights. You should clarify reproduction rights before signing a contract. Resources such as presenters, facilitators, suppliers, and design consultants have a right to protect their developed materials from unauthorized reproductions—whether these reproductions are found on your intranet or are distributed as hard copies.

For example, purchasing a course, intervention process, or video does not automatically give you the right to make copies. Specify in writing which of the following agreements satisfy the wishes of the author or producer:

- Vendor retains absolute copyright authority, which prohibits any reproduction.

- Vendor permits limited reproduction if permission is requested and granted.

- Vendor permits unlimited reproduction within the organization—the usual case with custom-packaged materials.

Outsourcing Determination Grid

To understand how outsourcing affects your organization as a whole, use this grid to look at the "big picture."

Factors	Things to Consider
Cost comparison and budget constraints	• Get as much information about the cost of the project or product as possible. Compare the cost of developing or delivering the project yourself with the vendor's cost. Do not forget to look at items like licensing fee.
Long-term versus short-term	• What kind of time and staff commitment can the vendor make? This is particularly important for a long-term project or need. • Ask questions about the vendor's staffing capabilities. Depending on the duration and complexity of the project, you probably want to know about administrative and project management staff as well. • You might want to ask about the processes used for project management (for example, what type of software programs do they use for project management).
Organization's culture	• Within the context of the outsourcing opportunity, compare your organization's culture to the culture, philosophy, or approach of the vendor. Are the two synchronous? • Ask questions about how the vendor will execute the project. For example, if diversity is important in your culture, inquire as to whom will be involved in delivering the project components. • Preview vendor materials that are potentially a part of the project to ensure consistency with what you want portrayed in your culture (including training manuals, videos, application models, and performance tools). This could include consistency in language (for example, using the word "leader" as opposed to "supervisor" or using the word "staff" as opposed to "subordinates") or setting (for example, video settings showing office workers for a training program for manufacturing workers). • Talk to others who have used the vendor.
State of the organization	• Consider the following questions in assessing the state of your organization: Is the organization currently involved in merger activities? Has there been a recent downsizing or is one expected? Is the organization involved in reengineering? Are there anticipated changes in key leadership positions or roles? • How you position the use of vendors and whom you select are affected by the answers to these questions. You might want to select a vendor with experience in these situations, even if the project does not directly relate to the situations.
Nature of deliverables or outcomes	• Is the product or program sensitive? Will it have high visibility? Are there political implications? Will there be a wide-scale implementation? • An incentive or disincentive fee in the contract might be appropriate as a deadline or quality control measure. Also, a systematic communication plan or process might be appropriate.
Decision-making autonomy	• Assess your decision-making autonomy. This may impact the vendor you select and how you present your selection to those involved in the final decision.
Audience receiving the service or product	• Do you anticipate audience acceptance will be a problem? Think it through, and identify ways to increase audience acceptance or at least make it more palatable.

Today, more than ever, outsourcing is part of how organizations do business. Savvy training and development professionals appreciate the strategic impact of outsourcing. Hallmarks of successful outsourcing endeavors include the following:

- creating true partnerships with vendors

- leveraging time and resources

- staying abreast of fast-evolving technology and information

New operational perspectives and a new demand on existing skills makes managing the training function an exciting task. In addition, making it all work is a process, not an event. It requires implementing key actions like those discussed in this *Info-line*. The bottom line is this: find the strategic advantage in every outsourcing opportunity.

References & Resources

Articles

Anderson, Merrill C. "Transforming Support Work into Competitive Advantage." *National Productivity Review,* Spring 1998, pp. 11-18.

Bassi, Laurie J., et al. "Training Industry Trends 1997." *Training & Development,* November 1997, pp. 46-59.

Byham, William C., and Sheryl Riddle. "Outsourcing: A Strategic Tool for a More Strategic HR." *Employment Relations Today,* Spring 1999, pp. 37-55.

Davidson, Linda. "Cut Away Noncore HR." *Workforce,* January 1998, pp. 40-45.

DeRose, Garry J., and Janet McLaughlin. "Outsourcing Through Partnerships." *Training & Development,* October 1995, pp. 51-55.

DiRomualdo, Anthony, and Vijay Gurbaxani. "Strategic Intent for IT Outsourcing." *Sloan Management Review,* Summer 1998, pp. 67-80.

Ellis, Teri. "The Future of Training." *Occupational Health & Safety,* June 1999, pp. 34-43.

Gordon, Jack. "The Great Outsourcing Stampede—That Never Happened." *Training,* February 1998, pp. 38-48.

———. "Outsourcing on the Web." *Training,* June 1998, pp. 98-100.

Kaeter, Margaret. "An Outsourcing Primer." *Training & Development,* November 1995, pp. 20-25.

Katz, Bruce E. "What a PEO Can Do for You." *Journal of Accountancy,* July 1999, pp. 57-61.

Klaas, Brian S., et al. "HR Outsourcing and Its Impact." *Personnel Psychology,* Spring 1999, pp. 113-136.

Laabs, Jennifer. "The Dark Side of Outsourcing." *Workforce,* September 1998, pp. 42-48.

Lonsdale, Chris, and Andrew Cox. "Falling in with the Out Crowd." *People Management,* October 15, 1998, pp. 52-55.

Maurer, Rick, and Nancy Mobley. "Outsourcing: is it the HR Department of the future?" *HRFocus,* November 1998, pp. 9-10.

Merrick, Neil. "Premier Division." *People Management,* August 19, 1999, pp. 38-39, 41.

Ozanne, Marq R., and Michael F. Corbett. "Outsourcing '98 Winning in Today's Global Marketplace." *Fortune,* July 20, 1998, pp. S1-S8, S28-S32.

Pickard, Jane. "Externally Yours." *People Management,* July 23, 1998, pp. 34-37.

Quinn, James Brian. "Strategic Outsourcing: Leveraging Knowledge Capabilities." *Sloan Management Review,* Summer 1999, pp. 9-21.

Rasmusson, Erika. "Getting Schooled in Outsourcing." *Sales & Marketing Management,* January 1999, pp. 49-51.

Salopek, Jennifer J. "Outsourcing, Insourcing, and In-Between Sourcing." *Training & Development,* July 1998, pp. 51-56.

Books

DeRose, Garry J. *Outsourcing Training & Education.* Alexandria, VA: ASTD, 1999.

Domberger, Simon. *The Contracting Organization: A Strategic Guide to Outsourcing.* Oxford University Press, 1999.

Greaver, Maurice F. *Strategic Outsourcing: A Structured Approach to Outsourcing Decisions and Initiatives.* AMACOM, 1999.

Info-lines

Callahan, Madelyn (ed.). "Be a Better Needs Analyst." No. 8502 (Revised 1998).

Darraugh, Barbara (ed.). "How to Conduct a Cost-Benefit Analysis." No. 9007 (Revised 1997).

Gilley, Jerry W. "Strategic Planning for Human Resource Development." No. 9206 (Revised 1998).

Murrell, Kenneth L. "Organizational Culture." No. 9304 (Revised 1997).

Overfield, Karen. "Developing and Administering Training: A Practical Approach." No. 9201 (Revised 1997).

Sparhawk, Sally. "Strategic Needs Analysis." No. 9408 (Revised 1999).

Thompson, Connie. "Project Management: A Guide." No. 8502 (Revised 1998).

Waagen, Alice K. "Essentials of Evaluation." No. 9705.

Assessing the Vendors

Use this job aid to help you assess the degree to which a vendor meets your requirements for three critical areas:

1. Performance ability relative to the 14 types of programs, products, or services listed below.

2. Project management ability.

3. Twelve key skills for training and organizational development professionals.

Use assessment strategies like reviewing the vendor's products, conducting structured interviews, collecting feedback from customers, observing the vendor's programs, and participating in the vendor's programs. Decide on an assessment scale. A simple three-point scale (adequate, good, and superior) is shown in the job aid. It is best to keep the scale relatively simple and straightforward.

Create a database to house the information (for example, a spreadsheet). Refer to the database when you need to identify an appropriate vendor (with the best skill fit) for a particular project. In addition, the database can support your efforts to build a virtual network of targeted vendors.

Scale: 1 = Adequate   2 = Good   3 = Superior

Program, Product, or Service Category	Name of Resource: Credentials: Contact Information (phone number, fax number, email address, address):	Assessment		
		Performance Ability (overall command of skills essential for the particular product category—for example, script writing, creating a learning hierarchy, using instructional media, or applying group theory)	**Project Management Skills** (meeting deadlines using resources appropriately, communicating updates or issues promptly, handling roadblocks)	**Comments** (observations or insights, review of products, feedback from internal customers)
Training Design				
Process Design (for example, behavioral-based interviewing model, telephone skills simulation)				
Training Customization of Existing Product				
Job or Performance Aid Design				
Training Evaluation				

(continued on next page)

Scale: 1 = Adequate   2 = Good   3 = Superior

Program, Product, or Service Category	Name of Resource **Credentials** **Contact Information** (phone number, fax number, email address, address)	**Assessment**		
		Performance Ability (overall command of skills essential for the particular product category—for example, script writing, creating a learning hierarchy, using instructional media, or applying group theory)	**Project Management Skills** (meeting deadlines using resources appropriately, communicating updates or issues promptly, handling roadblocks)	**Comments** (observations or insights, review of products, feedback from internal customers)
Training Delivery				
Individual Performance Coaching				
Executive Coaching				
Career Coaching				
Group Intervention				
Computer-Based Training				
Training Needs Assessment				
Distance Learning Design and Management				
Intranet or Web-Based Training Design and Management				

Writing Winning Proposals

Issue 0207

Writing Winning Proposals

AUTHOR

Steve Theobald
Productivity Partners
1111 Springfield Pike
Cincinnati, OH 45215
Tel: 513.821.7997
Fax: 435.518.1892
Email: stheobald@pptrs.com

Steve Theobald owns a proposal software and consulting company in Cincinnati.

Editor
Stephanie Sussan
ssussan@astd.org

Copy Editor
Ann Bruen

Production Design
Kathleen Schaner

Proposal Writing 101

A chore or a looked-forward-to experience? Drudgery or an opportunity to express your creative talents? Agony and anguish or energizing and uplifting?

Few would claim proposal writing as any of the enjoyable latter descriptions. Most of us approach the task with some dread, as we know it is an arduous effort. But we accept the necessity of it—who would try to get a potential client to rescind a request for proposal (RFP) because it's hard work for you?

Proposals *are* hard work. There is no way around that. Even the PC-based templates, macros, and wizards only help a little. Experience and a systematic approach are the only remedies to easing the effort. And that only helps some of the time, everybody gets writer's block—even Stephen King.

No two experiences are the same, and no two systematic approaches to proposal writing are the same either. One person may start on structure, another on content, and still another on style. All of these elements are equally important, and as long as the final product comes together on time and effectively states your proposition, the order in which you tackle the proposal effort does not matter.

That may sound like heresy to those who believe that any attention paid to format, graphics, and typestyles is fluff.

Content is the most important element—no argument. But you must get the reader's attention first and sustain it. Creating visual interest in your document does that.

In creating interest, you also may have to break some rules. Some of these are rules you learned in 6th grade, some are brought in by others on the proposal effort. Here are some general guidelines:

- Be consistent, but not to the point of repetition.

- Be conversational, but not colloquial.

- Borrow ideas from other venues (for example, journalism, newsletters).

Your client ultimately determines the latitude you can take with any of this so-called rule breaking. The more you can learn about his or her style and personality, the more you can tailor the proposal to keep his or her attention and remain professional.

This issue of *Infoline* outlines the steps involved in the proposal-writing process and identifies some common obstacles and techniques for overcoming them, as well as pitfalls to avoid. The issue is written for the training and development consultant who prepares service-related proposals for other companies.

Stages of Proposal Writing

There are six stages to the proposal-writing process. The steps are outlined in the most common chronological order. However, the latter steps can be conquered in the order most productive given your style and strengths.

Stage 1: Determine Scope and Structure

The first step is to determine how big this proposal is going to be, and what format it will take. That means how many pages and how complex it will be.

This effort will determine how much time and how many people it will take to complete it. This will establish your goal as well as your schedule.

Depending on the structure you've chosen, you have a general sense of how much text content and graphic examples you will have to assemble.

For example, if you have chosen a landscape orientation, bound at the top, and facing pages, you may have as many graphic elements as there are pages of text.

Stage 2: Outline the Content

The first step is to create a top-level outline. A generic outline can be found in the sidebar *Proposal Components* to the right. Once you have created a rough outline, further expand each section of the body with bullet points, references, and notes to yourself on the key points you want to make in each section.

Each section should tie back to others. For example, the benefits listed should not be general benefits of working with you, but should include specific and positive business benefits directly related to the statement of understanding/problem. Unless it's your intention, be careful that you don't guarantee specific measures of business improvement. Your role is to *help* create an environment that is conducive to positive change.

Whether you choose to state exactly how much improvement depends on the following:

1. Your knowledge of the specific causes of the underperformance and the client's potential to improve these statistics.

2. Your experience and confidence in achieving these results.

3. Your level of risk taking, that is, your willingness to expose yourself to the client's claim of nonperformance.

Components of a Proposal

The components listed in the sidebar *Proposal Components* lists the most common elements found in most service-based proposals. In a technical proposal, there also will likely be schemas, schedules, and diagrams, either embedded within the body or included as a separate attachment.

The relative sizes of the sections and their emphasis are as follows:

Cover letter—one page. The purpose of the cover letter is to introduce the proposal and set a follow-up or decision date.

Executive summary—three to five pages.

Body—no limit on total pages. Generally, this contains

- Statement of understanding—one to two pages.

- Project scope—contractually binding section, especially if a fixed-price bid.

- Method/approach—the bulk of this section. This is an important place for graphics. This is where you can develop your unique selling point.

- Benefits—generally one to two pages. This is what the client can expect from your training and or consulting.

- Schedule and fees—one to two pages.

Action/follow-up— one page.

Marketing exhibits—Brochures, inserts, and testimonials.

Stage 3: Finish First Draft

This stage consists of writing the full narrative for each of the sections you have outlined. The better job you do on outlining, the easier it will be to write the narrative component. You should not be laboring in this stage—if you are, go back and do more outlining.

The section that people most often cut corners in is the statement of understanding/problem. This is the worst area to shortcut. People often believe that the client understands the problem, so what's the point of restating it? Or, you really don't have a strong grasp of the problem and don't want to appear ignorant by making inaccurate or incomplete statements.

Actually, this section is your best, first, and maybe last, opportunity to show your potential client how good a consultant you are. People like to read about themselves. They will look to this section to confirm how well you understand their business and their problem. If you get that wrong, nothing else in your proposal really matters.

If you haven't completed enough fact-finding to write a knockout statement of understanding section, tell the client that and get his or her permission to complete this task. He or she usually will give it to you, but generally you can only go back to the well once.

A key element is consistency in style. An inconsistent proposal loses credibility with the client. Follow a style guide to keep a stable format. For more information on style guides, see the sidebar *Use of Style Guides* on the next page.

Another common problem faced during this stage is writer's block. To learn some techniques to mitigate this problem, see the sidebar *Overcoming Writer's Block*.

Proposal Components

There are several components that should appear in every proposal. Those five major sections are:

1. Cover letter.

2. Executive summary.

3. Body:

- statement of understanding/problem
- project scope
- method/approach
- benefits
- work estimate/schedule/fees/terms.

4. Action/follow-up.

5. Marketing exhibits.

Use of Style Guides

Large companies typically have standardized proposal formats and rules. In the trade, these are called *style guides*.

Following a style guide will add consistency to your proposal. Larger library branches will have style guide books in their business section.

Style guides contain a lot of useful information and examples on the use of:

- different graphics appropriate for various situations
- page layouts
- business grammar
- color recommendations (type, highlighting, and graphics).

A good guide will not provide a fill-in-the-blank proposal template, but rather, ideas and alternatives on all aspects of construction so that your proposal will be unique from that of another person using the same guide.

During the first draft, you can include your graphic examples, as they will look in the final version or a description of the exhibit.

At this point, circulate your first draft among trusted colleagues for review

Stage 4: Add Graphic Elements

Graphics are a powerful way to convey ideas and focus the reader's attention. You should give as much thought to selecting the graphics as you would to selecting your words. Readers may skip words, but they will not skip images.

When using stock clipart and photos, consider whether there are copyright or usage restrictions.

There are two primary forms of graphics that are appropriate in a professional service proposal.

Concept pictures/graphics, including clipart, photos, symbology, and logos (including watermarks). These are most effective when they show some creative association with the associated text, but not so creative that the reader cannot make the connection. For example, using a telescope or a dartboard bull's-eye in the executive summary is easily recognized as a metaphor for focus. Using a seashell is confusing.

Care has to be exercised when using your client's logo. In many cases, particularly for large companies, there are strict rules governing the pairing of the logo with specific typefaces and sizes. A little diligence in eyeing all of the examples of the use of their logo will tell you if this is a factor or not.

Charts, including graphs, tables, and data-based representations are the other forms of graphic treatment that are appropriate for a proposal.

Stage 5: Finalize Document

This stage covers final editing, cross-referencing, and ordering pages. It is very important to have several people proofread the document. We have all seen an otherwise flawless presentation marred by a small, innocent mistake. What does this say to your potential client about your attention to detail?

Stage 6: Choose Construction Elements

Assuming you are required to provide a bound, hard-copy proposal (as opposed to an electronic, or "soft" copy), you will have to address the issue of construction. This covers the decisions of paper weights, paper trimming, and binding. (For more information on soft-copy proposals, see the sidebar, *Soft Copy* on the next page.)

Anything you do beyond the standard 8.5 by 11 inches is a judgment based on your client's nature—conservative or progressive—and of course, his or her requirements if specified.

Here are some creative ideas to consider:

- Trim the upper left corner and ring-bind the proposal along this trim line.

- If using facing pages, half-size sheets (8.5 by 5.5 inches) bound at the top work well.

- Bind your proposal in a "stand-up" presentation folder.

None of these techniques requires any special equipment other than a paper cutter. The key point is to establish some unique and memorable elements to your proposal.

Some other decisions for you to consider are:

Choose a high quality paper. You did not go through all this work to print your proposal on plain 20 lb. bond. At the very least, use a 24 lb. weight, and make sure it has a brightness index of 90. Most common printer and copier paper has a brightness index of 84. You *will* notice the difference.

Be generous in your use of tabs. Even some sections within one page (for example, "Fees") deserve a tab.

Color-coordinate where possible. If your business card is on gray stock, use a light gray paper for cover or divider pages. Your printer or office supply store carries many stock colors.

Overcoming Writer's Block

Despite comic Steve Martin's belief that "writer's block is a fancy term made up by whiners so they can have an excuse to drink alcohol," it is a real problem—the curse of every writer. It's unavoidable, and most casual writers misjudge its extent.

Everyone has his or her own cure for writer's block, and if it works for you, great. But a deadline-driven project, such as composing a proposal, usually intensifies the so-called block effect.

Many believe that taking walks or some other activity unrelated to the proposal effort is a remedy. This is generally inefficient because it doesn't provide cues to get you through the block. Effective techniques are those that keep you rooted in the writing process, but in different contexts.

When writer's block hits, try the following:

- Write a newsletter article.

- Read a different proposal.

- Work on your web page.

- Get away from the computer. Instead, pick up a pen and paper, or a cassette recorder.

- Switch from content writing to proposal graphics and layout design.

- Switch to a different section of the proposal.

The key is to keep the thoughts of the blocking passage from entering your mind for a while. This seems contrary to the original purpose, but it is important to set aside a discrete amount of time when you will *not* be thinking of the section causing you trouble. Believe it or not, the ideas that come into your head that you're pushing off will be there later.

Soft Copy

Frequently, we are being asked to provide proposals in electronic document form. Here are some things to consider if you do this:

1. Are you providing your proposal as an HTML file or a Word file? In either case, you can hyperlink text or pictures to other areas within the proposal. Remember, though, that some Word files do not have a BACK function so the reader can return to the section they have left.

2. Test to make sure that all fonts and graphics are displayed properly on another computer before sending the document. It may be necessary to save the document with embedded fonts or to make sure the customer knows the graphics file format you have used.

3. Review the HTML header data or the Word properties box before the file is saved to delete any information you don't want the reader to see (revisions, authors, and so forth).

4. In Word documents, do you want to protect the document from changes or being distributed beyond the intended reader? You can do this with passwords. You can even protect it from someone "cut and pasting" from it, if that is a concern.

Because electronic files are so easily distributed, these are issues to consider, particularly if you are providing your "trade secrets" or confidential information.

Binding

Aside from stapling, almost any form of binding is acceptable (comb, ring, book). If using a three-ring binder, use one that *most closely* matches the number of pages in your proposal (this is the opposite of the rule when binding a workbook, which must be larger to accommodate handouts and notepapers). All that you can do to give the appearance that every component was especially selected for this proposal will improve its image.

If using a slip sleeve cover three-ring binder, make sure that your cover paper insert closely matches the dimensions of the sleeve. It is worth a few extra dollars to enlarge and trim the cover insert from 8.5 by 11 inches to 9 by 12 inches if that is your requirement. The copier at your local print shop should be able to handle this.

Ensure Readability and Create Interest

Just as in writing a newsletter article, a proposal or report must have some elements of visual interest to hold the reader's attention. Relevant graphics and facing pages can accomplish some of this.

Other elements you should consider adding to your document include:

- related concept pictures or clipart
- excerpted passages
- quotes (from famous sources or within text).

Many of the visual interest techniques can be borrowed from newsletters, pamphlets, manuals, and the like, but some generally don't work well with proposals. These include:

- sidebars
- frequent change of fonts and text treatments.

The key here is to always maintain the visual appearance of a professional proposal "from 20,000 feet." Overuse of above techniques invariably makes the document look like a newsletter, which you want to avoid. Here are some other things you should avoid:

- quotes from the infamous

- clipart or photos of all one style throughout — after the first few, your proposal becomes predictable and boring; mix them up a little

- identical text/graphic format on every page; vary pictures with excerpts or quotes.

The main objective is to strike a balance between consistency and redundancy.

Word Usage

Much has been written about using simple words and eliminating the so-called fog in business writing. As a rule, you should strive to achieve no higher than a 9th-grade reading level in your proposal. The executive summary should be even lower. This is not to "dumb down" your proposal—it is to make it readable at a pace that will keep your reader's interest.

Most word processors will calculate the reading grade index for you, and the grammar checking utility will suggest changes to simplify your text. Select the strictest grammar checking—you'll be surprised at the number of suggestions.

One thing most grammar checkers do not catch is the most common fault we all make—using our favorite words repeatedly. Get to know your program's thesaurus well, and vary your word choice.

Particularly avoid the word *proposal*. The more you use this word, the more the reader is reminded that you are asking them to take a leap of faith in you and in your fit with their business. *Proposal to Enhance the Business Benefit* could be simply reworded to *Enhancing the Business Benefit*.

One exception to the word repetition warning is using your potential client's company name. Mention it *often*. Don't forget the old adage that "the sweetest word to anyone is his or her own name." Apply this to the company name as well.

For more information, see the sidebar *Careful Word Choice* to the right.

Careful Word Choice

Unlike the spoken word, the written word "hangs around," so to speak. It doesn't get a chance to be withdrawn, so be careful in choosing one word over another.

Choose more positive or neutral words over those that have a negative tone.

Be on the lookout for words that are commanding (*stop, eliminate, don't*), disabling (*impair, impede*), idiomatic (*falling apart, breaking down*), or jargon. Jargon is words or phrases specific to your profession. It's all right to use them—sparingly—as long as the reader is provided with a definition of each at its first use.

These are not steadfast rules. For example, *impede success* sounds more positive than *fail*, despite the use of the disabling-word *impede*. The difference is its pairing with the positive *success*.

Commanding words like *stop* are permitted when used as an adverb, as in "the teams will stop working," but discouraged as a verb, as in "Stop the teams from doing this."

Tip: Avoid trying to word-edit everything as you go along. Write your proposal as you would speak it, and then run the "Find and Replace" utility on your word processor to replace these words.

Special Tips for Trainers

Training professionals, especially those in business for themselves, face especially difficult obstacles in creating winning proposals.

The basic issue is depicted by the following equation:

Customer Need = Minimum Identified Value from Training

What this means is that once your customer has determined their training need, they have established only the bare minimum business value that will come from a training session. That always is accompanied by a healthy dose of doubt that the training will actually have the desired effect. They have not explored the much larger value that can be realized with competent training, consulting, and follow-through. That is your job, and one way you do that done is through the proposal.

Remember that the proposal cannot establish the initial need for training—the customer must arrive at that conclusion on his or her own, perhaps with your help. The proposal's job is to confirm the business issue and expand the opportunity—and of course to win the job for you.

Be sure to include in your proposal:

● testimonials
● follow-up results from previous training sessions.

Remember, your focus should be on the business value achieved from the training, and not just on people's reaction to taking the class.

Think of this when soliciting testimonials. You may want to structure the questions as opposed to leaving them too open-ended. For example, you may want to ask your previous attendees:

● How many fewer errors are you tracking?
● How must faster is the task getting accomplished?
● How much improvement are you seeing?

Tailor the questions to those that can be plausibly related to the focus of your training class and the attendee's areas of responsibility.

Use of Color

Color adds a great deal to a proposal. However, this is an area where generally "less is more." At the very least, the cover should contain some color. Beyond that, it is up to your discretion. If you are having a printer make your copies, it will be expensive to have color throughout your proposal. And if you are printing the proposal on an inkjet printer, it will take quite a long time.

In order of efficiency (effectiveness vs. cost), the best use of color is as follows:

● cover
● preprinted running logo/icon/border
● exhibits at back of proposal
● embedded graphics.

Soft-copy proposals are not affected by cost, of course, and the use of color in these can be unrestricted.

A caution: You should test clarity of color graphics printed in black and white. It may be better to convert them to grayscale before printing.

Statement of Your Qualifications

When selling training and development you sometimes have to be the most creative.

If you have lots of specific, relevant experience, your need for creative editing is minimal. Simply including work citations and references in your proposal usually suffices. You should, though, invest a little effort to explicitly point out the relevance of each citation to your client's situation and not make them figure it out.

Think Creatively

If in fact you have experience in a relevant area, but are hesitant to cite it for any number of reasons, you usually can find a positive way to get your experience into the proposal.

For example, say you were selected to lead a new business initiative with a former employer, but that initiative never succeeded or got off the ground. You could still say that you "were selected to lead the initiative to…."

You probably will be asked about your experience during the interview, but you already got your strong point across—someone recognized your potential from among many others. You can use the interview to explain the mitigating factors of that assignment, and why it did not achieve completion or fulfillment of the business goals.

But what about the situation where your work experience is largely unrelated, at least directly, to the nature of the work that you're proposing? And what if you're relatively unknown to the client— that is, you don't have a mutual reference?

In these cases, it is vitally important to identify a unique selling point (USP) of doing business with you.

Identify Your USP

One way to create a USP is to "brand" your method, in essence transforming it into a methodology. Take your project plan or approach and give it a name. For example, you could call it LAMBDA, which is a Greek alphabetic symbol used in statistics to designate change. Or you can choose a word like ANLAGE, which is of German derivation and is related to "establishing a foundation."

A few keys to branding are:

- Choose a word that is uncommon but can be said and spelled easily.

- Choose a word that has a meaning relevant to your approach or USP.

- Develop some marketing collateral that references this word.

- Shun the trite acronym derived from the first letters of a series of words.

One final, important tip: Develop a graphic that is easy to remember and incorporates your methodology.

A key example of this is in the case of *The Octagon.*

A consulting firm once used an octagon to depict the eight operational and strategic areas of a retail business. It could be argued that were really six, seven, nine, or any number of areas, but eight was chosen. No clients ever argued the point.

For many years, the *Octagon* became instantly recognized as retail gospel and associated with the consulting firm. It was easy to remember. Further, it became a convenient tool for the firm to segment and target business opportunities within its customers.

Anticipate or Know Your Competition

Always assume that your proposal is being compared with others. Even if no others were requested at this time, your proposal will be casually judged against all that have been submitted in the past. You may find that your single-source opportunity has now been changed to a competitive bid. To avert this, ask your customer:

- Whom has he or she worked with before?

- What did he or she like and dislike about these other people and firms?

- What does he or she like most about you?

In short, no question is beyond asking (except for fees paid). If your client doesn't want to answer, he or she won't.

Know Your Client's Business

Here's one tip that will, above any other, impress your client:

Read a few issues of your potential client's leading trade journals. You can find back issues in most larger library branches or on the Internet.

Here are some examples of the power of this suggestion:

● Your client is a candy manufacturer or distributor. In reading one of their industry's trade journals, you learn that the current campaign in their industry is "*25 BY '05*," which is to succeed in getting U.S. consumers to increase their annual per-capita consumption of chocolate from 17 lbs. to 25 lbs. by the year 2005. Can this be tied into a course on creative thinking?

● Your client is a large U.S. retailer of packaged gifts of meats and cheeses. You read that Japan has a growing appetite for beef but has to pay high prices because fresh beef is imported on refrigerated ships. Start a conversation about the potential expansion of the chain to Japan.

● Your client is a printing company. You read that large timber-growing states are experiencing the fastest urban expansion in the country. What does this mean to loss of forests and their future prices?

If you cannot make a plausible connection between an industry-related issue and the service you are providing, you should leave it out of the proposal but bring it up in conversation. At the very least, it will demonstrate your industriousness.

Show Professionalism, Commitment

Sales professionals say that you should try to win work without encouraging competition. For many, this has been an argument against writing proposals unless first requested by the customer.

In contrast, offering a proposal shows your professionalism and commitment, and more often than not, helps to win the work.

A few final suggestions on becoming an expert proposal writer:

● Lend yourself out to business acquaintances to assist them in their proposal writing efforts.

● Don't hide your work-in-process. Show a few colleagues your proposal drafts or outlines and ask for their critique.

● Selectively break some of the rules you were taught in high school or college.

● Get out of your training and development venue. Collect proposals from industrial firms, product sales, public relations firms, and so forth. Visit your local printers for ideas and samples. You'll find useful ideas in many places.

References & Resources

Articles

Conger, Jay. "The Necessary Art of Persuasion." *Harvard Business Review,* May-June 1998.

Kantin, Robert. "Building Better Proposals." *The Small Business Journal,* Penguin USA, 2000.

Kennedy, Danielle. "Perfect Pitch." *Entrepreneur Magazine*, June 1996.

Peters, Tom. "The Brand Called You." *Fast Company,* 1997.

Perun, Cynthia. "Perfect Pitch." *Business Start-Ups,* January 1998.

Books

Bates, Jefferson. *Writing With Precision: How to Write So That You Cannot Possibly Be Misunderstood*. New York: Penguin, 2000.

Covey, Franklin. *Franklin Covey Style Guide for Business and Technical*. LaVergne, TN: Ingram-LaVergne, 2000.

Freed, Richard. *Writing Winning Business Proposals*. New York: McGraw-Hill, 1994.

Hamper, Robert. *Handbook for Writing Proposals*. Lincolnwood, IL: NTC Publishing Group, 1996.

Moreno, Mary. *The Writer's Guide to Corporate Communications*. New York: Allworth Press, 1997.

Roman, Kenneth. *Writing That Works*. New York: Harper Resource, 2000.

Williams, Robin. *The PC Is Not a Typewriter: A Style Manual."* Berkley, CA: Peachpit Press, 1992.

Williams, Robin. *The Non-Designer's Design Book*. Berkley, CA: Peachpit Press, 1994

Zinsser, William. *On Writing Well*. New York: HarperCollins, 1998

Job Aid

Proposal Workplan Checklist

Use the following checklist to ensure that you have considered all of the tasks and factors in completing a proposal.

☐ Secure appointment to conduct an informational interview about your potential client.

☐ Research issues relevant to your prospect's business

- trade journals

- industry associations

- website searches.

☐ Research issues relevant to your potential client's

- trade journals

- professional associations.

☐ Conduct pre-proposal informational interview to determine

- size of opportunity

- decision process (when made, who makes, and so forth)

- earliest training session needed

- political / sensitive issues.

☐ Establish proposal due date.

☐ Determine size and scope of proposal.

☐ Develop a schedule and plan for proposal completion.

Marketing Training Programs

Issue 0102

CONTRIBUTING AUTHOR

Teresa Davenport
Davenport Design & Development
P.O. Box 660711
Birmingham, AL 35266
Tel: 205.824.1501
Email:
  teresa@davenportdesign.com

Over the past 12 years, Teresa Davenport has provided professional development solutions to a wide range of industries and government organizations. She has an MS in instructional design and specializes in analyzing organizational needs and working with consultants to resolve training and performance problems.

Editor
Cat Sharpe Russo

Contributing Editor
Ann Bruen

Production Design
Kathleen Schaner

Internal Consultant
Karen Nishioki

Marketing Training Programs

What Is Marketing?

The word *marketing* brings forth different images for each of us. Whether we are being hit with television ads, print ads, direct mail pieces, or telemarketing phone calls that interrupt the dinner hour, marketing is without a doubt an enveloping phenomenon that affects everyone in the consumer world. In business today as well, the role of marketing encompasses every aspect of your work, no matter what business you are in. If you cannot sell your product to a buyer, any hope that you'll have a long and healthy business life will be cut short.

This is no less true for the training professional. The ability to understand and use marketing principles effectively will either jump-start your development program or cause you to stop dead in your tracks. How often have you heard comments like these?

- "Without buy-in from upper management, this program hasn't got a chance."

- "If you can't convince managers that their employees need this training to promote productivity . . . "

- "If you can't persuade learners that they want to come (rather than need to come) to this new product roll-out program, then . . . "

Probably too often. Well, let's find a method to help you solve your marketing problems.

At its most basic definition, marketing's principal function is to promote and facilitate exchange. In the training and performance business, this means promoting and facilitating the exchange of training and workplace learning. There is nothing complicated about this. Unfortunately, problems arise when trainers and workplace learning practitioners are asked to become marketers instead of trainers.

With this in mind, here is a practical, no-frills approach to implementing the promotion and facilitation exchange. *Promotion* and *facilitation* are two words every trainer is familiar with—any stand-up trainer has to promote himself or herself in front of a class, and without question, every trainer has to be a facilitator. So it will be no great leap to take those two skills and apply them to marketing. This issue of *Infoline* will focus on the techniques and strategies to help training and performance practitioners become better marketers of their products and services. When we apply a method to marketing that trainers are already familiar with—ADDIE (analysis, design, development, implementation, and evaluation)—the task becomes less daunting.

ADDIE steps enable you to integrate marketing principles into the already existing framework of training development. Because we are talking about marketing, we have added one important item to the mix—the marketing plan. Without a marketing plan, your efforts to increase program awareness or attendance will have no roadmap or milestones for guides. Because most training practitioners are not marketers by profession or background, it seems a logical consequence to apply a known quantity, ADDIE, to a lesser-known way of doing business.

Applying the ADDIE Template

Like all good instructional design, a successful marketing program depends on a thorough needs analysis—the results of which will lay the foundation for developing a good marketing strategy or plan. From start to finish, it really is about following a simple set of steps:

1. Conducting a needs analysis, which also includes a situation analysis.

2. Preparing the marketing strategy plan.

3. Designing the types of promotional materials to be used in your marketing campaign.

4. Developing or producing the actual materials.

5. Implementing or, in this case, deploying your promotional efforts.

6. Evaluating the effectiveness of your marketing efforts based on responses from various customer segments.

Targeting Your Audience

Identifying customers consists of two activities, segmenting your audience and targeting specific groups for your efforts.

■ *Segmenting*

This activity involves breaking your market down into discrete segments. The process will divide your audience into smaller pieces for specialized programs and efforts. For example, if your audience for a new product roll-out training program is aimed at all employees, you will separate or segment your audience (all employees) by their training needs, for example:

- sales staff
- customer technical support
- fulfillment
- telemarketing
- middle managers and administrative staff
- upper management.

■ *Targeting*

This defines the boundaries of your audience by identifying any significant customer variable (such as need, budget, location, gender, age, or staff size) that indicates how you should shape your promotional efforts to suit your audience. Identify your audience as above, but also include decision makers, influential persons, attendees, and sponsors (those who pay for training). List both individuals and groups under these categories. Although each will have specific concerns, you must persuade all of them to buy into the training and encourage participation in it.

Using the example above, a sales staff has completely different needs than a technical support staff. Although your training program's content may overlap for the different groups, how you target the various segments will influence their acceptance.

Decision makers. For each program you wish to market, determine who these people are and ask them what they think is most important about the program.

Participants. Decide which prospective participants are most likely to attend the training voluntarily. It is easiest to sell training to those who have supported or participated in training programs in the past.

Group leaders. Get these people involved at the outset. If you can persuade them that the training is worthwhile, you will have a ready-made public relations group to pass along positive advertising for your program.

Step 1: Analysis

In your first step, much like starting a training program, you need to find out what your needs are. For marketing purposes, this is accomplished through a situation analysis. The outcomes or results of the analysis will be the goals and objectives of your marketing plan.

A situation analysis defines how your current business stands and answers the question: "Where am I?" Often called a SWOT analysis, it examines the **s**trengths, **w**eaknesses, **o**pportunities, and **t**hreats to your business, and describes what you expect to happen in your business area in the short term—that period in which you are planning to have an impact.

Conducting this analysis enables you to prepare a marketing strategy. In terms of preparing a plan that can be applied to training and development programs, the analysis will answer the following SWOT elements:

- Program strengths—for example, staff subject matter experts (SMEs) can conduct the program rather than consultants.

- Program weaknesses—for example, it can only be offered on two sites, when needed at six.

- Program opportunities—for example, it can be packaged for deployment at remote sites.

- Program threats—for example, off-the-shelf software is available for just-in-time-learning.

Remember that many strengths can also be considered weaknesses. For example, having an in-house SME conduct your training offers you the benefits of historical knowledge and current application. On the other hand, having an in-house SME as your trainer could be a weakness, because the SME could have prejudicial methods of accomplishing tasks and not be open to different opinions.

In addition, your analysis will also include information on:

- The organization: What is its mission, values, goals, objectives, and culture?

- The decision makers: Who are they, how do they relate to one another, and what is their influence on budgets and approval processes?

- The audience: Who are they? What are their needs, current skills and educational levels, demographics, requirements?

For more details on how to define your audience segment, see the sidebar *Targeting Your Audience*.

Step 2: The Marketing Plan

Now that the analysis is complete, you can prepare a written statement of your strategy based on the data compiled. This will be your marketing plan—the roadmap to completing the project. Based on the information compiled, you will be able to set and realize your goals and keep on course. If you have not included the following information in your SWOT analysis, be sure that you have a clear idea of the following items that need to be included in the plan:

- the features and benefits of your program
- your target market
- competing programs
- the problem or need your program serves.

The components of a strong marketing plan include the following:

Executive summary: a short, preferably one-page, summary of the goals and designs presented in the plan.

Situation analysis: a description of the major factors affecting the training program (see previous page).

Goals and objectives: where you currently stand and where you want to go; a short-term document, covering six months or a year.

Marketing strategy: a set of decisions about target audiences, the marketing mix, and costs.

Conducting a Market Analysis

A market analysis is an in-depth study about a specific audience segment. The outcome of this analysis will allow you to compile information about the segment that will help you target the group for a specific promotion or effort. The analysis also can let you know if the particular segment is a worthwhile target audience. It may turn out that only 5 percent of one segment has a need for your program, while a different segment shows a 50-percent need. Based on a cost-benefit analysis, clearly the segment with a 50-percent need is a better target audience than the one with a 5-percent need.

Plan the market analysis similar to any research project. Identify your segment; then outline the elements to be researched. Do the research, but focus on the important points, not the minutiae. Then prepare a report based on the data collected. Although not a comprehensive list, the following topics will help you complete the necessary research to put the market analysis together:

- segment description
- needs and requirements
- distribution channels
- competitors
- best methods for communicating with the segment.

Goals and Objectives

When preparing goals and objectives for a training program's marketing plan, ask yourself the following questions. The answers will help you formulate objectives that are specific, measurable, and reasonable.

1. What is the primary outcome or result you are seeking from this marketing plan?

2. What is the primary outcome the organization wants from the training or performance program?

3. What, if any, are the secondary or tertiary outcomes the organization wants from the program?

4. Who are your clients?

5. What is the size of the target audience, and how much of it do you need to serve?

6. What image do you want your department and program to project in the organization?

7. What share of the training market do you want to have?

8. How many training courses do you want to offer?

9. What is your deadline for meeting the training or performance requirements of your organization?

10. What resources—such as time and money—do you have available to achieve your goals?

Action plan: a detailed description of the specific actions to be taken to accomplish the marketing goals, when they should be accomplished, and who should do them. (Refer to "Step 3: Design.")

Budget: a profit-and-loss statement based on goals, strategies, and actions to be taken. An accompanying cost-benefit analysis will always be helpful. For details on how to conduct this analysis, refer to *Infoline*, No. 9004, "How to Conduct a Cost Benefit Analysis."

Controls: how the progress of the program will be monitored. This will include goals reached, income and expenses, participant satisfaction, and so forth. (Please refer to "Step 6: Evaluation" for additional information on controls.)

A good marketing plan also provides a number of valuable aids in your promotional efforts by doing the following things:

- identifying needs and wants of customers
- determining demand for the product
- helping design needed programs
- identifying new training areas
- targeting new or potential customers
- providing measurements of success.

Now you will need to come up with marketing goals or objectives that are specific, measurable, and have a set time for completion. The purpose of these objectives is to give you a written statement that pushes you to put the marketing plan into effect and reach your desired outcomes. Similar to preparing a strategic plan, goals and objectives manage the gap between the current state and the desired future by defining where you want to be and the steps you need to take to get there. Goals need to be:

- reasonable
- specific
- measurable.

If you have multiple objectives, be sure that they are consistent and do not conflict with one another. Also, ensure that all parts of your marketing plan support your objectives.

Marketing Mix Worksheet

The following format is useful in defining and scheduling your marketing efforts:

Project name:

_____

Objective (What do you want to accomplish from this marketing effort?):

_____

Target market (Who are you trying to reach with this effort?):

_____

Promotion (How are you going to reach this audience?):

_____

Message (What benefits are you offering to the audience?):

_____

Budget (How much money do you have to spend, and how are you going to allocate it?):

_____

Schedule:

Date	Activity	Responsibility
_____	_____	_____
_____	_____	_____
_____	_____	_____
_____	_____	_____
_____	_____	_____
_____	_____	_____
_____	_____	_____
_____	_____	_____

Step 3: Design

Similar to the way training is outlined or storyboarded, marketing and promotional materials also need to be planned and delivered. This is called *marketing-mix planning*—the tactics that will be most effective in achieving strategic goals. (We have also referred to this as the "action plan" earlier.) This step involves the mix of four primary components: product, price, place, and promotion. Together, they will meet a targeted set of customer requirements.

■ *Product*

Product development—in this case, the training program—refers to the offering or group of offerings you will be making available to the customer. Sometimes training and development programs are pre-set. At other times, they are part of the analysis phase in which you determine just what programs are required, if this is the appropriate intervention.

■ *Price*

Price is usually something that has more influence when a customer has to purchase a product directly. With training programs, however, the price is a multifaceted item, rarely seen strictly in terms of the *cost* of the program. It is marketing's role to promote the cost-effectiveness of a program, both in terms of its benefits to the organization and its production cost.

■ *Place*

This refers to the location where the product, or program, is made available. In marketing language, you will also hear this referred to as *distribution*. For our purposes, programs need to be easily accessible to learners, whether they take place in a classroom environment or make use of technology for delivery.

■ *Promotion or Communication*

This element consists of the various methods used to communicate with and influence your customer segments. For training programs, the major tools you will use are advertising, sales promotions, and public relations.

For purposes of this *Infoline*, we will assume that you already have developed a training program, you are aware of the costs involved with producing the program (not to be confused with the costs of the promotion), and you know how and when the program will be delivered or distributed. This discussion will focus on the promotion and communication of your program.

A number of useful tools are available to you. Use them as key forces to influence customers. For example:

Employee Incentives. Your training budget for prizes and rewards might be very small, but if you tie training participation to larger performance goals, then the training stakeholders might be willing to offer more valuable incentives, such as more money, promotion, or time off for mastering new skills through training.

Endorsements from Decision Makers. When you develop a marketing plan for a specific training project, first find out *exactly* how much support the decision makers will lend. Will they publicly and formally endorse this training (that is, through newsletter testimonials, verbal support in meetings, and so forth)? If these people have the authority, will they make this training mandatory? Will they provide resources for completion of the marketing (funds, staff, technology)?

Celebrity Endorsement. While not every organization has the clout to invite Michael Jordan to a training event, inviting well-known public figures can provide another avenue to entice employees to participate in the training. These facilitators or speakers can lend professionalism, credibility, and an air of excitement to the training event.

Public Relations. A coordinated public relations effort is a good way to get the word out about your program to your audience. Its primary objective is to create a positive image of your training by emphasizing the quality of the program content and the advantages of learning new skills.

Word of Mouth. The most inexpensive and effective method of marketing your training is free—through positive word of mouth, where one satisfied client tells a colleague about your program. Use every opportunity to talk up your product and to stress that you are available to present it.

Technology. This has become a valuable component of successful marketing campaigns. The use of fax broadcasts, emails, web pages, intranets, and voicemail announcements is increasingly prevalent. Customers have become accustomed to the immediacy of technology, and marketers need to be able to deal with multiple responses to their promotions. For example, a hundred people could respond at the same time to a web announcement or a fax broadcast. On the other hand, technology poses a distinct challenge to marketers: They need to learn to write for the maximum effect when using these abbreviated communication formats.

Print Media

In the past, marketing has relied heavily on the printed word for getting its message out, and this method is still a valid means of promotion. Primarily used for direct marketing of products and services, each print piece will contain three vital elements:

- a definitive offer

- complete information required to make a decision about the offer

- a method of responding to the offer

Print media offer a wide range of products from which to select. For purposes of marketing training programs, we will focus on mailers (or brochures), newsletters, posters, and banners.

■ *Brochures*
These are typically sent through the mail or handed out. Good direct mail pieces can usually generate a 1 percent response rate, but if you are sending pieces to a targeted list, especially if this is internal to an organization, you can expect a much higher response.

Keep in mind that a brochure is not a catalog offering of your products. In our scenario, we are trying to elicit a response to a single course or program of courses—not your entire department or business's offerings. Because response rates from mailers are generally low, do not rely on brochures as your sole means of communicating with your customers. You will also need to take into account that print brochures have high production costs, long development cycles, and costly delivery (if done through the mail). Never discount the value of a well-produced brochure, but be prepared for the time, work, and costs associated with this media option.

Managing Your Promotion

What do you need to know about print materials to develop a marketing plan? Depending on what type of print media you plan to use, here are the elements that you will need to plan for: tasks, timeline, and budget and staff resources.

■ *Tasks*
Here is a sequence of tasks to follow when creating all types of print media.

- Create layout.
- Determine production method.
- Proof.
- Edit.
- Reproduce copies.
- Distribute to recipients.

■ *Timeline*
When should each task start and end? These timelines should parallel courseware development timelines. Some marketers release their mailers in several batches, all of which are coded for tracking purposes.

■ *Budget and Staff Resources*
Materials: You will need a realistic idea of how much your marketing materials will cost. To determine this cost, review the physical description and the number of print materials you plan to produce. Take this information to either your internal printing department or a reliable external vendor to determine the final cost of materials.

Staff: If you want to use staff members that report to other managers, clear the project through their managers before assigning them to the project. These staff resources can include:

- internal training staff
- in-house printing staff
- graphics department
- MIS
- staff in the department receiving the training.

Marketing Competencies

The effective marketing of training and performance programs requires proficiency in a number of competencies. Although most workplace learning practitioners will not be highly skilled in each competency, it is better to be aware of what you need to know. You can always acquire the needed knowledge—either through self-directed learning or by hiring people with the requisite skill set.

☐ Technology/computer proficiency

☐ Cost-benefit analysis

☐ Counseling

☐ Feedback

☐ Futuring

☐ Group process

☐ Industry knowledge and analysis

☐ Intellectual versatility

☐ Negotiation

☐ Preparing goals and objectives

☐ Comprehension of organization behavior

☐ Presentation

☐ Questioning techniques

☐ Relationship building

☐ Writing.

■ *Newsletters*

Newsletters are best used as periodic briefings to provide information about the organization's recent and future developments as well as to promote training and learning programs. A newsletter is its own best form of advertising. If you can get a newsletter out on a regular schedule as part of a departmental or business plan, you can then devote column space and sections specifically to promoting upcoming events or series of programs and initiatives. This is an excellent vehicle to feature endorsements from decision makers and celebrities; to employ personal testimonials and comments from previous participants; and to push motivational and inspirational content that encourages future participation in training.

■ *Posters*

Use large posters in common areas such as break rooms, rest rooms, kitchens, and lobbies. They should be large (at least 2 feet by 3 feet), made of rigid paper, and contain general information about the training. We don't want to go back to the days of junior high elections with hallways plastered with homemade posters, so use any of today's graphic programs that have features to make large-scale posters. If this is not easily available to you, most local print shops can make professional posters at a low cost.

■ *Banners*

Banners are effective tools for promoting new initiatives or training at the actual event itself. Use catch phrases, the name of the training, and times and dates. Banners can be located in high-visibility areas, such as main lobbies, cafeterias, or even in the parking lot or other outdoor areas. They are very large announcements (at least 3 feet by 8 feet) and are made of either cloth or plastic. Like posters, these are easily made by local print shops.

Step 4: Development

Once you have determined what the marketing mix of your promotions will be, you can begin producing the actual materials. Because some of your marketing plan includes direct communication that does not require development (phone calls, meetings with decision makers, and so forth), this section will focus on development of brochures, the piece you will most frequently need to develop.

Once created, the brochure can easily be adapted to serve other marketing materials such as emails or email attachments, faxes, posters, and more.

To develop your materials, you will need to decide what format you want to use and the appropriate size of the piece (this will be based largely on your budget constraints), and then, how to get customers' attention with content and language.

Format and Size

View any brochure as an opportunity to influence customers about you, your program, department, and organization. Brochures do not necessarily need lots of color, flash, and rich graphics to be successful—your objective is to elicit a positive response.

Decide on the format—brochure, newsletter, flyer, and so forth—but use something that is easily recognizable. By combining your corporate logo, slogan, or colors into a template, you can easily replicate pieces that will give your materials consistency and recognizability. Another advantage to using templates is that they save you time. Instead of creating each brochure from scratch, you can use the template and fill in information where content needs to be updated.

In terms of design, most brochures have a cover, which is used to grab customers' attention, followed by inside pages that are filled with copy, graphics, and usually a cut-out registration form or reply card. Following are some design tips to help you:

■ *Balance White Space*
White space is most effective on the brochure cover, where text and graphics need to be big and bold. The key to white space is *balance*. Beyond the brochure cover, use a limited mix of type sizes and fonts to explain your training. Don't make the common mistake of having all your columns jam-packed with type. You want to catch the reader's eye, not lose the reader's attention by including too much text.

■ *Typeface*
Again, follow your corporate guidelines. Typically, Roman or Universal typefaces are used. You can deviate from the norm, but use common sense. A script or gothic typeface, while attractive, is not necessarily appropriate for marketing copy.

■ *Use Artwork Artfully*
To make sure artwork takes its proper place in the brochure, do the following:

- Limit graphics, such as photos or clip art.

- Use lines to provide topical separations and sustain reader interest.

- Use background graphics to enhance the aesthetic appeal. The graphic should be very faint so as not to overpower the text placed over it.

■ *Color*
Color is a powerful, and often misused graphic tool. Color should enhance, not overpower. For internal organizational pieces, it is usually better to be conservative in your use of color. Take your cue from other successful pieces that have been published and used in your company. Use company colors when and if applicable.

Determining Brochure Size

In the best of all worlds, you would create all your copy and decide on graphic images and then sit down to determine brochure size. Rarely does this actually happen. Cost is a concern; so more often than not, size will dictate how much space you have for content and graphic images.

Most brochures are bifold or trifold. Sometimes, a brochure borders on becoming a booklet. A true brochure is a quick read and gets your points across in a clear, effective manner to elicit a positive response. Because size is determined by budget, it is vital that language and content be effectively communicated.

Writing to Get Attention

Language is a key to attracting customers. It seems that fewer people today know how to effectively use language to its best advantage. By applying the principles and steps set forth in *The Writing System Workbook* by Judith and Daniel Graham, it is easy to systemize a writing process that will get your points and message across to customers. Following are the steps as they apply to preparing marketing content:

Creating Brochure Content

What does your audience need to know to pique its interest, and to register for your training program? Here is a fairly comprehensive list to use as a guide when designing your brochures.

Attention-getting components (usually on cover)

☐ Headline

☐ Sub-headline (what you will learn)

☐ Presenter/sponsor and contact information

☐ Logo (corporate and/or training)

☐ Slogan (corporate and/or training)

☐ Incentive or reward for registering early and/or attending

☐ Logistics: where, when (repeat of information on registration form)

☐ Continuing Education Units (if applicable).

Details (usually in the body of the brochure)

☐ Course description

☐ Objectives

☐ Testimonials

☐ Benefits and features

☐ Materials

☐ Learning format

☐ About the facilitator (include photograph)

☐ Who should attend

☐ Related courses

☐ Self-test.

Registration form (usually on last page of brochure or a separate insert card)

☐ List and description of registration methods (this form, online, by phone, fax, email)

☐ Incentive or reward for early registration

☐ Cancellation policy

☐ Date/location for which participants are registering

☐ Payment methods (if applicable, that is, if an outside vendor is providing training through your department)

☐ Test codes (if you are testing certain elements of the mailing, such as date sent or who it was mailed to)

☐ Return address

☐ Contact name/email for questions.

1. Analyze the purpose of your task.

2. Analyze your audience and their needs.

3. Write a purpose statement.

4. Gather all relevant information.

5. Draft the content.

6. Revise and edit content for coherence.

7. Edit for clarity and economy.

8. Check for readability and correctness.

9. Proofread.

In addition, follow these tips to help you appeal to and influence your audience:

Use headlines and key words that specifically apply to your audience and describe the training program in a succinct but accurate manner.

Provide audience incentives. Instead of including incentives as a footnote on a registration form, make them the focal point of one of your pages.

Define program benefits and features. The quickest way to grab a reader's attention is to highlight program benefits and features that the customer finds attractive and suits his or her purposes.

Use a sample agenda or course content. A course agenda or content outline will quickly inform a potential customer about your program and help the customer make a decision as to whether or not to register. Using an agenda is often a good evaluation tool as to whether course content is an influencing factor in the decision whether or not to register for a program.

Reward referrals. Promote a "Referred By" program. If a registrant writes the name of the person who referred him on the registration form, they *both* get a reward.

Provide facilitators' biographies. This is an excellent method of influencing customers. If your presenter is a well-respected SME within the organization or a highly regarded industry practitioner, this is an advertising opportunity not to be wasted. If the facilitator is not well known, use brochure space to highlight his or her qualifications as a presenter.

Appeal to groups. If your program is designed to support entire teams, departments, or divisions, employ team building tactics to influence attendance by complete groups. Use organizational motivators, such as mission statements, driving forces, and productivity growth.

Step 5: Implementation

At this point in the process, you should set aside time for getting your marketing materials out to the potential audience. During the analysis stage, you identified your target audience. Now you must obtain the names of your target audience. Big or small, you still need to acquire "the list." Whether your program is targeted at internal employees of a particular division, or at all employees, or at non-employees, find the person(s) who can provide you the names. Internally, it is usually the human resource and training departments that are responsible for this data. Externally, you normally go to list brokers.

Traditionally, brochures are distributed via direct mail. You can always use this method, but internal to an organization, it is more economical to use the established distribution system. As an added incentive, you can set up kickoff breakfasts or information sessions that can garner support and give you the opportunity for one-on-one interaction with potential customers of your program.

In addition, you can create an email version of your brochure to advise potential participants about upcoming sessions. Use your local intranet to promote your program based on the brochure. When using any web-based media, remember to provide a response mechanism for registrants.

At the end of this issue, you will find a job aid that you can use as a guide to developing and implementing your marketing strategy. In it you will find all the elements that you need to address to pre-

Simple Tips to Avoid Common Marketing Mistakes

Some of these tips may seem elementary, but recognize that we often overlook the obvious. The following tips are exactly that, short reminders of common-sense items that frequently are omitted when putting together a promotional campaign.

■ *Be Sure Your Promotion Piece Requests a Response*
Now that you have gone through all the work to design and develop your marketing piece, make sure that people can reply to you. The reply can be a registration form, a telephone call, an email, a fax—any means of communicating with you. Be sure you have a return address, email, fax or phone number.

■ *Emphasize Features/Benefits in All Communications*
If every promotion piece, no matter how big or small, communicates the features and benefits of your program, the message being sent to customers is consistent and reiterated. Present the benefits and features in language that is understandable to the customer and reflects the customer's viewpoint—not the program planner's viewpoint.

■ *Distribute Sufficient Materials to Get a Response*
Calculate the correct quantity to be printed based on list totals and number of mailing (distribution) efforts. You may wish to add 5 to 10 percent more to have on hand in case a last-minute list is available or follow-up efforts for a particular target group are appropriate. Extras can be placed in meeting rooms and eating/kitchen areas, or used as giveaways to managers or preprogram reminders to registrants.

■ *Avoid Sending Promotional Pieces Around Holidays*
It's Thanksgiving week. You receive three direct mail pieces advertising various training programs. You are rushing to leave early Tuesday to drive 500 miles to your in-law's house. Are you really going to have time to study a marketing piece? No. Nor will you have time on the Monday after Thanksgiving—the piece will either land at the bottom of a never-to-be-read box or in the circular file. The lesson here—and most direct marketing experts will concur—is that if you want a customer's attention, get it when he or she is most open to receiving it.

■ *Simplify Registration Forms*
Design forms that are easy to fill in and provide plenty of space for customers to print their names, titles, addresses, phone and fax numbers, and email addresses. When asking customers to complete registration forms, try to put yourself in the customer's place—read the form as though you were filling it out.

As you review the copy ask yourself the following questions:

● Do you know what you're signing up for?
● Does it make sense?
● Are the times and dates of the program clear?
● What else do you want to know?
● Is there a number or website you can address questions to?

In addition, when requesting payment by credit card, provide sufficient line space for 20 digits, an expiration date, and a signature.

■ *Use a Proofreader*
In today's fast-paced environment of computers and spell-check programs, this essential part of the process is frequently omitted. Please don't be tempted to skip this step. Spell-check programs are not foolproof; programs are not intuitive—computers do not understand the essence of what your material is attempting to convey. If you can, hire a copyeditor; if you can't, a proofreader; and if that is not possible, ask a co-worker whose command of the written language is well respected. Nothing turns potential customers away more than poorly executed promotional content.

■ *Use the Web and Intranets to Advertise*
Technology is here to stay. Use it to your benefit. Ask for space on your company's intranet or website to promote upcoming programs. Use your internal email system for advertising, and direct customers to the web or intranet.

■ *Acknowledge Responses*
Once a participant has replied to your promotion by registering (whether by mail, fax, phone, or email) or requesting additional information before making a decision, let the participant know quickly that his or her reply has been received. If possible, send an acknowledgement

within 24 hours. Not only does this show the participant that you have good customer service skills, but more important, it sends the underlying message that your program is responsive to participants and their needs.

■ *Send Pieces Out with Plenty of Lead Time*
For in-house programs, send out the first round of notices four to five weeks ahead of the event. Send a second reminder notice three weeks ahead of the event. For programs conducted off site or with other groups, give potential participants at least two to three months of notification time so they can obtain approvals, make travel plans, and adjust personal schedules.

■ *Use Evaluations to Help the Next Promotion*
To improve future promotions, gather evaluation information from past or current programs. If you are creating new evaluation forms, be sure to include a couple of questions that will affect future promotional literature and program changes. For example:

● Did the content of the program meet the participant's expectations?

● Was the location convenient for participants?

● How easy was it for participants to register for the program?

■ *Determine Your Target Audience*
Targeting the perfect audience for your program will go a long way toward getting high response rates, excellent registration numbers, and meeting the expectations of your participants. Targeting also will save you money, because you will send promotional literature only to those individuals who really want it. Refer to the sidebar earlier in this issue that discusses how to target your audience.

pare and distribute your marketing materials. For each method you wish to use, begin by identifying exactly what it is you are going to market and when. That will lead you to the specifics of what needs to be done and by whom, as well as the resources available to help you accomplish your task.

Remember that implementation consists of these elements:

Timing. Try to meet the deadlines established in your marketing plan. This will ensure that your promotion efforts will reach prospects at the most opportune times.

Logistics of product and service delivery. Have sufficient staff available to produce and distribute your marketing materials.

Marketing data collection. Establish methods for gathering data about your marketing efforts, and a staff to maintain your records.

Step 6: Evaluation

Evaluation methods are called *controls*. These are used to measure the effectiveness of any promotion efforts. When evaluating a sales promotion, clearly the dollars brought in by the effort are an indicator of success or failure. For training program promotion, results are not as easily tracked—some of your advertising and networking efforts are not tangible, but you should always make note of these and your anticipated returns.

There are four types of marketing evaluation controls; each serves a different purpose.

1. Annual-plan control. This evaluates managerial objectives, and specific goals such as sales or numbers of attendees. Typically five different kinds of tools are used to monitor this control:

   ● sales analysis
   ● market share analysis
   ● marketing expense-to-sales analysis
   ● financial analysis estimates
   ● customer satisfaction surveys.

Most training professionals are familiar with customer satisfaction surveys, since they are the foundation for Level 1 evaluations. The other four items listed above, when applied to training program promotion efforts, will provide you with a complete evaluation picture.

2. Profitability control. This control allows an organization to closely monitor profits and expenditures in order to allocate its resources and effort efficiently.

3. Efficiency control. This entails a detailed analysis of the various elements of the marketing mix to determine productivity and cost-effectiveness.

4. Strategic control. This process allows managers to evaluate a marketing program from a long-term perspective.

Marketing Audits

Apart from the controls addressed above, which analyze one marketing activity (for example, training), an organization can conduct a comprehensive analysis of its strengths called a marketing audit. This process reviews the organization's marketing strategy, systems, and productivity. Someone independent of the marketing program should conduct these audits on a periodic basis in order to identify and solve problems before they arise.

Making It All Work

Once you have evaluated the effectiveness of your marketing strategy, you can take a step back and review the successes and shortcomings of the strategy. This will be your moment of truth, because it allows you to make decisions regarding future efforts, programs, and how to market new and current programs. You also will have a better knowledge base of who your audience is and why they attend training and learning programs.

For your next marketing effort, take this information and use it as a learning tool yourself, a way to modify and revise each of the steps, until you find a method that works best not just for you, but for your target audience. This information will always change; so evaluating the marketing effort outcomes will cause you to revise and change too.

References & Resources

Articles

Bruzzese, Anita. "Selling the Success." *Human Resource Executive,* October 20, 1996, pp. 15-17.

Clark, Kathryn F. "Marketing Savvy." *Human Resource Executive,* September 1997, pp. 36-39.

"Direct Marketing Tactics Resurrect Tired Training Programs." *Training Directors' Forum Newsletter,* May 1995, pp. 1-3.

Dust, Bob. "Marketing Training Services Internally." *Training & Development,* October 1996, p. 60.

Economy, Peter. "How to Attract Business via a Website." *Training & Development,* May 1998, pp. 97-98.

Hall, Brandon. "Reeling 'Em In." *Inside Technology Training,* May 1998, pp. 34-36.

Hipwell, Will. "Promoting Your E-Learning Investment." *Training & Development,* September 2000, pp. 18-19.

"How Sun Brings Along Doubters on Its New-Hire Intranet." *Training Directors' Forum Newsletter,* June 1998, pp. 4-5.

Kimmerling, George. "Surveying the Suppliers' Market." *Training & Development,* October 1995, pp. 34-39.

Laabs, Jennifer J. "HR for Profit: Selling Expertise." *Personnel Journal,* May 1995, pp. 84-92.

———. "Put Your Job on the Line." *Personnel Journal,* June 1995, pp. 74-88.

Lengnick-Hall, Mark L., and Cynthia A. Lengnick-Hall. "Expanding Customer Orientation in the HR Function." *Human Resource Management,* Fall 1999, pp. 210-214.

"Marketing Is Important to HR Survival." *HR Reporter,* May 1998, pp. 11-12.

"A Migration Training Success Story and How to Duplicate It at Your Organization. Part 3: Winning User Acceptance." *The Microcomputer Trainer,* October 1999, pp. 1-6.

Milite, George A. "HR and Marketing: An Overlooked Collaboration." *HRFocus,* October 1999, pp. 7-8.

Murphy, Jerry. "Market Your Wares to Prove Training Cares." *Technical & Skills Training,* October 1996, pp. 10-13.

"Online Learning from A to Z Part 4: If You Build It, Will They Come?" *The Microcomputer Trainer,* June 1999, pp. 9-10.

Ouellette, L. Paul. "Marketing Your Training Organization Internally." *Technical & Skills Training,* April 1993, pp. 27-29.

Parry, Scott B. "10 Ways to Get Management Buy-In." *Training & Development,* September 1997, pp. 20-22.

Raimy, Eric. "Fresh Airs." *Human Resource Executive,* February 1995, pp. 16-21.

"10 Ways to Stretch Your Budget, but Keep Training Quality High." *Training Directors' Forum Newsletter,* January 1996, p. 7.

Thompson, John. "Selling 'Soft' Issues to the CEO." *HRFocus,* June 1997, p. 12.

Books

Connor, Dick, and Jeff P. Davidson. *Marketing Your Consulting and Professional Services.* New York: John Wiley & Sons, 1997.

Graham, Judith H., and Daniel O. Graham. *The Writing System Workbook.* Fairfax, VA: Preview Press, 1994.

Knox, Alan B., ed. *Handbook of Marketing for Continuing Education.* San Francisco: Jossey-Bass, 1989.

Kotler, Philip. *Kotler on Marketing: How to Create, Win, and Dominate Markets.* New York: The Free Press, 1999.

Levant, Jessica. *HRD Survival Skills: Essential Strategies to Promote Training and Development Within Your Organization.* Houston: Gulf Publishing, 1998.

Lewin, Marsha D. *The Overnight Consultant.* New York: John Wiley & Sons, 1995.

Schrello, Don M. *How to Market Training & Information.* Long Beach, CA: Schrello Directing Marketing, 1994.

Wilcox, John, ed. *ASTD Trainer's Toolkit: HRD Marketing Materials.* Alexandria, VA: ASTD, 1994.

Infolines

Callahan, Madelyn R., ed. "How to Market Your Training Programs." No. 8605.

Darraugh, Barbara, ed. "How to Write a Marketing Plan." No. 9514.

Gilley, Jerry W. "Promoting Your Consulting Business: Techniques for Success." No. 9613.

Verado, Denzil. "Managing the Strategic Planning Process." No. 9710.

Internet Sites

http://www. MoreBusiness.com

http://idm.internet.com

Job Aid

Project Management Tool for Promotions

Use this matrix to guide you in developing your marketing mix. It contains all the guideposts that you need to follow to achieve a successful training promotion.

	Specifications/ Description	Completion Date	Distribution Date	Tasks	Responsible Person/Team	Budgeted Amount	Funds Source
Print Media							
Brochures							
Posters							
Banners							
Newsletters							
Technology							
Phone							
Fax							
Email							
Website							
Other							

Be a Better Manager

Issue 0607

Be a Better Manager

AUTHOR

Tora Estep
Associate Editor, ASTD Press
American Society for Training
& Development
1640 King Street
Alexandria, VA 22313-2043
Phone: 703.683.8138
Email: testep@astd.org

**Manager, Acquisitions &
Author Development**
Mark Morrow

Associate Editor, ASTD Press
Tora Estep

Editorial Consultant
Deborah Tobey

Copy Editor
Ann Bruen

Production Design
Kathleen Schaner

Managing Well

Managers are crucial to the success of organizations. While organizational leaders design forward-thinking strategies, managers make those strategies happen. Given the forces acting on organizations—such as globalization, outsourcing, the upcoming retirements of the Baby Boomer generation—organizations have to reinvent themselves as flexible learning organizations that can attract and retain the best and the brightest to stay competitive. Managers have a powerful role to play in that reinvention.

And yet, despite its importance, management development often receives less attention than leadership development. Where does this leave managers? Especially new or young managers who have been promoted up from the ranks because of skills in their functional areas? Often alone and unskilled in management techniques, floundering between the excesses of the micromanager whose employees feel second-guessed all the time and the passive, acquiescent manager whose employees struggle and whose goals go unachieved. And in the face of the changing business environment and manager role, even trained and experienced managers may need some additional development.

If you find yourself in the position of manager (or aspire to find yourself there) and feel that you could stand to learn some useful management practices and skills, this *Infoline* is for you. Although the list is not comprehensive, this issue describes a selection of competencies widely considered to be important for managers, including

- business management
- people management
- process management
- communication
- personal effectiveness.

Note that this issue is not intended to be a replacement for traditional management development; it is a guide to help you identify areas for improvement and plan for development as well as a supplement to any formal learning programs offered by your organization.

Prepare for Development

As a manager, you are a busy person. You don't have time to waste on learning what you already know or on competencies that don't have an impact on your work. However, constant learning is a hallmark of a great manager. The way to balance learning and a lack of time is to start by identifying your strengths and weaknesses. When you know your strengths, you will be better able to capitalize on them, and when you know your weaknesses, you can prepare an individual development plan (IDP) to improve them. To prepare for your development, follow these steps:

1. Complete the self-assessment in the sidebar *Management Competencies Self-Assessment*.

2. Select three or four of your lowest-scoring competencies and think of a time when lacking skills in these areas cost you or your organization. Describe the costs; this could include personal emotional costs, such as stress, or organizational costs, such as the loss of a high-performing employee and financial costs. From highest to lowest, rank order the selected competencies based on their costs.

3. Starting with the first competency on your rank-ordered list, prepare an IDP to address them, using the job aid at the end of this *Infoline*.

Develop Your Managerial Competencies

Once you have identified where you could use some improvement and determined which competencies have caused the most pain in the past, your next step is to improve your skills. The following sections provide brief overviews of the competencies as well as some tools, practices, and habits that can be useful in your quest to become a better manager. Feel free to skip some competencies and focus on others.

Management Competencies Self-Assessment

Consider the following statements and rate yourself on them according to the following key: (5) This is a real strength; (3) I have adequate skills in this area; (1) I could use some improvement in this area. Then add up your scores for each competency. Circle the three or four competencies with the lowest scores to focus on and assign priority to them (A, B, C).

Business Management	5	3	1	Priority (A, B, C)
I can describe my organization's goals and competitive environment.				
I understand principles of finance, budgeting, and accounting.				
I am skilled at preparing strategic plans that align with organizational goals.				
I understand relevant business regulations and procedures in my organization's industry.				
BUSINESS MANAGEMENT TOTAL:				
People Management				
I use an effective process to hire employees.				
I work with my employees to identify performance goals for them that align with the organization's goals.				
I am comfortable delegating work to my employees.				
I enable my employees to achieve their performance goals and more through effective coaching and motivation techniques.				
PEOPLE MANAGEMENT TOTAL:				
Process Management				
I run effective meetings that achieve their stated goals.				
I understand how change affects people and how to help them to embrace it.				
I am skilled at planning, organizing, and controlling work.				
I use resources effectively.				
PROCESS MANAGEMENT TOTAL:				

Communication	5	3	1	Priority (A, B, C)
I communicate well orally.				
I withhold judgment until I have completely and accurately heard what someone intends to say.				
I regularly provide both constructive and positive feedback that is specific and immediate.				
I communicate well in writing.				
COMMUNICATION TOTAL:				
Personal Effectiveness				
I practice excellent time management skills.				
Each day, I choose to first work on tasks that are highest priority to the organization and to me.				
My work space is well organized, and I always know where to find documents I need.				
I use effective problem-solving and decision-making processes.				
PERSONAL EFFECTIVENESS TOTAL:				

Business Management

According to Lisa Haneberg in "Reinventing Middle Management," today's managers "see themselves as business owners" and "know that they create and represent the organization; they establish the work context." In light of this, the need for a broad understanding of the organization as well as specific knowledge of business regulations and procedures becomes clear. The following are some examples of business knowledge you should know.

■ State of the Business
As a manager, you need to understand your organization's

- *business model,* which describes how an organization plans to serve its customers and its employees and includes both strategy and implementation plans

- *business objectives,* which state what your organization wants to accomplish; for example, a business objective might be to increase

profitability by five percent in the next year with the launch of a new product

- *factors that affect organizational growth,* including the competitive environment and the industry as well as the current culture and values of an organization

- *business drivers,* which are the internal (for example, product development) and external forces (for example, government or technology) that direct an organization's strategy, goals, business needs, and performance needs.

To complete the picture of the state of the business, you also need to understand corporate success measures and how the organization defines and measures success. All these factors determine how you will link your department's goals and objectives to overall business goals and objectives.

Basic Accounting Terms

To work effectively with your accounting department or with executives in the organization, you need to understand and learn to use basic accounting terminology.

- **Assets** refer to economic resources—in other words, what a company owns—that may be expressed in monetary terms.

- **Liabilities** are the debts or expenses a company owes.

- **Equity** is the value of the owners' or shareholders' portion of the business after all claims against it.

- **Balance sheet** is a statement of the firm's financial position, including assets, liabilities, and equity (liabilities + equity = assets).

- **Income statements** explain revenues, expenses, and profits over a specified period of time (revenues - expenses = net income).

- **Chart of accounts** is the listing of account lines maintained in the general ledger.

- **Cost-benefit analysis** is a comparison that weighs the costs of a training activity against the outcomes achieved and is carried out to determine the return-on-investment.

- **Expenses** are the costs incurred in the process of earning revenues and conducting business.

- **Incurred expenses** are the expenses in which obligations have been fulfilled but not paid.

- **Operating expenses** are expenses that relate directly to business operations, not to providing products or services.

- **Revenue** is the money a company earns by providing goods or services to its customers.

- **Financial statements** are the four statements that show the end results of an organization's financial condition: balance sheet, income statement, statement of cash flows, and statement of owners' equity.

Some ways you can identify these components of your organization include

- reviewing the organization's mission and vision statements and its annual report

- reviewing strategic plans (these will often be confidential) and talking to executives about the strategic direction of the organization

- maintaining knowledge of your industry through trade papers, conferences, and so forth.

■ *Budgeting and Accounting*

Creating a good budget is more than an annual event designed to document spending; it's a working plan that guides fiscal decisions. A well-designed and executed budget forms the foundation for developing next year's budget.

Although budgeting is often referred to as a process, in reality it's part of a larger accounting system (for some basic accounting terms, see the sidebar at left). A typical accounting system includes three steps:

1. Budget design and development (forecasting).

2. Budget execution (expense tracking, monitoring, and management).

3. Reporting and reconciliation.

In an optimal planning process, you would design a budget based on the business plan, not on other factors, such as available revenue to fund the plan or previous spending levels. The assumption is that business goals justify the expenditures. Note that it is good practice to work with your organization's accounting department to learn their preferences in terms of processes and documentation; this may help you to avoid having to redo your work.

■ *Organizational Structure*

Organizational structure refers to both formal and informal reporting structures as well as ways that information moves across the organization and work gets done. You can learn about formal structures from organization charts, but understanding informal structures requires personal observation and keeping your ear open. However, knowing the informal ways that things get done in an organization can be very powerful. For example, knowing who influences whom can be useful knowledge if you need to get something done.

■ *Strategic Planning*

Strategic planning can be defined as the process of systematically organizing the future, a process in which managers and other professionals use past experience as a filter for future decisions. When creating a strategic plan for your department, focus attention on department outcomes that link with the overall organization's mission and strategic plan and address these questions:

- Where is my department now?

- Where does my department want to go?

- How will my department get there?

- What are my department's strengths and weaknesses?

You can develop a strategic plan by using a four-phase process (see the sidebar *Strategic Planning* at right). Use strategic planning as a tool to accomplish more things that are critical to your department and to the overall business strategy. For that reason, don't think of strategic planning as a one-time event; it should be an ongoing process.

■ *Business Regulations*

Another important component of the business management competency is knowledge of business regulations and ethics. These may include

- employment law and regulatory requirements
- civil rights legislation
- workplace safety
- securities and financial reporting
- information technology compliance
- union relations
- intellectual property
- corporate policies and procedures
- ethical standards.

You can find information about these regulations through your human resources department, government websites, and any professional associations that you may belong to.

Strategic Planning

As a manager, you must be able to turn organizational goals into department goals. The way to do this is to carry out strategic planning for your department. Use this four-phase model to help you.

Phase	Task
1. Formulation	• Identify organizational mission, vision, and values. • Develop department mission, vision, and value statements based on this organizational review.
2. Development	• Conduct an analysis of strengths, weaknesses, opportunities, and threats (SWOT). • Establish strategic goals (two to three years to attain). • Identify strategies to attain those goals.
3. Implementation	• Establish long-term measurable goals to achieve strategies. • Establish short-term objectives (six months to a year) for each goal. • Create action plans to achieve those objectives. • Allocate resources to work toward those objectives. • Motivate employees to achieve those objectives.
4. Evaluation	• Review strategies. • Measure actual performance against strategies, goals, and objectives. • Take corrective action.

For more information on strategic planning, see "Managing the Strategic Planning Process," *Infoline* No. 259710, and "Strategic Planning for Human Resource Development," *Infoline* No. 259206.

Hiring Checklist

Hiring top performers is the culmination of effective recruitment and advertising, interviewing, and selecting. The following four areas cover the basics of the process.

Area 1: Requirements

☐ Focus on the few key attributes you are looking for.

☐ Have a plan. You must see how your employee needs link to the strategic plan of the organization.

☐ Look for *organizational* fit—not just job fit.

☐ Specify the job. Be clear about what the job entails.

Area 2: Hiring System

☐ Plan and prepare for interviews. Eliminate unnecessary duplication of questions, practice your approach, and test your questions beforehand.

☐ Develop the same basic questions for each interview so there will be a basis for comparison later on.

☐ Use both open-ended and closed-ended questions in an interview. Plan on talking about 25 percent of the time and listening about 75 percent of the time.

Area 3: Basics

☐ Be a good host. For example, make the interviewee feel welcome and offer refreshment.

☐ Make sure the interview and hiring processes are clear up front.

☐ Hone your interviewing skills and review federal guidelines for interviewing.

Area 4: Value-Added System

☐ Relate the interview to values and vision, not just to job experience.

☐ Meet across functions with people who will work with this person.

☐ Have a way to compare meaningful notes afterward.

Adapted from E. Stewart Hickman's "Hiring and Retaining Top Performing Employees," Infoline No. 250011.

People Management

The ability to manage people well is a crucial competency for managers, especially given that the job of managers is to achieve the goals of the department and the organization through the work of other people. Furthermore, it has become a truism that people don't leave organizations; people leave managers. How people are managed is a crucial factor in retaining employees.

For these reasons, it's important to develop strong people management skills. Some of these are discussed in the following sections.

Hiring and Retaining

How well your people perform starts with how well you selected them in the first place, and there are effective processes you can learn to interview candidates and hire the right employees (see the sidebar *Hiring Checklist* at left for an overview of an effective hiring process).

To prepare to interview candidates, ask yourself three questions:

1. What will make a candidate suitable for this job?

2. What are the signals that a candidate may be suitable for the job?

3. What are the signals that a candidate may not be suitable for the job?

Preparing an answer to the first question in advance will enable you to answer the second two during the interview itself. Although you will use the job description as a resource, note that the first question refers to more than job requirements; it refers to the culture of your organization and your department. In other words, what kind of person represents a good fit?

Once you have hired the right person, you need to work to retain that person. Losing employees is costly and disruptive to the smooth functioning of your department. One way to do this is to model your department on organizations with good track records for retention, which share certain characteristics. They

- value their workers

- tie workforce initiatives to organizational strategies

- understand the importance of employee growth and development

- link training to operations

- provide training and development for everyone

- use competencies

- track, measure, and evaluate their initiatives.

Managing Performance

Managing employees' performance goes beyond completing a performance review once or twice a year. Although formal performance reviews are an important tool in developing individual goals that will enable the department and ultimately the organization to achieve their goals, managing employees' performance should take place on a far more frequent basis, ideally weekly, or even daily.

This high level of engagement has become increasingly rare, according to Bruce Tulgan in "The Under-Management Epidemic," and represents a fear on the part of managers to appear to be the dreaded micromanager. Tulgan notes "that these under-managers often think they are being 'good guys' by soft-pedaling their authority, but their failure to provide leadership causes so many problems that they are not being good guys at all."

Tulgan describes these six characteristics of highly successful and engaged managers:

1. They know a lot about their employees' work, including how much, how fast, and how hard.

2. They have regular meetings with every employee, ideally once a day, but at a minimum, once a week, to talk about how the job is going.

3. They write everything down in a manager's notebook, which is a running log of employee meetings.

4. They do a lot for their employees—for example, provide training opportunities, recognition, different schedule arrangements—but they expect a lot in return.

5. They link rewards to specific instances of high performance.

6. They consider high performance to be the only option and work hard to achieve it through clear performance expectations, regular feedback, coaching for development, frank discussions, planning, and termination, if required.

Delegating

Delegation is often billed as a time-saving mechanism for the manager, but its benefits don't stop there. Successful delegation maximizes an organization's output, while producing competent employees, balanced budgets, and promotable managers. "Managers who delegate properly will always accomplish more than those who refuse to let go of projects their subordinates should be doing," says Eugene Raudsepp in "How to Delegate Effectively." Delegation has two goals: First, to free you up from routine tasks so that you can focus on more big-picture strategic tasks and, second, to develop employee skills so that they are learning and preparing for future tasks and positions.

Here is an effective process for delegating tasks:

- Decide what to delegate by identifying tasks that someone else can do just as well. (However, remember to always retain tasks related to overall planning, policy making, goal setting, budget supervision, confidential information, and subordinate relations.)

- Pick the right person for the task. To do this, consider your subordinates' characteristics, skills, and interests. The perfect assignment will challenge, but not overwhelm, your employee.

- Plan carefully and explain clearly. Communicate your priorities (speed or quality, for example), expected results, and performance criteria.

- Delegate both responsibility and authority. Make sure the employee has what he or she needs to get the job done. In the area of authority, that may mean contacting others with whom the employee will be working, requesting their cooperation, and letting them know the employee has full authority to complete the task.

- Monitor progress regularly, especially with employees who are undertaking unfamiliar assignments.

- Delegate a whole project. The employee will gain far more satisfaction and learn more from carrying out a complete project than he or she will from doing bits and pieces. If that isn't possible, explain the relevance of his or her contribution to the overall project.

- Encourage your employee. Provide constructive feedback and coaching as required.

- Evaluate the project together with the employee. Correct mistakes privately and tactfully, and reward success generously.

Motivating

Motivation is defined as a psychological force that determines what a person chooses to do, how hard he or she works, and how persistent he or she is in the face of a challenge. Understanding a variety of motivational theories and the different ways that different people are motivated is crucial to the successful work of a manager. The following two influences have a great effect on the motivation of your employees and should also be considered when integrating motivation into work planning, performance feedback, and relationship building:

■ *Management Recognition*
Instead of coming from some nebulous, ad hoc committee or corporate institution, the most valuable recognition comes directly from a person's manager. The sidebar *Rewarding Employees* provides a sampling of ways that you can reward your employees.

■ *Performance Incentives*
Your employees want to be recognized for the jobs they were hired to do. The most effective incentives are based on job performance—not on non-performance-related praise such as attendance.

Developing People

According to Haneberg, today's effective managers create work environments in which employees thrive. One important way to accomplish this is to provide challenging opportunities to learn and grow as well as to provide coaching and feedback.

To be a successful coach, you need to demonstrate certain behaviors, such as supporting employees' needs, creating choices, seeking commitment, and providing avenues of self-expression. Work toward a balance between being supportive and caring and being clear and direct about what is expected of the employee. Two categories of coaching behaviors are effective in developing employees: supporting behaviors and initiating behaviors.

Supporting behaviors demonstrate caring, concern, and acceptance and lead to reduced tension and more open communication. Examples include

- collaboration on solutions to problem areas
- help and assistance where needed
- concern about worker's needs and objectives
- empathy.

Initiating behaviors encourage the employee to discuss the work situation. A manager's initiating behaviors include

- providing feedback and analysis of issues
- clarifying goals and expectations
- planning solutions and changes
- outlining consequences of employee actions.

Process Management

Three processes are familiar to most managers: meeting management, change management, and project management. The following sections will describe some effective methods and tools to carry these out.

Meeting Management

Ineffective meetings that don't achieve their goals are some of the biggest time and money wasters in organizations today. Furthermore, they waste employee commitment and energy.

To make the most of meeting time, you need to do some planning and preparation. Before the meeting, you should

- determine what the meeting should accomplish

- identify who needs to be there and what he or she needs to do to prepare for the meeting

- prepare an agenda

- identify any tools you may need (whiteboards, markers, and so forth)

- invite participants, providing them with a description of what the meeting should achieve as well as any pre-work to accomplish.

At the time of the meeting, you should

- ensure that you have the space and tools that you need

- start on time

- introduce the participants to each other

- explain why you are meeting

Rewarding Employees

Research into why talented people stay in organizations is the basis for the following ways to show your employees that you appreciate them:

■ *Private Time With You*
Have lunch with an employee and ask questions like, "What can I do to keep you on my team?" "What might make your work life easier?" "What can I do to be more supportive to help you?"

■ *Frank Talk About the Future*
Hold a career conversation in a quiet, private place—off-site, if possible. Ask the following questions to start: "What do you enjoy most about your job? The least?" "Which of your talents have I not used yet?" "What jobs do you see yourself doing in the future?"

■ *Potential Growth*
Let employees choose from a list of potential projects, assignments, or tasks that could enrich their work.

■ *Submit to Pruning*
Ask the employee with whom you never agree to engage in some straight talk about how you can work together better. Listen carefully and don't defend yourself. Then take a step toward changing at least one behavior.

■ *A Unique Perk for Fun*
Give an employee a "kicks" coupon that entitles him or her to spend up to X amount of money to take a break or have some fun at work. It could involve the whole team.

■ *Blending Work and Passion*
Have a "Passion Breakfast" for all employees, a team, or one on one. Ask, "What do you love to do?" "At work?" "Outside of work?" Brainstorm and commit to helping them build more of what they love into their workday.

■ *Genie in a Bottle*
Ask an employee to write down six ways he or she would like to be rewarded. Anything goes. The only rule is that half of the ideas have to be low or no cost.

■ *A Chance to Download*
Give 12 coupons for listening time—one for each month, in which an employee can talk about anything for 20 minutes. Your job isn't to understand, just to listen.

Adapted from Beverly L. Kaye and Sharon Jordan-Evans's "The ABCs of Management Gift-Giving," Training & Development, December 2000.

● forecast the meeting process

● explain the ground rules

● display enthusiasm.

During the meeting, use meeting facilitation skills to keep to the agenda, ask all participants to contribute, and park topics that are not on the agenda.

And always follow up meetings by typing up notes and distributing them to everyone who participated, planning to follow up on commitments made in the meeting, and plan for a follow-up meeting to ensure that commitments are being upheld.

Change Management

Organizations make the decision to change for business reasons. But how change is implemented is based on "people reasons." It is important for managers to understand reactions to change and how to implement change effectively.

An organization's people are a critical component in ensuring that any organizational change initiative is successful. Management consultant, futurist, speaker, and prolific author Karl Albrecht described the *personal change response cycle* to help individuals work though the progressive psychological phases of change response, which are as follows:

■ *Threat*
In this phase, individuals are afraid to change the status quo because of fear of the unknown or fear of a state worse than the status quo.

■ *Problem*
At this point, individuals perceive change to be a lot of work and problems. Because they no longer know the rules, it's difficult for them to complete their jobs.

■ *Solution*
Overcoming the problems perceived in the previous phase starts to reveal some of the benefits of the change.

■ *Habit*
As old operating procedures are forgotten, the new become the norm.

Individuals progress through these phases at different rates. Your job as manager is to help people work through them as efficiently as possible. To do this, some of the tasks you have to achieve are to

● define the tasks that need to be done

● create management systems to help accomplish the tasks

● develop strategies for gaining commitment from employees

● develop communication strategies

● invite employee participation in the development of new processes and policies

● assign employees, resources, experts, and consultants to manage the change

● study present conditions

● collect data on employee attitudes toward the change

● create models of the end state

● state the goals of the transition and clearly describe the end state.

Project Management

Project management consists of planning, organizing, and controlling work. The goal of project management is to deliver a project that is on time, within budget, meets the required performance or specification level, and uses resources wisely. A project manager plans for a project's needs and then organizes and controls project resources as it progresses. Your tasks in managing projects are defined in the following sections.

■ *Defining the Project and Goals*

Regardless of the specific project goals and end deliverables, you, as project manager, are responsible for

● ensuring that the project work, and only the approved project work, is completed (scope)

● ensuring that the project schedule is planned, communicated, and monitored

● tracking an initial project budget and expenses incurred as the project progresses

● measuring and monitoring that the project deliverables meet the specified quality guidelines and standards

● scheduling and managing the appropriate use of resources.

■ *Project Planning*

The next task is establishing a plan for how the project will be accomplished. These are the steps in this process:

1. Select a strategy for achieving the objective.

2. Divide the project's tasks into subtasks and units (the work breakdown structure [WBS]).

3. Determine the standards for measuring the accomplishment of each subtask (specifications).

4. Develop a time schedule and sequence for performing tasks and subtasks (Gantt charts and program evaluation review technique [PERT] charts—also known as the critical path method [CPM]).

5. Estimate costs of each task and subtask and compile the entire project's cost budget (if not determined).

6. Design the staff organization needed to fulfill tasks and subtasks, including the number and kind of people required, their duties, and any necessary training.

7. Develop policies and procedures that will be in effect during the project's life cycle.

8. Acknowledge predetermined parameters imposed by the customer or organization, such as military standards or specifications.

Then carefully detail and document each element.

■ *Staffing a Project and Project Roles*

During the planning process, you compiled the tasks and subtasks that need to be performed. An important element of planning is finding and using the correct personnel to perform these tasks. Usually, in the interests of cost, time, and availability, you can find the personnel for a project within the organization. However, project managers often have the option of hiring expertise from outside the organization; hiring a consultant, for example, may be the best way to obtain the required skills without hiring full-time employees.

■ *Managing a Project*

You can use a variety of tools to prepare schedules and track work on a project. The following are three of the most important:

● The WBS not only identifies tasks, subtasks, and units of work to be performed, but also assists in estimating and tracking costs of each of these elements. A WBS represents a graphical hierarchy of the project, deliverables, tasks, and subtasks.

● A project's timeframe is derived from the plan and the WBS. The project manager lists the WBS components, arranges them in sequence, and determines how the elements mesh to form a milestone chart. Timeframe data is mapped into a chart called a Gantt chart, which graphically displays the time relationships of the project's steps and key checkpoints or deliverable dates, known as milestones. It's a valuable tool for project managers in planning, monitoring, and controlling projects.

● PERT and CPM charts are two widely used network-diagramming techniques. Network diagrams plot a sequence of activities (predecessor and successor tasks) to illustrate the interrelationships among activities and resources. PERT and CPM are also used to calculate the project duration.

Communication

Communication is an important competency in all areas of a manager's job, from presenting plans to executives, to interacting with subordinates, to communicating change initiatives, and more. Some facets of communication that a manager must master include presenting, listening, and giving feedback.

Presenting

In business, presentations are a fact of life. They can range from brief presentations to the executive team to a series of talks that constitute a training program. In any case, giving a presentation can be pretty frightening. *Communication Basics*'s authors Judy Jenings and Linda Malcak provide four steps to presentation success:

1. Focus on the participants. Find out who will be there and why, what they need to know and how they want to hear it, what makes them feel comfortable or uncomfortable.

2. Focus on the content. Now that you know who will be there, you know what kind of information they need and want to hear and how they prefer to hear it. Especially try to find out what the audience's pain points are and how what you have to say can relieve those pain points.

3. Focus on the structure of the presentation. Now that you know whom you are talking to and what you need to say to them, it's time to prepare your roadmap for how you are going to say it. Create an agenda that shows you where you stop and start, where you move on to a new topic, and where you provide breaks (if necessary). Then practice. And practice some more.

4. Finally, follow your plan. If you have focused on the right things by following the other three steps, then you can carry off your presentation with confidence.

Listening

The ability to listen well may be one of the most underappreciated and most powerful communication skills that anyone could have. Lyman K. Steil's sensing, interpreting, evaluating, and responding (SIER) model of listening is an effective method to ensure that you take full advantage of the ability to capture the full gist of that person's message before you respond. A brief description of the model follows.

■ *Sensing*
To listen effectively, you must first receive the message accurately. That means being silent and allowing yourself to hear what the other person has to say. But hearing the words is only one component of sensing the other person's message. You've also got to pay attention to the person's body language, tone of voice, and pattern of breathing.

■ *Interpreting*
Successful sensing lays the groundwork for the interpreting stage of the Steil SIER model. This is the stage in which you interpret the speaker's meaning. Considering the variety of meaning in words and the different ways that people use body language, this may be the most difficult stage of listening. To help you interpret correctly, rephrase what the speaker has said or ask for further clarification.

■ *Evaluating*
Only after you have fully sensed and interpreted the message are you in the position to evaluate it. This involves understanding your own reaction to the message: Did you like it? Dislike it? Think it was poorly argued? Think it was complete or incomplete?

■ *Responding*
The final stage of the model is responding. However, people often skip ahead to this point without taking the time and the focus to gather important information from the message along the way.

Giving Feedback

Feedback is a learned skill. Mastering its use can help you

- learn continually
- strengthen your communication skills
- develop more effective relationships
- improve your decision-making capabilities
- take advantage of opportunities for growth.

In your role as a manager, feedback is important in coaching, delegating, and managing performance. The sidebar *Giving Feedback* at right describes an effective feedback process.

Personal Effectiveness

Personal effectiveness is what enables you to stay organized, use your time effectively, and stay on top of your work.

■ *Time Management*
One way to get control of how you use your time is to keep a log of what you do for several days by writing down each task change that you make. Then review the log and determine if there are any obvious time wasters and work to eliminate them.

In "A Get-Real Guide to Time Management," Donna J. Abernathy cites research into time thieves that include telephone calls, drop-in visitors, lack of necessary resources, personal disorganization, indecisiveness, an inability to say no, procrastination, paperwork, and management by crisis. Once you have identified your biggest time wasters, determine ways to eliminate or minimize their effect. For example, if phone calls are your greatest time thief, set aside a portion of the day during which you send all calls into voicemail.

■ *Planning*
Closely related to time management skills are planning and prioritizing skills. To get the most of your time, practice focusing on the things that really make a difference at work. Abernathy describes the following categories to help you sort your work:

- A priorities: If you had nothing to do today, what should you work on that would improve your productivity in one to four weeks? What items on your to-do list are most closely related to organizational goals and strategies?

- B priorities: What things must be done today? Can you delegate any of them?

- C priorities: What things should be done today or tomorrow? Can you delegate any of them?

- D priorities: What things should you not do at all? (This may be the time to delegate, or you may want to let go of the item altogether.)

Giving Feedback

To be effective, feedback must be expressed in a manner that helps the receiver hear the message while keeping the relationship intact. To accomplish these goals, you must do the following:

■ *Show consideration*
One of the objectives of feedback is to help someone, not hurt someone. For that reason, you need to give feedback with care. To show consideration while giving feedback

- monitor your behavior
- practice active listening
- express concern and caring.

■ *Withhold judgment*
To reduce the receiver's resistance to feedback, make sure that you withhold judgment. Don't evaluate the behavior, don't assume its intent, but do describe specific behavior and its effects or consequences.

■ *Deliver at an appropriate time*
Most feedback literature states that you should give your message immediately after the behavior takes place or the next time there is a potential for recurrence. Generally speaking, this is the right approach to take. However, there are occasions when waiting is appropriate. One example is when either you or the receiver may lose emotional control. Another example is when the physical setting is inappropriate.

■ *Provide freedom to change or not*
It is important to acknowledge that the receiver is free to change or not. That decision belongs solely to him or her. However, make the effects of the behavior clear, because these effects may not be what the receiver intended. In addition, make clear what the consequences of continuing the behavior will be, whether positive or negative.

■ *Check for readiness*
Ideally, you should give feedback only when the receiver is mentally, emotionally, and physically ready to receive it. Feedback tends to work best when the receiver is open to it. However, circumstances aren't always ideal, and you may need to give feedback even when the receiver doesn't want to hear it. In those cases, double check your motivation: Do you want to give feedback, or are you just angry and want to sound off?

■ *Check for clarity*
Finally, check with the receiver to make sure that the message he or she received is the one that you intended to send.

Adapted from Holly DeForest, Pamela Largent, and Mary Steinberg's "Mastering the Art of Feedback," Infoline *No. 250308.*

■ *Organization Skills*

According to David Allen in *Getting Things Done,* "[h]aving a total and seamless system of organization in place gives you tremendous power because it allows your mind to let go of lower-level thinking and graduate to intuitive focusing, undistracted by matters that haven't been dealt with appropriately." One way to free up your mind for higher-level thinking is to empty your in-box regularly and use an efficient process.

Allen describes a simple process to empty your in-box regularly (and it applies to email also):

● Pick up or open the first item first. Don't look at any other items.

● Decide if you have to do anything with the item (whether now or later). If not, determine if you want to throw it out or file it for reference and do so immediately.

● If you do have to do something, determine exactly what that is, including any substeps. The action you decide on should be the next possible thing that you can do. For example, if you have received a tax form, and you realize that you need to file your taxes but you haven't received your W-2s, your next step may be to call your human resources department to get a copy.

● Then, determine how to do it. If it's an action that will take less than two minutes, do it immediately. If it will take longer than that, decide whether to delegate the task or do it yourself. If you need to do it, put a reminder into your schedule and file the paperwork. Never put anything back into your in-box.

■ *Problem Solving and Decision Making*

Solving problems and making decisions make up much of the day-to-day work of managers. Here is a six-step method for doing this that enables you to consider multiple options:

1. Define the problem. Simply stated, a problem is a discrepancy between what is and what should be. State the problem in the form of a question; for example, "How can we reduce the number of errors on the production line?"

2. Analyze the problem.

3. Establish a checklist of criteria to use in evaluating potential solutions.

4. List all possible alternatives (it can be helpful to get input from employees who are also involved in the problem).

5. Select the alternative that aligns best with the checklist of criteria and determine how to implement the solution.

6. Implement the solution. Monitor and evaluate the solution to ensure that it solves the problem.

■ *Influencing*

Basically, influence is communicating with the purpose of gaining support for your ideas. To exert influence over others, there are two habits you must develop. First, seek to understand what the other person wants (his or her priorities) and how he or she operates.

Second, examine how your own priorities may blind you to options. Although it is difficult to be objective, doing so liberates you to be more effective with others by enabling you to base discussions on organizational priorities.

When you can listen to others and understand what they want and what you should avoid, you will be able to predict more accurately their priorities and influence their decision making.

Move Forward

This *Infoline* provided a self-assessment to help you identify areas where you could use some improvement as a manager and brief overviews of some management competencies. This is only a beginning. As a manager, you must learn to embrace continual self-development. Start by identifying a competency or a skill to work on, practice the steps provided in this *Infoline* related to that skill, and look to the references and resources for more information. This is just your first step toward becoming a better and more efficient manager.

References & Resources

Articles

Abernathy, Donna J. "A Get-Real Guide to Time Management." *Training & Development,* June 1999, pp. 22-25.

Buckingham, Marcus. "What Great Managers Do." *Harvard Business Review,* March 2005, pp. 70-79.

Gosling, Jonathan, and Henry Mintzberg. "The Five Minds of a Manager." *Harvard Business Review,* November 2003, pp. 54-63.

Haneberg, Lisa. "Reinventing Middle Management." *Leader to Leader,* Fall 2005, pp. 13-18.

Hogan, Robert T., and Jorge E. Fernandez. "Syndromes of Mismanagement." *Quality and Participation,* Fall 2002, pp. 28-31.

Kaye, Beverly L., and Sharon Jordan-Evans. "The ABCs of Management Gift-Giving." *Training & Development,* December 2000, pp. 51-52.

Liccione, William J. "Balanced Management: A Key Component of Managerial Effectiveness." *Performance Improvement,* February 2005, pp. 32-38.

Lippitt, Mary. "How to Influence Leaders." *Training & Development,* March 1999, pp. 18-22.

McCrimmon, Mitch. "How Not to Waste Money on Leadership Development." *OD/Leadership News,* March 2006. Available at http://www.astd.org/astd /publications/newsletters/od _leadership_news.

McLagan, Patricia. "Management by Intent." *Leader to Leader,* Fall 2004, pp. 12-15.

Mittler, James E. "It's Management Quality That Matters—Not Style." *Quality and Participation,* Fall 2002, pp. 19-21.

Raudsepp, Eugene. "How to Delegate Effectively." *Machine Design,* April 20, 1995, p. 11.

Tulgan, Bruce. "The Under-Management Epidemic." *HRMagazine,* October 2004, pp. 119-122.

Books

Allen, David. *Getting Things Done: The Art of Stress-Free Productivity.* New York: Penguin Group.

ASTD (American Society for Training & Development). *ASTD Learning System.* Alexandria, VA: ASTD Press, 2006.

Blanchard, Ken, and Steve Gottry. *The On-Time, On-Target Manager.* New York: HarperCollins, 2004.

Blanchard, Kenneth, Patricia Zigarmi, and Drea Zigarmi. *Leadership and the One-Minute Manager.* New York: William Morrow, 1985.

Flaherty, Jane S., and Peter B. Stark. *The Competent Leader: A Powerful and Practical Tool Kit for Managers and Supervisors.* Amherst, MA: HRD Press, 1999.

Haneberg, Lisa. *High Impact Middle Management.* Avon, MA: Adams Media, 2005.

———. *Coaching Basics.* Alexandria, VA: ASTD Press, 2006.

Handy, Charles. *21 Ideas for Managers.* San Francisco: Jossey-Bass, 2000.

Jenings, Judy, and Linda Malcak. *Communication Basics.* Alexandria, VA: ASTD Press, 2004.

Radde, Paul O. *Supervising: A Guide for All Levels.* Austin, TX: Learning Concepts, 1981.

Russell, Jeffrey, and Linda Russell. *Strategic Planning Training.* Alexandria, VA: ASTD Press, 2005.

Steil, Lyman K., and Richard K. Bommelje. *Listening Leaders™: The Ten Golden Rules to Listen, Lead & Succeed.* Edina, MN: Beaver's Pond Press, 2004.

Infolines

Battell, Chris. "Effective Listening." No. 250605.

Darraugh, Barbara. "Coaching and Feedback." No. 259006 (revised 1997).

DeForest, Holly, Pamela Largent, and Mary Steinberg. "Mastering the Art of Feedback." No. 250308.

Estep, Tora. "Meetings That Work!" No. 250505.

Gaines, Kathryn. "Leading Work Teams." No. 250602 (revised 1998).

Gilley, Jerry W. "Strategic Planning for Human Resource Development." No. 259206.

Grosse, Eric F. "Interview Skills for Managers." No. 250206.

Hickman, E. Stewart. "Hiring and Retaining Top-Performing Employees." No. 250011.

Lauby, Sharlyn J. "Motivating Employees." No. 250510.

Verardo, Denzil. "Managing the Strategic Planning Process." No. 259710.

Wircenski, Jerry L., and Richard L. Sullivan. "Make Every Presentation a Winner." No. 258606 (revised 1998).

Younger, Sandra Millers. "How to Delegate." No. 259011 (revised 1997).

Job Aid

Better Manager IDP

To prepare your IDP, determine where you require additional development using the Management Competencies Self-Assessment. Write the competencies down in the following table. Then rank them. Give the one that is costliest to you and/or your organization the number 1, the next costliest the number 2, and so forth.

Competency Area	Description of Costs (Personal and/or Organizational)	Rank Order
Business Management		
People Management		
Process Management		
Communication		
Personal Effectiveness		

Next, create a table with the following headings to prepare your IDP (you can use a word processing program, a spreadsheet program, or simply write by hand—whatever format is most comfortable for you). Leave plenty of space to write your goals. In the first column, write the name of the management competency. In the second column, identify activities to help you improve your skills in the competency area. Make sure that these follow the SMART goal format: they should be **s**pecific, **m**easurable, **a**ttainable, **r**ealistic, and **t**ime bound. Use the third column to keep track of progress on your goals. In the fourth column, list some ways to apply your new knowledge or some new habits to form that will improve your skills in this competency. The first rows have been filled in with an example to help you get started. Aim to make some progress every day, even if it is something minor like purchasing a book on a relevant topic.

Competency Area	Goals (Are they SMART?)	Progress	Ideas for Application
Process Management	Complete change management training offered through the organization's training department by 5/12.	Change management course completed 5/12	Prepare communication strategy to help people transition to the new paradigm.
	Read *Infoline* on meeting management by 6/18.	In progress	Prepare an agenda for every meeting.
	Complete project management training offered by training department by 8/15.	Submitted training request to training department	

Leading Work Teams

Issue 0602

Leading Work Teams

A U T H O R

Kathryn Gaines
Leading Pace, LLC
6105 Twain Drive
New Market, MD 21774
Tel: 301.865.2960
Fax: 301.865.3688
Email: kgaines@
leadingpace.com
Website: www.LeadingPace.com

Kathryn Gaines has served as a management and organizational consultant, coach, and trainer for 15 years. She partners with client groups to improve performance, results, commitment, and accountability in the workplace. Gaines specializes in developing leadership and teamwork.

Associate Editor, ASTD Press
Tora Estep
testep@astd.org

Editor
Sabrina E. Hicks

Editorial Consultant
Chris Battell

Copy Editor
Ann Bruen

Production Design
Kathleen Schaner

Manager, ASTD Press
Mark Morrow

Leading Teams

Everyone works on teams. You work with co-workers within your department, with clients and customers, across organizational functions, and on temporary committees. Such collaboration is mandatory to achieve organizational goals. One benefit of the team structure is that you have the opportunity to hone your leadership skills, whether or not you hold the title of "team leader."

Every element of a team's success depends on its leadership processes: planning, clarifying roles, building relationships, accomplishing tasks, negotiating conflicts, navigating changes, making decisions, and solving problems. To complicate matters, the structure of today's workforce is complex:

- a team leader may work in a different time zone than his or her team members

- team members may report to more than one leader in a matrix operating structure

- a team, working on a knowledge-intensive project, may have a leader who has less technical expertise than some of his or her team members.

Cross-functional teams and geographically dispersed organizations—these are just a few of the current workplace trends that make the traditional command-and-control leader obsolete. Traditional conceptions of leadership focus on the top leader in the hierarchy selling a clear, compelling picture of the future to everyone in the organization. Present day notions of leadership center on a team of workers discovering a shared vision of the future. The best teams are those in which each member expresses some type of leadership—either formal or informal—to achieve team goals.

If you find yourself in a formal position of leadership, it's your responsibility to cultivate leadership—at all levels. Empowering all members of a team is important because, although you are the designated team leader, you may not be the expert, and you certainly won't always have the answers.

By becoming more engaged in leadership, with or without formal authority, you contribute greater value to, and have more impact on, your team.

Engaging in Leadership

Leadership is a process of influencing others to work toward the shared goals of the team. It is a collaborative relationship built through communication and influence behaviors.

While not everyone is a leader in the formal, traditional sense of the word, everyone shares an obligation as a member of a team. You have the responsibility to speak up, take action, and show initiative to mobilize your team to achieve results.

This *Infoline* will guide you in the application of basic leadership principles in a team setting. Whether you don the title of team leader or are one of many team members participating in the leadership processes, this *Infoline* offers tips and tools to help you

- break through barriers to effectively engage in leadership

- influence your team members by building and sustaining respect, trust, and credibility

- understand and strengthen the five core leadership behaviors and skills:
  — employing a *pulling* communication style
  — conveying information clearly and credibly
  — facilitating group learning and insight
  — envisioning an inspiring future
  — advocating action

- assess your skills and identify areas for improvement.

Basic Building Blocks

Respect, trust, and credibility are the fundamental building blocks of leadership. These basic elements inspire commitment and enlist the cooperation necessary to mobilize others to work together toward shared goals. Identifying, developing, and using behaviors that build respect, trust, and credibility can sometimes be challenging. You'll notice these behaviors in how you treat people and how you relate to others. But influence is not developed overnight. It takes time to build relationships and establish your reputation.

Obstacles to Leadership

To fully engage in leadership, you must first identify what obstacles are in your way. Consider how your perceptions, beliefs, and experiences could interfere with your participation in leadership.

☐ I am reluctant to speak up or take initiative because I do not feel that it is "my place." I worry that I will be seen as stepping outside the proper boundaries of formal authority.

☐ I have a formal position of leadership, but I do not want to be seen as pushy or aggressive.

☐ I have a formal position of leadership, but I am worried that I do not have the "right" answer or solution.

☐ I do not believe that it is my responsibility to participate in leadership unless I am officially given the title or position. Isn't that why people in formal leadership positions are paid more and given higher status?

☐ I am unwilling to accept the responsibility of engaging in leadership. It is not a risk I need to take. After all, isn't leadership the obligation of those in formal leadership positions?

☐ I do not participate in leadership because my team or organization does not provide any rewards or incentives for doing so.

☐ I do not participate in leadership because my team or organization punishes those who do so.

☐ I no longer participate in leadership. I have tried to do so in the past, but I ended up either overloaded or unappreciated. I felt exploited or taken for granted.

☐ I have tried to engage in leadership without formal authority. Others did not respond positively. I am afraid or unwilling to try again.

☐ I would like to participate in leadership; however, I am uncertain how to do it, so I just let it go.

Respect

If people respect you, they

- listen to what you have to say
- take you seriously
- seek your input
- demonstrate that they value your contributions.

But, respect is reciprocal. One way to gain respect is by showing respect to others. To build respect on teams, you should listen, support, and follow.

■ *Listen to Understand*
Demonstrate respect by listening to understand, not to respond. Using classic active listening behaviors (such as reflecting and paraphrasing) is an excellent way to do that.

■ *Ask Questions*
Convey an interest and a sense of value in others by asking questions (instead of giving answers) and taking the time to explore and probe to reach a deeper understanding. When you invest the time to fully understand what your team members are saying, you show not only that you care but also that you are open and objective.

■ *Do Real Work*
Directing, telling, advising, and ordering from the sidelines won't motivate modern work teams. But if you get down to business and put forth real effort—shoulder to shoulder—with your teammates, you'll inspire them. That shows respect.

■ *Provide Opportunities*
Another strategy for building respect is to provide opportunities for others to lead you. If you are secure enough to step aside and let someone who has more expertise lead the way, you show that not only are you open to learning from others but also that you respect your teammates. It also helps to admit your mistakes.

Trust

Respect is relatively easy to secure. You can convey it immediately as you interact with others. Trust is more difficult to build. Occasionally, people are generous and will trust you until there is some reason not to trust. Most of the time, however, people will trust you only after repeated positive experiences. Trust comes down to a simple mathematical equation: trust = your actions + your words.

- Do you do what you say that you're going to do?

- Have you established a reputation of following through on your promises—enough to make co-workers believe that you're likely to continue to do so in the future?

The level at which you are able to build trust with team members coincides with the consistency between your actions and your words.

■ *Walk the Talk*
One way to strengthen a connection is by making sure that your practices and behaviors align with your espoused values and beliefs.

■ *Assume the Best*
Another way to engender trust is by being predisposed to trust others. If you give people the benefit of the doubt, and are open and trusting of others, then others will more likely perceive you as trustworthy.

■ *Set High Expectations*
Finally, holding yourself and your teammates to the same high standards will help everyone achieve the consistency and fairness needed to build trust.

Credibility

Credibility inspires in others the conviction that is essential for influence and leadership. Respect and trust are both elements of credibility, but they are not the whole picture. Cultivate credibility by demonstrating that you have competence, sincerity, and integrity.

Leadership Skills Inventory

Consider each influence and leadership skill listed below in connection with your own behaviors and capabilities. Rate your strengths and opportunities for development.

1 = Strong   2 = Average   3 = Needs Development

1.	Listens openly to understand.	1	2	3
2.	Poses questions rather than tells information.	1	2	3
3.	Reports observations objectively.	1	2	3
4.	States position, thoughts, and feelings openly and objectively.	1	2	3
5.	Conveys information clearly and credibly.	1	2	3
6.	Offers group process feedback.	1	2	3
7.	Facilitates group learning and insight.	1	2	3
8.	Envisions an inspiring future.	1	2	3
9.	Advocates for action.	1	2	3

■ *Competence*

Stemming partly from technical expertise and education, competence also comes from the work experiences you bring to the team. In both respects, a sign of competence is not only being capable, but also being aware of your weaknesses and blind spots: Know what you do not know.

■ *Sincerity*

Credibility also comes from sincerely valuing the interests of others. It is built through honest, open, and authentic communication. Do you really care about those you lead and serve? Are you able to convey that care and interest sincerely?

■ *Integrity*

One way to demonstrate integrity and build credibility is by acknowledging and utilizing the strengths of your teammates. You're more apt to be viewed as credible if you are not threatened by their talents and expertise, and are willing to empower them. You must know when to step aside and allow others the chance to lead.

If people believe that you have a solid, moral character, their best interests at heart, and strong capabilities or expertise, then they're likely to see you as credible. Credibility, paired with trust and respect, is fundamental to leadership. The use of threats, rewards, coercion, or raw power will gain only compliance, not commitment.

Influence Behaviors and Skills

Leadership is not about being heroic, popular, powerful, or famous; it's about being wise, confident, and unafraid to do the right thing for those you serve. Leadership is a way of communicating (the act of speaking up) and behaving (how you speak up). Not only do you need to understand the characteristics that are necessary to influence others, but also you must practice certain behaviors. To have influence, you must increase your chances that people will be receptive to what you have to say. Connect their interests and goals with the needs and directions of the team, and you'll do just that.

Two communication skill sets are fundamental to influence. The first set—pulling communication—pertains to understanding; the second—authentic communication—concerns being understood and motivating others to action.

"Pulling" Communication Style

To best communicate with your team, it is better to "pull" than to "push."

A *pulling style* of communication means listening without providing an immediate response or reaction. It involves paraphrasing, reflecting, asking questions, and probing to get beyond the surface of the statement. Not only does a pulling approach provide a better understanding of the other person's needs, position, and situation, but also it conveys respect and demonstrates openness and objectivity. This approach prevents you from leaping to conclusions and helps you check your assumptions.

In contrast, a *pushing style* of communication involves telling, advising, directing, and giving information. Pushing is almost always met with resistance, especially if you don't have formal authority. If you're trying to influence a person or a group of people to move in a certain direction, then a pushing style is likely to be too forceful and create unproductive resistance. For example, if you disagree with a team member, your typical pushing responses might include

● evaluating, attacking, or judging his or her position

● offering data or arguments to explain why his or her position won't work

● telling him or her what should be done instead

● providing warnings or making threats about what will happen if the team goes in that direction.

Such responses create an adversary for you and inspire push-back from your team. In addition, your team might view you as a poor leader or a difficult team member. But you can avoid all that by using a pulling style of communication to demonstrate your respect, openness, and understanding. Such behavior increases the likelihood that your teammates will accept your position, and it helps to build a more collaborative, influential relationship.

You've probably heard of the pulling style of communication before. It is similar to Peter Senge's (known for his work on the learning organization and author of the book *The Fifth Discipline*) notion of balancing inquiry and advocacy. If you take a position and dig in your heels to defend it, then you get caught in destructive, unproductive interactions. If you're too forceful and pushing in your style of communicating, you're going to turn people off, construct walls, and limit your opportunities to influence others. Even if co-workers initially do what you want or fail to voice any opposition because they are intimidated, you still haven't succeeded in inspiring commitment or building ownership. In the long term, you fail to influence and lead.

Naturally, the pulling style of listening and working to understand is only half of the leadership equation. If you did nothing except observe, listen, and ask questions, you would merely serve as a facilitator—with minimum influence. You won't be valued as a contributor. You might understand others (an essential element of being influential), but you won't be understood or make an impact. To be influential, you need to convince others to discover or recognize what the team can do collaboratively to succeed. Only when the team is motivated to act together to achieve common goals have you achieved "leadership." For that, you need to be able to assert a clear, credible position.

Authentic, Inspiring Communication

The second skill set centers on the ability to state thoughts and perceptions directly, honestly, and objectively without attacking, judging, controlling, or threatening others. This skill must be paired up with communication that inspires others to action.

Authentic, inspiring communication behaviors include

- stating your position, thoughts, and feelings openly and objectively

- conveying information clearly and credibly

- facilitating group learning and insight

The Push-Pull Communication Continuum

The next time a co-worker brings a nontechnical problem to your attention, try to resist the urge to provide a solution straightaway (that's an outdated form of leadership). Instead, try the following pulling communication behaviors:

- Paraphrase and reflect back to your co-worker his or her description or feelings about the situation.

- Ask open-ended questions: "Tell me more about that." "Could you elaborate further?" "Could you help me understand better?"

- Summarize key points and continue to probe further with questions such as, "What else do you think could be going on?" or "What might be some other things contributing to this?"

- Ask your co-worker, when you're confident that you share a deeper understanding of the problem, "What do you think would help turn this situation around?" or "How do you think we should address this?"

Avoid or minimize the following pushing communication behaviors:

- telling co-workers what to do
- offering advice
- providing recommendations or solutions
- giving information
- sharing your own experiences.

If you use pushing behaviors to address a problem, you risk losing a chance to provide your co-worker with a learning opportunity. In addition, he or she probably won't feel as committed to the solution if it is provided by someone else.

Essential Components of Authentic Communication

It takes practice to state your position clearly and objectively, without judgment. Listed below are the six essential components necessary for authentic communication with your team.

- Influence others in a direct, positive way—not with tricks, coercion, or manipulation.

- Practice an active and initiating (rather than reactive) mode of behavior.

- Exhibit self-expression in which you stand up for your needs and wants without denying the needs and wants of others and without experiencing undue anxiety or guilt.

- Possess a nonjudgmental attitude that minimizes the use of labels, stereotypes, and prejudices.

- Take responsibility for yourself by not making other people responsible for who you are, what you do, and how you think and feel.

- Communicate wants, dislikes, and feelings in a clear, direct manner without threatening and attacking.

- envisioning an inspiring future

- advocating action.

You must possess self-awareness and self-control to make use of this skill set. You must also be able to assess and diagnose the situation and adapt your communication behaviors to the context.

■ *Convey Information Objectively*

You must be able to objectively relay information about what you observe, think, feel, want, or need. You can achieve that in several ways:

- report your observations and experiences without judgment or evaluation

- own your perceptions and feelings by using "I" statements

- describe the impact of specific team member behavior you observe or experience, which includes praise and encouragement for positive contributions.

In addition, you must acknowledge the needs, perceptions, thoughts, and positions of others. Empathizing and recognizing the constraints, frustrations, or obstacles other team members face is one way to show you understand; thus, you encourage others to be more understanding of your position and needs.

If you are aware of the needs and interests of others, you can use that knowledge to appeal to what is important to them and build influence toward meeting the overall needs of the team. Use these authentic communication skills individually or combine them. Remember, these skills are not just for team meetings; you can use them in one-on-one scenarios also.

When you effectively use these behaviors, you create communication that is clear, direct, and understood by others. However, you are not engaging in leadership until others are moved to act on behalf of the common goals of the team. Facilitating learning and awareness, envisioning an inspiring future, and advocating for action are ways to participate in leadership.

■ *Facilitate Learning and Awareness*

If you frame a problem or point out an issue, invite the team to reflect upon it (consider its causes and impact), and respond to it in some way, you've facilitated learning and awareness. The following are pulling communication behaviors that help to facilitate awareness:

- Solicit the team's perceptions first. Let each member speak to his or her behaviors by asking, "What do you notice about what is going on with the group now?" or "What are others observing or feeling right now?"

- Report your observations. Focus the team's attention on a specific pattern that you notice in the group. Don't overload team members, and don't become the judge or evaluator. State, "What I saw happening was…" or "What I heard (team member X) say was…." Most important, don't forget to offer praise, encouragement, and recognition for positive dynamics and contributions.

- Ask questions to verify your perception. Find out if the team agrees with you by asking, "Did anyone else see or hear that?" "Am I off target?" "Is there another way to interpret that?"

- Clarify the implications of the identified pattern. Find out what your team members think the impact of that pattern or behavior will be by asking, "What impact does that behavior have on the team's ability to perform?"

- Present possible solutions, and ask the team to prioritize or assess them. You facilitate learning and awareness by offering process comments that encourage team members to pay attention to how they interact and relate to others. Process comments should include statements that praise, support, and encourage the team.

Envision an Inspiring Future

Because constant, turbulent change is a daily reality for most organizations, the view of the future is often blurred. It's easy to lose sight of your ultimate destination. The steps below use pulling communication behaviors and group facilitation to encourage discussion and clarification of your team's shared vision.

1. Distribute sticky notes, index cards, or slips of paper to each team member.

2. Pose the following question to the team: "It is one year from now. We have succeeded at achieving our mission. Describe what it looks like and what is going on. What's it like to work on this team?"

3. Ask each person to write down one description or idea per sticky note or piece of paper.

4. Collect all the ideas and begin reading them out loud to the team, posting them on a wall or board, and grouping them into like categories.

5. Once all of the ideas are posted, invite everyone to silently review and move the items until the team is satisfied with how the ideas are organized and categorized.

6. As a group, title each category. This will reveal the central elements of the team's shared vision.

7. Based on these elements, the team can craft a powerful, compelling picture of the future.

With this ultimate vision in mind, the team will make decisions, allocate resources, and take action. If it is not motivating, inspiring, shared, and understood by all, the team is not likely to achieve its potential.

Case Scenario: Leadership as a Team Attribute

You are a research physician employed by a global pharmaceutical company. You are serving on a cross-functional drug development team. The project team comprises biologists, chemists, statisticians, marketing professionals, and regulatory affairs officers. You are the only MD on the team.

The team has spent considerable time, money, and other resources to develop a compound that showed great promise in the early stages of clinical development. However, as further testing was performed, the drug proved to have only slight positive effects. Because so much had been invested in early testing and development of the drug, the team leader decided to press forward. He is convinced that the drug will be this year's breakthrough blockbuster and feels that his career as a project leader and his future with the organization is riding on its success. Earlier in the development process, preliminary data suggested the weak positive effects of the drug. The team leader refused to take the data seriously and transferred to another team the individual who pointed out the data.

The drug is now far into the final development stage, and, as you review the results from several clinical trials, you come across disturbing information that points to serious, though non-life-threatening, side effects of this drug. You are questioning the payoff of taking this drug through full development.

Discussion

1. Which response below is closest to how you would handle the situation—not how you think you should handle it?

Option A: Speak up adamantly at the next meeting. Share your concerns and doubts with the team. Point out the potential costs and impact of the team's decision. Demand that the team reconsider its decision and take the findings more seriously.

Option B: Schedule a one-to-one meeting with the team leader. Share your concerns and doubts with him. Point out the potential costs and impact of the team's decision. Appeal to the possible impact on his career if this drug is a failure. Ask him to reconsider the decision and to take the findings more seriously.

Option C: Let this one go. You need to pick and choose your battles. You have reported the data from the clinical trials. It is the team leader who is ultimately responsible and accountable. Why should you stick out your neck and risk being transferred from the team?

Option D: Refuse to work on this project. Resign from the team on ethical grounds.

Option E: Pose some questions for the group at the next meeting. Point out your concerns and doubts by raising them as questions for the team. Seek the team's input and reaction.

2. What is the potential impact of each option on you, on the team, and on the organization?

Option A: This approach uses a *pushing* style of communication that gives information, tells people what to do, and can often be seen as aggressive. The team leader might view it as an attack and could be threatened by this approach. This response could easily create a defensive, adversarial climate on the team, rather than an open, collaborative climate. The team could be less open to your arguments and naturally resist if you push or demand too adamantly. The team leader might transfer you from the team as he did the other team member who voiced opposition. Bottom line: The team is not likely to listen or seriously consider the issues you raise.

Option B: This approach allows the team leader to save face. Depending on your relationship with the team leader, it could be a direct and honest way of bringing up your concerns. But this "behind closed doors" approach still incorporates a pushing style of communication. Even if you use a respectful tone, the team leader could view this as a direct challenge. The team leader could be less open to your arguments and naturally resist if you push or demand too adamantly. The team leader might transfer you from the team as he did the other team member who voiced opposition. Bottom line: The team leader is not as likely to listen or seriously consider the issues you raise. There's a good chance that this will never be brought up with the rest of the team.

Option C: This approach might seem the safest and most comfortable. It is also the most passive. As the only physician on the team, it is critical to consider your responsibility for ensuring the clinical safety of the drug under development. This approach will protect you, but what are the implications for patients and other stakeholders? As with all options, it is important to weigh the costs and benefits.

Option D: This response makes your position clear, but what result does it achieve? The team is likely to feel relieved that one more obstacle is moved out of its way. Team members are likely to continue on the path they've chosen. Bottom line: Nothing is likely to change, and you will have abdicated any responsibility.

Option E: This approach puts the concerns on the table and offers them to the team for consideration. It strikes a nice balance between an aggressive and a passive response. It does not abandon responsibility, but it is not pushy or domineering. This is the action that most closely resembles leadership. It puts the spotlight on the issue and offers it to the entire team to own and handle.

The Next Step

There are no clear-cut right or wrong answers. All situations requiring leadership are complex and values-based. You need to consider your intentions, the potential impact of your actions, the larger goals of the team, and the costs and benefits of every alternative.

Although there is no magic recipe, there are some important ingredients. You need to strike a balance between forceful, aggressive behavior and passive, laissez-faire behavior. Your objective is to influence the decisions and actions of the team in ways that move the team toward achieving its overall goals. You need to know how and when to intervene. Consider where on the continuum your response would fall: Do you use more of a pushing or pulling communication style?

You also might need to identify and challenge your assumptions about leadership. For example, as the physician on this team, would you feel an obligation to act or speak up, or do you feel it is the sole responsibility of the designated team leader? Would you worry about stepping on toes because you are not the official leader? Do you feel that it is your right to speak up or intervene?

■ *Envision an Inspiring Future*

A shared vision of the future can motivate people to work together toward a common goal. Any person can help his or her team envision an inspiring future by appealing to the shared values, needs, and priorities of the team. Invite the team to begin creating its shared vision of the future by describing an ideal or imagined scenario for the group. Another approach is to pose a question to the group: "What does success look like for us?" The objective is to have a clear, shared understanding of an inspiring vision of the future.

■ *Advocate Action*

Ultimately, leadership is not happening if people are not influenced to take action to achieve the common goals of the team. Advocating action is a key leadership skill. Use one of the following approaches to inspire action:

● Argue for a specific course of action. Take a position and present reasons and arguments for why the team should pursue that course of action. Lay out the costs and benefits or the pros and cons. Appeal to the needs, priorities, values, and emotions of the team. Assuming you have established credibility with the group, you will persuade them.

● Prompt the team to closure. Encourage the group to make a decision or take action, but not necessarily in a particular direction. This approach uses communication skills reviewed earlier (such as providing process comments, reporting observations, and posing questions). It can often be as simple as saying: "We seem to be going back over the same ground here. Are we ready to make our final decision?"

● The third approach combines aspects of the first two approaches. It involves building dialogue and group discussion in order for the team to reason through alternatives and make a choice. Asking the following questions provides an opportunity for the team to think through the application of each approach:

  — What actions are you advocating?
  — Who are the stakeholder groups that will be affected?
  — What are their needs, priorities, values, and expectations?

Stages of Team Development

Teams go through predictable stages of development, and different types of leadership are needed at each stage. The text below describes the characteristics of each stage and lists the various leadership skills required to help a team progress to the next stage. By identifying what stage your team is in, you'll be able to pull from the broad range of leadership capabilities to meet the needs of the team.

Stage: Forming

Team members discover what behaviors are acceptable to the group during the forming stage. For newly established groups, this is a stage of transition: from individual to team member. The forming stage is a time in which members will test behaviors and dependence on formal or informal group leadership—especially for teams with new leadership, a new mission, or new members. Other characteristics of this stage are:

- identification of tasks and decisions about how the group will accomplish those tasks

- decisions on the type of information needed and how it will be used

- participation that is hesitant

- tests of behavioral expectations and ways to handle behavioral problems

- feelings of initial attachment to the team

- discussions of problems peripheral to the task

- complaints about the organizational environment

- suspicion, fear, and anxiety about the new situation

- minimal work is accomplished (people are not clear about objectives, and there can be false starts).

Leadership Needed

- Provide more direct, hands-on leadership.

- Pay attention not only to the tasks but also the relationships.

- Dedicate time to define the mission, goals, boundaries, resources available, and roles.

- Allocate space for the group to begin building trust and open communication. (Team members need to get to know one another better; clarify hopes and fears about the team; and understand each other's strengths, needs, and expectations.)

- The tools that are essential to the forming stage are icebreakers, team builders, team norms and ground rules, a strategic or operational plan, and role descriptions.

Stage: Storming

During the storming stage, team members may become aggressive or overzealous as a way to express their individuality and resist the group. Members recognize that the team's task is demanding, and they respond emotionally to the perceived requirements for self-change and self-denial. This is particularly relevant for cross-functional teams in which team members over-identify with their function or discipline and cultivate an "us/them" mindset, rather than a "we" mindset. Other characteristics of this stage are:

- in-fighting, defensiveness, and competition

- establishment of unattainable goals

- disunity, increased tension, and jealousy

- resistance to task demands because they are perceived to interfere with personal needs

- polarization of group members

- fluctuations of relationships and reversals of feelings

- concern over excessive work

- establishment of pecking orders

- low to moderate work accomplished because energy is spent on resistance and conflict.

Leadership Needed

- Provide active, hands-on leadership if you are in a formal leadership position.

- Be less directive and more facilitative than in the forming stage.

- Use process comments and facilitation behaviors to help the team surface, discuss, and resolve the dynamics that are diverting energy from the real purpose of the team.

- Expect the storming stage. It is normal, so you should schedule the time needed to work through it.

- Recognize that charging forward, without dealing with this stage, means that you bog down the team and detract from productivity.

Stage: Norming

The norming stage is when you notice team members accepting the team, team norms, their roles, and the idiosyncrasies of fellow members. Emotional conflict is minimized as the team norms and relationships are developed. Other characteristics of this stage are:

- an attempt to achieve maximum harmony by avoiding conflict

- a high level of intimacy (characterized by team members confiding in each other, sharing personal problems, and discussing team dynamics)

- a new ability to express emotions constructively

- a sense of team cohesiveness with a common spirit and goals

- the establishment and maintenance of team boundaries

- moderate work accomplishment.

Leadership Needed

- Use a hands-off, facilitative leadership style.

- Spotlight issues and conflicts that the team may be avoiding or ignoring for the sake of cohesion.

- Continue to provide feedback to the group, but do it on a process level rather than task level.

- Recognize that the team will see directive, task-oriented communication as mistrust and micro-management.

- Continue to offer praise and make sure that the team members know you are there to support them and advocate for them.

Stage: Performing

Now that the team has established its interpersonal norms, it enters the performing stage. It is capable of diagnosing and solving problems and making decisions. Other characteristics of this stage are:

- insight into personal and interpersonal processes
- constructive self-change
- a great deal of work is accomplished.

Leadership Needed

- Formal leadership recedes into the background as a leader-aware team is cultivated.

- Team members lead themselves and each other.

- Leadership emerges collectively, and team members step into and out of leadership roles as needed.

- Formal leaders do not abdicate leadership responsibilities; they continue to offer support, advocacy, and feedback.

Although the stages are described as separate and distinct, it's important to remember that you'll experience a considerable degree of overlap. In fact, you'll often notice elements of one stage present in every other stage. However, it's the dominant behaviors that determine the developmental stage of the team.

During the life cycle of the team, it's common to add or lose members, get a new mission or task, or experience a change in leadership. Any of those events will cause some change in the team development cycle and will require reassessment and modification of behavior. In general, when a significant change occurs, it's likely that the team will move backward through the development stages. A good leader will notice the effect of a change on a team and will modify his or her behavior to reflect the appropriate stage of the team.

Identify a Stage

- Consider your work team. What stage of team development seems most predominant? What behaviors do you see?

- How can you help the team successfully negotiate that stage? What does the team need?

— What emotional or persuasive appeals could you use to connect with those needs, values, priorities, or expectations?
— How will this course of action benefit the stakeholders?
— What are the potential risks or costs of this course of action for each stakeholder group?
— How will you avoid or minimize those risks or costs? How are they outweighed by the benefits?
— How does this course of action compare with alternatives?
— How can you establish your credibility with stakeholders in order to convince them to take this action? What knowledge, experience, sincerity, or integrity do you bring to the argument?

If the team is persuaded or inspired to act, then securing or providing needed resources to support the action can be another way of exerting leadership.

Leadership in Action

All leadership behaviors are communication and influence activities. None relies on formal authority or position power. Any member of a team, organization, or community—regardless of title, rank, or position—can use these behaviors and engage in leadership. But it's not simple or easy. Leadership is a complex process that requires skill-building, practice, experience, perceptiveness, and flexibility. You must overcome obstacles, develop capabilities, diagnose each situation skillfully, and become adept at combining the correct mix of skills to suit the context. After reading this *Infoline*, you should have the information and resources you need to engage in leadership on work teams.

References & Resources

Articles

Barry, D. "Managing the Bossless Team: Lessons in Distributed Leadership." *Organizational Dynamics,* vol. 21 (1991), pp. 31-47.

Dotlich, D.L., and S.H. Rhinesmith. "The Unnatural Leader." *T+D,* March 2005, pp. 27-30.

Goldstein, M. "Building Speak-Up in Corporations." *T+D,* July 2005, pp. 37-42.

Hollander, E.P. "Leadership, Followership, Self, and Others." *Leadership Quarterly,* vol. 3 (1992), pp. 43-54.

Hollander, E.P., and L.R. Offerman. "Power and Leadership in Organizations: Relationships in Transition." *American Psychologist,* vol. 45 (1990), pp. 179-189.

Manz, C.C., and H.P. Sims Jr. "Superleadership: Beyond the Myth of Heroic Leadership." *Organizational Dynamics,* vol. 19 (1991), pp. 18-35.

Marion, R., and M. Uhl-Bien. "Leadership in Complex Organizations." *Leadership Quarterly,* vol. 12 (2001), pp. 389-418.

Pearce, C.L., and H.P. Sims Jr. "Shared Leadership: Toward a Multi-Level Theory of Leadership." *Advances in Interdisciplinary Studies of Work Teams,* vol. 7 (2000), pp. 115-139.

Raelin, J. "Preparing for Leaderful Practice." *T+D,* March 2004, pp. 64-70.

———. "The Myth of Charismatic Leaders." *T+D,* March 2003, pp. 46-52.

Schwarz, R. "Becoming a Facilitative Leader." *T+D,* April 2003, pp. 51-58.

Walston, S.F. "Courage Leadership." *T+D,* August 2003, pp. 58-60.

Books

Badaracco, J.L. Jr. *Leading Quietly: An Unorthodox Guide to Doing the Right Thing.* Boston: Harvard Business School Press, 2002.

Bennis, W. *On Becoming a Leader.* Reading, MA: Addison-Wesley, 1989.

Bergman, H., K. Hurson, and D. Russ-Eft. *Everyone a Leader: A Grassroots Model for the New Workplace.* New York: Wiley & Sons, 1999.

Block, P. *Stewardship: Choosing Service Over Self-Interest.* San Francisco: Berrett-Koehler, 1993.

———. *The Empowered Manager: Positive Political Skills at Work.* San Francisco: Jossey-Bass, 1987.

Cohen, A.R., and D.L. Bradford. *Influence Without Authority.* 2nd edition. San Francisco: Jossey-Bass, 2005.

Drath, W. *The Deep Blue Sea: Rethinking the Source of Leadership.* San Francisco: Jossey-Bass, 2001.

References & Resources

Hakim, C. *We Are All Self-Employed: A New Social Contract for Working in a Changing World.* San Francisco: Berrett-Koehler, 2004.

Heifetz, R.A. *Leadership Without Easy Answers.* Cambridge, MA: The Belknap Press of Harvard University Press, 1994.

Hesselbein, F., M. Goldsmith, and R. Beckhard, eds. *The Leader of the Future: New Visions, Strategies, and Practices for the Next Era.* San Francisco: Jossey-Bass, 1996.

Huszczo, G.E. *Tools for Team Leadership: Delivering the X-factor in Team Excellence.* Palo Alto, CA: Davies-Black, 2004.

———. *Tools for Team Excellence: Getting Your Team Into High Gear and Keeping It There.* Palo Alto, CA: Davies-Black, 1996.

Katzenbach, J.R., and D.K. Smith. *The Wisdom of Teams: Creating the High Performance Organization.* New York: HarperCollins, 1993.

Kouzes, J.M., and B.Z. Posner. *Credibility: How Leaders Gain and Lose It, Why People Demand It.* San Francisco: Jossey-Bass, 1993.

———. *The Leadership Challenge.* San Francisco: Jossey-Bass, 1995.

Lencioni, P. *The Five Dysfunctions of a Team.* San Francisco: Jossey-Bass, 2005.

———. *Overcoming the Five Dysfunctions of a Team.* San Francisco: Jossey-Bass, 2002.

Marquardt, M. *Leading With Questions: How Leaders Find the Right Solutions by Knowing What to Ask.* San Francisco: Jossey-Bass, 2005.

Raelin, J.A. *Creating Leaderful Organizations: How to Bring Out the Leadership in Everyone.* San Francisco: Berrett-Koehler, 2003.

Senge, P.M. *The Fifth Discipline: The Art and Practice of the Learning Organization.* New York: Doubleday, 1990.

References & Resources

Infolines

Butruille, S.G. "Listening to Learn;
   Learning to Listen." No. 258806
   (revised 1997).

DeForest, H., P. Largent, and M.
   Steinberg. "Mastering the Art of
   Feedback." No. 250308.

Russell, L. "Leadership Development."
   No. 250508.

Sindell, M., and T. Hoang. "Leadership
   Development." No. 250101.

Thomas, S.J. "Developing Thought
   Leaders." No. 250410.

Job Aid

An Action Plan for Engaging in Team Leadership

Use this worksheet to develop a personal action plan to help you participate in leadership on your team.

Topic/Skill	Potential obstacles and challenges	How I will strengthen and develop this element	Resources needed and how I will access them	Target date
Basic building blocks: respect, trust, credibility				
Listening openly to understand				
Posing questions rather than telling or giving information				
Reporting observations objectively				
Stating my thoughts and position directly and openly				
Conveying information clearly and credibly				
Facilitating group learning and insight				
Envisioning an inspiring future				
Advocating action				

Succession Planning

Issue 9312

AUTHORS

Marilyn Buckner, PhD
Lynn Slavenski
National Training Systems, Inc.
P.O. Box 8436
Atlanta, GA 31106
Tel: 404.875.1953
Fax: 404.875.0947

Editorial Staff for 9312

Editor
Barbara Darraugh

Revised 1998

Editor
Cat Sharpe Russo

Contributing Editor
Ann Bruen

Succession Planning

Succession Planning

In today's dynamic world of mergers, acquisitions, downsizing, shrinking markets, and flattening organizations, many companies are asking two key questions about succession planning:

- Do we have qualified people ready to fill key positions now and grow the business in the next three to five years? (Short-term emphasis.)

- Will we have a sufficient number of qualified candidates ready in five to 10 years to fill key positions? (Long-term emphasis.)

Because many organizations are challenged by ever-evolving work environments, the implementation of a succession planning program requires the use of change management strategies. It is well known that **changing organizations succeed by having the right people in the right places at the right times.** Research done by the Center for Creative Leadership in Greensboro, North Carolina, on how executives develop stresses the importance of planning structured activities that will allow individuals to acquire leadership skills as a part of their natural rate of development.

In addition, research conducted in 1997 by the Advisory Board, located in Washington, D.C., emphasizes the shortage of leadership at all levels and its impact on the future of organizations. The key to designing a successful succession planning program is not accomplished by copying somebody else's. The key is asking the questions that pertain to the specific issues of your changing organization now and continuing to ask these questions as your organization progresses through inevitable transformations. A good succession planning program is always part of continuous improvement.

What Is Succession Planning?

Succession, or replacement, planning entails the identification of those employees who have the right skills to meet the challenges the organization faces. During this process:

- key positions are identified and analyzed

- candidates are assessed against job and personal requirements

- individual development plans are created

- people are selected.

Succession planning normally focuses on replacements for specific, top positions. In some cases where a number of people can fill certain positions (for example, general managers, business leaders, domestic or international representatives), organizations use a pool or group approach. In this situation, a group of individuals is groomed to fill any number of similar positions. This approach has become more prevalent as specific positions change within organizations, but at the top executive levels, traditional succession planning for specific positions still takes place.

Succession planning is used to help organizations solve real business problems, such as the following:

- Who will move into this key financial position when Ron retires?

- In view of our vulnerable domestic situation, who can be spared to open the new European market?

- Pat could move into any of these three positions, but if we place her in one, who will fill the other two?

- Why aren't more female and minority employees in the executive suite?

- Joan is not quite ready for this assignment, but if we hire externally, will we lose her?

- How can we keep John from leaving us? He is a key player.

If your company raises questions like these and finds no ready answers or solutions, it is probably time to develop and implement a succession planning process. Obviously, every organization needs to develop its own culture-sensitive system. While no one system fits all, this *Infoline* can provide the framework for system design.

System Components

There are five basic succession planning components: replacement planning, human resource audit, high-potential employee identification, employment input, and development programs. Some systems incorporate all five, while others may rely on only one or two.

Replacement Planning

The primary component of a succession planning system is the identification of replacement personnel. At its simplest, this is a statement of who will fill a given job because it comes open. At its best, replacement identification includes an evaluation of the quality and "readiness" of the named successors.

Although the group approach to succession planning is currently being implemented in many large companies, at the very top, basic replacement planning still occurs. In fact, according to Jeffrey Sonnenfeld in *The Hero's Farewell*, boards of directors of large companies increasingly want to know not only who the replacements for key positions are but also their qualifications. In small to medium-sized companies, traditional succession planning for managerial positions may take place throughout the organization. Because of the increased need for technical expertise across all organizations, a form of replacement planning for filling key technical positions is also occurring.

A useful tool for succession planning is the *Succession Summary* work sheet opposite, which can be used by a manager of a unit to choose successors.

Planning Tips

When conducting your replacement planning, follow these suggestions:

- Create a bottom-up approach—either specific positions or a pool for similar positions—whereby managers at lower levels make initial recommendations as to who can be replacements for their direct reports.

- Have each higher level of management review the recommendations and make revisions. (If a cross-movement strategy is being used, managers should include recommendations from other parts of the organization.)

- Identify competencies for all key positions in highly technical, detailed, and stable organizations through a formal job analysis process. Managers, or a panel of managers, can evaluate individuals against these standards (see *Infoline* No. 9503, "Understanding Core Competencies").

- Use group meetings in more flexible organizations to discuss replacement skill level, readiness, and potential to get a fairly accurate judgment of a person's capability. Use group consensus for general skills for the future.

Human Resource Audit

The human resource audit, the second component of a succession planning system, builds on the identification of successors and addresses assessment of employee mobility to various positions. This process identifies whether employees at various levels should stay in their current positions, or move to other positions, and distinguishes key developmental strategies. It also helps designate the pools of people qualified for specific positions.

Each manager conducts a human resource audit by reviewing each direct report, including his or her:

- time in current position
- performance
- readiness for advancement
- potential to move to a new position
- development required.

This plan ensures that all employees are reviewed whether they are successors or not, alleviating management's concern that succession planning is an elitist program that ignores the development of all employees.

If your system is linked to a staffing process, you must then collect information on "recommended next positions." A job-function code (sales, manufacturing, legal, human resources, or quality control, and so forth), combined with salary information, can help you locate candidates for open positions in other parts of the organization. This way, a person who is not a "natural" successor in his or her own unit could be considered in another part of the organization.

Succession Summary

The position is listed first on the form because it is the focus of the planning process. Some optional pieces of data can be collected on the incumbents and replacements, such as Social Security or other employee identification numbers that are used in computer systems for retrieval of information. (International organizations often have employees who do not have Social Security numbers, so they would have to develop a numbering system.)

A job-function code identifies the type of job that an incumbent occupies or can fill in the future. This code is helpful if the system is expected to do candidate searches for similar positions. The probability of vacancy (PV) rating alerts the organization if a manager will be leaving in less than one year. The successor(s) are listed on the right of the form with their potential (PO), readiness (RE), and performance (PR) ratings.

Division: _____

Department: _____

Unit: _____

RATING MANAGER (Manager of Unit)	**JOB FUNCTION CODE** _____ SUCCESSION NAMES	**PV**	**PO**	**RE**	**PR**
POSITION:	(List candidates in order of preference.)				
NAME:	**1.** NAME:	____	____	____	____
ID#	ID#				
	2. NAME:	____	____	____	____
	ID#				
	3. NAME:	____	____	____	____
	ID#				

DIRECT REPORT POSITIONS	**JOB FUNCTION CODE** _____ SUCCESSION NAMES	**PV**	**PO**	**RE**	**PR**
POSITION:	(List candidates in order of preference.)				
NAME:	**1.** NAME:	____	____	____	____
ID#	ID#				
	2. NAME:	____	____	____	____
	ID#				
	3. NAME:	____	____	____	____
	ID#				

NOTE: If you do not have an ID# for a person on the list, please contact your personnel or human resources representative for assistance.

PROBABILITY OF VACANCY
1. Within 12 months
2. Within 1-2 years
3. Beyond 2 years

POTENTIAL
1. Advance 2-3 levels
2. Advance at least 1 level
3. Move to a lateral position

READINESS
R. Ready now
F. Ready 1-3 years
Q. Promotability within 5 years is questionable
? Too early to evaluate

PERFORMANCE
1. Exceptional
2. Exceeds expectations
3. Meets expectations
4. Does not meet expectations
X. New in Position

JOB FUNCTION CODES

01	Finance/Accounting	**09**	Data Processing	**16**	Publications
02	Contracts Administration	**10**	Library	**17**	Technical
03	Sales	**11**	Purchasing	**18**	Technical Support
04	Account Management	**12**	Material Handling & Distribution	**20**	Airplane Operations
05	Public Relations & External Affairs	**13**	Facilities & Plant Maintenance	**21**	Manufacturing Managers
07	Human Resources	**14**	Communications & Administrative Services	**23**	General Managers & Executives
08	Security	**15**	Executive Support & Planning & Business Development	**40**	Legal

Succession planning should be supported by performance appraisal programs or other means of providing viable, dependable employee skill information. With high-quality assessment information, managers can provide employees with effective development for future assignments.

Audit Tips

Apply the following principles to human resource audits:

■ *Use Multiple Reviewers*
This is effective, particularly with a good supply of promotable employees. In such a process, at least two levels of management review the employees and agree on their candidacy for specified positions. More formal evaluation processes, such as the following, may be warranted under these conditions:

- Manager judgments or experience levels are weak.

- There is a shortage of identified talent.

- The organizational culture supports structured programs.

■ *Use Assessment Centers*
Because employees are evaluated on job-sample exercises that closely resemble the actual job, assessment centers provide extremely accurate measures of performance and capability. Organizations using assessment centers have seen a high degree of predictability of employee success at more senior levels. These can be used for selection or development purposes, but the trend is more to use the assessment center for development.

■ *Ensure Managers Have Good Judgment Skills*
The quality of the judgment skills of the managers in your organization is critical. If hiring and promoting employees are infrequent events, managers may need training in performance appraisal and assessment to identify the most promotable employees.

Identifying High-Potential Employees

Experts recommend including a high-potential identification process for the next generation of leaders. These high-potential programs can either be stand-alone or incorporated into the entire succession planning process. The more comprehensive programs utilized by many successful groups generally integrate high-potential identification. In addition, high-potentials can even be grouped into pools of successors.

The simplest definition of a high-potential employee is someone who has the ability to move into (and perhaps above) a particular level, such as a vice president or other key position in an organization. This definition becomes increasingly selective by identifying necessary competencies (based on previous or future success) and failure factors associated with certain positions.

To narrowly define *high-potential*, look at critical competency areas for leaders. High-potentials need to have management, as well as growth, potential. Predicting leadership capacity potential has led some experts to observe a set of common factors possessed by these individuals:

Results driven—has completed many challenging assignments.

People skills—influences, motivates, works with a wide range of people.

Mental ability—street smart, asks insightful questions.

Lifelong learning—seeks challenging opportunities for new knowledge, learns from successes and failures.

Integrated thinking—links ideas, sees essence of problem.

Flexible—adjusts priorities, takes risks, embraces change.

Energy—gets energy from work and energizes others.

In addition to the above-listed personal skill competencies, there are also organization competency requirements. According to corporate strategy experts C.K. Prahalad and Gary Hamel, managers need to

High-Potential Definitions

Only 5 percent of those in a salary range mentioned below should be high-potential. (This is the norm in many organizations.) The following are definitions of high-potential employees:

Potential to be a senior-level officer in any sector

- Can advance two job levels within five years.

- Demonstrates quantifiable accomplishments.

- If in field, willing to relocate.

- If at headquarters, willing to get field experience (relocate) if needed to become senior officer in their career ladder.

- Has potential for at least 10 to 15 more years with the company.

These candidates should have the following characteristics:

- People skills.

- Management skills (decision making, planning and organization, leadership, oral communication).

- Background, knowledge (understand business, technical knowledge, experience).

- Traits such as results orientation, ability to deal with change, flexibility.

- Willingness to move from sector to sector.

Potential to be at least regional or staff executive

- Can advance two job levels within five years.

- If in field, willingness to relocate.

- If at headquarters, willingness to relocate if needed in their career ladder.

- Demonstrates quantifiable accomplishments.

These candidates should have the following characteristics:

- People skills.

- Management skills (decision making, planning and organization, leadership, oral communication).

- Background, knowledge (understand business, technical knowledge, experience).

- Traits such as results orientation, ability to deal with change, flexibility.

- Willingness to move from sector to sector.

Potential to be general manager, department head

- Same criteria as above.

In some cases, sectors will also provide definitions of sector high-potentials.

identify employees who possess skills related to the core products of the organization. These people are corporate resources, to be shared throughout the company.

As a result, an organization may need more than one classification of "high-potential." A second classification might be high-potentials who can be general managers. A third classification might include a pool of employees lower down in the organization who can move upward at least two levels. A fourth category might even be necessary if your organization needs employees who can move into specialty areas, such as international positions, key technical management, or nonmanagement positions. Even with precise definitions, most organizations can never expect to have total accuracy in identification. As a result, people will drop off the high-potential lists in successive years. Generally, most organizations target 5 percent of their population as "high-potential." For a listing of high-potential definitions, see the sidebar on the preceding page.

Another driving force is the globalization of companies, which demands that employees possess a broad spectrum of specific personality and character traits. Recent research conducted by the Canadian Imperial Bank of Commerce has identified the factors that best produce global executives. It cites the following 10 key competencies as a requirement for increasing global business:

1. Cross-cultural awareness.

2. Ability to value differences in people.

3. Flexibility.

4. Language skills.

5. Emotional adaptability and stability.

6. Interpersonal skills in listening and coaching.

7. Sensitivity.

8. Ability to deal effectively with conflict and ambiguity.

9. Social intelligence.

10. Ability to understand nonverbal communication styles.

Identification Tips

When conducting high-potential employee identification programs, follow these guidelines:

- Define high-potential employees.

- Determine whether you have a large supply of high-potentials or a minimal supply (use this information to define the scope of the program).

- Assess candidates against competencies and criteria.

- Hold group meetings for final selection at which managers discuss their high-potential employees.

- Determine if you need to "grow" or "buy" high-potentials and at what organizational levels.

- Create developmental plans (see opposite) and corresponding follow-up plans.

- Track the loss of high-potentials and establish a retention plan.

- Determine whether to tell high-potential employees that they are considered high-potentials.

Employee Input

The fourth component of succession planning is employee input via a career development process. Successful planning must respond to workforce demands, and this includes employee input. Such responsiveness is a vital link between human resource planning and business strategy. Employees list career interests, qualifications, and willingness to relocate on an employee input form. This form should trigger a career development discussion between the manager and the employee. If a computerized system is used, candidate information for the employee can be combined into career profiles. You can use this career profile in review meetings and for selection information when openings occur. It contains information generated by both the employee and the organization.

Gathering Tips

When seeking employee input for career development programs, consider the following:

- Obtain employee data through manager-employee career discussions that focus on employee interests, goals, and development. Managers can capture the data informally by taking notes during these discussions.

- Have employees complete career interest forms—which address relocation, dual career issues, language fluencies, and career objectives—for formal information gathering.

- Enter job preference data into a database. This data can be searched to fill positions that have no successors or to assist management in finding future replacements in other parts of the organization.

- Use computer networks/intranets to make career information accessible to all employees. (Some organizations have set up career websites that contain job information, company information, assessment capability, and a planning process.)

Development Programs

The fifth component of succession planning is the design and implementation of career development programs for employees. As a result of the accelerated rate of change, development is becoming increasingly critical. Organizations need more people faster to fill key positions—and they must have them ready now. The skills needed for positions are changing so rapidly that people cannot keep up without having planned development. Many organizations use leadership development programs to fast-track their high-potentials. Some of the more innovative and effective programs use action learning (participants diagnose, discuss, and resolve actual business challenges) and business simulations. In addition, managers are being asked to coach and mentor people in more intensive ways than they have in the past.

Unless development is a strong part of a succession planning program, the actual replacement will not be able to move into a designated position, and high-potentials will not be prepared. Development

Developmental Plan

Name: _____

Date: _____

Current Position: _____

Department: _____

Manager: _____

Possible Future Positions	Skill or Functional Development Area
1.	1.
2.	2.
3.	3.

Development Activities	Time Frame
Innovation/Creativity (Attend senior-level meetings)	
Strategic Planning (On-the-job training)	
International Key Experiences (Job rotation)	
Corporate Knowledge (Job enrichment)	
Financial Knowledge (Training and development programs)	
Interpersonal/Leadership Skills (Task force assignments)	

takes succession planning from a plan to a process. (See *12 Development Strategies* for more methods of developing employees.)

Use a format that emphasizes key assignments to encourage people to think beyond just the use of their education. For further information, refer to *Infoline* No. 8804, "Training and Learning Styles." Another important ingredient of development is a vehicle for measuring accomplishments (see *Learning Plan*).

Development Program Tips

When devising a development program, follow these guidelines:

● Determine if you should use a skill-based plan or a job strategy-based plan focusing on the proper mix of job experiences—or a combination of the two.

● Use instruments to assess the skills of high-potentials and to identify their developmental needs. (A popular trend is to use instruments that collect data from subordinates, peers, and supervisors, called 360-degree feedback. See *Infoline* No. 9508, "How to Build and Use a 360-Degree Feedback System.")

● Match content of development plans to reflect how people actually learn. People learn primarily from challenging assignments, relationships with people outside their regular environment, and hardships. Some examples of challenging assignments include turnaround, fix-it, starting things from scratch, and significant shifts in scope and scale of activities.

Factors for Success

Simply knowing the necessary components of succession planning is not a guarantee of success. What does it take to really make a succession planning program work? Below is a list of best practices from organizations with successful programs.

■ *Get Top Management Support*
This is obtained by clearly identifying needs within the organization and tying programs to business strategy and results. A sense of urgency and importance in getting things done is probably the single

most important factor in running a successful program. (For example, the business strategy may call for anticipating the staffing of future positions because of organizational growth, decline, or changes. A clear identification of business strategies is needed to obtain proper resources and commitment to ensure your program will be successful.)

Management also needs to realize that it takes time to put these programs into operation. An organization must commit the time and resources necessary to get the plan moving. Many organizations find that it takes three to five years to fully implement a planning process, and even longer to make the development process a part of the fabric of the organization. Managers will be committed if they can see the problems the process is beginning to solve.

■ *Conduct Management Review Meetings*
Review meetings create energy for completion of the process and give top management the opportunity to provide support. They address only the most critical issues: top-level successors, a few high-potentials, cross-organizational movement, international candidates, progress of candidates, or diversity programs. These discussions are necessary because actual job movements and developmental actions are more likely to happen when managers are talking about candidates frankly. Review meetings should include representatives from all parts of the organization involved in the succession planning process and be facilitated by a human resources representative, who takes notes on action items and provides follow-up to make sure there is progress.

■ *Put Development First*
Succession planning can be successful only if high-potential employees are given the opportunity to develop their skills, knowledge, and attitudes through an ongoing learning process. Key decision makers in an organization need to make development a priority and hold managers accountable for emphasizing people planning in their departments. One way to ensure accountability for development is through reporting measurements of progress or tying development to a bonus or appraisal system. This will ensure that managers take the development of their employees seriously.

■ *Move People Effectively*
Organizations must have systems in place that ensure smooth moves of employees either within a department, across the organization, or across the

12 Development Strategies

Many people think that development is something that just happens in the classroom. But only 1 percent of people's time is actually spent in the classroom, suggesting that the bulk of development takes place during the other 99 percent of the time. In other words, people develop on the job; the expenses associated with "learning while doing" are part of the investment in development. Following is a list of development strategies and activities that will help you learn:

1. **Variety of Job Assignments**
   People learn lessons from different job assignments—line to staff switches, starting from scratch, fix-it opportunities, larger- or smaller-scope jobs, project or task force assignments—and even from setbacks.

2. **Training Sessions**
   These can take several forms: inside courses relating to professional, management, and technical programs; courses contracted from sources outside the organization; or business-specific training provided from within the organization.

3. **Self-Study**
   This employs a variety of media from which to learn—CD-ROM, audio, print, and video.

4. **On-the-Job Coaching**
   This approach is particularly useful for developing improved job performance and involves day-to-day discussions between the manager and individual. It may be used to upgrade skills or technical knowledge and may involve progress discussions, question-and-answer sessions, or working through an actual problem with the individual to provide direction and guidance.

5. **Understudy**
   Here, the employee works closely with a manager as an "understudy" to develop potential for assuming a manager's position or understanding his or her supervisor's job better. This technique is particularly useful for developing both knowledge and skill areas.

6. **Shadowing**
   Following another person around and watching what they do—"shadowing" them—can be helpful in learning about a particular area or function. The process could entail an hour, a day, a week, or a month of observing, going to meetings with the person, and so forth.

7. **Job Enrichment**
   This involves expanding present responsibilities to include a wider variety of assignments and duties. It is effective for improving both skill and knowledge areas, but should be limited to those who already are effective in their present positions, since it requires expanding work performance rather than simply adding more of the same work.

8. **Job Rotation and Lateral Moves**
   This involves moving to other, same-level jobs within the organization. Different functions increase employees' knowledge of the organization and require a different skill set. This is becoming a common development move and is particularly useful for exposing employees to new areas.

9. **Task Force Assignments**
   Here, employees are assigned to committees or task forces composed of specialists from a single functional area or a combination of functional areas. This is beneficial to acquiring skills for complex problem resolution or issues that involve broad organizational scope. This strategy develops current job performance and promotion potential.

10. **Higher-Level Meeting Attendance**
    Here, employees attend and participate in selected meetings. Involvement may include preparation of materials, participation in discussions, or just observation. Knowledge or management skills can be acquired, depending on the role of the individual at such meetings as well as exposure to the thinking and procedures of higher management.

11. **"Acting" or Replacement Assignments**
    Employees are given temporary assignments that are vacant because of illness, vacation, or other reasons. This strategy is particularly useful for developing skills and knowledge critical to promotion potential.

12. **Serving As a Conference Leader or Instructor**
    This is beneficial to developing both skills and knowledge. Preparation and research for teaching can provide valuable knowledge, while serving as a leader or instructor may provide development in a range of skill areas. Employees who attend training classes should be encouraged to return and share this knowledge with fellow employees.

globe. If employees go to new areas and cannot transition well, replacement plans cannot be effective. All managers must be involved and supportive of moving people between organizational areas. To implement this, having a policy of mandatory release of candidates may be necessary. Such a policy might state that a manager may refuse to release a candidate the first time for business reasons, but that on the second request, the employee must be released.

Avoid common problems associated with moving employees by having these solutions in place:

- a good placement and development process

- funding to allow people to move between areas

- a talent pool to move

- policies for employees to move from their locations in a timely and appropriate manner.

Another problem is moving people too often. In his study of general managers in *The Dynamics of Taking Charge*, John J. Gabarro found that it takes anywhere from two to two and one-half years for managers to acquire an in-depth understanding of their new situation and become truly effective. Moving them in less time does not allow them to develop sufficiently.

■ *Link Programs and Staffing Needs*

To meet the organization's overall business goals, you need to align succession planning with other organizational programs and staffing decisions (see the sidebar, *Identifying Critical Human Resource Issues*).

Changes in an organization's structure or workforce require an overall human resource strategy that links employee development programs. For example, a high-potential program is connected with career development, whereby employees provide input into deciding what types of positions they would like to fill. The high-potential program also is linked to a management development training program, which moves people through a series of training programs, from the professional ranks through supervisor and middle-management levels, until they can reach senior management.

Providing managers with viable candidates may be the most important product of a succession planning and high-potential system as well as the most effective way of gaining long-term management support. An effective human resources manager is able to influence staffing decisions, including those that involve external staffing in which the decision may be made that talent needs to be bought when internal talent is not available.

■ *Develop Leadership Skills*

Leadership is the main reason for successful employee development programs. The chief executive officer and senior executives have to show active leadership by holding people accountable for achieving goals and communicating that succession planning and high-potential development are essential to the management process. Senior management should identify leaders who not only possess those qualities required to develop people but also are committed to making identification programs work.

Organizations that are good at developing future talent identify people early in their careers, give them challenging assignments, and move them around to different departments. Managers tasked with developing their employees' leadership potential can identify solutions to common problems by reviewing the *Key Issues* sidebar.

■ *Use Computer Capability If Appropriate*

Computers are helpful, but not critical to the success of the replacement planning and high-potential identification process. You can use computers to simplify data collection and documentation and to integrate personnel information from different sources to create documents for presentations. You also may use them for analysis and review. Various succession planning software packages are available, but if you decide to buy a computer program, make sure it is flexible in changing the data elements as well as the reporting features. Most programs need to change as the succession planning and high-potential identification system evolves.

Learning Plan

Name: _____ Area: _____

Date: _____ Name of Coach: _____

Assignments
- a project with senior levels
- job scope increase or change
- start-up project
- key presentation
- represent manager
- benchmarking other companies
- fix-it project
- project team leader
- project in another area.

Coaching
- specific ongoing behavioral coaching
- practice presentations
- watch role models
- refer them to other colleagues as advisers
- schedule follow-up meetings.

Education
- courses
- self-study
- books
- periodicals
- videos
- audios
- CD-ROMs
- professional associations.

Future Career Goals (not exact positions) _____

Learning Objective _____

	Actions	Target Date	Date Completed	Involvement of Others	Type **A, C, E**
1.					
2.					
3.					
4.					

Learning Objective _____

	Actions	Target Date	Date Completed	Involvement of Others	Type **A, C, E**
1.					
2.					
3.					
4.					

Learning Objective _____

	Actions	Target Date	Date Completed	Involvement of Others	Type **A, C, E**
1.					
2.					
3.					
4.					

Learning partners who will observe you and give candid feedback_____

Evaluation of Plan: _____ % of activities completed as of _____ (date)

Completed Review Meetings (dates) _____

Identifying Critical Human Resource Issues

Answer the following questions to identify and probe the critical human resource (HR) issues existent in each key business objective:

Organizational Structure

☐ What changes in the organization's structure are suggested?

Workforce Planning

☐ What changes are needed in the number and types (diversity) of people who will be needed in the future?

☐ Is a planning process in place to help answer this question?

Management Skills

☐ What is the significance of changing business strategies to current management skills?

☐ What new management capabilities and resources will be required?

☐ What are the implications for attracting high-talent individuals to the organization?

☐ What current management strengths or capabilities will require a change in priority and emphasis?

☐ What HR emphasis will be needed to change the focus? (Consider performance appraisal, compensation, training, labor relations, and other management strategies to accomplish needed changes.)

Consequences of Not Implementing Programs

☐ What is the impact of loss in competitive edge of continuing without change?

☐ What external factors (government, unions, and so forth) will influence your ability to attract, retain, and grow productive employees?

Recent research has uncovered the following trends in organizations that are reexamining their current succession planning processes. These companies are:

- developing a leadership framework for executive development

- using the pool approach for flexible employee selection

- redefining the involvement of the senior management team

- preparing the leadership cadre to create successful selection programs that are linked to mission and values.

The implementation of these programs will help ensure that organizations are ready and able to deal with the constantly changing workplace of the future.

Key Issues

As you develop your succession planning program, a number of issues will arise. Here are some solutions to common problems.

Issue	Solution
Managers may feel unsure as to whether the best candidates are filling positions.	A systematic process of review will reassure them.
Employees may perceive that you get ahead by whom you know.	Knowing there is a complete review process for staffing will help alleviate their concerns.
Losing high-potential professionals may be a problem.	A targeted development and retention program can address this situation.
You may have a lack of candidates at certain levels.	A plan to fast-track people or buy talent may be needed.
Some high-potentials may become "bottle-necked" and frustrated and may need to be moved laterally to keep them challenged.	You will need to communicate that it is OK to move laterally and create opportunities.
Some organizations get so large that managers do not really know whom they need to promote.	A refined list of names for job openings will be the key to meeting this need.
High-potentials may sometimes be identified, but there may not be a targeted management development program.	You will need to link your design to obtaining internal or external training resources.
High-potentials may or may not be willing to move to other locations.	You will need a career development component to integrate this vital piece of information into the staffing process.
You should determine whether you should buy or grow high-potential individuals.	Very often in some organizations the grass looks greener on the outside. You may need to look at assessment centers to help prove to your managers that internal people are as good as those outside the organization.
You have a major problem with bias toward internal candidates from other divisions.	A management development program in which you give people exposure to employees from other divisions may help to break down the biases.

References & Resources

Articles

Brookes, Donald V. "In Management Succession, Who Moves Up?" *World of Banking*, Summer 1996, pp. 30-32.

Caudron, Shari. "Plan Today for an Unexpected Tomorrow." *Personnel Journal*, September 1996, pp. 40-45.

Fulmer, Robert M., and Kenneth R. Graham. "A New Era of Management Education." *Journal of Management Development*, vol. 12, no. 3 (1993), p. 35.

Hayes, Cassandra. "Passing On the Baton." *Black Enterprise*, September 1996, p. 52.

Johnson, Randall. "Downsizing Presents New Challenges for Succession Plans." *Training Directors' Forum Newsletter*, February 1995, p. 5.

Joinson, Carla. "Developing a Strong Bench." *HRMagazine*, January 1998, pp. 92-96.

Kelley, Bill. "King Makers." *Human Resource Executive*, February 1997, pp. 18-21.

Liebman, M., et al. "Succession Management." *Human Resource Planning*, vol. 19, no. 3 (1996), pp. 16-29.

McConnell, Charles R. "Succeeding with Succession Planning." *Health Care Supervisor*, December 1996, pp. 69-78.

Nowack, Kenneth M. "The Secrets of Succession." *Training & Development*, November 1994, pp. 49-54.

Prahalad, C.K., and G. Hamel. "The Core Competence of the Corporation." *Harvard Business Review*, May/June 1990, pp. 79-91.

Richards, Randall R. "Lending a Hand to the Leaders of Tomorrow." *Association Management*, January 1997, pp. 35-37.

Vicere, Albert A., and Kenneth R. Graham. "Crafting Competitiveness." *Human Resource Planning*, vol. 13, no. 4 (1990), pp. 281-295.

Werther, William B. Jr., et al. "Global Deployment of Executive Talent." *Human Resource Planning*, vol. 18, no. 1 (1995), pp. 20-29.

Books

Bell, Chip R. *Managers As Mentors*. San Francisco: Berrett-Koehler, 1996.

Buckner, M., and L. Slavenski. "Succession Planning." In *Human Resources Management and Development Handbook*, edited by William R. Tracey. New York: AMA-COM, 1993.

Burack, Elmer H. *Creative Human Resource Planning & Applications*. Lake Forest, IL: Brace-Park, 1994.

Dalton, Maxine A., and George P. Hollenbeck. *How to Design an Effective System for Developing Managers and Executives*. Greensboro, NC: Center for Creative Leadership, 1996.

Davis, Brian L., et al. *Successful Managers Handbook*. Minneapolis, MN: Personnel Decisions International, 1996.

Eastman, Lorrina J. *Succession Planning*. Greensboro, NC: Center for Creative Leadership, 1995.

Gabarro, John J. *The Dynamics of Taking Charge*. Boston: Harvard Business School Press, 1988.

Hill, Linda A. *Becoming a Manager*. Boston: Harvard Business School Press, 1996.

Kotter, John P. *Leading Change*. Boston: Harvard Business School Press, 1996.

Potts, Tom, and Arnold Sykes. *Executive Talent*. New York: Irwin, 1992.

Rothwell, William J. *Effective Succession Planning*. New York: AMACOM, 1994.

Sonnenfeld, Jeffrey. *The Hero's Farewell*. New York: Oxford University Press, 1988.

Ulrich, Dave, and Dale Lake. *Organizational Capability*. New York: John Wiley & Sons, 1990.

Vicere, Albert A., and Robert M. Fullmer. *Crafting Competitiveness*. Oxford, UK: Capstone Publishing, 1996.

Walker, James W. *Human Resource Strategy*. New York: McGraw-Hill, 1992.

White, Randall P., et al. *The Future of Leadership*. Southport, UK: Pitman Publishing, 1996.

Wolfe, Rebecca L. *Systematic Succession Planning*. Menlo Park, CA: Crisp Publications, 1996.

Infolines

Russell, Susan. "Training and Learning Styles." No. 8804 (revised 1998).

Shaver, Warren, Jr. "How to Build and Use a 360-Degree Feedback System." No. 9508 (revised 1998).

Younger, Sandra Millers. "Understanding Core Competencies." No. 9503 (revised 1998).

Career Interest Form

Employee Name/Title_____

Social Security Number _____

Manager Name/Title_____ Company/Sector _____

Department/Branch_____ Location _____

1. Company Experience (most recent jobs first)

From _____to _____   From _____to _____

Title _____   Title _____

Department/Branch _____   Department/Branch _____

2. Product Experience

_____

_____

_____

_____

3. Additional Experience (relevant experience only)

From _____to _____   From _____to _____

Title _____   Title _____

Organization _____   Organization _____

4. Education—Formal Education/Degree

Year _____ Degree _____

Institution _____Major or Specialization _____

Certification/Licenses/Memberships _____

_____

_____

_____

5. Other In-Depth Training. List long-term assignments, courses, or programs through which you have increased your work skills and abilities (for example: Management Institute, Insurance Associations Claims course, extended university programs).

_____

_____

_____

_____

_____

_____

(continued on next page)

Job Aid

6. **Career Interest.** As you look ahead, what do you see as your "ideal" career future? Please describe long-range goals, as well as intermediate and short-range options and assignments that may be interesting, challenging, or that you see as prerequisites for helping you accomplish your goals within the company.

_____

_____

_____

_____

7. **Language.** Indicate which languages you write and speak fluently.

_____

_____

_____

_____

8. **Mobility.** Are you willing to geographically relocate?_____ Are you willing to move to another sector?_____
Please describe any special circumstances that affect your geographic mobility at this time.

_____

_____

_____

_____

8a. **Career Achievements/Skills.** As you look back over your career, what key achievements have you accomplished? Please briefly describe two or three of these here and the results accomplished. Use numbers where applicable. Be specific. Also describe key skills you feel you have developed.

_____

_____

_____

_____

9. **Development Strategy.** What do you see as your development strategy/plan?

_____

_____

_____

_____

Employee's Signature _____ Date _____

Reviewing Manager's Signature _____ Date _____
(denotes that preceding information is accurate to your best knowledge)

This Career Experience Employee's Statement does not constitute or create an express or implied employment contract, but rather is intended for information purposes only. No representative of the company has the authority to enter into any agreement for employment other than on an at-will basis, unless specifically agreed to in writing and signed by an officer of the company.

INFO LINE

Basic Trainer Competencies

Issue 0606

Basic Trainer Competencies

AUTHOR

Jennifer K. Mitchell
Sr. Associate Editor
American Society for Training
 & Development
1640 King Street
Alexandria, VA 22313-2043
Phone: 703.683.8152
Email: jmitchell@astd.org

**Manager, Acquisitions &
Author Development**
Mark Morrow

Associate Editor, ASTD Press
Tora Estep

Contributing Editor
Sabrina Hicks

Production Design
Kathleen Schaner

Foundational Competencies

The core competencies of a good trainer are the skills that will always sustain the profession and ultimately allow trainers with those abilities to increase their effectiveness in organizations. In the parlance of today's new breed of trainers, possessing the core competencies outlined in this *Infoline* are your keys to success, whether your goal is to become a learning executive with a "seat at the table" or a highly effective trainer in a traditional classroom.

According to the *2005 ASTD State of the Industry* report, "The perception of the value of learning in driving organizational performance is increasing, as is the level of investment in learning. The learning function is being run like any other business function with increased attention to operational efficiency, accountability, and connection to organizational strategy."

This trend is supported by the increasing number of training professionals who seek out formalized training, specialized certificates, and even formal certification such as the Certified Professional in Learning and Performance (CPLP) program.

Creating a list of the qualities that all effective trainers need is a simple matter for anyone who has ever experienced a great training session or spent a semester with a talented teacher. On the list would be phrases such as articulate and effective communicator, trustworthy and fair, motivating and entertaining. In the current business climate, trainers and workplace learning and performance (WLP) professionals are being called upon to relate the value of training to key stakeholders, which thrusts the WLP professional into the realm of bottom-line thinking, organizational analysis, and strategy.

When ASTD did its own competency study in 2004, it came as no surprise that these skills were key to success for WLP professionals. The *Foundational Competencies* sidebar contains an explanation of the study and results. Also see the sidebar *The ASTD Competency Model.*

While this *Infoline* draws from the competency study, the focus of this issue is on the baseline qualities (or competencies) that all successful trainers must possess. In fact, those qualities are called foundational competencies in the 2004 study because they are just that: a *foundation* for success in the WLP field. The competencies were identified in three areas: business management (understanding the basics of business), interpersonal (being a great communicator and influencer), and personal (possessing an adaptable and forward-thinking personality).

This *Infoline* will examine competency and show you how to

- develop and demonstrate these important competencies on the job

- chart a path for future growth using the competencies

- assess the competencies you may need to develop further.

Although several of the competencies describe qualities that many people naturally possess, most of them can be developed—or even acquired—through training and personal development. For example, to be a successful trainer, it helps if you are naturally extroverted, but you can improve your business acumen over time.

If you are an experienced trainer, these competencies probably come as second nature—you don't even think of them as skills anymore. This *Infoline* will serve as a refresher on the importance of developing those skills even further and can act as a reminder to continue developing the Foundational Competencies. In addition, this *Infoline* can serve as a starting point when explaining training roles and competencies to a non-trainer.

Foundational Competencies

The *ASTD Competency Study* defined 12 foundational competencies for trainers. Those foundational competencies are found on the bottom tier of the ASTD Competency Model and define the relevant behaviors for all WLP professionals. The competencies are grouped into three areas: interpersonal, business/management, and personal. They describe the knowledge, skills, and attitudes needed to deliver success in the WLP profession.

Business/Management

- Applying business acumen

- Analyzing needs and proposing solutions

- Thinking strategically

- Driving results

- Planning and implementing assignments

Interpersonal

- Building trust

- Communicating effectively

- Leveraging diversity

- Networking and partnering

- Influencing stakeholders

Personal

- Demonstrating adaptability

- Modeling personal development

Business/Management Competencies

In keeping with the demand for organizational strategic knowledge, trainers must have up-to-date knowledge of business strategy, finance, and products and services. Whether you work in a for-profit, not-for-profit, or government organization, you have no doubt seen an increased demand for training professionals who possess business savvy. Developing this competency means perfecting your ability to analyze needs, propose solutions, and institute training that contributes to the bottom line.

■ *Applying Business Acumen*
One way to strengthen your business acumen is to try to communicate that skill to others. So, it follows that if you communicate the value of strategic thinking to employees and leaders—through training—you will enhance your own business acumen skills. See the sidebar, *Strategic Thinking*, on page 201.

There are three main areas in which to focus your business knowledge acquisition:

- *Industry knowledge* enables you to know what kind of pressures your organization faces, from competition from other organizations to government regulations. Ask yourself, What is your organization's primary product or service? Who are your organization's major competitors? Is there oversight or regulation by outside agencies? Are there technological, social, environmental, or political pressures on your organization?

- *Strategic positioning* defines the way that your organization distinguishes itself from its competition. It affects how your performance supports the needs of the organization, including speed, innovation, price, quality, customer service, and image.

- *Perspectives of value* are different for different people; for example, executives typically look at the bigger picture; middle managers care about productivity and how well their employees are achieving the goals of the unit; and employees are concerned with their own productivity, success, and skills and knowledge.

The ASTD Competency Model

The ASTD Competency Model serves as an excellent resource for professional growth and development for anyone in the WLP field. Comprehensive enough to guide career development at all levels of the profession, this model covers a wider spectrum of roles than any previous ASTD model and presents three layers of knowledge and skills: foundational competencies, areas of expertise, and WLP roles. This *Infoline* focuses on the bottom tier—the foundational competencies.

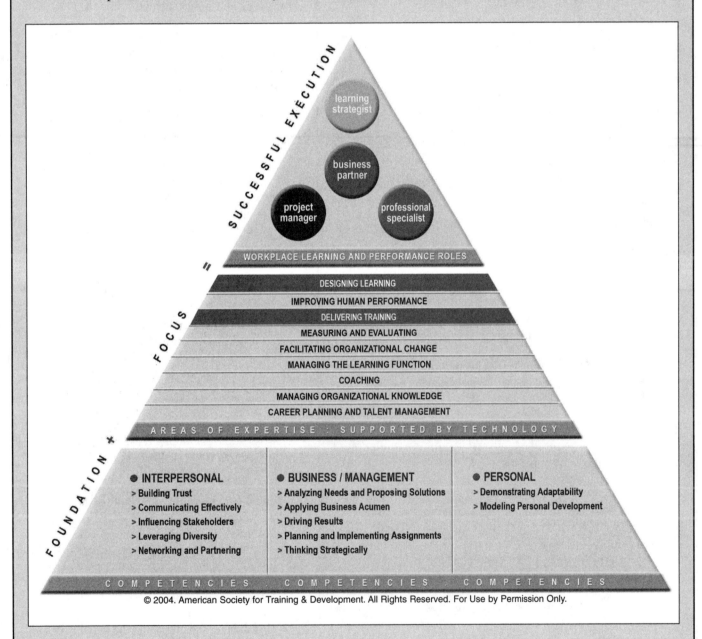

SUCCESSFUL EXECUTION

FOCUS

FOUNDATION +

learning strategist

business partner

project manager

professional specialist

WORKPLACE LEARNING AND PERFORMANCE ROLES

DESIGNING LEARNING

IMPROVING HUMAN PERFORMANCE

DELIVERING TRAINING

MEASURING AND EVALUATING

FACILITATING ORGANIZATIONAL CHANGE

MANAGING THE LEARNING FUNCTION

COACHING

MANAGING ORGANIZATIONAL KNOWLEDGE

CAREER PLANNING AND TALENT MANAGEMENT

AREAS OF EXPERTISE · SUPPORTED BY TECHNOLOGY

● INTERPERSONAL
> Building Trust
> Communicating Effectively
> Influencing Stakeholders
> Leveraging Diversity
> Networking and Partnering

● BUSINESS / MANAGEMENT
> Analyzing Needs and Proposing Solutions
> Applying Business Acumen
> Driving Results
> Planning and Implementing Assignments
> Thinking Strategically

● PERSONAL
> Demonstrating Adaptability
> Modeling Personal Development

COMPETENCIES · COMPETENCIES · COMPETENCIES

Needs Analysis Know-How

In *Strategic Thinking: A Guide to Identifying and Solving Problems*, author Roger Kaufman offers the following guidelines for thinking, talking, and writing about performance needs:

● Define a need as a gap between current and desired results—not as insufficient resources, means, or "how-to-its."

● Distinguish between needs and wants.

● Prioritize needs in order to focus on the most important.

● Steer clear of the phrases *need to, in need of, need for, needed,* and *needing*. They lead to conclusion-jumping caused by equating a problem with its solution. Instead, use "need" as a noun. For instance, say, "The primary need is to find ways to improve cross-functional communications" as opposed to, "We need to reorganize."

Kaufman also classifies four scales of measurement:

Nominal: name or label; in measuring and evaluating some performance behaviors, it's only possible to name an action and then note whether it did or didn't happen.

Ordinal: ranking as *greater, equal, less desirable,* and so on—without describing, for instance, how much greater.

Interval: ranking by markers of equal variation from an arbitrary point, such as plus or minus dollars of sales from a sales-projection target.

Ratio: similar to interval measurement except that the point of comparison occurs naturally, such as the zero freezing-point of water in the centigrade temperature scale.

These scales may measure performance gaps (describe performance needs) or achievement (evaluate whether or how well needs have been met). Kaufman cautions against using a scale that is inappropriate to what is being measured. He says that interval-scale terms are the most precise scale generally applicable to human behavior.

Adapted from Infoline *No. 259713, "The Role of the Performance Needs Analyst."*

■ *Analyzing Needs*

The *ASTD Competency Study* ranked analyzing needs and proposing solutions as the most important skill a trainer can possess in the future. This means that WLP professionals foresee the need to do a better job of monitoring internal and external influences on learning and performance and tracking new industry trends.

In their book *Performance Consulting: Moving Beyond Training,* Dana Gaines Robinson and James C. Robinson describe the types of business needs trainers should be aware of:

1. Business needs that relate to goals of a unit, department, or organization.

2. Performance needs that relate to on-the-job behavioral requirements of a person or people performing a particular job; in other words, what people need to do to meet business needs.

3. Work environment needs that relate to systems, processes, conditions, and tools required to support successful performance.

4. Training needs that relate to what people must learn if they are to perform successfully.

5. Customer needs and wants that are the impetus for business needs. (The sidebar at left outlines the basics of needs analysis.)

The following two sections will describe the value of a training needs assessment and help you prepare your own assessment.

Conducting a training needs assessment has six main purposes:

● It places the training need or request in the context of the organization's needs. Training adds value only when it ultimately serves an organizational need.

● It validates and augments the initial issues presented by the client.

- It ensures that the ultimate training design supports employee performance; thereby, conducting a training needs assessment helps the organization meet its needs.

- It results in recommendations regarding non-training issues that affect the achievement of desired organizational and employee performance goals.

- It helps ensure survival of the training function.

- It establishes the foundation for back-end evaluation.

Now that you know the value of conducting a training needs assessment for your organization, here are the seven steps involved in conducting your assessment:

1. Perform an external and internal organizational scan.

2. Perform data collection to identify business needs.

3. Identify potential training solution.

4. Collect data to identify performance, learning, and learner needs.

5. Perform data analysis.

6. Deliver data analysis feedback.

7. Transition step that begins the training design process.

■ *Thinking Strategically*
In *Strategic Planning Training*, authors Jeffrey and Linda Russell define strategic thinking: "Although strategic planning offers a formalized plan to realize a desired future, strategic thinking enables the spontaneous discovery and creation of innovative approaches (strategies) that more formal planning could never have imagined." In other words, strategic thinking means looking for fresh, untraditional ways to improve processes and think about goal attainment and organizational success. See the sidebar, *Strategic Thinking*, at right.

Strategic Thinking

Strategic thinking involves all of the following:

- holding an image of the vision or ideal future in your mind

- drawing on and being shaped by the organization's core values

- scanning the environment continuously, looking for opportunities and threats

- seeing the patterns and relationships in events and circumstances

- recognizing the interconnection and interdependencies before making decisions and taking action

- making decisions and taking actions for the long term that are shaped by the vision, core values, awareness of the environment, and awareness of the interdependencies.

Adapted from Jeffrey and Linda Russell's Strategic Planning Training.

Developing and managing a strategic learning process is nearly impossible without first becoming a strategic partner in your organization. To become a strategic partner, complete the following steps:

- Provide services that support the organization's business strategy.

- Improve the visibility of your activities and accomplishments.

- Measure results or at least tie results to other internal measures.

- Become educated in strategic planning.

- Educate others in the strategic planning process.

Effective Communication Skills

To create an effective communication plan for implementing strategic learning and to relate the message about business case, timeframes, and anticipated impact to stakeholders and leaders, follow these steps:

Step 1: Define your audience.

Start by segmenting the learning audience to identify stakeholders, leaders, and various levels of end users. If not everyone needs the same learning, identify the groups that require various levels or timing of learning. Then get the message out early.

Step 2: Design a diversified strategy.

Develop a communication strategy for all phases of the learning that uses several methods of communication, such as newsletters, emails, voicemail, and so on, to ensure that people take notice. Each stage of the process needs to have a communications component. Only then can you design and develop a detailed communication plan for each phase of the learning process and each audience.

Step 3: Gain feedback.

Throughout the communication process, it is beneficial to build ways for the target audience to provide feedback on communications. Communication should be a two-way process. You can obtain feedback by using surveys, focus groups, posting flipcharts on walls for people to comment on, question-and-answer sessions, and so on. The feedback you get will provide valuable information about how the initiative is going and where there might be issues that you need to address.

Step 4: Broadcast your message.

Finally, communicate your successes. Celebrating the successful rollout of the strategic learning opportunity is not enough. End users need to be reminded of what is coming, when it is coming, and what they can expect along the way.

■ *Driving Results*

If you can prove that your skills and abilities as a trainer can be connected to the financial well-being of your organization, you will communicate your effectiveness and ensure future personal and organizational success. *Quick! Show Me Your Value* author Teresa Seagraves writes, ". . . to communicate value, the WLP professional . . . needs the ability to continuously scan the financial horizon, the courage to propose new initiatives in terms of his or her contribution to the bottom line, and the tenacity to drive that contribution to reality."

Here are the key steps in understanding what drives your organization:

- Identify the business case driving the strategic goals of the organization. For example, is the organization trying to gain market share by being the most cost-effective provider, a market innovator, or more customer focused? Or is the organization preparing for future opportunities or problems?

- Customize the business case for the employees and key stakeholders by communicating the business case at a level that relates to each individual's level of responsibility. For example, if the organization wants to be more customer-focused, define who the customers are, both internally and externally.

- Establish connections between activities and outcomes. For example, if the operations department produces timely reports, customers will submit fewer complaints. Fewer complaints may in turn mean increased profitability and eventual bonuses. The sidebar at right describes an effective way to communicate these connections.

Ask these questions to assess the organization's issues and objectives:

- What key issues is the organization facing?

- What effects are those issues having on your unit?

- How is your unit addressing those issues for the company?

- What supports are necessary to get the desired results?

- What are the challenges or barriers to getting the results you want?

- Whom do you need to enlist or convince to get the desired results?

- What is going well for you? What is not?

Remember that the business climate, while changing almost constantly, is different for each organization. You should take care to assess not only your organization's goals, but also the state of the industry in relation to your organization, as well as current WLP industry conditions. In doing so, you can relate the value of your training to the goals of the organization, while assessing the need for future programs.

■ *Implementing Assignments*
Of all the hats you wear as a trainer, your project management skills are crucial to the effective achievement of your organization's learning and performance goals.

Planning your change management or learning project might involve tasks such as creating Gantt charts, risk analyses and roles/responsibilities matrices to develop an action plan; managing a budget; determining tasks and delegating responsibility; planning for contingencies; and tracking progress. For more detailed information, see *Infoline* issue 250512, "Managing Training Projects."

■ *Putting Competencies into Action*
Here are a few specific actions you can take to improve your skills in the business/management competency:

- Step outside your usual way of thinking to create a different type of proposal for a client's training need.

- Create a value proposition for your organization.

- Provide leadership as a learning and performance professional by taking a stand and following through to support a business objective.

- Review your project management habits and skills to ensure the timely outcome of future initiatives.

- Be a forward-thinker; anticipate how trends and new developments will affect the industry and your organization.

Interpersonal Competencies

Within the five interpersonal competencies, one underlies all key actions. Without good communication skills, you will find it impossible to build trust, influence people, support diversity initiatives, or establish an effective professional network.

While reading through the following description of interpersonal competencies, keep two goals in mind: how to communicate the value of each area to others in the organization, and how to develop your communication skills within each area.

■ *Communicating Effectively*
As a trainer, you must not only be able to speak clearly and effectively, but should be truly passionate about what you are saying and why you are saying it. After all, why should participants care about what a trainer is saying if he or she doesn't care? Speaking with conviction is integral to gaining the trust of participants. *Communications Basics* authors Judy Jenings and Linda Malcak offer three ways to build trust through effective communication during training:

- Recognize participants and their needs and be confident enough to change paths or directions to achieve better overall results.

- Demonstrate that you have a passion for what you do. Good trainers are not only passionate about content but also about the people who attend their workshops and seminars, and the proof of that passion is found in the solid information you provide that is immediately applicable on the job.

- Show that you possess the strength to step out from behind the agenda and the content, to truly connect with the learners in a results-oriented way.

Naturally, many of those skills overlap with other competencies, creating a solid basis for overall proficiency as a trainer. For example, an underlying concept present in each of the above statements on trust is the ability to demonstrate adaptability, which is one of the two personal foundational competencies.

■ *Building Trust*
To freely give of their time and resources, an organization's employees must also understand the business case for learning—and trainers help to convey that understanding. Employees need to know why they should care and what is in it for them. Once employees understand how learning contributes to the overall strategy of the organization, they are more willing to commit to the process. Again, your communication skills are essential in relating the importance of training and its expansive scope for the organization and its people.

By treating all people fairly and with dignity, you will build trust throughout your career. You will find building trust comes easily if you maintain confidentiality and model ethical behavior at all times. For more information on ethics, see the *Ethics and Standards* sidebar at right.

■ *Leveraging Diversity*
Communicating the importance of a positive climate of diversity—an environment in which people listen to each other's perspectives, understand cultural differences, and work to accomplish common goals—is another essential aspect of a trainer's responsibility. Being a model for others in the organization and championing diversity is one of the most effective ways you create that message. You have the important role of ensuring that educational opportunities that explore the many aspects of workforce diversity exist within your organization. Being aware of changes in demographics that affect the way organizations do business is also vital.

From the "Diversity Programs That Work" issue of *Infoline* (No. 250312), here are some examples that show an organization's commitment to diversity:

- Establish external diversity advisory boards.

- Develop internal diversity employee advisory councils.

- Measure progress.

- Encourage community involvement.

- Benchmark best practices.

- Conduct culture assessments.

- Examine trends in litigation.

- Address formal and informal communication processes for internal and external customers.

- Develop and implement a diversity strategic plan.

- Recognize and reward the skills and accomplishments of all employees.

Think about your communication skills and diversity awareness, and reflect on how you would handle a training program in which all of the participants originated from different cultures. How should you adapt your communication style for those participants? Would you vary your style when talking with individuals, but revert to your comfort zone when addressing a group? Keeping cognizant of your delivery is an essential aspect of maintaining a climate that contributes to your diversity programs.

■ *Networking and Partnering*
The WLP field is undergoing tremendous change and advances; thus it is essential for trainers to communicate with one another, as well as with key players within a particular organization. By building a varied and widespread group of peers and influential individuals, you can be confident that you are aware of any trends in the industry; this includes the opportunity to benchmark and share best practices with other professionals in your field, but outside of your own organization. Networking is a skill that you have to nurture continually; it takes time to build contacts and relationships. Be patient but persistent, and remember that for any help someone can give you, you can offer valuable advice or support in return.

■ *Influencing Stakeholders*
A positive side effect of your personal and professional networks is the ability to gain visibility and influence key stakeholders by building those relationships and contributing to important projects.

Ethics and Standards

As a trainer, it is important to be aware of any legal and ethical policies specific to your or your clients' organizations. Helping others implement these standards might also be part of your responsibilities. Some organizations have developed guidelines and codes of conduct that they want their managers and employees to adopt. The ASTD Code of Ethics (right) is an example.

You can also develop a focus on the basic values that help lead people to more consistently ethical behaviors by modeling integrity and guiding individuals toward the right choices.

Copyright Law

WLP professionals must set an example that does not encourage others to use material requiring previous permission for use. The design and development of training requires using, updating, or incorporating various sources of information, so care must be taken with copyright requirements.

Rehabilitation Act

In 1998, the U.S. Congress amended the Rehabilitation Act to require federal agencies to make their electronic and information technology accessible to people with disabilities. The law applies to all federal and information technology, which includes training materials. (To further your understanding of The Rehabilitation Act, Section 508 and how to support its implementation, go to www.section508. gov.)

ASTD Code of Ethics

The ASTD Code of Ethics provides guidance to individuals to be self-managed workplace learning and performance professionals. Clients and employers should expect the highest possible standards of personal integrity, professional competence, sound judgment and discretion. Developed by the profession for the profession, the Code of Ethics is the public declaration of workplace learning and performance professionals' obligations to themselves, their profession, and society.

I strive to . . .

● recognize the rights and dignities of each individual.

● develop human potential.

● provide my employer, clients, and learners with the highest level quality education, training, and development.

● comply with all copyright laws and the laws and regulations governing my position.

● keep informed of pertinent knowledge and competence in the workplace learning and performance field.

● maintain confidentiality and integrity in the practice of my profession.

● support my peers and avoid conduct which impedes their practicing their profession.

● conduct myself in an ethical and honest manner.

● improve the public understanding of workplace learning and performance.

● fairly and accurately represent my workplace learning and performance credentials, qualifications, experience, and ability.

● contribute to the continuing growth of the profession.

Revised November 2005

Building Influence

The ability to influence people is an important skill in getting your ideas heard and being able to contribute to important work. To develop your influence-building skills, the following table presents a set of general strategies and some key steps for success.

General Strategy	Key Steps for Success
● Adapt to other people's styles.	● Know people's preferences for communication and collaboration.
● Gain trust and credibility.	● Keep your word.
	● Under promise and over deliver.
● Manage other people's perceptions of you.	● Present a professional and consistent image.
	● Be helpful and cooperative.
● Manage mutual expectations.	● Communicate, negotiate, and agree on expectations.
	● Understand other people's point of view.
● Develop personal versatility.	● Be flexible in responding and reacting to people, situations, and opportunities.
	● Imagine yourself in other people's positions.
● Leverage your skills and talents.	● Know and use your strengths and talents in situations and relationships.

Stakeholders are the individuals in your organization who will be most affected by the outcomes of your learning programs. You need to identify their concerns about the learning process and clarify the business case for the strategic learning. Although stakeholders might not need to be engaged in the actual learning, they must understand and be willing to deal with the impact it will have on their staff and their short-term division goals. (See *Building Influence* sidebar at left.)

As you make connections with leaders and stakeholders, remember the importance of expanding your understanding of training from your individual results, to the effect your training has within your group, to its effect outside your group, to its effect on the organization's overall goals and strategy. Your broad understanding of organizational goals is critical to enable you to contribute effectively and in a way that supports your personal goals and ambitions.

■ *Putting Competencies into Action*
Here are some of the key actions you can take to improve your skills in the interpersonal competency:

● Review the legal, ethical, and regulatory requirements that affect your processes and organization. If your organization does not have a formal code of ethics, take the initiative to create one.

● Practice active listening.

● Rework the current marketing strategy for your training to reflect those competencies in which you excel.

● Choose a culture that you know little or nothing about and research that culture's practices and customs. Reflect on how your new knowledge might affect your communication style with someone from that culture.

● Commit to finding a networking opportunity within the next three months (or other reasonable time frame), and follow-up by contacting at least one person you met through the event to share information, exchange favors, or activate a partnering opportunity.

Personal Competencies

The last group of foundational competencies relates to those *personal* qualities that you should possess (or develop) to achieve success as a trainer. Adaptability and the drive to continue personal development are not necessarily inherent characteristics, but they are advantageous if you generally feel comfortable with flexibility and are motivated to move forward with your career.

■ *Demonstrating Adaptability*

As a trainer, you know that organizations and their people are constantly undergoing change. From large-scale mergers and leadership changes to new internal departmental processes, change is part of the work environment. An adaptable personality, patience during upheaval, and an ability to "see" changes on the horizon are all important qualities for a trainer.

To help those in your organization through any change process and to build awareness of your attitudes toward change, you'll find it helpful to know how the mind adapts to change. In his book *Organization Development: A Total Systems Approach to Positive Change in Any Business Organization,* Karl Albrecht described the personal change response cycle to help individuals work though the following progressive psychological phases of change response:

- **Threat:** In this phase, individuals are afraid to change the status quo because of fear of the unknown or fear of a state worse than the status quo.

- **Problem:** At this point, individuals perceive change to be a lot of work and problems. Because they no longer know the rules, people find it difficult to complete their jobs.

- **Solution:** Overcoming the problems perceived in the previous phase starts to reveal some of the change benefits.

- **Habit:** As old operating procedures are forgotten, the new become the norm.

In *Changing for Good,* James O. Prochaska, John Norcross, and Carlo DiClemente note that people go through several stages of readiness before they can make a true commitment to change. In the first stage, people deny that they need to change. In the next stage, people engage only in contemplation. They see a need to improve and are willing to think about it, but they are ambivalent and tend to put off making a decision. Preparation is the focus of the third stage: Here, employees recognize individually that a problem exists and that there are ways of dealing with it. Only at this third stage is the individual ready to sit down and make a specific, concrete plan. The fourth stage is when the person acts on the plan.

Recognize that an organization's need for change often conflicts with its employees' needs to maintain their sense of personal security is important. When a change is first introduced, what is the first instinctive reaction? Survival, or "How will the change affect me?" Competency in this area means understanding that need for surviving the fallout that will occur, not only for employees, but also for yourself as a key figure in change management.

Adaptability—or more specifically, the ability to think and react "on your feet"—is just as important for trainers as the understanding of organizational change. Think not only about the WLP professional who is faced with an organization full of employees undergoing a major shift in leadership, but also think of the facilitator whose slide presentation is rendered inoperable because of a technological glitch. Such situations that call for a flexible frame of mind and the courage to face challenges with a positive and results-focused attitude.

■ *Modeling Personal Development*

As a training professional, you face delivering training that targets the personal and professional development of an organization's employees, and your professional development as well. You have the unique opportunity to model the very behavior that is part of your training. Taking the responsibility to initiate your own learning and development will reflect your commitment to its importance. Seeking new opportunities for learning, maximizing found opportunities, and taking risks in order to learn are key actions within the personal competency.

WLP professionals face continuing demands, in regard to both employee retention and human resources issues, and their careers as well. Some of the ever-present challenges are

- access to decreasing resources

- increasing levels of accountability

- increasing levels of competition

- increasing responsibilities and top-down expectations

- increasing exposure to positioning, posturing, and politics.

Possessing the skills and abilities outlined in this *Infoline* will help you stay at the top of the WLP field and ensure continued success, regardless of fluctuating job market conditions. An individual development plan can help you focus your strengths and map immediate goals.

With that in mind, below are some basic definitions of what it means to thrive or succeed in an organization:

- being challenged and growing in experience and skills

- seeing the bigger picture and contributing to the effort

- experiencing job satisfaction and fulfillment

- receiving good performance reviews and raises

- getting increased responsibility and authority

- supervising others

- advancing in the organization.

Keeping abreast of learning trends and emerging learning technologies by maintaining professional memberships, attending meetings and conferences, and reading journals and professional publications are more proactive actions of the personal competency. All of these behaviors, including the "success" descriptions are another part of what you can connect to the larger organizational strategy; and to your continued success.

■ *Putting Competencies into Action*
Here are some of the key actions you can take to improve your personal competency skills:

- Demonstrate adaptability by remaining open to a new way of dealing with a changing situation; consider new lines of thought and approaches.

- Put yourself in a new or possibly uncomfortable situation in order to learn; take on a challenging or unfamiliar assignment.

Competencies at Work

Now that you have an understanding of the foundational competencies for trainers, start putting that knowledge to work. For example, if you feel you need a greater understanding of your organization, gather information on those needs to create the appropriate solution—or to simply learn more about the organization's long-term goals.

The job aid in this *Infoline* will help you assess the areas you may need to focus your efforts in building your skills even further. Reflect on which competencies are important in your current job, and which areas will be important in the future. Assessing your level of competency in all three areas is of great benefit, whether you are new to the profession or an advanced trainer.

References & Resources

Articles

Davis, Patty, Jennifer Naughton, and William Rothwell. "ASTD's Competency Study: New Roles and New Competencies for the Profession." *T+D.* April 2004, pp.26-36.

Rothwell, William, and Rich Wellins. "Putting New Competencies to Work for You" *T+D.* May 2004, pp. 94-101

Books

Albrecht, Karl. *Organization Development: A Total Systems Approach to Positive Change in Any American Organization.* Upper Saddle River, NJ: Prentice Hall Trade, 1983.

Bailey, Rita F., and Scott Cawood. *Destination Profit.* Mountain View, CA: Davies-Black, 2006.

Biech, Elaine. *Training for Dummies®.* Indianapolis: Wiley Publishing, Inc., 2005.

Bernthal, Paul R., et al. *Mapping the Future: ASTD Competency Study.* Alexandria, VA: ASTD Press, 2004.

Jennings, Judy, and Linda Malcak. *Communications Basics.* Alexandria, VA: ASTD Press, 2004.

Lyerly, Barry, and Cyndi Maxey. *Training From the Heart.* Alexandria, VA: ASTD Press, 2000.

McArdle, Geri E. *Training Design and Delivery.* Alexandria, VA: ASTD Press, 1999.

Piskurich, George M. *Trainer Basics.* Alexandria, VA: ASTD Press, 2003.

Piskurich, George M., and Ethan S. Sanders. *ASTD Models for Learning Technologies.* Alexandria, VA: ASTD, 1998.

Piskurich, George M., Peter Beckschi, and Brandon Hall, eds. *The ASTD Handbook for Training Design and Delivery.* Alexandria, VA: ASTD Press, 2000.

Phillips, Patricia Pulliam, and Jack J. Phillips. *Return on Investment Basics.* Alexandria, VA: ASTD Press, 2005.

Prochaska, James O., John Norcross, and Carlo DiClemente. *Changing for Good.* New York: William Morrow and Company, 1994.

Rosania, Robert J. *Presentation Basics,* Alexandria, VA: ASTD Press, 2003.

Russell, Jeffrey, and Linda Russell. *Strategic Planning Training.* Alexandria, VA: ASTD Press, 2005.

Russell, Lou. *Project Management for Trainers.* Alexandria, VA: ASTD Press, 2000.

Seagraves, Theresa. *Quick! Show Me Your Value.* Alexandria, VA: ASTD Press, 2004.

Sugrue, Brenda, and Ray J. Rivera. *The 2005 ASTD State of the Industry Report.* Alexandria, VA: ASTD, 2005.

Ukens, Lorraine L. *What Smart Trainers Know.* San Francisco: John Wiley & Sons, 2001.

Infolines

Biech, Elaine, and Jennifer Naughton. "12 Habits of Successful Trainers." No. 250509.

Callahan, Madelyn R., ed. "Be a Better Needs Analyst." No. 258502.

Callahan, Madelyn. "From Training to Performance Consulting." No. 259702.

Cowan, Stella Louise. "Change Management." No. 259904.

Holt, Katherine E. "Innovation at Work." No. 250303.

Johnson, Jennie. "Ethics For Trainers." No. 250406.

Kamin, Maxine, Cristina de Mello-e-Souza Wildermuth, and Ron Collins. "Diversity Programs That Work." No. 250312.

Kirranne, Dianne. "The Role of the Performance Needs Analyst." No. 259713.

Larsen, Nan Gesche. "Implementing Strategic Learning." No. 250210.

Pietrazak, Theodore, and Mike Fraum. "Building Career Success Skills." No. 250501.

Reitman, Annabelle. "Take Charge of Your Career." No. 250305.

Russo, Cat Sharpe, ed. "Basic Training for Trainers." No. 258808.

Sparhawk, Sally. "Strategic Needs Analysis." No. 259408.

Spitzer, Dean, and Malcolm Conway. "Link Training to Your Bottom Line." No. 250201.

Toenniges, Lisa, and Karyn Patterson. "Managing Training Projects." No. 250512.

Foundational Competency Assessment

Use the table below to rate your level of expertise in each competency area. Next, rate how important you think each key action will be to your career in the future. To rate your level of expertise, complete the statement: "In my current situation, I...." To rate the importance to your career, complete the statement, "For future success in the workplace learning and performance field, a practitioner should...." After completing those two ratings, you should be able to assign a priority (A, B, or C) to each skill.

Foundational Competencies and Key Actions	Rate your level of expertise					Rate importance to your position					Assign Priority
	1	2	3	4	5	1	2	3	4	5	(A, B, C)
Business/Management											
■ *Applying Business Acumen*											
Understand the business	☐	☐	☐	☐	☐	☐	☐	☐	☐	☐	_____
Understand business operations	☐	☐	☐	☐	☐	☐	☐	☐	☐	☐	_____
Apply financial data	☐	☐	☐	☐	☐	☐	☐	☐	☐	☐	_____
Use business terminology to gain credibility	☐	☐	☐	☐	☐	☐	☐	☐	☐	☐	_____
Recognize business priorities	☐	☐	☐	☐	☐	☐	☐	☐	☐	☐	_____
Create a value proposition	☐	☐	☐	☐	☐	☐	☐	☐	☐	☐	_____
Advance the learning and performance business agenda	☐	☐	☐	☐	☐	☐	☐	☐	☐	☐	_____
■ *Analyzing Needs and Proposing Solutions*											
Gather information about client needs	☐	☐	☐	☐	☐	☐	☐	☐	☐	☐	_____
Diagnose learning and performance issues	☐	☐	☐	☐	☐	☐	☐	☐	☐	☐	_____
Generate multiple alternatives	☐	☐	☐	☐	☐	☐	☐	☐	☐	☐	_____
Search for innovative solutions	☐	☐	☐	☐	☐	☐	☐	☐	☐	☐	_____
Choose appropriate solutions	☐	☐	☐	☐	☐	☐	☐	☐	☐	☐	_____
Recognize impact	☐	☐	☐	☐	☐	☐	☐	☐	☐	☐	_____
Propose solutions	☐	☐	☐	☐	☐	☐	☐	☐	☐	☐	_____
■ *Thinking Strategically*											
Understand external factors affecting learning and performance	☐	☐	☐	☐	☐	☐	☐	☐	☐	☐	_____
Understand the organizational context for learning and performance	☐	☐	☐	☐	☐	☐	☐	☐	☐	☐	_____
Recognize and act on emerging opportunities	☐	☐	☐	☐	☐	☐	☐	☐	☐	☐	_____
Build strategic alignment	☐	☐	☐	☐	☐	☐	☐	☐	☐	☐	_____
Develop learning and performance strategies	☐	☐	☐	☐	☐	☐	☐	☐	☐	☐	_____
Operate from a systems perspective	☐	☐	☐	☐	☐	☐	☐	☐	☐	☐	_____
■ *Driving Results*											
Target improvement opportunities	☐	☐	☐	☐	☐	☐	☐	☐	☐	☐	_____
Establish goals and objectives	☐	☐	☐	☐	☐	☐	☐	☐	☐	☐	_____
Orchestrate effort to achieve results	☐	☐	☐	☐	☐	☐	☐	☐	☐	☐	_____

Foundational Competencies and Key Actions	Rate your level of expertise					Rate importance to your position					Assign Priority
	1	2	3	4	5	1	2	3	4	5	(A, B, C)
Business/Management (continued)											
■ *Driving Results (continued)*											
Overcome obstacles	☐	☐	☐	☐	☐	☐	☐	☐	☐	☐	_____
Provide courageous leadership	☐	☐	☐	☐	☐	☐	☐	☐	☐	☐	_____
■ *Planning and Implementing Assignments*											
Establish parameters and forecasts outcomes	☐	☐	☐	☐	☐	☐	☐	☐	☐	☐	_____
Use planning tools to create project plans	☐	☐	☐	☐	☐	☐	☐	☐	☐	☐	_____
Manage budget	☐	☐	☐	☐	☐	☐	☐	☐	☐	☐	_____
Determine tasks and resources	☐	☐	☐	☐	☐	☐	☐	☐	☐	☐	_____
Plan for contingencies	☐	☐	☐	☐	☐	☐	☐	☐	☐	☐	_____
Mobilize resources	☐	☐	☐	☐	☐	☐	☐	☐	☐	☐	_____
Manage time	☐	☐	☐	☐	☐	☐	☐	☐	☐	☐	_____
Track progress and ensure completion	☐	☐	☐	☐	☐	☐	☐	☐	☐	☐	_____
Interpersonal											
■ *Communicating Effectively*											
Develop and deploy effective communication strategies	☐	☐	☐	☐	☐	☐	☐	☐	☐	☐	_____
Deliver clear messages	☐	☐	☐	☐	☐	☐	☐	☐	☐	☐	_____
Present with impact	☐	☐	☐	☐	☐	☐	☐	☐	☐	☐	_____
Adjust message content and delivery	☐	☐	☐	☐	☐	☐	☐	☐	☐	☐	_____
Demonstrate active listening	☐	☐	☐	☐	☐	☐	☐	☐	☐	☐	_____
Invite dialogue	☐	☐	☐	☐	☐	☐	☐	☐	☐	☐	_____
Create clearly written communication	☐	☐	☐	☐	☐	☐	☐	☐	☐	☐	_____
Master multiple communication methods	☐	☐	☐	☐	☐	☐	☐	☐	☐	☐	_____
■ *Building Trust*											
Operate with integrity	☐	☐	☐	☐	☐	☐	☐	☐	☐	☐	_____
Disclose position	☐	☐	☐	☐	☐	☐	☐	☐	☐	☐	_____
Maintain confidentiality	☐	☐	☐	☐	☐	☐	☐	☐	☐	☐	_____
Lead by example	☐	☐	☐	☐	☐	☐	☐	☐	☐	☐	_____
Treat people fairly	☐	☐	☐	☐	☐	☐	☐	☐	☐	☐	_____
Ensure compliance with legal, ethical, and regulatory requirements	☐	☐	☐	☐	☐	☐	☐	☐	☐	☐	_____
■ *Leveraging Diversity*											
Convey respect for different perspectives	☐	☐	☐	☐	☐	☐	☐	☐	☐	☐	_____
Expand own awareness	☐	☐	☐	☐	☐	☐	☐	☐	☐	☐	_____

(continued on next page)

Job Aid

Foundational Competency Assessment (continued)

Foundational Competencies and Key Actions	Rate your level of expertise					Rate importance to your position					Assign Priority
	1	2	3	4	5	1	2	3	4	5	(A, B, C)
Interpersonal (continued)											
■ *Leveraging Diversity (continued)*											
Adapt behavior to accommodate others	☐	☐	☐	☐	☐	☐	☐	☐	☐	☐	_____
Champion diversity	☐	☐	☐	☐	☐	☐	☐	☐	☐	☐	_____
Leverage diverse contributions	☐	☐	☐	☐	☐	☐	☐	☐	☐	☐	_____
Accommodate global differences	☐	☐	☐	☐	☐	☐	☐	☐	☐	☐	_____
■ *Networking and Partnering*											
Network with others	☐	☐	☐	☐	☐	☐	☐	☐	☐	☐	_____
Benchmark and share best practices	☐	☐	☐	☐	☐	☐	☐	☐	☐	☐	_____
Establish common goals	☐	☐	☐	☐	☐	☐	☐	☐	☐	☐	_____
Develop partnering relationships	☐	☐	☐	☐	☐	☐	☐	☐	☐	☐	_____
Generate new collaborative possibilities	☐	☐	☐	☐	☐	☐	☐	☐	☐	☐	_____
■ *Influencing Stakeholders*											
Analyze stakeholder perspectives	☐	☐	☐	☐	☐	☐	☐	☐	☐	☐	_____
Establish a marketing strategy	☐	☐	☐	☐	☐	☐	☐	☐	☐	☐	_____
Communicate a strong value proposition	☐	☐	☐	☐	☐	☐	☐	☐	☐	☐	_____
Build energy and support	☐	☐	☐	☐	☐	☐	☐	☐	☐	☐	_____
Gain commitment to the solution	☐	☐	☐	☐	☐	☐	☐	☐	☐	☐	_____
Personal											
■ *Demonstrating Adaptability*											
Seek to understand changes	☐	☐	☐	☐	☐	☐	☐	☐	☐	☐	_____
Approach change positively	☐	☐	☐	☐	☐	☐	☐	☐	☐	☐	_____
Remain open to different ideas and approaches	☐	☐	☐	☐	☐	☐	☐	☐	☐	☐	_____
Adjust behavior	☐	☐	☐	☐	☐	☐	☐	☐	☐	☐	_____
Adapt to handle implementation challenges	☐	☐	☐	☐	☐	☐	☐	☐	☐	☐	_____
■ *Modeling Personal Development*											
Model self-mastery in learning	☐	☐	☐	☐	☐	☐	☐	☐	☐	☐	_____
Seek learning activities	☐	☐	☐	☐	☐	☐	☐	☐	☐	☐	_____
Take risks in learning	☐	☐	☐	☐	☐	☐	☐	☐	☐	☐	_____
Maximize learning opportunities	☐	☐	☐	☐	☐	☐	☐	☐	☐	☐	_____
Apply new knowledge or skill	☐	☐	☐	☐	☐	☐	☐	☐	☐	☐	_____
Maintain professional knowledge	☐	☐	☐	☐	☐	☐	☐	☐	☐	☐	_____

Adapted from Mapping the Future: The ASTD Competency Study. *ASTD Press, 2005.*

Ethics for Trainers

Issue 0406

Ethics for Trainers

AUTHOR

Jennie Johnson
ASTD
1640 King Street, Box 1443
Alexandria, VA 22313-2043
Tel: 703.683.8168
Email: jjohnson@astd.org

Jennie Johnson joined the staff of ASTD in 1997 as an area manager, working in the Eastern and Mid-Atlantic regions of the United States. She is currently a senior manager in international relations. She speaks regularly at conferences and meetings outside the United States.

Prior to joining ASTD, Johnson worked for 15 years in various management and specialist roles in human resources, employee development, and organizational development. She has master's degrees in organizational behavior and development from the college of business at Eastern Michigan University and is currently a doctoral candidate in human development, specializing in adult learning and human resource development at Virginia Polytechnic Institute and State University. Her research interests are adult moral development and professional ethics.

Managing Editor
Mark Morrow

Editor
Tora Estep
testep@astd.org

Copy Editor
Ann Bruen

Production Design
Kathleen Schaner

Why Ethics?

Today more than ever the media is filled with stories of corporate scandals and ethical dilemmas in organizations. These stories often reflect poorly on the organizations and individuals involved, which not only brings ethics to the forefront of the public's attention, but also provides you, the workplace learning and performance (WLP) practitioner, an opportunity to think about ethical issues related to your own areas of practice. Use the renewed focus on business ethics to remind those of you involved in learning, change, and performance of your responsibilities to one another, to learners, to your organization, and to the public.

In most organizations, WLP professionals are charged with creating ethics programs, designing interventions to address ethical issues, and helping managers and employees grapple with workplace ethics. In J. Joseph and E. Esen's study, *SHRM/Ethics Resource Center 2003 Business Ethics Survey,* 70 percent of the respondents indicated that they—professionals with roles in human resource-related functions—were considered the primary source of ethical expertise. The same study revealed that 40 percent of these same professionals were called in to "clean up ethical messes" after they occurred.

What a challenge this responsibility imposes upon professionals involved in the human side of business! Do you feel equipped to handle it? If the organizations and people you work with count on you as an important resource in terms of ethics, what do you need to do to develop yourself in this area? Are you experiencing your own ethical messes?

R. Clement, P. Pinto, and J. Walker's article "Unethical and Improper Behavior by Training and Development Professionals" revealed that many WLP practitioners have observed colleagues behaving in ways they consider unethical. Among the most common unethical behaviors observed were:

● delivering "one size fits all" solutions to clients

● accepting work they are not qualified to perform

● breaking client confidentiality

● ignoring their professional development.

This *Infoline* will enable you to learn more about ethics and to tackle your own professional development in this area. It suggests including ethics development in professional development plans for all areas of practice and provides information, materials, and tools to make this development possible. In addition, much of the information, materials, and tools provided can be applied, with minor modifications, to the organization as a whole.

Ethics: A Little Background

Some common attitudes regarding ethics and reasons given to justify unethical behavior in organizations include:

● pretending that an act is not really unethical

● excusing an action by saying it is in the organization's best interest

● assuming the behavior is okay if no one finds out about it

● expecting a supervisor to support and protect the wrongdoing.

J. Joseph and E. Esen's study *SHRM/Ethics Resource Center 2003 Business Ethics Survey* indicates that the major reasons employees in organizations report they engage in unethical behavior are:

● to meet organizational goals and schedules
● to help the company survive
● to comply with a management directive.

Several of these reasons imply misunderstandings about ethics and what ethics are. Ethics involve a complex set of internal and external variables. To successfully navigate these variables, this section will help you get to know the language of ethics and understand an ethical model.

The Meaning of Ethics?

Values, ethics, morality: What's the difference? Is the lack of clarity a problem or an opportunity?

Philosophers, lawyers, theologians, scholars, and businesspeople do not agree totally about what the terms *values, ethics,* and *morality* really mean and what the differences are.

You can view this either as a problem, or as an opportunity to work with living, evolving concepts.

The most important factor, however, in determining what is ethical is to remember that it is not simply an individual exercise, but a collective exercise. Whether you are creating a professional code of conduct or an organizational code of ethics, the richness of multiple perspectives adds meaning to the end product.

This collective approach is more salient than ever in the global economy where diversity and multiculturalism are becoming a bigger part of everyday life, both personal and professional.

The Vocabulary of Ethics

The word *ethics* comes from the Greek word *ethos,* which means character. The Greek philosopher Aristotle was the first to make a distinction between intellectual virtue and character, or moral virtue. Knowing how to do something, such as possessing the knowledge and skills to perform the technical and interpersonal activities involved in business or a profession, is an intellectual virtue. Intellectual virtues are the skills and behaviors that people in the workplace tend to focus on.

However, to guide intellectual virtues toward their proper ends, workers need moral virtues, or ethics. Ethics are commonly defined as the set of (individual or organizational) core values used to make decisions and take action. Other common definitions of ethics include the following:

- the study of what is good and right and how people make the decision to do what is good and right

- a set of principles used to make decisions and take action based on core values

- decisions, behaviors, and choices that reflect personal or organizational values.

However, people do not always agree on the definition of ethics. The sidebar *The Meaning of Ethics?* at left discusses this disagreement.

In practice, ethics or ethical dilemmas relate to situations that involve making choices. Ethics are in play daily in the workplace as well as in all phases of adult learning, change management, and performance improvement. Ethics underlie most of your decisions and behaviors related to learning, change, and performance. Some words or terms often associated with professional or organizational ethics follow.

■ *Aspiration*
An aspiration is the desire to achieve something good or great. Professional codes of ethics often are considered aspirational, or intended to reach an ethical standard that surpasses simple compliance. For more clarity on the differences, see the sidebar *Compliance and Aspiration* at right.

16

■ *Codes of Conduct or Codes of Ethics*

These synonymous terms refer to documents that convey organizational values and a stated commitment to uphold them. They are used as central guides for employees to support day-to-day decisions. They often clarify the organization's mission and values and may contain references to available resources related to ethics.

■ *Compliance or Compliance Codes*

Compliance involves adapting actions to a rule, policy, or law. Compliance codes comprise codified behaviors intended to meet legal requirements.

■ *Conflict of Interest*

A conflict of interest is a situation in which an individual has a vested interest in the outcome of a decision, but tries to influence the decision-making process as if he or she did not. Disclosing or acknowledging potential conflicts is often required when persons in positions of trust (such as those who exercise judgment on behalf of others) have interests or obligations that may interfere with those judgments.

■ *Credo*

A credo is a statement that outlines the fundamental beliefs or guiding principles of a group.

■ *Ethical Dilemmas*

These are situations that require a judgment call. A number of right answers may exist, but no solution in which everyone gets all that they want.

■ *Integrity*

Integrity means making decisions that are consistent with each other and with one's values.

■ *Morals*

These are values specifically related to defining right versus wrong or good versus bad. Typically, they get their authority from outside the individual (higher authority or higher being).

■ *Standards*

Standards may be guidelines, rules, or a model to follow.

■ *Values*

Values are the fundamental beliefs an individual or organization holds regarding what is worthwhile, important, right, and fair in terms of actions and interactions with others.

Compliance and Aspiration

For most people and organizations, what emerges daily is not necessarily a question of whether or not an action is legal or illegal (although it can be). Instead, ethical issues arise when decision making is more subtle and goes beyond compliance with the law to adherence to a personal value system, set of beliefs, and sense of right and wrong. While compliance emphasizes rules and prohibitions, value-driven ethics are aspirational in nature.

To some degree, industries and professions that are highly governed by regulations and legalities may be in an easier position to capture what is "right" and what is "wrong," and handle infractions through the legal system or some other governing body. Aspirational ethics are not as easily enforceable by external entities and require the individual to be the first point of governance.

However, each person's basic system of personal values serves as a guide to everyday behavior, including professional behavior. These values give direction to life and become particularly important in situations where the need to choose among two or more possible courses of action exists. Adulthood, like professionalism, is characterized by the desire to be competent and to bring knowledge and skills to fruition in one's life. This entails increasing one's capacity to change by developing a more in-depth and comprehensive understanding of self, work, and the world. This requires re-examining significant mores and values and revalidating one's value structure in the context of the workplace and a professional body.

■ *Value-Centered Codes*

Differing from compliance codes, value-centered codes offer a set of ethical ideals to which professions want members to aspire, or an organization wants employees to adopt in their work practices.

A Model of Ethics

The figure presented in the sidebar *An Ethics Model* at right offers a schematic way to understand the complexities inherent in ethical practice. The model consists of three main areas:

1. A value system.

2. Responsibility to others.

3. Behaviors, actions, policies, and practices.

The model is applicable in multiple contexts, including the professional ethics of the individual practitioner, the individual behavior of employees, and the organization's overall ethical climate.

■ *A Value System*

At the core of the model is a value system. Both individuals and organizations operate from a value system (for more on the bases of value systems, see the sidebar *Three Ethical Bases*). The system may be explicit or implicit, but exists nonetheless. Individuals at work operate based on personal work values, including:

- honesty
- friendliness
- respect
- self-directedness
- trust
- self-interest
- helpfulness
- balance between work and family life.

Value systems may or may not be articulated in organizations, but ethics are nonetheless part of an organization's culture. Some typical organizational values are:

- service
- safety
- quality
- diversity
- respect
- profit.

Awareness of the value system depends upon the degree to which values have been internalized by employees and the degree to which an individual feels inconsistency within the organizational value system, or with his or her own value system.

One way to understand the degree of internalization is to think about the value along a continuum that spans acceptance, preference, and commitment. Acceptance is at one end of the continuum and represents the most basic level of understanding, while commitment, at the other end of the continuum, represents the strongest belief, perhaps expressed as conviction or strong loyalty.

Value systems are at the center of all ethical situations, so thinking about and writing down values are important first steps for both the individual professional and the organization thinking about developing ethically.

■ *Responsibility to Others*

In the model, responsibility to others is the layer between the core of the model—value system—and the outer or visible part of the model—behavior, actions, policies, and practices. For an individual, this layer represents responsibilities to family, friends, the community, and society at large. For practitioners, the audiences are numerous and diverse: self, clients, colleagues, employees and bosses, the employing organization, the profession, and society. For the organization, this audience generally includes shareholders or members, employees, suppliers, customers, and society. The potential for conflict among these audiences is significant.

■ *Behaviors, Actions, Policies, and Practices*

In the outermost ring of the model are the behaviors, actions, policies, and practices that the individual and the organization carry out. This outer area is the part of the model where the two other areas—core values and responsibilities—are made manifest through individual behaviors, professional practices, and organizational decisions and actions. The core values and responsibilities are at the center of ethical decision making. A common way to depict this outer layer for a profession is through a formal code of conduct or ethics, or through credo statements or standards of performance.

An Ethics Model

The figure below illustrates the multi-layered quality of ethical behavior. Ethics are expressed in behaviors, actions, policy, and practice, which are represented in the outermost ring of the figure. At the center of ethical behavior is a value system. Mediating between these layers is a layer identified as "responsibility to others." This central layer is the greatest source of potential ethical conflict.

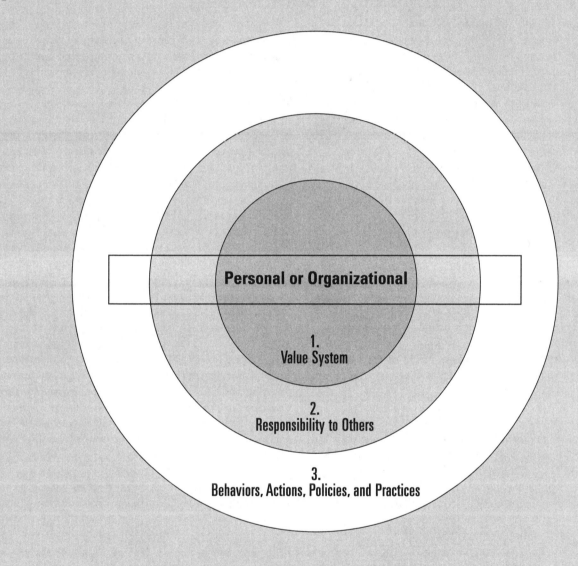

Personal or Organizational

1.
Value System

2.
Responsibility to Others

3.
Behaviors, Actions, Policies, and Practices

Three Ethical Bases

Ethical frameworks help practitioners involved in learning, change, and performance to think through the situations and dilemmas they face in their practice. Practitioners benefit by developing awareness of their primary operational framework when confronting ethical dilemmas to understand and honor the opinions of those with different perspectives. This does not necessarily make decision making easier, but it enables respectful dialogue about ethics.

Three ethical frameworks exist: the ethic of justice (right and wrong), the ethic of care (good and bad relationships), and the ethic of evaluation. These perspectives are not mutually exclusive. You need to understand all three to build ethical environments for learning and change in individuals and organizations. Because most people operate from more than one of these bases most of the time, you need a multidimensional look at work in an adult learning setting, or organization in general.

The Ethic of Justice

The ethic of justice asks the question, "How shall we govern ourselves?" and manifests itself in adult learning through attention to issues such as equal access, due process, and promotion of fair and equitable policy and procedure formation and implementation.

Lawrence Kohlberg, who emphasized fostering higher levels of moral development, is often considered a spokesperson for the ethic of justice. He outlined six stages of moral development in his book *Essays on Moral Development Volume 1: The Philosophy of Moral Development*. Each represents a concept of justice and each builds upon the previous stages. The six stages are:

1. The stage of punishment and obedience: This is the most basic level of justice in which an individual unquestioningly follows a set of rules and laws that are handed down by an authority. A critical motivator behind ethical behavior here is the threat of punishment, as opposed to an intrinsic sense of right and wrong.

2. The stage of individual instrumental purpose and exchange: At this stage a person learns that his or her own interests may not agree with the interests of the authority that makes the rules. In *Theories of Development,* W. Crain explains that in stage 1

"punishment 'proves' that disobedience is wrong. At stage 2, in contrast, punishment is simply a risk that one naturally wants to avoid." Ethical behavior at this stage is characterized by fair exchanges or deals between individuals.

3. The stage of mutual interpersonal expectations, relationships, and conformity: At this stage, the right thing to do is that which is "good" at an interpersonal level.

4. The stage of social system and conscience maintenance: As at stage 1, rules and laws bear more weight on ethical behavior at stage 4. However, here the person is not simply motivated by punishment, but has learned a system perspective that has enabled him or her to understand the greater good to his or her society.

5. The stage of prior rights and social contract or utility: At this stage of ethical thinking, a person asks generally "what makes a good society?" Here, a person may see conflicts between what is ethical morally, as defined by rights such as life and liberty, and what is right legally and try to integrate laws with what he or she perceives to be morally right.

6. The stage of universal ethical principles: At this stage, a person bases his or her ethical thinking on principles of respect for other people. A key differentiator between this stage and stage 5 is the absolute commitment to the principle over the law. An example of such ethical behavior is civil disobedience, in which a person refuses to obey a law that does not respect people equally.

Kohlberg stresses moral development through these stages to arrive at ethical solutions to situations in which values are challenged or in conflict.

The Ethic of Care

The ethic of care has to do with quality of life and fidelity to individuals. It asks the question, "What is good here for the other person and what is bad?" and "What do our relationships require of us?" This ethical framework requires acknowledging and honoring the dignity of each person.

In adult learning, an ethic of care can take the form of mutual respect between learner and educator or the empowering of people to be all they can be. An example of someone operating within the framework of the ethic of care would be a trainer making a point of establishing an open and trusting relationship with participants, enhancing the strengths of each participant, developing a personal relationship with participants, or taking a counseling stance to find ways to help each learner based on his or her circumstance and needs.

The focal points of the ethic of care are cultural enrichment, individuality, loyalty, human potential, human dignity, empowerment, and environment.

The Ethic of Evaluation

Practitioners operating within this framework ask questions like, "Who controls?" "What legitimates?" and "Who defines?" Critical issues within this ethical construct relate to what groups dominate in determining the programs to offer and when; who defines value in a situation; and what groups, if any, have advantages over others.

Persons with this orientation are likely to be concerned if practitioners use privileged positions in their roles or if materials and methods make the learning process more difficult for some. Those operating based on the ethic of evaluation are aware of the injustices embedded within the systems of society, for example, the injustices represented by racism, classism, and sexism.

Someone with this orientation may be particularly interested in the controversy that surrounds single-identity training, which provides programs to train women and minorities within the context of their own needs and experiences. A long-raging debate exists about the benefits of single-identity programs, especially leadership programs.

The focal points of the ethic of evaluation can be summarized as hierarchy privilege, class distinctions and distortions, power definitions, and cultures of silence and domination.

Ethics Awareness

Behaving ethically enacts a complex set of internal and external variables and requires an individual level of awareness that the situation should be questioned or examined. Absent that awareness, developing and using codes of ethics, participating in dialogue, and engaging in reflection can be used to create future awareness.

Ethical Codes

Codes of ethics or conduct and standards for performance and integrity provide frameworks for helping practitioners think through the ethical dilemmas they face in practice. Although debate exists among both academics and practitioners regarding the need and usefulness of such codes, they are generally accepted as important for establishing identity and credibility for professions. In most cases, credentialing for professionals includes some code of conduct related to the credential. Examples of codes of conduct are presented in the sidebars *ASTD Code of Ethics* and *Ethics and Integrity*.

Although codes of ethics can have legal benefits for businesses, they have other benefits as well. The National Business Ethics Survey in 2000 reported that the benefits of an ethical working climate include reduced job dissatisfaction, fewer observations of misconduct by other employees, and decreased perception of pressure to violate published ethical standards.

Codes specifically serve as central guides to support day-to-day decision making at work. They clarify values and principles and help practitioners operationalize those values. Codes are not designed to limit action, but to liberate and empower so that effective decisions can be made with greater confidence.

ASTD Code of Ethics

The ASTD Code of Ethics provides guidance to members to be self-managed human resource development professionals. Clients and employers should expect from ASTD members the highest possible standards of personal integrity, professional competence, sound judgment, and discretion. Developed by the profession for the profession, the ASTD Code of Ethics is the Society's public declaration of its members' obligations to themselves, their profession, and society at large.

Personal Declaration

I strive to:

- recognize the rights and dignities of each individual

- develop human potential

- provide my employer, clients, and learners with the highest-quality education, training, and development

- comply with all copyright laws and the laws and regulations governing my position

- keep informed of pertinent knowledge and competence in the human resource field

- maintain confidentiality and integrity in the practice of my profession

- support my peers and avoid conduct that impedes their ability to practice their profession

- conduct myself in an ethical and honest manner

- improve the public understanding of human resource development and management

- fairly and accurately represent my human resource development or human resource management credentials, qualifications, experience, and ability

- contribute to the continuing growth of the Society and its members.

Rules of Behavior for Members

Members of the Society shall:

- refrain from any overt statements or pointed humor that disparages the rightful dignity and social equity of any individual or group when presenting from any Society platform

- when using the Society's name or in introductions to presentations, make clear that the ideas presented are personal and do not represent those of the Society

- refrain from using the Society's platform to directly sell, promote, or otherwise encourage participants to purchase or use the speaker's products or services.

Rules for Leaders

Leaders of the Society:

- will not solicit or receive anything of value for services rendered in the Society's name or using the Society's materials

- will not use any Society funds for their personal gain

- are defined as the board of directors; national advisers for chapters; council of governors; and members of committees, task forces, teams, and special projects.

Adapted from The Member's Guide to ASTD Governance, *American Society for Training & Development, November 1999.*

Professional codes of ethics may include value statements and be called credos, standards or codes of conduct, or compliance codes. A list of common components of codes is presented in the sidebar *Components of Codes*. They may be compliance based, value based, or aspirational. Most commonly they are hybrids, combining adherence to enforceable standards of rules, regulations, policies, and procedures and aspiration to the standards set by lofty principles and values.

Do not view codes of conduct as formulas for providing simplistic answers to complex ethical dilemmas. Developing individual and organizational ethics is a process, not a destination. Codes and models offer ways to discuss and reflect upon the issue of ethics, a concern for all professionals.

Dialogue

Simply speaking about ethics in organizational settings can be difficult. A natural reluctance exists to talk openly about values, beliefs, or ethics, especially at work. Ways to get the dialogue started and improve dialogue can take many forms.

- Use the word ethics and talk about ethical conduct. Encourage employees to seek guidance whenever they have doubts or concerns about a situation.

- Take time during staff gatherings to acknowledge someone who has demonstrated ethical conduct.

- Make expectations about ethical behavior clear.

- Keep communication open and be available to employees. In particular, if you are a manager, you should always make time to talk about anything related to ethics and avoid putting it off.

- Use case studies as a basis for discussing ethics issues or dilemmas (see the sidebar *The Case of the Evaluator's Dilemma* for an example).

Ethics and Integrity

In 1999, the Academy of Human Resource Development published a comprehensive document entitled "Standards on Ethics and Integrity." It covers the following:

General Principles

- competence
- integrity
- professional responsibility
- respect for people's rights and dignity
- concern for others' welfare
- social responsibility.

Standards

- general standards
- research and evaluation
- advertising and other public statements
- publication of work
- privacy and confidentiality
- teaching and facilitating
- resolution of ethical issues and violations.

The Academy intends its document to be guiding principles—or values—that practitioners can use as a basis for the professional and ethical conduct of human resource development (HRD) activities. The Academy considers HRD to be an interdisciplinary field focused on systematic training and development; career development; and organization development to improve processes and enhance the learning and performance of individuals, organizations, communities, and society.

Adapted with permission.
© Academy of Human Resource Development

Components of Codes

Codes of ethics can have legal benefits, but other benefits exist as well, including greater job satisfaction, decreased observation of misconduct, and decreased pressure to violate ethical standards.

A less tangible, but also valid, benefit is that codes of ethics legitimatize discussions about ethics, enabling discussion about ethics or gray areas in the workplace. Codes of ethics also can provide a vocabulary for employees to ask questions and seek guidance, as well as for managers to set expectations and requirements. Over time, codes can make the discussion of ethics in organizations as commonplace as discussion about customer satisfaction, job safety, and product and service quality. Ethics policies or codes help to remind employees what the organization deems is the right thing to do even if other documentation related to the employee's job does not.

Typical topics addressed in formal codes of conduct in organizations are:

● confidential information

● definitions of conflicts of interest

● policies related to product and service pricing

● policies related to use of company assets

● employment policies and procedures, including time sheet reporting

● policies and procedures related to relationships with other employees and with suppliers and contractors

● policies related to gifts, gratuities, and entertainment

● policies related to political contributions and activity

● procedures related to international business

● regulatory and compliance matters.

You can approach dialogue from an experiential perspective and thereby encourage individual development. Formal dialogue at work allows you to hear and understand a situation from a perspective other than your own. This technique can help you develop awareness of your own perspectives, upon which you can later reflect. The characteristics of dialogue are:

● It is not a solitary activity; it engages at least one other person and can be done effectively in a small group.

● As in the case of brainstorming, participants should suspend judgment when someone's perspective is different from their own.

● It builds upon others' perspectives and ideas.

● It involves active listening and participation.

● It does not involve analysis or finding the right solution.

Use some of the following questions to help facilitate dialogue:

● What did you hear that confirmed what you know?

● What did you hear that was interesting or challenging?

● What was missing for you?

● What insights or "aha's" did you have?

Reflection

Reflection, sometimes referred to as critical thinking, is a generic term for those intellectual and affective activities in which individuals engage to explore their experiences. Reflection is a purposeful and deliberate activity in which the individual engages to discover new understandings and appreciation of self and others.

The Case of the Evaluator's Dilemma

Keen Ideas is a U.S. retail high-end general merchandiser with a focus on quality customer service. With more than 100 stores (mostly in large cities), Keen Ideas employs 15,000 people. Each store has 100 to 150 workers and 10 departments ranging from clothing and toys to hardware and electronics. Each department has a supervisor who oversees six to 11 people.

Each new employee is given orientation training consisting of a series of videotapes on customer service product familiarity and information systems. In addition, supervisors use role play to train new employees individually, and they place employees with a mentor for their first three months of employment.

The corporate vice president (VP) of operations has recently noticed an unusually high number of customer service complaints in three of the large urban Midwest stores. The standard survey form for measuring customer satisfaction indicates that customers feel they are being ignored and that employees aren't interested in assisting them. Several customers noted that employees seem unwilling to approach them because of their appearance or ethnicity. Another complaint is that employees are often conversing with each other rather than attempting to help customers.

The VP of operations called a teleconference with the three store managers to discuss the complaints. Managers assured her that they would take care of the situation by talking with the department supervisors and trainers. A month later, complaints had increased 10 percent. Now, the VP contacts you.

As a corporate training evaluation specialist, you agree to devise a plan that focuses on the extent customers are satisfied with their experience at Keen Ideas' three Midwest stores and the extent to which employees are using the customer service skills they have been trained for. You:

- Design the pilot test, a multi-item customer satisfaction survey, to elicit quantitative and qualitative data about the quality of customer service and also plan observation of customer service skills at the three stores.

- Contact the customer service department and request several mystery shoppers, Keen Ideas employees, who pose as typical customers. Each shopper visits each store twice a week over a one-month period and completes a survey after each visit. The shoppers are told not to identify any employee by name.

- Collect and analyze the data and then present the results.

Only the three store managers and a few supervisors are told about the evaluation; employees are not told. The results: Nearly 70 percent of the mystery shoppers report having negative experiences and not observing customer service skills. After reviewing the results with the operations VP, you share them with the store managers and selected supervisors, who react negatively and say the results are inaccurate and unrepresentative of the quality of customer service training in their stores. You reiterate that the data is valid, but they are adamant.

Puzzled and concerned by their zeal, you meet again with the operations VP, who insists that you contact the mystery shoppers and find out the names of the employees who failed to provide quality service. Her justification is that you could provide specific feedback to the managers and help them find ways to reward, further develop, remediate, or dismiss certain employees. You remind her you both agreed that employees' names wouldn't be provided on the surveys or final report—and that her plan is a reversal of what was promised to the store managers and supervisors. The VP persists. You ask for 24 hours to consider the issue.

Adapted with permission from Tim Hatcher's "Is It an Ethical Dilemma for Sure?" T+D May 2002.

Ways to engage in reflection relating to ethics are:

- writing down personal values

- identifying ways that these values are manifested both personally and professionally

- keeping a learning journal related to values and ethics issues

- paying attention to affective (feeling) responses experienced in situations and recognizing if they are related to values or ethics

- writing down a situation from another person's point of view; writing in the third person versus the first person

- writing unsent letters to others involved in an unresolved ethical situation.

Case studies, personal experiences, and the experiences of others provide great material for you to use in a reflective manner.

Note that reflection and dialogue are two sides of the same coin. One is an individual activity, while the other allows for dyad or group discussion. They are highly complementary techniques, because for some individuals group discussion can lead to more individual reflective thinking, or at least questioning, especially when awareness levels are low.

Individuals and groups vary in their comfort and motivation to participate in dialogue and reflection. However, both techniques are important for all levels of ethics development: individual, group, and organizational.

Ethics Applied

In the end, understanding and developing ethics matters little if you don't apply ethics to your personal behaviors and actions or if the employees of your organization don't apply ethics to organizational policies and procedures. The following section will provide some guidelines for making ethical decisions as well as creating a comprehensive system in support of organizational ethics.

Decision-Making Process

Underlying the following seven-step process are the decision-making steps presented in "Ethics for Training and Development," *Infoline* No. 259515, which provide a comprehensive way to think about work, solve ethical dilemmas, and make ethical decisions. These steps don't necessarily occur as distinct links in a chain, but are distinguishable from one another.

1. Define the problem. What are the goals and objectives you hope to reach at the end of the process?

2. Identify the stakeholders and get the facts. Accurate information from a variety of sources is essential to making any reasonable decision. Who should be involved in the decision? How much time will you allocate for fact finding?

3. Identify alternatives. Usually more than one solution will arise from the information you have gathered. Organize your material into options.

4. Evaluate the alternatives. Rank the options you have developed based on what happens to be the strongest or weakest solution.

5. Make a decision and test it. Once you have selected an option, a trial program will help test how good a choice it was. If the trial effort goes poorly, reconsider your options and test another plan until a realistic solution emerges.

6. Implement the decision. Prepare the detailed steps required to support the chosen plan. The steps should include timeframes, budgets, and personnel requirements.

7. Evaluate the decision. Prepare assessment tools to determine how well the plan is functioning and how to make future updates. Consider further adjustments as the plan unfolds.

What distinguishes this process from other decision-making models is the application of an ethical component. At each step, apply filters to the thinking or discussion. Four filters are relevant for decisions in organizational settings. They are:

■ *The Compliance Filter*
This has to do with legal and regulatory issues. Will the decision be legally acceptable?

■ *The Policy Filter*
Are there organizational policies, procedures, or guidelines (code of ethics) that can help in this situation? Is this action or decision acceptable in light of these?

■ *The Values Filter*
Will the decision or action conform to the organization's values?

■ *The Self*
Will this decision or action satisfy my personal values? Will it be consistent with what I feel is right and good?

At key steps in the decision-making process, the decision maker or group can run each consideration through these filters and be able to separate the ethical implications from the remainder of the decision. This ensures that the ethical issues imbedded in the decision can be given consideration.

The application of these filters won't necessarily guarantee that an ethical decision will be made, but that the ethical dimensions of the situation decision will be surfaced, thus enabling a choice to be made based on known factors. The job aid at the end of this *Infoline* presents a model of this decision-making process.

Decision Making Questions

There also are very simple and quick ways to judge the quality of a potential decision, by asking oneself a few simple questions at the time of a decision.

1. Is what I am about to do legal?

2. Would I be ashamed if my mother knew that I had done this?

3. Will this decision pass the scrutiny of my manager?

Although highly simplistic, in today's busy workplace, where change is rampant and rapid and where employees do more with less, workers report that they are not always thinking about what they are doing until it is too late. Using simple filters like the questions above can help prevent major ethical missteps.

A Comprehensive System

Part of an effective organization is the existence of systems for work to be done effectively and efficiently. If you assume that "ethics is good business," then your organization will have a system to align actions with specific values and beliefs.

Compare such a system to generally accepted accounting principles. If an organization's purpose is to communicate its financial performance clearly, using accounting techniques is one useful way for doing this. If the organization's intent is to mislead, accounting techniques can be adapted to that as well.

The same holds true for an organization's vision, mission, and values. Missions should describe why an organization exists; why it is in business. Values stream from the mission. They should be few and prioritized and describe the belief system that forms the basis upon which the organization, its leaders, and its employees are expected to act.

These values provide a common sense of rightness, fairness, and goodness for the organization. At best they form the foundation that helps everyone in the organization steer through the complexities, uncertainties, and pressures faced in the daily activities of the organization's business.

Unfortunately, employees often see ethics interventions as just another organizational program that will eventually go away, or apply to only a few. Codes are good first steps. A comprehensive system to support organizational ethics would include many, if not all, of these components:

- ethical leadership

- a vision statement

- ethics training for employees at all levels of the organization

- a values statement

- a code of ethics

- a designated ethics officer

- infusion into employee orientation, exit interviews, and all training program and communication vehicles

- an ethics hotline

- daily conversations about ethics

- formal and informal rewards for ethical behavior

- a response system, investigations, and sanctions

- a cross-functional taskforce or committee to develop or periodically review ethics initiatives and programs

- periodic evaluation and pulse taking via mini-surveys and employee climate and trust surveys.

Ethics is a very challenging topic for individuals, professions, and organizations and can generate skepticism and debate. Nonetheless, it's a topic that won't go away; its salience and challenge only seem to grow. Many professionals and organizations think about and take steps to address ethics within their professional body or business only after problems occur, but, clearly, preventing ethical problems from occurring by developing ethical practices in the organization is preferable.

Addressing ethics requires individual reflection, group dialogue, and creation of a supporting system that reflects the ethics of the community of practice or work organization. Practitioners involved in workplace learning, performance, and change have increasing responsibility within their organizations to develop all or part of comprehensive ethics programs, as well as act as adviser and consultant to management and employees within the organization regarding ethics issues. This makes it even more important for practitioners to routinely think about their own professional ethics and model not only exemplary ethical behavior but
also exemplary ethical development practices.

References & Resources

Articles

Argan, S., T. Hatcher, and R. Swanson, eds. "Ethics and Integrity in HRD: Cases in Research and Practice." *Advances in Developing Human Resources,* vol. 3, no. 1 (2001).

Clement, R., P. Pinto, and J. Walker. "Unethical and Improper Behavior by Training and Development Professionals." *Training and Development,* vol. 32, no. 12 (1978), pp. 10-12.

Connelly, R., and K. Light. "An Interdisciplinary Code of Ethics for Adult Education." *Adult Education Quarterly,* vol. 41, no. 4 (1991), pp. 233-240.

Hatcher, T. "New World Ethics." *T+D,* vol. 57, no. 8 (2003), pp. 42-47.

———. "Speaking of Ethics: Is It an Ethical Dilemma for Sure?" *T+D,* vol. 56, no. 5 (2002), pp. 106-109.

———. "What Do You Do When Your Consulting Integrity Is on the Line?" *T+D,* vol. 56, no. 2 (2002), pp. 71-74.

Hatcher, T., and S. Aragon. "A Code of Ethics and Integrity for HRD Research and Practice." *Human Resource Development Quarterly,* vol. 11, no. 2 (2000), pp. 179-185.

McDonald, K., and G. Wood, Jr. "Surveying Adult Education Practitioners About Ethical Issues." *Adult Education Quarterly,* vol. 43, no. 4 (1993), pp. 243-257.

McLean, G. "Ethical Dilemmas and the Many Hats of HRD." *Human Resource Development Quarterly,* vol. 12, no. 3 (2001), pp. 219-221.

Books

Brockett, R., ed. *Ethical Issues in Adult Education.* New York: Teachers College Press, 1988.

Brown, M. *Working Ethics.* San Francisco: Jossey-Bass, 1990.

Crain, W. *Theories of Development.* Englewood Cliffs, NJ: Prentice-Hall, 1985.

Himstra, R. "Translating Personal Values and Philosophy Into Practical Action." In R. Brockett, ed., *Ethical Issues in Adult Education.* New York: Teachers College Press, 1988.

Joseph, J., and E. Esen. *SHRM/Ethics Resource Center 2003 Business Ethics Survey.* Alexandria, VA: SHRM Research, 2003.

Kohlberg, L. *Essays on Moral Development, Volume. 1: The Philosophy of Moral Development.* San Francisco: Harper & Row, 1981.

Merriam, S., and R. Brockett. *The Profession and Practice of Adult Education: An Introduction.* San Francisco: Jossey-Bass, 1997.

Rion, M. *Everyday Ethics: Putting Values Into Action.* Washington, D.C.: Resources for Ethics and Management, 2003.

Infolines

Gordon, E., and J. Baumhart. "Ethics for Training and Development." No. 259515 (revised 1997).

Poore, J., and L. Lottier. "Ethics for Business." No. 259103.

Websites and Other Resources

Academy of Human Resource Development. Available at http://www.ahrd.org.

ASTD, Certified Performance Technologist Code of Ethics. Available at http://www1.astd.org/cpt/code_of_ethics.aspx.

2000 National Business Ethics Survey. Ethics Resource Center. Available at http://www.ethics.org.

Michael Rion. Available at http://www.rionethics.com.

The Nonprofit Good Practice Guide. Available at http://www.nonprofitbasics.org.

Seven-Step Decision-Making Process

The four ethical filters in an organizational context are compliance, policy, organizational values, and self. Apply each filter to each step in the process for the ethics situation at hand.

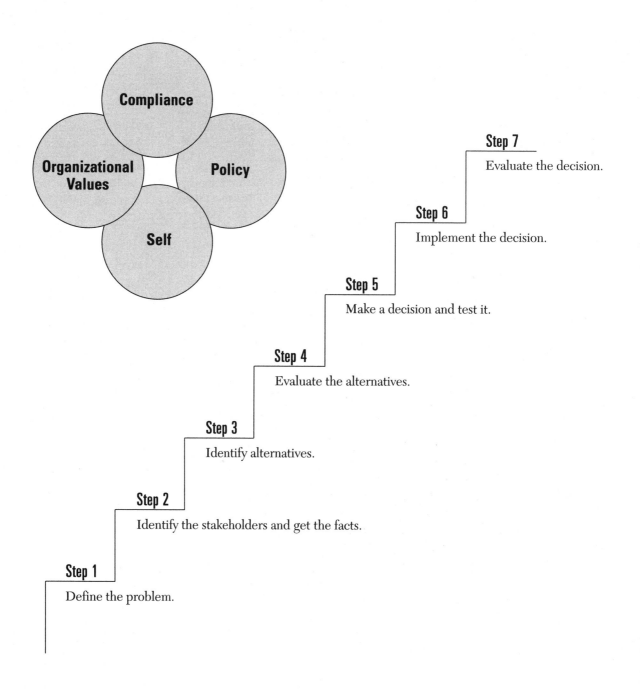

Step 7
Evaluate the decision.

Step 6
Implement the decision.

Step 5
Make a decision and test it.

Step 4
Evaluate the alternatives.

Step 3
Identify alternatives.

Step 2
Identify the stakeholders and get the facts.

Step 1
Define the problem.

Essentials for Evaluation

Issue 9705

Essentials for Evaluation

AUTHOR

Alice K. Waagen, PhD
Workforce Learning
1557 Hiddenbrook Drive
Herndon, VA 20170-2817
Tel: 703.834.7580
Email: WorkLearn@aol.com

Alice Waagen has more than 18 years of experience in designing and implementing corporate training. She has developed full systems of training measurement and evaluation, including cost of training, training volume and activity, training customer satisfaction, and ROI. She holds MS and PhD degrees in education.

Editor
Cat Sharpe

Associate Editor
Patrick McHugh

Designer
Steven M. Blackwood

Copy Editor
Kay Larson

ASTD Internal Consultant
Dr. Walter Gray

Essentials for Evaluation

We all know the lingo: reengineering, downsizing, rightsizing, competition, globalization—the list seems endless. What all the "ations" and "isms" represent is the accelerated climate of change in corporate organizations today. Faced with maturing markets and global competition, corporate leadership has become extremely critical in its analysis of existing business processes and procedures.

One aspect of this introspection is the desire to eliminate waste and redundancy. Corporate overhead—or those support functions not directly responsible for generating revenue—has come under great scrutiny. The support functions that have survived this scrutiny best are those that, early on, learned how to operate like independent businesses themselves—providing optimal customer service while emphasizing value for the dollars spent.

Leading-edge training and development organizations, whether internal staff or contractors providing services to many corporations, know that the success of their businesses depends on demonstrating the value of training investment. The simplest way to prove training's value to a client is to document that the training has achieved its desired outcome.

Herein lies the fundamental secret to evaluating training: The evaluation process and procedure must be incorporated at the start; it must be an integral part of any program development process. If program development follows the classic steps of assessing needs and generating objectives, the evaluation criteria that follow are then based on measuring how well the program components—students, instructors, and materials—have met these objectives and answered the needs.

For more information on needs analysis and objectives refer to the following *Infolines*: No. 258502, "Be a Better Needs Analyst"; No. 259808, "Task Analysis"; No. 258505, "Write Better Behavioral Objectives"; No. 259611, "Conducting a Mini Needs Assessment"; No. 259401, "Needs Assessment by Focus Group"; No. 259712, "Instructional Objectives"; and No. 259713, "The Role of the Performance Needs Analyst."

A broad range of methods and tools is available for every evaluation approach. Options include direct observation, comparisons of tests taken before and after training, interviews, reports, follow-up testing, questionnaires, and surveys. The most effective approach includes combinations of the aforementioned methods. Depending on your objectives, the nature of the training, and focus of the evaluation, some methods are more appropriate than others. For example, the best choice for measuring machine repair skills is direct observation, the worst evaluation tool is a survey.

This chapter outlines the basics of training program evaluation. Different methods of evaluation will be discussed and matched to assorted training program designs. You will learn the advantages and disadvantages of the various types of evaluation. And finally, the emphasis on reporting results to management will be discussed, as well as keeping the evaluation process *client focused* and closely tied to business results.

Benefits of Evaluation

Evaluation methods help determine whether training achieves its objectives. Programs that are structured and designed properly have objectives or elements that specify what the training must accomplish and in what time period these accomplishments must be realized.

A sound system of evaluating training provides valuable information for the client, training management, and senior corporate management. The information elicited from training evaluations should be the final instrument upon which training decisions such as program additions, changes, or deletions should be made. Good evaluations document results of training programs, which subsequently can be used to prioritize training needs at the corporate level. Then, financial and other resources can be shifted from training that has less impact on corporate goals to those objectives that have the most favorable cost-benefit ratio.

Some specific benefits of evaluation are:

- a tool to assess the value of courses, seminars, and workshops

- built-in quality control of training programs that documents whether or not course objectives have been met

- a method for identifying programs that need improvement

- a basis upon which decisions to continue or eliminate a program can be made

- a way to identify the proper audience for future programs

- a method for managing training programs

- a mechanism to review and reinforce essential program points

- a way to get top management and participants to buy in to the program.

When structured to elicit open-ended comments, training evaluations can serve two purposes: first, as a demonstrator of present-day benefits, and second, as an indicator of future training program needs.

Finally, summary or "macro" evaluation information can be proffered to senior management or key clients on a regular basis. This educates them as to the value of the training enterprise. Good evaluation reports should also document, in both statistical and qualitative terms, how training has helped the organization meet its goals.

Evaluation of Training

There are a number of ways to evaluate training and each method is designed to elicit different information. These various methodologies are often described as "levels" of information, from the simplest that obtain and quantify (reaction surveys), to the more complex and detailed (corporate results).

There are several levels of program evaluation criteria based on participants' reactions: what they've learned, their skills performance, their on-the-job behavior, and the effects and results the training has had on the entire organization.

The main evaluation methods will be discussed in terms of their strengths and weaknesses. Rather than thinking of these methods as a hierarchy from least valuable to most valuable, think of them all as useful tools in your training tool kit. If your client is most interested in seeing reaction data, this is a perfectly acceptable and useful form of evaluation; it should not be passed over for something more complex.

Following is a breakdown of how each level can be applied to help you develop a systematic approach to evaluating what your programs have accomplished.

Participant Reaction Surveys

Participant reaction surveys or "smile sheets" are questionnaires that are typically distributed at the end of each training program. They ask students to rate their perceptions about the quality and impact of the specific program. These questionnaires can range from a simple handful of questions regarding program design, instruction methods, and facilities to elaborate multipage forms for students to rate all facets of the program and provide input on future programs. This evaluation tool can serve as a valuable measure of attendee satisfaction and is relatively easy to administer, tabulate, and summarize in a results report.

Guidelines for Designing Reaction Surveys

Reaction surveys can provide quantifiable customer service data, giving you direct information from your program consumers. When designed with uniform overall questions, these surveys produce data that can be used to make comparisons between courses and participants. This allows program design decisions to be based on a broad range of perceptions, not just the responses of a few disappointed or disgruntled participants.

Reaction surveys provide the following results:

- Protection against making decisions based on a limited number of either satisfied or disappointed participants.

- Clues for improving programs, but no indication of how the training will affect job performance or organizational results.

Steps for Evaluating Reactions

The best instruments for reaction evaluations focus on points that are most important to the evaluator. They are straightforward and simple to fill out.

Evaluate reactions by using the following steps:

1. Determine what you want to know. Concentrate on specific areas such as methods, facilities, materials, and so on.

2. Design a comment sheet for tabulating and quantifying reactions. Experts suggest using a form designed for the particular program rather than a standardized or generic form.

3. Include sufficient space for questions and comments that cannot be quantified or tabulated.

4. Do not require participants to sign their evaluation forms. If participants are forced to identify themselves, they may feel obligated to be overly positive.

5. Keep the form simple and make sure it takes only a short time to complete. If you are interested in reactions, design sheets focusing on program content, not administration, for example.

6. Use a final comment sheet to gather additional or follow-up information. If you have already collected two or more previous evaluations, use a final one to clarify and complete information.

7. Establish standards of performance by converting reactions to numerical ratings. An example of this is a scale with numbers representing grades of quality: 1 = poor, 2 = adequate, 3 = good, 4 = very good, 5 = excellent.

What Have Participants Learned?

A number of different tools can be designed to measure what participants have learned in the training program. Paper and pencil tests, administered before and after training, can be used to measure acquisition of knowledge and information. Skills can be evaluated concurrently with the training through simulations or in-class activities, which allow students to demonstrate instructed skills. Regardless of the assessment method used, all of these tests must be designed to relate directly to the course objectives.

Participant learning evaluations are difficult and more time consuming to develop and administer, but they are essential if the nature of the training requires that the learning be demonstrated and documented. Learning assessments are most commonly used in training programs that lead to licensing, certification, or involve skills that contain elements of risk. Computerized simulators, used for airplane pilot and locomotive engineer training, are examples of learning assessment tools. One reason learning evaluations are difficult to design is that they must be customized for every instructional program and *must* reflect the conditions of the specific job.

It is important to remember that learning evaluations accurately measure the amount of knowledge and skills acquired *at the time the test is administered*. In no way do these tests indicate long-term knowledge or skill retention, nor are they an indicator of how knowledge and skills are applied to the job. They simply serve as a snapshot in time denoting that students have mastered the course objectives at the time the instruction was offered.

Components of Learning Evaluations

Effective tests must be thoroughly and thoughtfully designed. Most course developers will design questions as they author the course rather than wait until they are done. All evaluation instruments must be "dry run" on subject experts as well as sample student audiences. Be especially watchful for unclear or ambiguous wording in questions and instructions.

Paper and pencil tests and performance tests are the standard methods for measuring knowledge and skills. The first type measures knowledge, the second measures skills. The material in these tests relates directly to program objectives and the specific knowledge and skills learners work to acquire during training.

Evaluation tests may be based on standardized tests, but the ones that yield the best results are custom written for each specific program.

Designing Paper and Pencil Evaluations

You may want to use the following suggestions for designing and administering effective tests:

Increase your research resources by drafting sample questions before and during program development. Use these questions to make sure you have touched on all program areas; delete the ones pertaining to areas you could not cover during the session.

Plan thoroughly. Tests must be planned out in complete detail. Pay close attention to every part of the test including the schedule, timing breaks, review of instructions, administration, and scoring.

Give participants the opportunity to show what they have learned. Tests should be representative of the training, allowing learners to demonstrate their new knowledge. Relevant tests are more meaningful to learners and yield more valid results to instructors.

Use objective questions such as multiple-choice and true or false instead of open-ended essays.

Present only one correct answer. More than one right answer confuses test-takers, makes scoring more difficult, and reduces the validity of the test.

Never present misleading information. Trick questions invariably result in wrong answers, and are a waste of time for you and your learners. If trainees will be faced with difficult on-the-job decisions, represent these situations with challenging but fair questions.

Write questions for easy comprehension. Remember, your objective is to test participants' knowledge of the training material, not their reading skills.

Write questions to reveal how well the participants understand the material, not how well they can memorize it.

Use a random arrangement of answers to keep test-takers from guessing the pattern of correct responses (two false, three true).

Use multiple-choice items that do not allude to answers of subsequent questions. A block of answers that are tied together seriously affects a participant's score if he or she incorrectly answers the first question. Again, this kind of situation can affect the results and validity of your test.

Vary the level of difficulty throughout the test. Use a mixture of challenging, relatively difficult, and comparatively easy questions.

Try not to cue or signal the correct answer by varying the size of fill-in spaces or by letting one multiple-choice item stand out from the rest of the list as the only reasonable possibility.

Make the mechanics of test-taking simple. Remember, your objective is to measure participants' knowledge, not their ability to follow complex test instructions.

Review the test before you administer it. Is it valid? Does it meet the objectives of both the program and the evaluation process? Ask training colleagues to review the test and make suggestions for improving it.

Provide thorough and consistent directions.
All learners must receive identical, clear, and concise instructions. Poor instructions can influence the outcome of the evaluation. When administering tests, be sure to provide whatever information is necessary such as blueprints, tables, charts, diagrams, reference books, and so on. If possible, the instructor should use a beta test to present samples of how trainees are expected to answer evaluation questions.

Use procedures for objective evaluations.
Determine standards in advance and prepare learners so they will understand the requirements for satisfactory test performance.

Evaluating Skills Performance

Follow these suggestions to evaluate how well new skills have been learned:

- Design performance tests to objectively measure skills in quantifiable terms.

- Ensure that tests cover key requirements of the skills performance specified during training.

- Present the test to participants by clearly and simply explaining instructions, tabulation methods, and performance standards. Tell trainees precisely what they are expected to accomplish.

- Concentrate on improving participants' job performance rather than giving them more training material or information.

- Be sure evaluations reflect how the training has changed skill levels. To do so, carefully prepare and design evaluations. Research your procedures during program pilots and use "control" as well as "experimental" groups to gather data.

- Consult with design experts and other resource people to check the validity and value of your design methodology.

If the test is to be used to qualify a person for a specific job, use outside expertise to evaluate the test for validity and fairness. If test scores can be used to deny employment or promotion opportunities, they must be demonstrably sound or you will open your employer to discrimination charges. If you do not have the expertise yourself or in your staff to validate tests, seek validation from an industrial psychologist or other professional possessing this expertise.

A final note on testing: Be cautious of managers who ask for test results on individual students. Some managers may want to use learning evaluation scores as grounds for discipline, termination, or even promotion. Remember, these tests document a snapshot view of knowledge and skill acquisition. By no means do they accurately reflect on a person's job performance. Using test results as performance indicators can be misleading and even illegal. When in doubt, consult with your human resource or legal department.

On-the-Job Behavior Evaluation

The ultimate goal of any training program is to improve job performance. Often, training clients want to know more than "has the student acquired new knowledge and skills by the end of the program?" They also want to know if the student can apply the knowledge and skills on the job. Behavior evaluations are designed to measure changes in on-the-job behavior and document improved performance directly related to training.

Job performance evaluations measure whether or not the trainee can accomplish program objectives. These evaluations must be based on the actual task or job performance. This can be documented by observing on-the-job behavior; managers, peers, or subordinates can serve as observers, plus offer oral and written reports regarding performance changes.

If available, performance data can also be gathered and analyzed. For instance, most manufacturing facilities have detailed records of work units produced by employees. In the "soft skills" training programs, action plans can be developed based on observable results. Again, co-workers can be used to record the presence of these observable behaviors.

Evaluation Checklist

Training evaluations can make the difference between a company's losses and gains. Accurate methods and tools for measuring training outcomes can mean significant improvement in organizational performance—increased productivity and savings, decreased costs and personnel problems. To get valuable data from an evaluation, plan your approach by thinking through the following checklist:

☐ What questions do you want to answer? How did participants feel about the training? What did they learn? How did the training affect their attitudes and behavior? What were the organizational results?

☐ How will you measure the items addressed in your questions? Will you administer paper and pencil tests, questionnaires, or surveys? Will you require participants to demonstrate their new knowledge and skills in a role play or simulation?

☐ What are the objectives of your training program? Are your evaluation criteria based on these objectives?

☐ Do the criteria indicate improvement between expected and actual performance when measured against the results of your needs analysis?

☐ What data sources are already available to help you measure results (productivity reports, sales and revenue analyses, and so on)?

☐ Are there alternative methods for gathering this data such as interviews and on-site observations?

☐ What are the best and most cost-effective methods for measuring the results of training? Can you think of less costly, more efficient ways of administering the evaluation?

Components of Behavior Evaluations

The key to developing effective behavior change evaluations is to have clear, observable objectives. These objectives must be based on a systematic appraisal of on-the-job performance as well as interviews with employees and management about requisite levels of the task's performance. Essentially, the difference between current performance and desired performance should correlate to the content of the training.

Methods for gathering this kind of information include:

● on-site observations of performance by trained observers (supervisors, co-workers, or professional observers)

● analyses of individual performance records

● observable results of action plans developed during training to improve specific performance areas

● comments from managers, employees, or subordinates, describing behavior changes of their supervisors, co-workers, or support staff.

Steps for Data Collection

To determine the effectiveness of a program in behavioral terms, follow these steps and be sure measurements are objective and quantifiable:

1. Make a systematic appraisal of on-the-job performance both before and after the training.

2. Collect comments and performance appraisals from trainees, superiors, subordinates, and co-workers.

3. Compare pre- and posttraining performances and how they relate to the program's instruction.

4. Conduct posttraining evaluations at least three months after program completion to allow trainees sufficient time to practice and test their new skills and knowledge. Additional appraisals will add to the validity of your evaluation.

5. Use control groups that do not receive training to compare against those that do receive training. This helps you measure the effectiveness of your program and its impact on job performance.

One note of caution: In addition to skills or knowledge, behavior change is based on many factors. Training programs can be successful in knowledge and skill transfer yet not result in changed behavior on the job. Participants may choose not to change their behavior due to various reasons: lack of management support for the new behavior, lack of sufficient rewards to motivate change, or perhaps the workplace itself may not be conducive to change.

Because the cause-and-effect relationship between training and behavior change is complex, one should elicit more than just performance observations to have an accurate evaluation system. Posttraining interviews with employees can be used to discover why there has been a behavior change or resistance to change. If there has been no change, ask employees why they have not used the new skill or knowledge on the job. Keep this information confidential. The answers may reveal significant environmental barriers to the change. Until these barriers are identified and eliminated, performance measures will fail to produce positive results. Once the barriers are removed, training can more effectively produce the desired performance objectives.

Evaluation of Organizational Results

Evaluating organizational results measures and documents the effects of training interventions as they relate to the achievement of corporate goals and objectives. Essentially, this documents the overall "macro" result of training programs and is frequently sought when senior managers ask the question: "What real difference does training make? If we stopped training tomorrow, what effect would I see on my bottom line?"

Trainers who need to document their program's impact on the corporation should first look at the corporation's annual goals and strategic direction. They also need to examine any measures that are currently used at divisional or departmental levels to support these goals. Some of these metrics might include the following: new or existing reports and records covering profits and production, quality, sales, customer service, costs, waste, defects and efforts, efficiency, employee absenteeism, turnover, and so on.

After determining corporate objectives, trainers can relate the evaluation of results to organizational gains and improvements. The benefits of training can include:

- increased productivity
- increased savings
- better quality
- decreased absenteeism
- fewer errors, grievances, and safety problems.

To analyze the effects of the training program on the organization, practitioners compare pre- and posttraining data. Results evaluation measures the fiscal or financial impact of a program and is much more difficult than the simple reaction measurement, but possesses the highest value for an organization.

There is an inherent difficulty when measuring training in terms of results. This is because training is only one of many variables that affect organizational performance. In addition, because many corporate performance metrics are developed irrespective of the training, they can measure factors that may not directly relate to employee performance. These include things such as stock prices or equipment efficiency. Trainers must be cautious when stating that training affects a measure not directly linked to the objectives of the program. For this reason, many organizations opt only for reaction, learning, and behavior evaluations.

Choosing the Right Format for Questions

Selecting the right kind of questions for your particular program evaluation is essential for obtaining good results. Tests may consist of one or all of the following types of questions:

Multiple-choice. This format provides a selection of possible responses; the trainee is told to choose the most accurate one.

Open-ended. These tests offer unlimited responses. Learners write lengthy answers in blank spaces following each question. For example: "An angry customer arrives at your office complaining about your delivery service. How would you calm the customer down and resolve the situation?"

Checklist. This type of test presents the learner with a situation and a list of items which may or may not apply. The trainee must choose those items most applicable to the given situation. For example:

"Match the proofreader's symbols to their proper use."
  a. paragraph
  b. insert comma
  c. let it stand
  d. capital letter
  e. lower case letter

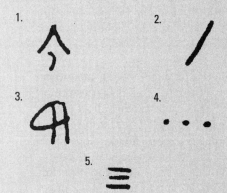

Two-way. This format poses alternate answers. Learners choose *yes* or *no* or else *true* or *false* responses. For example:

"Adult learners are mainly interested in highly job-relevant training."
  a. True
  b. False

Rating scale. This type of test asks learners to rank lists of items according to particular scale.

Guidelines for Measuring Results

Evaluations measuring the impact of training on the organization require hard data—new or existing reports and records covering profits and production, quality, sales, customer service, costs, waste, defects and efforts, efficiency, employee absenteeism and turnover, and so on.

Use the following guidelines to assist you when gathering evaluation material:

1. Gather accurate data from results evaluations; isolate the effects of the program in order to evaluate them objectively.

2. Be aware of external factors that are not related to training. Some of these include:

   - changes in procedures, processes, and new technology

   - the job experience and maturity of trainees

   - the trainee recruitment method; volunteer participation usually results in more positive performance than mandatory attendance.

3. Ensure validity by using the following methods:

   Control groups. These are employees who have not received training. Check organizational gains, such as increased productivity and decreased errors, against a performance comparison of trained and untrained employees. Note differences in on-the-job behavior and whether they are related to training or other factors.

   Sampling. This is a representative selection of the entire trainee population. Choose a sample that represents different backgrounds and levels of experience.

4. Analyze evaluation data carefully before making connections between training and organizational achievements. Review the data to make sure it is consistent and accurate. Scan reports and studies for excessive and unrealistic values and eliminate incorrect or incomplete items.

5. Never exclude relevant data. Valid, though often negative, information that does not support the desired outcome must be included with the positive data.

6. Keep your statistical and data analyses as simple as possible. Limit your methods and interpretations to a particular focus for drawing accurate conclusions.

7. Focus on bottom-line results directly related to organizational goals. Increased production or sales, for example, are frequently essential objectives for many companies. Calculate changes by comparing totals before and after the training program.

8. Determine the benefits of reducing time in production, processing, and construction. The valuable and visible result is improved service, or a decrease in the amount of time it takes to deliver products and services to customers.

9. Calculate the value of improved quality by comparing pre- and posttraining reports on the numbers of mistakes and necessary corrections, client dissatisfaction, and product liability.

Be sure to evaluate results in quantifiable and accountable terms. For example, assign a dollar value to cost savings, remembering to adjust costs experienced over time because they are likely to increase beyond the value of actual savings. Assign dollar values to the time saved by employees trained to perform their jobs faster and more efficiently. To calculate time savings, multiply the labor costs per hour by the amount of hours saved.

A final note on results evaluation: Many training managers have concluded in recent years that there is "no return-on-investment (ROI) when measuring the ROI of training." Results measurement is by far the most difficult, complex, and costly evaluation methodology. Be cautious of building elaborate systems of measurement and reporting unless your clients and management have specifically requested them.

If management requests that you demonstrate training's impact on corporate goals, research thoroughly the resources you will need, in staffing, computer power, statistical and analytical support, and so on. Prepare a cost analysis of the results evaluation project and present it to management before you begin.

Testing Methods

Comparisons of pre- and posttest scores are very good indicators of program effectiveness. Higher test scores show that the program has improved and strengthened trainees' skills, knowledge, and abilities. Following are types of tests used in human resource departments:

■ *Norm-Referenced*
Rather than rate learners according to program objectives, these tests compare individuals or groups to the norm, the average trainee performance. This kind of test identifies the best and weakest performers, the class rank of each person, the median score for the group, and the percentile standing of each participant. Norm-referenced tests are most useful in a program with a large learner population where score average and individual ranking are significant.

■ *Criterion-Referenced*
These are objective tests that require specific and precise responses based on program objectives. Criterion-referenced tests (CRTs) have predetermined cut-off scores and measure according to precisely defined program objectives. Rather than analyze how learners rank among one another, the CRT focuses on assessing, analyzing, and reporting what learners have achieved based on the combination of performance standards and program objectives. For example, the criteria for a typing test would follow from a program objective such as: "At the end of training, learner will be able to type 60 words per minute with no more than two errors." If the learner successfully meets this standard and accomplishes the objectives, he or she will have mastered the typing skills as specified in the training program.

■ *Performance or Simulations*

These tests permit the learner to physically demonstrate skills or the uses of knowledge in a program. Some types of skills exhibited may include analytical, manual, interpersonal, verbal, or any combination of the aforementioned. Most often, practitioners use performance tests to demonstrate activities in specific job-related training; for example, "Demonstrate the correct procedures for coding an HTML document for a web page."

Supervisory and management training involves performance testing as role plays and skill practice exercises. Learners may be asked to demonstrate problem-solving or communications skills by acting out scenarios with each other.

Evaluation Tips

1. The basic steps for evaluation can be used in any kind of organization. The techniques and procedures have broad application, but never try to overlay evaluation results from one department or organization onto another department or organization.

2. Always give your participants enough time to complete evaluation forms in class. Experts agree that "take-home" forms usually stay at home. If you save only the last few minutes of the session for evaluations, the forms will show tell-tale signs of the time crunch—hurried and incomplete responses. Before the wrap-up segment of the program, put aside some time to review the program and answer questions about the evaluation forms.

3. To get a comprehensive picture of your program, try to ask the same number of questions about strengths and weaknesses. A "mixed review" can be more accurate and helpful than overly positive or negative responses.

4. Share responses with the group. Express your interest in their opinions and ideas by preparing a summary of the written evaluations and discussing the issues that seem most important. This gives individuals a sense of how others responded as well as how their own reactions compare with the group's response.

5. Conduct evaluations more than once during the training no matter how long or short the program. An eight-hour workshop can be evaluated at midpoint and improved for the remaining half. If you evaluate only at the end, you will not be able to share comments, use suggestions, or follow up for additional information.

6. When it is not feasible to stop and evaluate the program at different points, use a method of ongoing evaluation. Instead of evaluating only at the end of the program (during long programs it can be difficult to remember important details), hand out evaluation forms at the beginning and instruct learners when and how to fill them out. Give them a few minutes after each topic to evaluate the material, presentation, and presenter.

7. Review your evaluation methodology with your human resources and legal professionals to ensure that your tests are valid and nondiscriminatory. This is especially important if the test results are used to qualify a person for hiring, promotion, or to serve in a specific job. An invalid or discriminatory test can create a legal risk for the corporation. Also, determine with your legal partners how long test results must be stored for future reference.

8. Legal departments also use training attendance and completion records to demonstrate "due diligence" effort of corporations in sexual harassment or Equal Employment Opportunity (EEO) types of litigation. If a corporation can demonstrate that it takes an active role training its employees on appropriate behavior in the workplace, the organization can shift responsibility for subsequent misbehavior from the corporation to the individual. Partner with your legal staff to determine how training results need to be documented.

9. Keep all employee test results confidential and secured. Misuse of this information, especially low or failing scores, can be devastating to the employee and to the credibility of your entire training effort. Again, seek legal counsel as to the length of retention for this type of information and destroy it once obsolete. Keep all paper records locked and secured; password protect all electronic files.

Follow-Up Evaluations

After the last program evaluation, conduct a related follow-up evaluation that involves feedback questionnaires, interviews, and observations.

Use follow-up evaluations to:

- measure lasting results of training

- identify areas where learners show the greatest and the least improvement

- compare follow-up and end-of-program evaluation responses.

Guidelines for Follow-Up Evaluations

To find out the degree of improvement since the program, measure the success of the training according to participants' on-the-job accomplishments and how they are using the training to improve performance.

- Make sure learners are prepared for the follow-up. At the end of the program, announce your intention to conduct a follow-up evaluation and explain what kind of information you need. Providing this type of explanation will increase your response rates.

- Explain that the follow-up is mandatory, not optional; the evaluation is crucial in determining the effect and value of the program.

- Pose questions that are the same or similar to those that appeared on the end-of-program evaluation forms.

- Find out if the training worked.

- Share follow-up data with all managers and supervisors.

- The kinds of questions you ask will give you a reliable basis for accurate data comparison and analysis. For example, if learners were asked to estimate their increase in productivity resulting from the training, follow up by asking about their actual rate of increase.

- Encourage participants to identify reasons why they have or have not improved and what factors obstructed their progress. Isolating the negative effects can be as useful as identifying the positive ones.

- It is vitally important to share follow-up evaluations with participants' managers or supervisors. These individuals need to know the program results and follow-up information and should also be involved with the participants' practice and application of the training.

- As a final effort, assign follow-up activities when and if appropriate. For example, if a learner needs clarification in some aspect of the training, practitioners can instruct them to complete a task or achieve a goal related to the program's content. This helps learners to better evaluate the program.

Reporting Results to Management

At a minimum, training evaluation data should be reported to the training manager and on up to the senior level. At each level, the data should be increasingly summarized and extracted. No manager wants to wade through tomes of data, so reports should be condensed to provide the most relevant information for each level.

The fundamental question to ask in reporting any data is, "What business decision will the reader make after reading this information?" To answer this question, you need to determine the decision-making authority and span of control belonging to the reader. If the manager cannot use the report to assist in his or her decisions, it is "nice to know" information and will probably end up discarded and unread.

Evaluation Methods

Paper and Pencil Test. This method measures how well trainees learn program content. An instructor administers paper and pencil tests in class to measure participants' progress.

Attitude Surveys. These question-and-answer surveys determine what changes in attitude have occurred as a result of training. Practitioners use these surveys to gather information about employees' perceptions, work habits, motivation, value beliefs, working relations, and so on. Attitude surveys also reveal respondees' opinions about their jobs, the workplace, co-workers, supervisors, policies, procedures, and the organization. If you conduct a program to change attitudes, before and after surveys can assess improvement.

Simulation and On-Site Observation. Instructors' or managers' observations of on-the-job performance in a work simulation indicate whether a learner's skills have improved as a result of the training.

Productivity Reports. Hard production data such as sales reports and manufacturing totals can help managers and instructors determine *actual* performance improvement on the job.

Posttraining Surveys. Progress and proficiency assessments by both managers and participants indicate perceived performance improvement on the job.

Needs/Objectives/Content Comparison. Training managers, participants, and supervisors compare needs analysis results with course objectives and content to determine whether the program was relevant to participants' needs. Relevancy ratings at the end of the program also contribute to the comparison.

Evaluation Forms. Participants' responses on end-of-program evaluation forms indicate what they liked and disliked about the training.

Professional Opinion. Instructional designers critique and assess the quality of the program design.

Instructor Evaluation. Professional trainers administer assessment sheets and evaluation forms to measure the instructor's competence, effectiveness, and instructional skills.

Cost Analysis. The training manager compares costs of instructor's fees, materials, facilities, travel, training time, and the number of trainees to determine the hourly cost of training for each participant.

Consider using these suggestions for including management in the evaluation process:

- Involve line managers in developing evaluation objectives and determining criteria.

- Explain the process to managers and use their input to develop data collection methods and techniques that focus on the criteria and indicate the effects of training.

- Include managers in identifying significant results. They also can help determine the best ways to report results.

- Reach agreement on a reporting method—written, formal presentation, or informal discussion.

- Decide who should receive the reports (participants, administrators, department managers, supervisors), as well as the best times for distributing or presenting the reports.

Essential Corporate Partners

To the new trainer, developing good training evaluations can be a daunting task. But there are many skilled professionals within a corporation who can help you with this task. In return, you can make them special clients of training, offering them your training counsel and expertise. Actively seek out partners in the following departments:

■ Information Systems Specialists

These are the computer hardware and software gurus who can help you automate all your record-keeping and reporting. And no, there is no one miracle computer program out there that will do it all. Once you get into the intricacy of data collection and retrieval, you will need expert help in setting up programs to manage it.

■ Human Resources

Talk regularly with your corporation's recruiters. Ask them what positions are difficult or costly to fill. Then talk to the organization development (OD) staffing experts about the possibility of retraining existing staff for these positions. OD, leadership, and executive development professionals can also provide you with keen insight about organizational difficulties that might be addressed through training.

Inquire from the compensation staff whether there are any requirements for training in the performance review process. If so, this will affect your training volume shortly before review time. The words trainers hate to hear are: "My performance review is next week and I have to take Course XYZ before then. Why aren't you offering it?"

Likewise, talk frequently with the employee relations and EEO people. They hear a lot of the negative stories about management and employee behavior; sometimes training can raise awareness and alleviate some of these problems.

■ Legal

Partner with the legal department to obtain help regarding the legal side of testing, surveying, record retention, and reporting.

■ Finance/Accounting

Somewhere in every finance department are people with expertise on statistics and modeling. They also are well versed on reporting complex statistical information in ways that are easy for management to comprehend. Get their advice to fine-tune your data reporting.

Financial experts can also provide you with models that determine the cost of training. Many corporations use standard algorithms to compute average employee salary costs. You need to use the same calculation for your reports.

■ Employee and Corporate Communications

These people not only have vehicles (email lists and newsletters) to reach all employees, they are often the consummate wordsmiths. They can help you with the appearance and readability of your reports.

This is but a small sampling of the corporate staff that can help you with training evaluation and reporting. Network frequently with these people, and they will help ease your reporting burden.

References & Resources

Articles

Barron, Tom. "Is There an ROI in ROI?" *Technical & Skills Training,* January 1997, pp. 21-26.

Benabou, Charles. "Assessing the Impact of Training Programs on the Bottom Line." *National Productivity Review,* Summer 1996, pp. 91-99.

Bernthal, Paul R. "Evaluation That Goes the Distance." *Training & Development,* September 1995, pp. 41-45.

Birnbrauer, Herman. "Improving Evaluation Forms to Produce Better Course Design." *Performance & Instruction,* January 1996, pp. 14-17.

Blickstein, Steve. "Does Training Pay Off?" *Across the Board,* June 1996, pp. 16-20.

Bushnell, David S. "Input, Process, Output: A Model for Evaluating Training." *Training & Development Journal,* March 1990, pp. 41-43.

Dixon, Nancy M. "New Routes to Evaluation." *Training & Development,* May 1996, pp. 82-85.

Dust, Bob. "Understanding Financial Terminology." *Training & Development,* May 1996, pp. 99-100.

Geber, Beverly. "Prove It! (Does Your Training Make a Difference?)" *Training,* March 1995, pp. 27-34.

Jedrziewski, David R. "Putting Methods to the Madness of Evaluating Training Effectiveness." *Performance & Instruction,* January 1995, pp. 23-31.

Lapp, H.J. "Rate Your Testing Program." *Performance & Instruction,* September 1995, pp. 36-38.

Lewis, Theodore. "A Model for Thinking About the Evaluation of Training." *Performance Improvement Quarterly,* vol. 9, no. 1 (1996), pp. 3-22.

McLinden, Daniel J. "Proof, Evidence, and Complexity: Understanding the Impact of Training and Development." *Performance Improvement Quarterly,* vol. 8, no. 3 (1995), pp. 3-18.

Phillips, Jack J. "How Much Is the Training Worth?" *Training & Development,* April 1996, pp. 20-24.

————. "ROI: The Search for Best Practices." *Training & Development,* February 1996, pp. 42-47.

————. "Was It the Training?" *Training & Development,* March 1996, pp. 28-32.

Pulley, Mary Lynn. "Navigating the Evaluation Rapids." *Training & Development,* September 1994, pp. 19-24.

Shelton, Sandra, and George Alliger. "Who's Afraid of Level 4 Evaluation?" *Training & Development,* June 1993, pp. 43-46.

Smith, Jack E., and Sharon Merchant. "Using Competency Exams for Evaluating Training." *Training & Development Journal,* August 1990, pp. 65-71.

Williams, Leigh Ann. "Measurement Made Simple." *Training & Development,* July 1996, pp. 43-45.

Willyerd, Karie A. "Balancing Your Evaluation Act." *Training,* March 1997, pp. 52-58.

Books

ASTD. *The Best of the Evaluation of Training.* Alexandria, VA: ASTD, 1991.

————. *The Best of the Return on Training Investment.* Alexandria, VA: ASTD, 1991.

Basarab, David J., and Darrel K. Root. *The Training Evaluation Process: A Practical Approach to Evaluating Corporate Training Programs.* Norwell, MA: Kluwer Academic, 1992.

Bassi, Laurie J., et al. *The ASTD Training Data Book.* Alexandria, VA: ASTD, 1996.

Dixon, Nancy M. *Evaluation: A Tool for Improving HRD Quality.* Alexandria, VA: ASTD, 1991.

Fisk, Catherine N., ed. *ASTD Trainer's Toolkit: Evaluation Instruments.* Alexandria, VA: ASTD, 1991.

Head, Glenn E. *Training Cost Analysis: The How-To Guide for Trainers and Managers.* Alexandria, VA: ASTD, 1994.

Kirkpatrick, Donald L. *Evaluating Training Programs: The Four Levels.* San Francisco: Berrett-Kohler, 1994.

References & Resources

Medsker, Karen L., and Donald G. Roberts, eds. *ASTD Trainer's Toolkit: Evaluating the Results of Training.* Alexandria, VA: ASTD, 1992.

Phillips, Jack J. *Handbook of Training Evaluation and Measurement Methods.* Houston: Gulf Publishing, 1997.

Rae, Leslie. *How to Measure Training Effectiveness.* Brookfield, VT: Gower Publishing, 1991.

Robinson, Dana G., and James C. Robinson. *Training for Impact.* San Francisco: Jossey-Bass, 1989.

*Infoline*s

Austin, Mary. "Needs Assessment by Focus Group." No. 259401 (revised 1998).

Cheney, Scott. "Benchmarking." No. 259801.

Gupta, Kavita. "Conducting a Mini Needs Assessment." No. 259611 (revised 1999).

Hacker, Deborah Grafinger. "Testing for Learning Outcomes." No. 258907 (revised 1998).

Kirrane, Diane. "The Role of the Performance Needs Analyst." No. 259713.

Long, Lori. "Surveys From Start to Finish." No. 258612 (revised 1998).

Plattner, Francis. "Instructional Objectives." No. 259712.

Robinson, Dana Gaines, and James C. Robinson. "Measuring Affective and Behavioral Change." No. 259110 (revised 1997).

Sharpe, Cat, ed. "Be A Better Needs Analyst." No. 258502 (revised 1998).

———. "Write Better Behavioral Objectives." No. 258505 (revised 1998).

Waagen, Alice K. "Task Analysis." No. 259808.

Internet Sites

ASTD:
http://www.astd.org

Evaluation and Training Institute (ETI):
http://www.otan.dni.us/webfarm/eti/

Job Aid

Evaluation Guide

I. Client Needs

A. State the objectives of the program.

B. Describe evaluation criteria based on these objectives.

II. Participant Reaction

A. How will participants' reactions during and after the program be measured? State what methods will be used: questionnaires, surveys, interviews, observations.

B. Describe what measurement standards will be used. Examples of these are relevance ("Was the program relevant to your specific job needs?") and ease of learning ("Were you able to complete the activities and exercises with relative ease, or were they too difficult?").

C. List specific issues to be addressed. Some examples include program design, class size and arrangement, and the value of program's content.

D. How will the information be collected and tabulated?

E. State and describe back-up sources for information. These may include participants' remarks to the trainer, and their questions concerning program exercises and content.

III. Performance Skills and On-the-Job Behavior

A. List the methods for evaluating learning during and at the end of the training. Examples include tests, questionnaires, and company documents.

B. Describe the measurement standards. Use these questions to help establish standards. How much of the material do the participants understand? How well do they understand it and apply it?

C. List specific program areas that will be questioned. Focus on program structure, presentation, activities, and examples.

D. How will the information be collected and tabulated?

E. List and describe back-up sources. Look at the amount of time the training program required and note whether all or some of the content was covered. Check trainee performance on exercises, during demonstrations, and on the job. (Are trainees using the new skills and information successfully?)

IV. Organizational Results

A. How did the training affect the organization. Did it have a positive impact on organizational performance?

B. Using annual reports, corporate, strategic, and annual plans, list the organization's goals or objectives against which you will measure the training's impact.

C. Describe the measurement standards that will be used to evaluate organizational results.

D. How will the information be collected and tabulated?

E. List back-up data sources. Some of these may be interviews and discussions with management, personnel, and clients.

F. Include observations of procedures and processes.

Be a Better Needs Analyst

Be a Better Needs Analyst

Editorial Staff for 8502

Editor
Madelyn R. Callahan

ASTD Internal Consultants
Ron Zemke
Allison Rossett

Revised 1998

Editor
Cat Sharpe

Contributing Editor
Ann Bruen

Reprinted 2006

Be a Better Needs Analyst

Question:
What is the last thing a needs analyst should be expected to do?

Answer:
Read minds.

In today's business market, analysts must have strong communication and technical skills, proficiency in the use of time-tested assessment instruments, and a fair amount of ingenuity. If they possess these qualities and have a firm commitment from their client, they will not need be clairvoyant.

Successful needs analyses rely on good strategies and the support of the client organization. This is the ideal foundation for beginning a needs study. Effective analysts can start out with a clear focus: to find the right problem and the right solution.

The classical approach to determining needs or problems is **identifying the discrepancy between the desired and actual knowledge, skills, and performance (and specifying root causes).** That difference is the training need. A variety of methods including interviews, observations, questionnaires, and tests may lead to identifying needs.

Using these methods effectively involves accurate gathering, analyzing, verifying, and reporting of data. Critical competencies for the analyst's role include the following:

- understanding organizational structure, power, culture, and communication systems

- understanding the factors that contribute to and hinder group and individual changes in organizations

- identifying the knowledge and skills necessary to perform jobs; assessing individuals' abilities

- using technology (such as computers, web-based training, the Internet, intranets, CD-ROM) to assist training and evaluation

- observing and describing behavior objectively

- developing sound data collection and analysis methods

- processing, synthesizing, and forming appropriate conclusions about the data

- providing constructive feedback

- designing presentations and communicating information, recommendations, suggestions, and ideas.

What this means is that skilled analysts are now among the most important professionals in the training, development, and performance fields. Technological advances and expanding industries continually create new workplace training requirements, increasing the demand for skilled analysts and accurate assessment methods. With unrelenting budget cuts hitting training departments, today's trainers have bigger jobs, yet correspondingly smaller budgets than they did in the past. For many organizations, a sound needs analysis is essential to a return on training investment dollars and reduces the risk of funding inappropriate programs.

This issue of *Infoline* will help you improve your needs analysis techniques, paying special attention to administering interviews and questionnaires. It provides a beginning for the trainer who wants to conduct, report, and justify effective needs assessments.

Conducting the Needs Analysis

As with any analysis, there are procedures to be followed in order to produce a useful product. Here are six basic steps to help you focus your needs analysis.

Step 1: Define Your Objectives

Determine your purposes and objectives for the analysis. These factors are the bases for management planning and development decisions. Some objectives for conducting a needs analysis are as follows:

- Distinguish employees who need training.

- Identify performance problems, deficiencies, and the root causes.

- Determine whether training is the best solution to the problems.

Nailing Down Needs Assessment

Across the nation trainers hear words like these:

Brad, in just a little over five weeks, our new blockbuster sandwich will be available to the public in 2,600 stores and franchises across the nation. I want to be certain that this sandwich is done right everywhere. It has to taste exactly the same in Boise and Boston. That's where you come in. Get some training ready to go so that our people know how to make that sandwich and make it good. Start with a needs assessment. But don't spend too long before you start writing that training.

Wilma, see that box over there? It's full of illustrated manuals that pretty much describe how the new system will work. Well, actually, that documentation is for the hospital, which is one-third our size, but the vendor swears that we'll be able to use it here. And here's Sharon Murray's number. She is the vendor rep who can help you out. We need this course and we need it fast. No time for a whatchamacallit, a needs assessment, this time.

The phrase *needs assessment* is everywhere, and everywhere it means something different. That makes it difficult to learn about, challenging to do well, and nearly impossible to explain to a skeptical colleague.

Fortunately there are some things about needs assessment that most experts recognize:

1. It comes at the beginning of any systematic approach to training, prior to teaching anybody anything in any setting or technology.

2. It is done to understand more about a performance problem—some gap between what is happening and what ought to be happening. This means that needs assessment is the systematic search for details about the difference between optimal and actual.

3. There is a lot of verbal support for the idea of needs assessment, far more than for the time and resources it takes to do it well. When people want trainers to solve problems, they want them solved yesterday. If a needs assessment stands between the problem and a snappy new course, then needs assessment is suspect.

4. People who conduct needs assessments usually do so using in-person and telephone interviews and questionnaires. Training literature clearly presents the leading characteristics of these two techniques: ease of data analysis, anonymity, opportunity to follow up responses, and cost.

5. Needs assessments usually ask for people's feelings. The inquiry should focus on what sources feel is causing the performance problem and whether or not the trainees could perform successfully under pressure. Training resources should not be used on problems that better supervision or powerful incentive plans can dispatch.

6. Training and therefore needs assessment is not about performance problems as much as it used to be. Now it is about new systems and technologies, necessitating expanded ways of understanding the situation before training.

These areas of accord provide little solace to people like Wilma and Brad who need to know what needs assessment is, why it is important, and how to do it. It is not just one act like sending out a survey. It is several stages of assessment, using several techniques, each of which gets you closer to knowing what is going on, and why.

Needs assessments are used to discover the following things:

Optimal performance. Both of the trainers described above need to seek out the details of what constitutes excellent performance.

Actual performance. How well is each employee performing? How have middle managers conducted their performance appraisals? New systems and technologies involve little examination of current, actual performance. These training needs assessments will be based primarily on information about optimals.

Attitudes on subject, skills, or technology. This search is crucial for training design. Will Wilma walk into the hospital training center and be greeted with hostility? Do middle managers believe that the old appraisal system was perfectly adequate? Are they confident of their ability to master a computerized behavioral rating scale?

The cause or causes of the problem. There are still those old-fashioned performance problems caused by poor incentives, motivation, skills, knowledge, or work environment. Which of these is the obstacle in Wilma's situation? Needs assessment must tell you that.

Trainers perform needs assessments until they know, in detail and conclusively, the nature of the mission (optimal minus actual), the attitudes or feelings, and the causes of problems. The search for information varies, depending on what got you started: a performance problem, or a new task, system, or technology.

Allison Rossett

- Secure the support and commitment of management in the process of building and evaluating effective training programs.

- Generate data that will be useful in measuring the impact of the training program.

- Provide specific recommendations for training programs: scope, methods, frequency, cost, and location.

- Decide priorities for the upcoming year and for long-range strategic planning.

- Justify spending to top management by determining the value and cost of training. Calculate the difference between "no training" costs (the expenses incurred or monies lost by continuing with the same problems) and the costs of the training solution.

Step 2: Identify the Necessary Data

A thorough needs assessment requires information to identify:

- the need
- the solution
- the population requiring training
- the strategies for delivering training.

Know the nature and quantity of the information you require for a useful assessment study. You may need opinions, attitude surveys, financial statements, job descriptions, performance appraisals, work samples, or historical documents from the company's archives.

Step 3: Select Data Collection Method

Choose or design a method for gathering data. Use various combinations of the following methods, alternating between their structured and unstructured versions: interviews, questionnaires, observation, group discussion, key consultation, work samples, records, reports, and tests.

Base structured or formal assessment methods on the necessary data as outlined in step two and also on a comparison of each method's degree of effectiveness for gathering the data. Validate all instruments (questionnaires, surveys, and so forth) used in this approach.

Step 4: Collect the Data

If you are dealing with a sample or study group, administer the questionnaires, conduct the interviews, observe performances, and so forth.

Step 5: Analyze and Confirm the Data

Compare the new data with past years' information and analyze to uncover problems and related trends or patterns. Confirm results and check for accuracy by consulting with the persons who originally provided the information.

Step 6: Prepare the Final Report

Point out problems, needs, weak areas, and recommend strategies for improvement. Using tables, graphs, and other support data for findings, design a clear and interesting presentation with well-written materials and attractive visuals. Some presentation skills are also necessary. Refer to *Infoline*s No. 8410, "How to Prepare and Use Effective Visual Aids"; No. 8606, "Make Every Presentation a Winner"; and No. 9409, "Improve Your Communications and Speaking Skills".

Needs Analysis Guidelines

Following are a number of guidelines to keep in mind as you undertake a needs analysis. While all these suggestions may not be appropriate for your situation, many can help ease the task and simplify the process.

1. Use a model of human performance that is relevant and useful for your particular organization. The model should take into account the company's culture, climate, objectives, availability and allocation of resources, and specific factors that affect performance.

2. Use a comprehensive and flexible approach. A good needs analysis should address the total organization, a department, division, group, or a single individual.

3. Plan a well-timed analysis. Do not schedule assessments during difficult periods of structural change, transfer of ownership or executive management, or major policy revisions that affect all organizational levels. Analysts must assess the current needs of individual departments and divisions on their own terms but also on the basis of how these groups can be affected by changes in other areas of the organization.

4. Use your analysis to indicate if an actual, significant problem or need exists and, if it does, to develop an appropriate solution. Start by identifying the concerned members of the organization:

   - Why are they interested in the problem?
   - How do they perceive the problem?
   - Why do they support training as a solution?

   To find the individuals responsible for that problem or need, begin at the top of the organizational structure and continue through the lower levels. Include the concerned individuals in every step of the process; they must assist in determining the needs and approve the analysis results.

5. Know your study subjects. To reduce the possibility of prescribing inappropriate training, analyze the performance level of your group. Do this by identifying discrepancy factors, the important differences between high and lower performers. Use this information in determining training program content and emphases. Enhance strong points discovered during the analysis.

6. Vary techniques for gathering data. Habitual use of a few approaches may trap you into inappropriate applications. Several kinds of independent performance studies are more likely to produce accurate needs assessments than one. For example, surveys may indicate a number of needs, but multiple group or one-on-one interviews may negate those findings.

7. Keep studies short. It is preferable to survey a small sample of high and low performers than to attempt an analysis of the entire workforce. Large-scale studies create unrealistic expectations of your work and high costs to the client. One good rule of thumb is that studies should be completed within 20 to 40 working days.

8. View front-end analysis costs as an investment in the future. Strong technical skills, effective assessment methods, accurate scoring, and a lucid, substantial final report are vital for successful analyses. Always schedule enough time to prepare a good presentation of your needs analysis results, even if you must stop the process before completing some additional data analyses. At the end, it is better to spend time and money on polishing rather than hastily constructing a presentation.

9. In reports and presentations, convey the right amount of information to the appropriate audience at the appropriate time. Reports are typically long and comprehensive, indicating results of surveys, questionnaires, and other methods for gathering data. They may also include explanations of methods and samples of data-gathering devices. Following are some groups that may be in your presentation audience:

- study subjects

- employees of the client organization

- funding agencies

- top and middle management

- professional colleagues

- other needs analysts.

10. In presentations, use a variety of strategies for presenting results. Some include:

Graphics. Illustrations, photographs, boxes, different typefaces, and white space are effective design elements and contribute to the appearance of all printed material. Slides, overheads, and videotapes are useful for large presentations.

Needs Analysis Planning Checklist

Unfortunately, many companies lose time, effort, and funds on unsuccessful needs studies, and all too often, their failures can be traced to poor planning. Sound decisions at the beginning guarantee a strong foundation throughout the analysis. Start making wise choices by thinking through the following issues:

☐ Who is being trained? What are their job functions? Are they from the same department or a variety of areas in the organization?

☐ What are their deficiencies? Why are they deficient?

☐ What are the objectives of the needs analysis?

☐ How will a needs analysis assist in solving problems and benefit the organization?

☐ What are the expected outcomes? Will they have a pervasive effect on many organizational levels (departmental, divisional, regional, and corporate)?

☐ Will assessment instruments (questionnaires, surveys, tests, and so forth), interviews, or a combination be most appropriate? Who will administer these, in-house personnel or external consultants?

☐ Will the analysis interrupt the work process? What effect will this have on the workforce and on productivity?

☐ Will there be a confidentiality policy for handling information? Will the individuals working with the information honor this policy?

Summaries. A separate sheet of research briefs or condensed sections of the text can be the most important information for fast, easy reading. These may be executive (introductory) or report (concluding) summaries, abstracts, or overview quotations.

Oral Reports. A short presentation of essential information should give the highlights of results, clarify questions concerning methods or findings, and encourage all concerned to act on the recommendations of the report with interest and commitment.

Data Collection Instruments

Instruments are tools such as questionnaires, tests, checklists, surveys, and scales that systematically gather data about individuals, groups, or entire organizations. In a needs analysis they indicate both weak and strong areas. Answer the following questions to determine your needs and then you can select the type(s) that best suits your needs, time constraints, and budget requirements from the below listed descriptions of the most commonly used instrument types.

- What are the stated goals or expectations of the personnel being studied? How do they relate to the organizational goals?

- What is the organizational climate?

- What are the backgrounds and educational profiles of the personnel being studied?

- Who will administer, score, and interpret results?

- Does the use of follow-up of instruments require special training? If so, is this training available?

- Is the scoring objective, or will it require special skills? (Objective scoring eliminates the need for such skills, and respondents more easily accept the results as accurate.)

- How complicated is the scoring? Complex scoring scales are costly and time consuming.

Instrument Formats

All instruments share certain characteristics. They can be easily and quickly administered, usually without special training; they can be administered in groups and do no disrupt the workplace; they can be scored quickly and accurately using computer software designed for data collection, and the results obtained are objective; so training departments do not need interpret them. Here is a listing of several instrument formats from which you can select to conduct your data collection.

■ *Likert Scale*

This is a linear scale used to rate statements and attitudes. Respondents receive a definition of the scale ranging from one to 10 with, for example, one indicating least important and 10 indicating most important.

■ *Semantic Differential*

In this format, participants rate two contrasting ideas or words that are separated by a graduated line, either numbered or unnumbered. They indicate frequency of behavior or depth of opinion by circling points on the line. An example measuring the value of new equipment would be:

VALUABLE – – – – – – – – – – – – – – – – USELESS
  1 2 3 4 5 6 7 8 9 10

■ *Alternate Response*

This is an inventory format that forces respondents to choose between two acceptable statements. The choices present a pattern of responses indicating tendencies toward particular behaviors or attitudes. This is the hardest type of instrument to construct because both statements must be plausible enough to present a difficult choice, but sufficiently different to distinguish two separate sets of beliefs and attitudes.

■ *Multiple-choice*

Also difficult to construct, this format consists of choosing one item or statement from several well-planned and well-written choices. Each choice must be logically consistent with all elements of the instrument. The results indicate a person's style, behavioral patterns, and attitudes. For example, with this format it is possible to identify and analyze styles of leadership, communication, training, problem solving, management, and sales.

■ *Open-ended*

This essay question format also may be difficult to construct. Questions must be objective, free of the questioner's biases, and clear enough for respondents to complete the questionnaires or surveys without a great deal of assistance. These questions are not limited to preselected responses.

■ *Completion*

This format presents well-designed completion questions that encourage participants to disclose opinions and perceptions about themselves, their jobs, careers, and other workers and managers. Some experts have found that completion helps to focus and stimulate respondents' thinking, more so than the open-ended format, because it forces them to use their own thoughts and language to complete or fill in the blanks.

Designing and Using Instruments

Before you begin your needs analysis, you must do considerable planning. Follow these suggestions to achieve optimum results:

Become familiar with instruments. Study the different formats and respond to a variety of instruments. Analyze for style, tone, word choice, and language patterns. How do the words stimulate thoughts and feelings?

Gather preliminary information for your instrument. Interviews, observations, reports, and print media will provide excellent background material. From these sources select key issues for your focus.

Choose the most important issues and arrange them in logical sequence. For example, assessing sales skills would require organizing ideas on communication, presentation, and negotiation.

Select an appropriate format. If this is your first effort, use an easy format such as the completion questionnaire or rating scale.

Write questionnaire items and statements clearly and logically. Write clear and simple instructions: "Read through the list of duties and indicate how often you perform these jobs by circling 'frequently,' 'occasionally,' 'infrequently,' or 'never.'" Do not ask wordy or combined questions such as, "Do you have sufficient time to keep up with production standards, or should you petition for weekend overtime and temporary outside assistance?" Separate these into two questions.

Provide spaces for comments next to or following each question.

Focus your questions to gather information and responses that are more specific than "yes" or "no." For example: "What training exercises are most useful to you on the job?" "What practice activities would improve the training program?"

Emphasize important distinctions to avoid misinterpretations of questions. For example, "What exercises are *not* helpful?" "Does the training program address both problems *and* workers' needs? "Are the statements true *or* false?"

Assign descriptions to numerical scales to help participants answer questions. For example: "In comparison to your old machinery, how helpful are the new computer terminals?"

1	2	3	4	5
not helpful	less helpful	no change	more helpful	very helpful

Carefully examine the instrument and items it is designed to measure; these should be clearly and logically related.

Administer the instrument at different times to the same participants under the same conditions to establish the tool's reliability. If the results are the same, the instrument is reliable.

Look for valid content. The instrument should measure the items as it promises.

Evaluate instruments based on whether they are appropriate for the study subjects: For example, is the instrument written in a clear jargon-free style? Are there any statements or questions in it that will cause negative reactions? How well known is this particular instrument? Will participants be familiar with the format? Too familiar?

Introduce participants to the instrument by pointing out that it is not an examination form but an assessment tool for determining training needs. The instruments help individuals assess department operations, managers' performance, and their own individual job performance.

Provide a simple scoring system. Complex systems may cause confusion and frustration. Systems that subtract points for unacceptable answers will be seriously questioned. Use *general* scores to call attention to tendencies or patterns. Precise computations and percentages are not meaningful in this context. Inform respondents that scores are general guidelines indicating patterns rather than final judgments.

De-emphasize the numbers. Groups must understand that the objective is to focus on behavior, attitude, and values. Provide precise scoring instructions if groups are more comfortable with numbers and "how much" qualifiers.

Periodically try different procedures. Get a feel for when precise or general scoring is most useful, depending on the background of the group, the training goals, and your own training standards.

Questionnaires

In this instrument, individuals respond to a printed question-and-answer format—such as surveys, polls, and checklists—by choosing from lists of prepared answers or writing in original responses. Questionnaires may solicit factual information ("How many overtime hours do you work per week?") or opinions ("How do you feel about working two shifts?").

Use questionnaires to accomplish the following goals:

- reach a large or geographically dispersed population in a limited period of time

- determine areas of inquiry that require further investigation through other assessment methods

- verify information gathered from other sources

Following are the advantages and disadvantages of using questionnaires:

Advantages

- Comparatively inexpensive to administer and easy to construct, questionnaires yield data that can be tabulated and reported without difficulty.

- Respondents may freely give confidential information without fear of reprisal.

- No special training is necessary to administer the questionnaire or tabulate results.

- Many standard questionnaires are available, eliminating development time and effort.

Disadvantages

- Since communication is one way, respondents may not properly interpret questions. Results may also be misinterpreted.

- The questionnaire may not get at causes of and solutions to problems. It may not ask the most effective questions, missing the point of the analysis.

- The development of effective and reliable instruments requires strong technical skills and may be costly.

- Low return rates and inappropriate responses hinder the accuracy of questionnaires.

Electronic Questionnaires

The increased use of email and intranets has opened new options for gathering information. The electronic questionnaire can be completed online, promising a quick turnaround of responses. The information can be submitted directly to a database, thereby reducing or eliminating data entry. There are, however, disadvantages to using electronic questionnaires. Your target population is limited to those who have access to email or the intranet, and therefore, your results may be biased. In addition, the investment of time and money necessary to purchase the necessary software and learn how to use it may be prohibitive.

Tips for Effective Questionnaires

When preparing and administering questionnaires, follow these tips for success:

1. Before developing the questionnaire, gather preliminary information. Interview a small sample of people to get a sense of the language and emphases that must be part of the questionnaire.

2. Determine the kind of results you expect from the questionnaire. Then identify the questions that will produce this information.

3. During development, clearly focus the questionnaire. Lengthy and broad questionnaires will be answered grudgingly and hastily, if at all. Developers should establish a reasonable amount of time for gathering necessary information.

4. When considering formats and questionnaire design, keep the following factors in mind: the background and job of the respondent, the kind of information that is required, the purpose for gathering the information, and its application.

5. Select the appropriate type of questionnaire based on the number of respondents. With large groups, use a checklist or alternate response questionnaire for simple processing and data comparison. Checklists are suitable for presenting data in quantified form.

6. Avoid using open-ended questionnaires with large groups. The responses are very difficult to quantify. Small groups benefit most from this format. Questionnaires provide them with substantial information worth the processing time and effort.

7. If you plan to use questionnaires on a regular basis, develop question files for the companies and jobs you will be assessing most often. The files will help you construct questionnaires to suit the particular requirements for each job, ascertain the effectiveness of the questions in prior situations, and adjust the questions according to current changes in the organization or department.

8. Give every assurance to respondents that the questionnaire is confidential. Besides verbal assurances, you can offer them the opportunity to use code numbers instead of their names on the questionnaires. Avoid asking for biographical data such as age, gender, or marital status. If this data is required, however, word the question in general terms. For example, a question about age would be:

    Indicate the age bracket to which you belong.

    (a) 18 to 35   (b) 35 to 50   (c) over 50

9. If responses are grievances and complaints, address these in a straightforward manner. Explain your plans to improve or alleviate problem situations and let respondents know that management recognizes and understands the problems, including those they may not have the power to solve.

10. Keep questionnaires simple and relevant to employees' performances. Do not use the questionnaire as an opportunity to gather information about other segments of the organization. This wastes time and creates doubts in respondents' minds about the stated purpose of the questionnaire.

11. Always use questionnaires in conjunction with a variety of other methods.

12. Do not regard questionnaire results as ends in themselves but as stimulation for additional discussion and analysis of problems. For example, during interviews solicit participants' opinions with questions based on the questionnaire results. Do participants agree with the findings? What are their reasons for agreeing or disagreeing?

13. Do not administer questionnaires to low literacy groups. A negative experience with this method will set the tone for your entire study. Choose instead interviews or observation—methods that do not involve reading or writing—or use questionnaires as outlines in structured interviews.

14. Be sure that respondents are able to supply the required answers before administering the questionnaire. For example, word processing assistants would not be able to offer an improved software design for their computer work. They could make useful recommendations for more efficient software options, but they should not be expected to have program design skills.

15. To determine if the data will be usable, test the questions by anticipating possible responses. Well-designed questions receive few unproductive responses, such as: "I can run this department better than my supervisor;" or "This new equipment keeps me from doing a better job—I suggest buying other machinery by a different manufacturer."

16. Always test the questionnaire. Ask a sample group or at least two individuals to comment on clarity and format. This feedback indicates which questions and instructions should be reworded or edited, reducing the possibility of misinterpretation. Questionnaires going to more than 200 people should be tested by 10 to 20 respondents, and the results subsequently analyzed. Easily misinterpreted or leading questions should be reworded as well as any questions that solicit strictly positive or negative responses.

17. When appropriate, share the results with respondents ether in a letter to them or by addressing them in small groups. Their valuable feedback on the quality of the data and the experience of analyzing and discussing the data establishes trust and confidence, essential qualities for additional successful activities. If you cannot share the results with participants, send a letter thanking them for their participation and telling them how you intend to use the information they contributed.

18. Investigate using a commercially prepared questionnaire for standard assessments.

Interviews

The interview is an active interchange, either in person or via telephone with one individual or a group. It may be a first step or the central means of gathering data in a needs analysis program. Interviews may be formal and highly structured, with prepared questions, or they may be casual and flexible, directed mainly by the interviewee and focused on topics that may evolve spontaneously during conversation. Suggested discussion topics include the following: problems on the job; ideas for improvement or solutions; the most and least liked parts of the job; working relationships with co-workers, managers, and staff; job achievements; personal goals; and interest in obtaining more knowledge and skills.

Use interviews to accomplish these goals:

- gather background data at the beginning of analysis or supplement and expand data from instruments and observations

- obtain input from those people who better express their views in person than on written surveys or questionnaires (this input can be used to construct more effective instruments)

- identify causes of problems and possible solutions by encouraging interviewees to reveal their feelings and opinions on these matters

- give participants pride of ownership in the analysis process by inviting them to provide the data for diagnosing training needs.

Following are the advantages and disadvantages of using interviews.

Advantages

- Interviews clarify expectations and assumptions about the process for both the analyst and the group being studied. They enable parties to become familiar with one anothers' language and jargon and help uncover root problems yet untreated.

- Interviews are good opportunities to build rapport. They demonstrate that decision makers value employees' opinions and empathize with staff. In open-ended and nondirective interviews, participants and interviewers can relax and be themselves.

- Interviewers receive additional information in the form of nonverbal messages. Interviewees' behaviors, their gestures, eye contact, and general reactions to questions are additional data or cues for the next questions.

- Good questioning techniques focus data and produce solid, manageable evidence. Interviewers use these techniques to probe ambiguous responses and unexpected leads.

Disadvantages

- Interview-generated data can be affected by the interviewer's biases. In some cases interviewers become too involved with clients' problems and turn the interviews into counseling sessions.

- It can be very difficult to organize and analyze the data results accurately, especially with unstructured interviews. Frequently, wide variation exists between clients self-assessed and actual performances.

- Unskilled interviewers sometimes make clients feel self-conscious. In such cases, interviewees will say whatever they think the interviewer wants to hear.

Tips for Conducting Effective Interviews

Interviews require thorough preparation. You must plan out in detail exactly what you want to accomplish during the interview and the steps you will take to accomplish those goals. Here are some tips for success:

1. Conduct interviews in private, comfortable environments, such as conference rooms, that are free of traffic and interruptions. Opt for a neutral space instead of a work site or supervisor's office where having a desk between you and the interviewee may be an obstacle.

2. Prepare for the interview by observing the department and gathering information. What are the specific problems and difficulties that are immediately apparent? How frequently do they occur?

3. Determine the number of interviews required for a successful study. If interviews are your only source of data, schedule more than the amount needed to develop questionnaires and surveys. Experts suggest conducting only four to six interviews when studying a homogeneous group. The first interviews may give you up to 98 percent of the necessary information.

4. Be well prepared with solid interviewing techniques and a plan for conducting the interview. Decide whether you want it to be structured or flexible and open ended.

5. Prepare participants and allay their anxieties by fully explaining the purpose of the interview and the process. Let them know that you have been asked by management to prepare a training program based on information derived from these interviews.

6. Set the climate for the interview and put interviewees at ease with general questions that can be easily answered by the interviewee, such as "What does your job entail? What do you like most about it?" Gradually incorporate more specific inquiries about problems, for example: "If you had the authority, what changes would you make in the organization?"

7. As interviewees enter the room, ask them if note-taking, audio- or videotaping during the interview will make them uncomfortable. If they do not feel self-conscious about recording, proceed carefully. If you tape the interview, use a counter so you can access salient information without running through the entire tape.

8. Keep questions broad based enough not to indicate how they should be answered. They should be short and to the point.

9. Create a good environment for understanding and communication. Strong listening skills help you gather detailed and accurate information.

10. Keep the interview focused and stay on course. To avoid having your interview change into a counseling session, maintain a friendly distance from clients' serious personal problems by suggesting they speak in detail with qualified professionals such as counselors, personnel specialists, advisers, or therapists.

11. Never make interviews mandatory. If participants feel threatened, the interview data will reflect their self-consciousness and half-hearted cooperation.

12. Conduct group interviews when *group* behavior determines job performance. Although individual interviews may give you the information you need, they may also signal an effort to break up the group, resulting in reduced morale and effectiveness.

13. Make necessary provisions for group interviews during *and* after work. If the workday must be interrupted for interviews, affecting workers with interdependent jobs, provide assistance such as rescheduling the extra workload or bringing in temporary help.

14. Clarify misunderstandings about interviews scheduled after work hours. Assumptions that administrators do not think the process warrants company time sharply reduce the validity of findings and data. Determine whether to compensate off-the-clock interviewees with pay or compensatory time.

15. Remember to get the entire, accurate story and all the facts. If an interviewee requests that information be kept off the record, accommodate that wish.

16. If appropriate, interview at least three other persons who can offer useful information about a participant in an individual needs assessment. Others, such as supervisors, subordinates, and customers, may provide valuable insights into the subject's behavior.

17. Never betray your clients' trust. Confidentiality is crucial for a successful analysis; it is also the basis of your credibility.

18. End the interview in a comfortable, straight-forward manner.

19. Analyze and summarize the data. Maintain objectivity; do not let your analysis be over-shadowed by your own theories.

20. Report the analysis of the data. Follow a confidential reporting procedure that is comfortable for each interviewee.

Observations

The needs analyst obtains data directly by observing behavior and interacting with the workforce (employees, managers, clients, and field representatives). Observation is a fundamental tool with both broad and highly specific applications. Use observation to accomplish the following objectives:

- obtain background information on topics such as group dynamics, the organization's culture, or the work climate

- supplement interviews and questionnaires

- validate information derived from interviews and questionnaires

- investigate possible communication problems; inefficient use of time, resources, and personnel; declining operational standards; ineffective procedures; and conflicts between management and staff

- identify positive or strong characteristics.

Following are the advantages and disadvantages of using observation as a data-collection tool.

Advantages

- Observation gives observers an idea of a typical workday.

- Observation is unobtrusive; it may be as unstructured as a walk down the hall or a casual chat with workers. It minimizes disruptions of the work process and activity.

- Observation provides direct contact with situations. It yields on-the-job reports and is, therefore, highly relevant and valid.

- Administrative costs may be low if the observation is casual and relatively unstructured.

Disadvantages

- It is difficult to record data and to observe large numbers of people when using this tool.

- Employees may feel that they are being scrutinized and consequently may alter their performance.

- When observation is restricted to the work setting, data may be limited.

- It can be time consuming. Many jobs are part of cyclical operations that take place on a weekly, monthly, or yearly basis. A great deal of time would be necessary to observe all of these operations.

Tips for Effective Observation

To get an overall sense of the organizational climate, you can observe the work environment and interact with personnel. Following are some suggestions for successfully using observation as an information-gathering tool:

1. Explain the purpose and process of the observation to all supervisors and subordinates. This will alleviate any fears about "spying."

2. Describe actions with narrative statements or checklists.

3. Stay close to activity but remain unobtrusive.

4. Check at various points during the process to make sure that you are gathering meaningful and accurate information. Cross-check for validity by consulting reports, records, and staff.

5. Avoid returning for additional observation. This is disruptive and nonproductive, particularly in plant or factory environments where the work routine varies only slightly from day to day.

6. Reduce false expectations and waste in training expenditures by using observation to distinguish those employees who are most likely to benefit from training.

7. Restrict activity to *watching* the workforce. In cases where individual coaching would improve and raise performance to company standards, ask supervisors to handle the coaching. This will let supervisors know you are not trying to usurp their responsibilities.

8. Assess reliability of the data. Two or more observers of the same operations should have coinciding ratings. Agreement among raters is the basis for determining the validity of the data.

9. Share the results of the observation with the group *before* this data becomes part of the needs analysis report.

Work Samples

This front-line information can be in the form of tangible work samples such as the manager's reports, a secretary's typing, a repairman's mending of equipment, or a computer programmer's new software design. Or, it can be less tangible, for example, a teacher's presentation of a lesson or a manager conducting a meeting. Work samples can also be advertising layouts, market analyses, training designs, or program proposals.

Use work samples to identify problem areas that may require further analysis. If a department's or individual's products are found unsatisfactory on a regular basis, then an investigation may be necessary. Work samples also may be used to supplement other assessment methods, to validate other data, and to gather preliminary information for the study.

Here are some of the advantages and disadvantages to using work samples for gathering data.

Advantages

- The method is unobtrusive.

- As is the case with records and reports, this method provides clues to trouble spots.

- It also provides direct data on the organization's actual work.

Disadvantages

- Using this method may be costly and time consuming. The wrong sample will provide little or no information.

- In order to use this data-gathering method, the trainer's skills must include specialized content analysis.

- Workers may alter their behavior if they know that some kind of observation is in progress.

Records and Reports

Company archives contain useful historical data in the form of the following: personnel, productivity, and financial records; government, planning, audit, budget, and program reports; policy handbooks; organizational structure charts; program evaluations; minutes of meetings; memorandums; documents explaining the organization's history; exit interviews; grievance files; quality control; career development information; and conference proceedings.

Use records and reports to accomplish the following goals:

- gather background information and acquire a general sense of the organization's culture and traditions

- verify information generated by other assessment methods

- understand how particular problems have influenced individuals and organizational competency.

Following are the advantages and disadvantages of using this method of information gathering:

Advantages

- It can indicate potential problem areas.

- This method is unobtrusive; researchers work on their own schedules without interrupting the workplace and routine.

- If stored, filed, and updated at the work site, these data can be collected easily, quickly, and inexpensively.

- This method has high validity, because the data is quantifiable, historical, and objective evidence.

Disadvantages

- Reports may be adjusted or "selectively edited."

- It may be difficult to obtain materials if access is restricted to authorized persons or if record-keeping procedures have changed over time.

- Documents are limited to a historical focus. This method requires skilled analysts to apply pertinent information to current problems.

- This method risks misinterpretation by unskilled analysts. Patterns and trends may be difficult to interpret from the data. Causes of problems and solutions may be unclear.

Tips for Using Records and Reports Effectively

In order to successfully employ this method of data gathering, do the following:

1. Find out what kinds of records and reports are kept in the company archives.

2. Decide whether these particular documents will give you the necessary information. For example, minutes from the monthly directors' planning meetings and studies of the turnover rate may not offer direct insight into the impact of the word processing training program.

3. Use reports such as turnover studies to indicate trouble spots. For example, if the turnover rate is higher than the average, a problem may exist requiring a needs analysis. Other kinds of documents, such as planning reports or career development materials, may directly identify training needs.

4. If the material is not immediately accessible, determine whether it is worth spending the time searching through files.

5. Use production records to find information about sales, customer complaints, back orders, and other production data.

6. In non-manufacturing companies, look for documents, such as strategic planning reports, explaining how the company is achieving its mission and objectives.

References & Resources

Articles

Brethower, Dale M. "Rapid Analysis: Matching Solutions to Changing Situations." *Performance Improvement,* November/December 1997, pp. 16-21.

Darraugh, Barbara. "It Takes Six." *Training & Development Journal,* March 1991, pp. 21-24.

Kaufmann, Roger. "Auditing Your Needs Assessment." *Training & Development,* February 1994, pp. 22-23.

Kaufmann, Roger. "A Needs Assessment Audit." *Performance & Instruction,* February 1994, pp. 14-16.

Kimmerling, George. "On Target: Needs Assessments and Organizational Goals." *Technical & Skills Training,* May/June 1992, pp. 26-30.

McClelland, Sam. "A Systems Approach to Needs Assessment." *Training & Development,* August 1992, pp. 51-53.

Moseley, James L., and Mary J. Heaney. "Needs Assessment Across Disciplines." *Performance Improvement Quarterly,* vol. 7, no. 1, 1994, pp. 60-79.

Rossett, Allison. "Have We Overcome Obstacles to Needs Assessment?" *Performance Improvement,* March 1997, pp. 30-35.

Sleezer, Catherine M. "Training Needs Assessment at Work: A Dynamic Process." *Human Resource Development Quarterly,* Fall 1993, pp. 247-264.

Watkins, Ryan, and Roger Kaufman. "An Update on Relating Needs Assessment and Needs Analysis." *Performance Improvement,* November/December 1996, pp. 10-13.

Zemke, Ron. "How to Do a Needs Assessment When You Think You Don't Have Time." *Training,* March 1998, pp. 38-44.

Books

ASTD Trainer's Toolkit: Needs Assessment Instruments. Alexandria, Virginia: ASTD, 1990.

Bartram, Sharon, and Brenda Gibson. *Training Needs Analysis: Resource for Identifying Training Needs, Selecting Training Strategies, and Developing Training Plans.* Aldershot, Hampshire, United Kingdom: Gower Publishing, 1994.

The Best of Needs Assessment. Alexandria, Virginia: ASTD, 1992.

Goldstein, Irwin L. *Training in Organizations: Needs Assessment, Development, and Evaluation. (3rd edition.)* Pacific Grove, California: Brooks/Cole Publishing, 1993.

Kaufman, Roger, et al. *Needs Assessment: A User's Guide.* Englewood Cliffs, New Jersey: Educational Technology Publications, 1993.

McClelland, Samuel B. *Organizational Needs Assessments: Design, Facilitation, and Analysis.* Westport, Connecticut: Quorum Books, 1995.

Phillips, Jack J., and Elwood F. Holton (eds.). *In Action: Conducting Needs Assessments.* Alexandria, Virginia: ASTD, 1995

Reay, David G. *Identifying Training Needs.* East Brunswick, New Jersey: NJ Nichols Publishing, 1994.

Robinson, Dana Gaines, and James C. Robinson. *Performance Consulting: Moving Behone Training.* San Francisco: Berrett-Kohler, 1995.

Swanson, Richard A. *Analysis for Improving Performance: Tools for Diagnosing Organizations and Documenting Workplace Expertise.* San Francisco: Berrett-Kohler, 1994.

Warfel, Sam L., and Robert L. Craig (eds.). *The ASTD Training and Development Handbook: A Guide to Human Resource Development.* New York: McGraw-Hill, 1996.

Wilcox, John (ed.). *ASTD Trainer's Toolkit: More Needs Assessment Instruments.* Alexandria, Virginia: ASTD, 1994.

Infolines

Austin, Mary. "Needs Assessment by Focus Group." No. 9401 (revised 1998).

Gupta, Kavita. "Conducting a Mini Needs Assessment." No. 9611.

Sparhawk, Sally, and Marian Schickling. "Strategic Needs Analysis." No. 9408.

Job Aid

Checklist For Designing Instruments

When designing a needs analysis, it is very important to select the instrument or combination of instruments that best support your analysis objectives as well as your respondents' objectives. Regardless of your choice, however, each type of item requires special consideration during the design phase. The checklist that follows will help you determine whether your items are well written and are likely to help you gather the data you need for your analysis.

Directions: Complete the checklist appropriate to each type of item included in your analysis. Note that "no" answers may indicate potential problems in item construction that may bias your results.

	Yes	No	Comments

Multiple-Choice Items
1. The central question or problem is stated in the stem of each item.
2. The response choices for each item are grammatically correct.
3. All the response choices within each item are approximately the same length.
4. There are no ambiguous statements in the stems or the choices.
5. All the choices for each item are feasible.
6. The items are written at the language level of the respondents.
7. The items are constructed so that clues cannot be obtained from other items.
8. The items are constructed to measure the level of knowledge, specific skills, or attitudes.

Completion Items
1. Only significant words, feelings, or attitudes are omitted in incomplete sentence items.
2. Each item is grammatically correct.
3. Any question asked is explicit enough to be easily understood by the respondent.

True-False Items
1. All statements are entirely true or entirely false.
2. No trivial details are included in any of the statements.
3. The statements are concise without more elaboration than is necessary to give clear meaning.
4. The statements avoid using specific determiners that signal the desired response.

Essay Items
1. The language in each item is precise and unambiguous.
2. All problems or tasks are clearly stated.
3. All special conditions are stated.
4. The items clarify any additional directions needed beyond the general set of directions.
5. No item may be answered with a simple "yes" or "no" response.
6. All items are written at the respondent's comprehension level.

Oral Items
1. The possible response could not be a simple "yes, I agree," or "no, I don't agree."
2. The response will not be embarrassing for the respondent to make.
3. Specific directions are planned that would be helpful to the respondent in structuring a response.
4. Wording of the oral question is at the respondent's level of comprehension.
5. Possible follow-up questions are planned.

Structured Interview Items
1. The items for the interview are in a logical sequence.
2. Each item is worded at the respondent's comprehension level.
3. A method of recording responses is specified.
4. Possible follow-up questions are planned.

Attitude Scales
1. All items are at the comprehension level of the respondent.
2. Directions are clearly stated and define or describe the ratings to be used.
3. Items are logically sequenced.
4. The scale includes at least three, but no more than seven, ratings for each statement or set of words or ideas.

■INFO LINE■

Data Collection for Needs Assessment

Issue 0704

Data Collection for Needs Assessment

AUTHOR

Deborah Davis Tobey
Vice President of Organization
Development, Comdata Corporation
Principal, Deb Tobey LLC
Email: dtobey@mindspring.com

Dr. Deborah Tobey has been in the human resources development field for more than 20 years. She owns a solo consulting practice and is vice president of organization development at Comdata Corporation in Brentwood, Tennessee.

Editor
Justin Brusino
jbrusino@astd.org

Copy Editor
Ann Bruen

Production Design
Kathleen Schaner

Collecting Data

A training needs assessment is the foundational process that ensures training is grounded in the needs of the organization. It identifies how training can help an organization reach its business and performance goals. Without a needs assessment, human resource development (HRD) professionals risk developing and delivering training that does not support organizational needs and provides no value to the organization.

A training needs assessment results in identification of both training and nontraining factors that affect achievement of business and performance goals. The training needs assessment also identifies training indicators such as learning objectives, learning activities, background, and content and defines the metrics used to determine the success of the training.

Thorough data collection is vital to the needs assessment process and helps HRD professionals avoid some common mistakes that affect training outcomes including

- *treating only presented problems:* assuming an organization is aware of all its needs

- *conducting improper data collection:* using too few collection tools, resulting in insufficient data or too many tools, leading to "analysis paralysis"

- *trying a quick fix:* over-responding to the client's stated needs without taking time to focus on potentially larger problems

- *applying the wrong fix:* delivering what the client wants rather than what the client needs

- *assuming one problem/one solution:* thinking a performance issue is the result of a single problem; there are nearly always multiple issues requiring multiple solutions

- *disregarding nontraining issues:* allowing clients to think that training is the only solution to performance problems; failing to address nontraining issues and close the performance or learning gap both undermines your credibility and limits your success.

Implementing a proper training needs assessment helps the organization see the value of the training function and its role as a business partner. By establishing a collaborative relationship with the client, a pattern of involvement and joint decision making is developed that can continue throughout the entire design, delivery, and evaluation of the training process.

This *Infoline* will focus on one piece of the needs assessment process: data collection. You will learn how to know your client, plan data collection, implement data collection, and report your findings.

Know Your Client

Clients can be a great resource throughout the needs assessment process. Who else knows their business better? It's important to get some information from your client before you begin your assessment. Have a conversation that addresses:

- business needs
- performance needs
- learning needs
- learner needs.

The goals of this conversation are to get an idea of the client's expectations and deadlines for the assessment, as well as what the client perceives to be the training problem. This also helps build a collaborative relationship with the client, which can be a valuable resource throughout the entire needs assessment process. The sidebar *Initial Client Discussion* has examples of successful questions.

Initial Client Discussion

Use this discussion to gauge your client's desires and expectations for the needs assessment. Keep these expectations in mind so that you can address them later if they are not met. Ask questions that consider needs at each stage of the assessment.

Needs Assessment Stage	Questions
Stage 1: Business Needs	• What current business needs or strategies are being affected or perhaps caused by the present problem? • What business problems exist? What is going on in the external environment that is related to this present problem? • What other data exists that may provide information regarding this business need? • What business strategy are you seeking to support with this requested training intervention? • What's happening in your business that shouldn't be happening? • What's not happening in your business that should be happening?
Stage 2: Performance Needs	• What results should employees achieve? What is their current level of achievement? • What should people be doing differently? • What should they stop/start/keep doing? • What does perfect performance look like? What does current performance look like? • What else might be getting in the way of employees performing as they should, other than lack of skills and knowledge? • What will be the nature of management support for job application and practice after training?
Stage 3: Learning Needs	• What knowledge and skills do you think the targeted employees need to learn to perform the way they should? • How important is each knowledge and skill that you have listed? • How well should they be performing the skills by the end of the training?
Stage 4: Learner Needs	• What are the targeted learners' backgrounds and experience in this subject matter? • What are their learning styles? • What is their job environment like (fast-paced, stressful, routine)? • What are the expectations regarding when and how they will attend the training (during work, after hours, paid, unpaid)?

Plan Data Collection

A substantial portion of training needs assessment encompasses gathering information from learners, their managers, and other sources. This information is used to identify skill-based learning objectives, develop relevant learning activities, and ensure that the training design and its delivery replicate the learners' jobs.

Thorough data collection is vital to the needs assessment process. Data collection

- augments and validates the client's perceived business needs

- links the business needs to the client's goals and the desired training intervention

- defines the business gap between the current needs and the desired goals

- identifies the gap between the current performance level and the desired performance level

- defines the gap between the current skills level to the desired skills level

- identifies learners' needs—the conditions that make the learning environment most conducive to learning for the specific audience.

Planning your data collection consists of four separate thought processes:

- choosing data collection questions

- identifying data sources

- understanding potential data collection methods

- selecting methods to implement.

It is important to keep these thought processes separate. Jumping to identify a method too quickly closes down your options. In particular, it is tempting to combine data collection sources and data collection methods. Choosing your data sources is an independent decision while choosing collection methods is influenced by external factors. When one of those decisions cannot be applied, the other three collapse with it. Whether you call it data collection tunnel vision, jumping to conclusions, or narrowing the process too soon, it's difficult to regroup and think about alternative methods.

Breaking down the choice of a data collection method into distinct thought processes results in a narrowing-down process that culminates in the selection of the best, most effective data collection methods. See the job aid *Data Collection Plan* for a useful tool to help organize your data and separate your thought processes.

Choose Data Collection Questions

Develop your data collection questions based on your initial client conversation. What do you want to know at these stages—business needs, performance needs, learning needs, and learner needs? Some of these questions will appear similar to the questions suggested earlier in your initial conversation. In the client conversation you are finding out what the client thinks in response to your questions, but here, you are gathering data to augment and validate the client's initial responses.

Identify Data Sources

Now that you have developed some data collection questions, a data source must be identified for each question. Remember, this decision is not yet about identifying the data collection *method,* for example a focus group; it is about identifying the data *source,* such as department managers. This can be a tough distinction to make. Think about it as *where* and *who* you are going to get your information from, not *how.*

Different data sources provide different types of data and have their own inherent advantages and disadvantages. See sidebar *Data Sources* to identify the sources best suited to your assessment.

Data Sources

This chart will help you compile a list of potential data sources. Use a variety of sources as each has its own advantages and disadvantages.

Data Source	Type of Data and Needs Assessment Stage	Advantages	Disadvantages
Extant data: annual reports, benchmarking studies, sales figures, complaints, HR data	Business needs information	Data has already been collected and is easy to obtain; you may need your client to provide an entrée to the data source	Data was not collected for your purpose; must extrapolate from the data to find indicators of the information you need.
Upper management/ client	Business needs information	Identify the priorities and goals of the business.	Access may be limited or even non-existent as you go higher in the organization.
Learners' managers	Desired performance / Current performance	Speak very clearly to the results learners are to achieve on the job and to expected on-the-job behaviors.	They may try to dictate what the learning should look like; must keep managers on track to address only performance.
Subject matter experts (internal or external, or resource materials)	Desired performance / Desired knowledge and skills	Give a clear picture of what performance looks like and what knowledge and skills it takes to get that performance.	Expertise may not translate into learning terms; needs assessor must be able to do that.
Extant data: job descriptions, aggregate performance evaluation data, 360-degree aggregate data	Current performance	Data has already been collected and is easy to obtain; you may need your client to provide an entrée to the data source.	Data was not collected for your purpose; must extrapolate from the data to find indicators of the information needed.

Data Source	Type of Data and Needs Assessment Stage	Advantages	Disadvantages
Customers	Desired performance Current performance	Give a clear picture of what customers want, which is a key performance driver, and a clear picture of what they are getting and their level of satisfaction.	Customer feedback is without organization context of performance expectations, logistics, and feasibility of doing what they want.
Learners	Current performance Learning needs Learner needs	Provide a great deal of information at multiple levels: what they do now, what they need to learn, how they need to learn.	Can be uncomfortable with giving certain information.
Other training professionals	Learning needs Learner needs	Other trainers who have trained the target group can give information about skill levels and what learners need to learn, as well as about techniques and activities that do or don't work.	Their feedback can be influenced by their own training methods or other biases.
Extant data: previous training evaluation information	Learning needs Learner needs	Gives information on learners' own perceptions regarding their learning needs and what works for them in the learning environment.	Depth of information depends on context of when learners filled out training evaluations; if it was in the last five minutes of a previous training course, the data won't have much meaning.
Star performers	Desired performance	These employees are the best source of information on what excellent performance looks like because they do it every day.	Performance may be so second nature that they can't identify components; needs assessor must do that.

Understand Data Collection Methods

You are now ready to consider potential data collection methods for your needs assessment. You need to know about the methods, how they are used, and their advantages and disadvantages. With that information in hand, you will be able to choose the optimal methods for your situation.

Training, performance, and human resource development professionals use many of these common data collection methods:

Extant data is existing, written information. It provides quick, reliable data, but because it was not collected for training purposes, it must be carefully analyzed.

Observation of trainees or jobholders is especially useful to determine skill deficiencies or to set performance standards. On the training side, observation may provide valuable data on average task completion time or the average utilization of training equipment.

Questionnaires are a popular way to collect data because they are inexpensive and the results are easy to tally. But it can be difficult to construct questions that give accurate data. The development of effective questionnaires is addressed below.

Interviews are used when the data is considered sensitive, when the data needs to be acquired quickly, or the purpose is to prove opinions or attitudes as opposed to quantifying opinions. Interviews also provide more detailed information than questionnaires. Guidelines for conducting an interview are addressed below.

■ *Tips for Constructing Questionnaires*
Questionnaires are best used to gather broad, quantitative, nonsensitive data. Use these tips when preparing your questionnaire:

- Be careful with descriptive adjectives and adverbs that have no agreed-upon meaning, such as "frequently," "occasionally," and "rarely." Different respondents will define these relative terms differently.

- *Italicize* or **bold** a word you want to emphasize.

- Beware of double negatives. A respondent must study these carefully to answer properly. (Example: "Are you opposed to not requiring students to take showers after gym classes?")

- Provide adequate alternatives. "Yes" or "No" responses to the question "Are you married?" do not allow for possibilities such as "widowed," "divorced," or "separated."

- Place scale points in negative-to-positive order, for example, "Strongly Disagree" through "Strongly Agree." This will overcome the "positive-response bias," that is, respondents' tendency to be more lenient in rating their true opinion.

- Avoid double-barreled questions, such as "Should trainees be placed in separate groups for instructional purposes and assigned to different classrooms?" These questions ask for two different pieces of information, and the respondent may be in favor of one part and opposed to the other.

- Avoid questions that assume knowledge or experience that the respondent may not have.

■ *Guidelines for Interviews*

Create a detailed outline for your interview using these guidelines:

● Write one or two simple and interesting "Yes" or "No" questions for the start of the interview to put the respondent at ease and gain interest; make the remaining questions open ended.

● Alternate tough and easy questions to give respondents necessary breaks from thinking so hard.

● Write a few different versions of key questions so you can ask them more than once (without irritating the respondent); this will ensure that you get full answers. Space out different versions of the same question.

● Cluster questions on like topics together.

● Do not put sensitive questions at the beginning of the interview. They are better asked after the respondent answers other questions and feels comfortable with you.

● Sequence questions from general to specific.

● Do not put important questions at the end of the interview. The respondent may become tired and may answer inaccurately; or the respondent may terminate the interview due to lack of time before you ask an important question.

● Put demographic questions at the end. They are easy to answer, and they flag the interview's finish.

Data collection methods are either qualitative or quantitative. Quantitative methods result in hard data. Hard data is objective and measurable, stated in terms of frequency, quality, proportion, or time. Qualitative measures yield soft data. These measures are more intangible, anecdotal, personal, and subjective, as in opinions, attitudes, assumptions, feelings, values, and desires. Qualitative data cannot be objectified, giving it a unique value. For example, knowing how job performers feel (qualitative measure) about a skill will be just as important in the ultimate training design as knowing how well (quantitative measure) they perform it. Use the sidebar *Data Collection Methods* as a guide to determine your best collection methods.

Select Methods to Implement

You should choose both quantitative and qualitative methods to ensure data sets complement one another. There are several factors to consider before selecting data collection methods:

Time needed

● How much time do you have available to conduct the data collection?

● How much time do employees have for data collection?

● How much time does each method take?

Data Collection Methods

This chart will help you compile a list of data collection methods. Use a variety of methods for the best results as each has its own advantages and disadvantages.

Method	Definition	Advantages	Disadvantages
Extant Data *Quantitative*	Provides existing data including records and reports; examples include job descriptions, annual reports, financial statements, staffing statistics, 360-degree feedback, turnover rates, absenteeism, customer complaints, training evaluation data, and so on.	• Examines trends and patterns in the data over time • Provides consistent measurements, giving reliable data • Does not involve individual employee confidentiality issues because data is used in aggregate form	• Usually collected for purposes other than training needs assessment, so training issues must be inferred from patterns in the data • No control over the methodology that was used to collect the data • Can be mixed in with data that is extraneous to your purpose so it must be "sifted"
Questionnaires *Quantitative and Qualitative*	Ask respondents a series of focused questions, can be administered in paper or electronic form.	• Inexpensive to create and administer • Results are easy to tally • Easy for respondents to participate • Give quick results • Provide both qualitative and quantitative data: soft data questions yield qualitative data; while the answer tally is quantitative	• Challenging to construct questions that get the desired data • Wording of the questions must mean the same thing to all respondents to be successful • Choosing an appropriate answer scale can be difficult • Respondents can skew the results by simply checking all one type of answer without really reading the questions • A large sample is needed for reliable data
Tests and Assessments *Quantitative*	Gauge what the respondents know, can do, or believe regarding the training need being investigated; types include, knowledge assessments, true/false, fill-in-the-blank, or essay questions.	• Objective • Specifically identify gap between current and desired performance, knowledge, and skills • Focus on finding specific performance gaps	• Don't always reveal the thought processes behind why a participant performed a certain way • Some participants can "freeze" and perform poorly due to test anxiety • Can be challenging to include both knowledge and skill assessments due to time constraints in the training

Method	Definition	Advantages	Disadvantages
Interviews *Qualitative*	Elicit reactions of the interviewee to carefully focused topics through one-on-one discussions; usually accompanied by note-taking or recording.	• Provide rich detail • Produce consistent data across interviews that can be compared to identify patterns and trends • Can be used to "flesh out" quantitative data collected in a survey	• Time-consuming for the volume of data gained • Interviewees must truly represent the targeted population or the data will be skewed • Frequency of responses does not get at the reason behind the responses • Interviewer must be careful to record, not interpret interviewee responses
Focus Groups *Qualitative*	Provide data through group interviews regarding job environment, current level of skill and performance, and perceptions of desired skill and performance level.	• Develop hypotheses that can be tested with a larger population through surveys or observation • The facilitator can make note of nonverbal behaviors that accompany statements • Skilled facilitation results in all focus group members being heard rather than just the more verbal participants	• Very time- and resource-intensive • Can fall under the influence of particularly verbal members and give a false impression of unanimity • Difficult to conduct with just one facilitator to run the group and make notes
Observation *Quantitative and Qualitative*	Examines and records the behaviors of job performers; advanced versions include time-and-motion studies and human factors studies.	• Excellent for assessing training needs for physical/psychomotor skills • Creates a step-by-step procedure that can be standardized for all learners in the form of a flowchart, diagram, graphic, list of steps, or a job aid • Identifies job environment conditions that help or hinder performance • Allows the observer to hypothesize nontraining issues in the job environment that are important • Can be augmented with a critical-incident interview to "observe" job performer's mental processes	• Difficult to identify where a specific task begins and ends • Misses the performer's mental processes in making choices at each step unless accompanied by a critical-incident interview • Some performers will act differently than normal because they know they are being watched. Interviewing the performer after observation can help control for this effect

Nontraining Issues

It is also the job of the needs assessor to address nontraining issues. These issues are not skill-related but do affect performance; some examples are lack of tools or resources, poor working environment, inappropriate rewards, and lack of motivation to use a desired skill.

When identifying findings, the training professional should ask, "What else is going on in the organization that, even if the training program is an unparalleled success, might prevent the attainment of performance and business goals?" There are several reasons for doing this:

- to address all factors affecting job performance; this comprehensive approach promises the highest likelihood that job performance goals will be achieved

- training has the best chance of succeeding when other contributing factors are also addressed

- to focus on the big picture of job performance, not just on meeting a training need.

If the business fails to address nontraining recommendations and performance goals are not met, training often becomes the scapegoat. It's important to be on record saying that other factors should have been addressed.

Costs

- How much will it cost to buy equipment, software, tools, and so on?

- Are there fees for services conducted?

- What travel expenses will be incurred?

Essentialness

- Could other data collection methods yield the same results?

- Is a specific data collection method the only one that can obtain a needed data set?

Availability

- What data sources are easily accessible?

- How open is access to sources?

- When is the organization's busiest time of the year?

Logistics

- Are sources located at multiple sites? How much travel is involved?

- Is there appropriate space in the organization to conduct each data collection method? Are private rooms available for interviews? Space to observe work without being obtrusive?

Skill Level

- How familiar are you with data collection methods being used?

Implement Data Collection

You are finally ready to collect your data. Here are some tips to help you execute the process efficiently and effectively.

- *Double-check.* Make a quick pass over your choices and your reasons for choosing each method. Don't be afraid to make last-minute adjustments. Be sure you have chosen methods that optimize your time and access to resources.

- *Create a plan.* Develop a calendar, timeline, or some other tool to help you stay on track and remind you of deadlines. Monitor your progress as you go along.

- *Be flexible.* One of the nice things about having a plan is that you'll know when to deviate from it. Accept the fact that things happen in organizational life that are out of your control, and prepare to adjust your data collection as needed. Implement the most essential methods first; if circumstances force you to cut the data-gathering process short, you will still have useful data.

- *Include your client.* It goes without saying that your client must approve your data collection plan. By sharing information gathered along the way, you encourage the client's interest in the process and the results. If you discover contradictory data items, the client can provide context and meaning.

- *Be objective.* Keep your own interpretations and experiences out of the data collection. Your data must be objective or analysis will not be accurate. It is tempting to augment data with your own views. For example, avoid interpreting for an interviewee by saying, "What you really mean is...." Instead try, "Tell me more."

- *Utilize extant data correctly.* Extant data is rarely collected for your purposes, so you must infer from that data and validate it. For example, if exit interviews indicate that employees are leaving because of a weak benefits package, this is important information. It may not necessarily be true, but many employees who have left *believe* that it's true. Check with other data sources, or address the problem in your recommendations.

- *Involve others.* If possible, use other people in some of the data collection to help control any bias you might have. Have others conduct some of the interviews or look at extant data. You can use co-workers from the training or human resources department, or a manager who has an interest in the project.

- *Share data.* Decide with your client how the data will be shared with the sources who cooperated with the collection process. Nothing bothers people more than being asked for their opinion and then hearing nothing about it. You and your client have the prerogative to decide what and how much data to share, but some kind of follow-up must happen or credibility can be damaged.

- *Review data.* Examine your data as it is gathered. If any unique or significant information appears, there will still be time to focus subsequent data collection on validating that information or gathering more of it.

- *Know when to stop.* There's no rule saying you must complete all the data collection methods in your plan. Stop when the data trends become clear. If the first 10 interviewees have said the same thing, the last five will probably do the same.

Presentation Tips

Don't make the mistake of thinking that your data can speak for itself or that the answers are so glaringly obvious that you don't need to point them out. These are the most influential factors in your presentation:

- a level of detail that matches the audience's expectations

- your ability to answer questions that arise

- organization of information in such a way as to build evidence, so that the answers logically present themselves to the audience

- your ability to link disparate points of information on the spot, making it obvious to the client that you truly understand the business issues and challenges

- your level of confidence.

Here are tips for preparing and delivering your presentation.

- *Know your audience.* Address the interests of all concerned in the presentation, and tailor your presentation media and style accordingly.

- *Separate findings from recommendations.* Clarify that findings and recommendations are two separate phases of the project. This fact should be reflected in the outline of the presentation, in handouts, and any other media. Follow through by addressing findings and recommendations separately during the presentation.

- *Allow silence.* Provide your client with enough time to digest and think about the information. Don't feel pressure to fill dead air; you may end up making the client feel rushed.

- *Structure your time.* Use no more than half of the allotted time to present findings. The most important part of the presentation is your recommendations.

- *Plan ahead.* Think about what could be cut from the presentation. If the client is unexpectedly called away or walks in and says, "I know we scheduled an hour, but I'll have to leave in 30 minutes," you'll have to be able to adjust.

Report Your Findings

After you analyze the data, you must present your findings and recommendations to your client. The goals of your presentation are to 1) persuade the client to approve the recommended training intervention, and 2) take ownership of the nontraining issues and recommendations. As you plan and deliver your presentation, these goals must be foremost in your mind. Present comments that draw the audience back to the goals of the presentation.

Behaving as if "this information is so interesting, and I am sure the trends and patterns are as obvious to you as to me" is more convincing to the client than behavior that communicates "I must convince you that this is correct." See sidebar *Presentation Tips* for more helpful information.

Presentation Steps

Use these steps to develop your presentation.

1. *Begin with a summary.* Share briefly the methods that were chosen and why, as well as any significant developments that occurred during the data collection.

2. *Present findings.* Ask for the client's opinion about key findings. The client may arrive at some of the recommendations during the discussion of the findings. Should this happen, the client's ownership of these recommendations is assured. Validate what the client has done right in working on this business need, and position your study as augmenting and supplementing the client's efforts. Present information that contradicts the client's initial problem or beliefs in a "Guess what I found?" mode, not a "You were wrong" mode.

3. *Transition to recommendations.* Make your transition obvious to all. Turn the page; change the slide; take a break; make a verbal transition: "Now that we have discussed the findings, I'd like to get into suggestions for what actions we can take based on this information."

4. *Identify recommendations.* Relate each recommendation directly to findings. In the case of nontraining recommendations, it will be the client's prerogative to determine what actions to take. If a client is unwilling to address a nontraining issue, it is crucial for you to obtain the client's acknowledgement that the issue exists.

5. *Be flexible.* Move more quickly or more slowly through information as needs require. Change media if needs dictate. Move from PowerPoint slides to a flipchart or whiteboard if the audience wants to generate ideas on the spot.

Have confidence in your abilities to expand the perception and role of the training professional in your organization. When a training program adds value, the training function is appreciated for its impact and results. A comprehensive data collection will ensure your training program adds significant value to the organization and considers all factors that affect performance.

References & Resources

Books

Barbazette, Jean. *Training Needs Assessment: Methods, Tools, and Techniques.* San Francisco: Pfeiffer, 2004.

Bartram, Sharon, and Brenda Gibson. *Training Needs Analysis Toolkit.* Amherst, MA: HRD Press, 2000.

Block, Peter. *Flawless Consulting,* 2nd ed. San Francisco: Pfeiffer, 2000.

Carliner, Saul. *Training Design Basics.* Alexandria, VA: ASTD Press, 2003.

Charney, Cyril, and Kathy Conway. *Trainer's Tool Kit.* New York: AMACOM, 1998.

Eitington, Julius E. *Winning Trainer: Winning Ways to Involve People in Learning,* 4th ed. Boston: Butterworth-Heinemann, 2001.

Gupta, Kavita. *Practical Guide to Needs Assessment.* San Francisco: Pfeiffer, 1999.

Justice, Tom, and David W. Jamieson. *Facilitator's Fieldbook.* New York: AMACOM, 1999.

Kinlaw, Dennis. *Facilitation Skills: The ASTD Trainer's Sourcebook.* New York: McGraw-Hill, 1996.

Kirkpatrick, Donald L. *Evaluating Training Programs: The Four Levels.* San Francisco: Berrett-Koehler, 1994.

Knowles, Malcolm S. *Adult Learner: A Neglected Species,* 4th ed. Houston: Gulf Publishing, 1990.

Knowles, Malcolm S., Elwood F. Holton, and Richard A. Swanson. *Adult Learner: The Definitive Classic in Adult Education and Human Resource Development,* 5th ed. Houston: Gulf Publishing, 1998.

Mager, Robert F. *Analyzing Performance Problems,* 3rd ed. Atlanta: Center for Effective Performance, 1997

———. *Making Instruction Work,* 2nd ed. Atlanta: Center for Effective Performance, 1997.

McClendon, McKee J. *Statistical Analysis in the Social Sciences.* Stamford, CT: Wadsworth Publishing Company.

Merriam, Sharan B., ed. *New Directions for Adult and Continuing Education.* San Francisco: Jossey-Bass, 2001.

Merriam, Sharan B., and Rosemary S. Cafarella. *Learning in Adulthood: A Comprehensive Guide.* San Francisco: Jossey-Bass, 1998.

Phillips, Jack J. *Handbook of Training Evaluation and Measurement Methods,* 3rd ed. Houston: Gulf Publishing Company.

———. *In Action: Measuring Return on Investment.* Alexandria, VA: ASTD Press, 1994.

Phillips, Jack J., and Elwood F. Holton, III. *In Action: Conducting Needs Assessment.* Alexandria, VA: ASTD, 1995.

Phillips, Lou. *Continuing Education Guide: The CEU and Other Professional Development Criteria,* 3rd ed. Dubuque, IA: Kendall-Hunt Publishing Company, 1994.

Pike, Bob. *Managing the Front-End of Training.* Minneapolis: Lakewood Books, 1994.

Piskurich, George M., ed. *HPI Essentials.* Alexandria, VA: ASTD Press, 2002.

Rossett, Allison. *Training Needs Assessment.* New York: Educational Technology Publishers, 1987.

Rummler, Geary A. *Serious Performance Consulting According to Rummler.* Alexandria, VA: ASTD Press, Silver Spring, MD: ISPI, 2004.

Rumsey, Timothy A. *Not Just Games: Strategic Uses of Experiential Learning to Drive Business Results.* Dubuque, IA: Kendall-Hunt, 1996.

Silberman, Mel., ed. *Consultant's Tool Kit.* New York: McGraw-Hill, 2001.

Sprinthall, Richard C. *Basic Statistical Analysis.* Boston: Allyn & Bacon, 2002.

Swanson, Richard A. *Analysis for Improving Performance.* San Francisco: Berrett-Koehler, 1996.

Swanson, Richard A., Ed Holton, and Elwood F. Holton. *Results? How to Assess Performance, Learning, and Perceptions in Organizations.* San Francisco: Berrett-Koehler, 1999.

Tobey, Deborah. *Needs Assessment Basics.* Alexandria, VA: ASTD Press, 2005.

Tracey, William R. *Designing Training and Development Systems,* 3rd ed. New York: AMACOM, 1992.

Vella, Jane. *Learning to Listen, Learning to Teach: The Power of Dialogue in Educating Adults.* San Francisco: Jossey-Bass, 2002.

Witkin, Belle Ruth, and James William Altschuld. *Planning and Conducting Needs Assessments: A Practical Guide.* Thousand Oaks, CA: Sage Publications, 1995.

Willmore, Joe. *Performance Basics.* Alexandria, VA: ASTD Press, 2004.

Zemke, Ron, and Thomas Kramlinger. *Figuring Things Out: A Trainer's Guide to Needs & Task Analysis.* Reading, MA: Addison-Wesley, 1982.

References & Resources

Infolines

ASTD Press. "Infoline Guide to Performance." No. 240101.

Conway, Malcolm. "How to Collect Data." No. 259008 (revised 1998).

Long, Lori. "Surveys from Start to Finish." No. 258612 (revised 1998).

Sparhawk, Sally, and Marion Schickling. "Strategic Needs Analysis." No. 259408.

Job Aid

Data Collection Plan

Get organized before you begin collecting data for your needs assessment. Use this chart to separate the four aspects of data collection and specifically address each need. When your plan is completed, you can transform column four into a proposal for your client requesting permission to implement the collection methods and obtain access to necessary individuals or data. Then use this plan as your roadmap for implementing your data collection. Later, it can serve as part of the outline for reporting your findings and recommendations.

Project: _____

Needs Assessment Stage	1. Questions to Be Answered	2. Data Sources	3. Potential Data Collection Methods	4. Selected Data Collection Methods
Stage 1: Business Needs				
Stage 2: Performance Needs				
Stage 3: Learning Needs				
Stage 4: Learner Needs				

The material appearing on this page is not covered by copyright and may be reproduced at will.

Evaluating Trainer Effectiveness

Issue 0103

AUTHORS

Mal Conway
IBM Learning Services
8 John Lenhardt Road
Trenton, NJ 08690-1812
Tel: 609.890.7772
Fax: 609.890.7762
Email: malcolmc@us.ibm.com

Michael F. Cassidy, PhD
Principal, Performance
Improvement Services &
Associate Professor,
Marymount University
2807 N. Glebe Road
Arlington, VA 22207
Tel: 703.450.9408
Email: cassidym1@aol.com
Web:
www.measurement-intl.com

Editor
Cat Sharpe Russo

Managing Editor
Stephanie Sussan

Production Design
Kathleen Schaner

Evaluating Trainer Effectiveness

Effective Training

While e-learning is on the rise, classroom training is far from being outdated. Our increasing use of technology for the various forms of e-learning, including satellite TV, web-based training, CD-ROMs, and intranet training, makes it very easy to overlook the continuing importance of instructor-led classroom training. James Sharpe, an IBM executive noted when recently announcing Mindspan, a new global initiative in e-learning, "We decided on a blended solution—incorporate classroom to motivate students through the process." Instructor-led training still is very much with us. When successful, instructor-led training can result in enhanced performance. When unsuccessful, not only is the investment of time, money, and opportunity lost, but the process can frustrate and demotivate trainees.

The challenge is to recruit, select, train, and develop trainers and instructors who possess the necessary subject matter content, adult education knowledge, motivation, self-direction, and presentation skills to facilitate learning. Meeting these objectives requires an understanding of teaching skills and competencies, and an expertise in measuring them in reliable and valid ways.

The relatively recent development of trainer certification programs described in this issue of *Infoline* is but one attempt to ensure that corporate and public sector trainers possess the necessary content and delivery skills and knowledge to effectively facilitate learning. But certification, per se, is not the complete answer to evaluating trainer effectiveness, nor is passing a certification examination an ironclad guarantee of instructional quality. It is not uncommon for instructors, who know their subject matter and can pass knowledge-based content examinations, to be uncomfortable, or even panicked, in front of a class, despite coaching and experience. The behavior goes well beyond the fear of public speaking.

This *Infoline* presents a generic model to evaluate the effectiveness of trainers. The issue will discuss everything from developing trainers' skills to evaluating their competencies and how to select the best trainers for your project. The job aid at the end of the issue will help you with this process by providing simple training evaluation forms.

Developing Performance Skills

A common solution to developing strong performance skills is to ensure that certification examinations include a performance component, such as submitting a videotaped lesson, in addition to the content component of the examination.

AT&T's Corporate Training Support Group captured the essence of its vision of a professional instructor by emphasizing the instructor's ability and commitment to accomplish the following:

- Examine personal strengths and weaknesses; work with colleagues to design self-development strategies; and follow through on those strategies.

- Reflect on one's own personality style and express enthusiasm.

- Understand the variety of learning styles and be flexible.

- Facilitate resolution of conflict through appropriate levels and methods of intervention.

Reflected in these objectives is a commitment to continuous improvement, grounded in data and self-reflection and achieved through specific plans executed collegially. The vision is noble, but it begs the question of *how* it should be achieved.

What, then, are the necessary skills and competencies of the professional trainer, and how can they be evaluated and developed? These are the fundamental questions this *Infoline* will address. Also this issue will:

- Differentiate skills and competencies and the value of defining them for instructors.

- Present a strategy for evaluating trainer effectiveness and give guidelines and tactics for implementing the strategy (for example, the major types of instruments for measuring trainer effectiveness).

- Discuss methods for selecting and recruiting instructors.

- Describe how to use evaluation data for the professional development of instructors.

Instructor Competencies

Before considering how to evaluate instructor competencies, it is helpful to look at what some experts have written about the nature of those competencies.

The construct of competence is often attributed to psychologist David McClelland, who published a paper in 1973 reviewing studies suggesting that traditional aptitude and content tests, as well as school grades and diplomas, did not predict job performance or later success in life. Some in the training community credit this paper with launching the competency movement. The paper spurred further research to identify competency variables, which could predict superior job performance. For McClelland, a competency is "an underlying char-acteristic of an individual that is casually related to effective and/or superior performance in a job or situation."

Competency models exist for a variety of professions, including instruction. Such models are useful in evaluating trainer effectiveness because they potentially aid the:

- appraisal of competence based not only on what employees contributed to the bottom line, but also on how they did it

- successful selection of trainers by fitting training candidates' competencies to the job requirements

- development of trainers' competencies through experiential education, motivation, social learning, and self-directed change.

ASTD Models for Excellence

An ASTD study produced a critical model for the training and development field. This model can be used as a standard of professional performance and development. The following list produced from that study denotes the 31 essential components of training and development. Competencies shown in italics are associated with the trainer role.

1. Adult Learning Understanding.

2. A/V Skill.

3. Career Development Knowledge.

4. Competency Identification Skill.

5. *Computer Competence.*

6. Cost-Benefit Analysis Skill.

7. Counseling Skill.

8. Data Reduction Skill.

9. Delegation Skill.

10. Facilities Skill.

11. *Feedback Skill.*

12. Futuring Skill.

13. *Group Process Skill.*

14. Industry Understanding.

15. Intellectual Versatility.

16. *Library Skills.*

17. Model Building Skill.

18. Negotiation Skill.

19. *Objectives Preparation Skill.*

20. Organization Behavior Understanding.

21. Organization Understanding.

22. Performance Observation Skills.

23. Personnel/HR Field Understanding.

24. *Presentation Skills.*

25. *Questioning Skill.*

26. Records Management Skill.

27. Relationship Versatility.

28. *Research Skills.*

29. Training and Development Field Understanding.

30. *Training and Development Techniques Understanding.*

31. Writing Skills.

Select Competency Models

Following are three competency models; the first two were developed by professional training organizations and the third by the National Highway Institute (NHI). Each is relevant to understanding what constitutes instructor competency.

■ *ASTD Models for Excellence*

This study produced a descriptive model for the training and development (T&D) field. It was developed to produce a detailed and updateable definition of excellence in a form that will be used as a standard of professional performance and development by organizations, institutions, training and development departments, and individuals in the training and development field. The study produced various products, including 15 T&D functions—such as needs analysts, group facilitator, evaluator, program designer, *not* job titles—and the T&D Competency Model, which is the core product of the study presenting behavioral anchors for 31 competencies most critical to T&D. (See the *ASTD Model for Excellence* chart on the previous page.)

■ *IBSTPI*

Founded as a not-for-profit board in 1984, the International Board of Standards for Training, Performance, and Instruction (IBSTPI) is a service organization for training and development practitioners, managers, educators, and vendors. To date, they have developed competencies for professional instructional/training designers, instructors, and competencies training managers, as well as supporting materials. The 14 core instructor competencies are shown in the IBSTPI chart to the right.

■ *NHI*

Responding to a perceived need to shift focus from trainers as disseminators of information to catalysts of learning, the Federal Highway Administration's training organization, the NHI, developed the following list of six competencies, drawn from the ASTD set of competencies written by Kopinski:

1. Positive behavior modeling.

2. Communication.

3. Classroom management.

4. Facilitation and trainer skills.

IBSTPI Core Competencies

The International Board of Standards for Training, Performance, and Instruction has developed their own competencies for professional trainers. The following lists IBSTPI's core instructor competencies.

1. Analyze course materials and learner information.

2. Ensure preparation of the instructional site.

3. Establish and maintain instructor credibility.

4. Manage the learning environment.

5. Demonstrate effective communication skills.

6. Demonstrate effective presentation skills.

7. Demonstrate effective questioning skills and techniques.

8. Respond appropriately to learners' needs for clarification or feedback.

9. Provide positive reinforcement and motivational incentives.

10. Use instructional methods appropriately.

11. Use media effectively.

12. Evaluate learner performance.

13. Evaluate delivery of instruction.

14. Report evaluation information.

---

5. Knowledge of adult learning theory.

6. Technical knowledge.

The ASTD and IBSTPI models demonstrate the similarity in the competencies they stress. The NHI list illustrates the importance of using lists of competencies as a point of departure. By adapting ASTD's list, NHI made it its own. This point is worth stressing. Any evaluation effort with a hope of success must be customized to reflect the priorities of its stakeholders and the environment within which it will be used.

The ASTD and IBSTPI models are similar not only in what they encompass, but in another regard as well, one that is potentially problematic: They are inherently abstract and, as such, are open to wide interpretation. To be practically useful, they need to be translated into operational or measurable terms. Much of what follows addresses this issue.

Evaluating Instructors

The variables that potentially influence a successful learning experience are numerous and include those related to the learner (motivation, preparedness, and so forth), the course design, the subject matter of the training, the environment, materials, and, of course, the trainer. This *Infoline* is limited to the trainer, but any training evaluation effort must consider *all* relevant variables.

While presented as a series of steps, the following strategy need not be followed in lockstep fashion. The strategy is, however, grounded in several important premises, widely supported by research, that should not be ignored. The following is strongly advocated:

Acknowledge instructors' competencies. These competencies are multidimensional. While relatively few general factors adequately evaluate an instructor, formative evaluation—aimed at helping the trainer diagnose areas of improvement—requires consideration of a large number of competencies.

Collect data from multiple sources. Trainees, for example, are an excellent source of perceptual data about pacing, enthusiasm, and the value of examples to make concepts real. They are often biased, however, by such factors as a trainer's personality and the difficulty of the subject matter. In addition, trainees are not a particularly good source for assessing a trainer's command of the subject matter. Consider collecting data from many sources: peers, trainees, trainees' management, the trainer's management.

Employ multiple methods. Don't rely on an end-of-course evaluation form alone. The complexity of what is being evaluated demands the use of multiple, integrated methods, such as observation, learner performance measures, and interviews.

Avoid the competitive mentality. While publicly stating that the purpose of the evaluation effort is to improve instructor performance, its real purpose in some situations is to prove that some instructors are better than others. Such unspoken agendas create unnecessary and unproductive competition within an organization.

Distinguish meaningful from meaningless. There are two points here. First, meaningful and useful evaluation data is collected at multiple points in time. Second, random variation is a part of life and will manifest itself in random ups and downs in data, including instructor performance data, tracked over time. Identifying meaningful variation requires statistically based techniques.

Tactics

There are six essential steps for evaluating instructors:

■ *Step 1: List the Purpose of the Evaluation*
What decisions might be made as a consequence of the evaluation data? For example, will the data be used to assist the instructor in identifying areas for improvement, for decisions related to compensation and retention, or both?

■ *Step 2: Identify Relevant Competencies*
As suggested earlier, a good place to begin is with competencies developed by professional organizations. A second source is the research literature on instructor performance. Use these as a foundation from which to develop the competencies important to your situation. Involve key stakeholders, including trainers, in choosing the competencies.

■ *Step 3: Translate into Meaningful Measures*
There are two options that, ideally, should be used in combination with one another. First are direct measures, that is, those that are quantifiable and specific to the competency. For example, a measure of a trainer's course management skills might be the number of times course materials arrive at the training site in time for the start of training. A second option is the use of indirect measures. These measures are inherently subjective. For example, asking trainees on a course evaluation sheet the extent to which they agree with a statement about perceived learning, is an indirect measure of actual learning.

■ *Step 4: Choose Data Collection Methods*

These methods could be in the form of rating sheets or observations. Also choose from whom the data will be collected, and with what frequency it will be collected. At this stage, it is also prudent to consider who will have access to the data, where it will be stored, and how it will be reported. In other words, deal with the effort as a system.

■ *Step 5: Implement the System as a Trial*

The purpose of this stage is to evaluate the tools, methods, and procedures you are using, not to evaluate the instructor. While beyond the scope of this *Infoline*, the reliability, validity, and sensitivity of the instruments used to collect data should be assessed and revised as needed.

■ *Step 6: Deploy the System*

Keep in mind that periodic evaluation of the evaluation system will be needed to ensure that it's doing what was intended.

Data Collection Methods

The following section describes some commonly used data collection methods for evaluating trainer effectiveness.

Rating Scales

Rating scales are a form of written questionnaire. Bona fide subject matter experts (SMEs) often use them to observe trainers. Training and development professionals commonly use them because they are easy to tabulate. However, developing effective questionnaires is part art and part science (see *Infolines* No. 8502, "Be a Better Needs Analyst," and No. 0001, "How to Measure Customer Satisfaction," for more information).

The following are critical success factors in developing effective questionnaires (that is, questionnaires that produce useful information and are technically sound from a measurement standpoint). Consistent with the strategy previously outlined, begin by defining what you wish to measure with the rating scale.

Instruments for Measuring Trainer Effectiveness

A variety of methods and sources exist for collecting data about trainer effectiveness. The *methods* include:

- rating forms
- interviews
- trainee learning.

The *sources* include:

- trainers
- trainees
- fellow trainers
- training management.

They are depicted in the table below, which also shows which methods are most appropriate for which sources.

Methods/Sources	Rating Forms	Interviews	Tests of Learning
Trainers	✔	✔	
Trainees	✔	✔	✔
Fellow trainers	✔	✔	
Training management	✔	✔	

You can do this in the following manner:

- Agree on an appropriate scale to use in measuring the competencies.

- Pilot-test the draft questionnaire before using it.

- Ensure that the questions are both reliable (consistently interpreted) and valid (measuring what they are intended to measure).

As widely recognized in the measurement literature, rating scale reliability depends on the type of question used. Global questions, such as the example below, are preferable to specific questions because they are more reliable. In addition, they permit the use of multivariate statistical techniques such as multiple regression, which is useful in identifying specific behaviors and attributes that explain or predict overall ratings.

Overall, I would rate the trainer as:

☐ *Very poor*
☐ *Moderately poor*
☐ *Neither poor nor good*
☐ *Moderately good*
☐ *Very good*

More specific questions, however, have the advantage of providing diagnostic feedback about what should be changed. For example:

How effective was the trainer in illustrating concepts with job-specific application examples?

☐ *Very ineffective*
☐ *Moderately ineffective*
☐ *Neither ineffective nor effective*
☐ *Moderately effective*
☐ *Very effective*

You should also note that if trainee ratings have sufficient validity you can use them in personnel/human resource (HR) decisions. Be wary, however. The recruitment and selection literature strongly emphasizes the importance of using statistically reliable and valid measures, both to contribute to sound decision making and to avoid legal complications. In other words, instructor rating should have demonstrably high criterion validity.

Interviews

While more expensive to implement than trainer rating forms, some training and development organizations use interviews. They conduct phone, in-person, or focus group interviews to evaluate trainer effectiveness. (Diaries kept by trainers, a form of self-interview, are less common.) You can have an interview format that is structured or relatively unstructured, and you can use the results

for personnel/HR decisions or for professional development. But you should be aware that interviewing requires special skills on the part of the interviewer to probe beyond superficial answers. Recent literature supports the superiority of a structured interview format over an unstructured one in making hiring decisions.

Because interviews yield qualitative (non-numerical) data, they require more effort to analyze and summarize the comments given by the interviewees. Interviews used for personnel/HR decisions should use a standardized set of questions, and you must fully document them. You should have SMEs review the written interview guide to determine if your questions measure what you intend them to measure. When used for professional development, the interview guide can be less structured.

Tests

Many trainers and training managers believe tests that gauge the learning that results from training are the best measures of the trainer's and program's effectiveness. We have all probably worked with trainers who were charismatic, but from whom we learned little. Learning, therefore, is a more defensible measure than just positive reaction to the training.

When used for personnel/HR decisions about trainers, tests need to be systematically developed, appropriate, and have documented validity and reliability. This requires that the training manager or lead trainer have a background in measurement or access to this expertise internally or externally.

Training Evaluation Sources

Another evaluation method uses four sources in measuring and evaluating trainer effectiveness: trainers, trainees, fellow trainers, and training management. This process is analogous to the concept of 360-degree feedback, in that it uses performance feedback from all sources who have experience with the performer and can comment on his or her competency.

As noted earlier, however, you must observe some cautions when using each of the sources, as well as follow some of the following check items:

☐ Preserve the confidentiality of the data.

☐ State how the data will be used.

☐ Document the evaluation.

☐ Make sure to name the data source.

When using *trainers* as a data source to self-assess their competency:

☐ Make sure you provide an environment in which the trainer is comfortable assessing his or her own competency. When used for professional development, this assessment usually is easier than when used for personnel/HR decisions.

☐ Stress that you will be using multiple data sources to get a more complete picture.

When using *trainees* as a data source to evaluate trainers:

☐ Make sure that you indicate the input will be used for personnel/HR decisions.

☐ If the training program lasts beyond a week, and you are interested in collecting formative, diagnostic data, make sure that you sample trainee opinions throughout the training. This will provide a more realistic picture and more valid data than if you were to measure only at the end of a training program.

☐ Make sure that at least 75 percent of the trainees, preferably more, complete the instrument.

☐ As Larry Braskamp also noted in his book, *Evaluating Teaching Effectiveness: A Practitioner's Guide,* when comparing one trainer with another make sure you understand and take into account factors out of the control of the trainer (for example, new content being taught for the first time).

When using *fellow trainers* as a data source:

☐ Make sure you establish an open atmosphere for the feedback.

☐ Preserve confidentiality.

☐ Probe to make sure that the evaluating trainer and the evaluated trainer have a professional relationship and that there are no known factors that could bias the feedback.

When using *training management* as a data source:

☐ In addition to following the guidelines for using fellow trainers as data sources, make sure you determine the degree to which the training manager has the experience to accurately evaluate the trainer. Sometimes, those in training management positions have strengths in the content/subject matter and not in delivery competencies.

☐ Make sure you clearly indicate if you plan to use the data for personnel/HR decisions or professional development.

☐ Probe for normative data, that is, ask the manager to think not only about the individual trainer, but also about other trainers whom he or she has managed or dealt with to provide a comparison point.

Using Data for Development

Many large organizations, such as AT&T, Xerox, and federal agencies have instituted training as a formal career path or profession. In this case, instructors "on assignment" for a few years often choose to stay in training and advance through various career levels available to them in both the design and development and the delivery of training. For example, IBM trainers can progress through various job roles with increasing responsibility.

Trainer Certification

Trainer certification is becoming an increasingly common selection/promotion criterion for some training positions. Two main certification routes exist for trainers:

1. Individual vendors who certify trainers to teach their programs.

2. Programs such as the Certified Technical Trainer (CTT) and Certified Professional

Development Trainer (CPDT) that are cross-industry certifications of instructor skills based on the IBSTPI standards.

Vendors like Langevin Learning Services, Wilson Learning, and Creative Training Techniques are among those who offer such programs. (In information technology [IT] there are various tests administered by vendors like Oracle, IBM, Microsoft, and Novell that assess content knowledge.)

Vendor certification processes are fairly straightforward. After reviewing the program materials, the prospective trainer usually performs the following three steps:

1. Observes the program as taught by an experienced trainer.

2. Teaches a unit or co-teaches the entire program.

3. Teaches the specific program with feedback from the experienced instructor.

CTT is intended for instructors who deal with technical subjects, while CPDT is for trainers who teach interpersonal, or so-called soft skills. They are offered through groups such as Chauncey Group International, Ltd., a subsidiary of the Educational Testing Service. Each test consists of a computer-based multiple-choice test and a performance test given in the form of a 20-minute videotape of the trainer instructing a class of at least five students.

IBM is a company that has fully embraced certification. The company requires both staff and contract instructors to earn the CTT certification, as well as content certification in their subject matter area. IT professionals must earn both vendor and internal certification.

Not all training and development professionals view trainer certification positively. An example is William Coscarelli, professor at Southern Illinois University, who participated in an effort by the International Society for Performance Improvement to analyze the need for an instructional-design certification. In Chris Lee's article, "Certified to Train," Coscarelli said, "I don't see these [certifications as] a response to any huge demand in the field for this kind of credential."

Mentoring

Mentoring is a very effective method for improving trainer skills. However, our experience has been that mentors should be identified by the protégé and not pre-assigned. This provides a better match between relevant experience and the protégé's development needs. A structured partnership approach to mentoring, wherein goals and success measures are agreed to by both parties, is suggested. Under ideal circumstances, evaluation data provides diagnostic information that facilitates the substance of the mentoring process. (See *Infoline* No. 0004, "Mentoring.")

According to a recent article by Chip Bell in *Training & Development*, mentoring from a partnership perspective entails four stages:

1. Level the learning field.

2. Foster acceptance and safety.

3. Give learning gifts.

4. Bolster self-direction and independence.

The first two stages are aimed at creating a readiness for the main event: gifting. The final stage is all about weaning a protégé from any dependence on his or her mentor.

Level the Learning Field

The first challenge a mentor faces is to help a protégé experience the relationship as a true partnership. It requires removing the mask of supremacy and creating kinship. The tone created in the first meeting can determine whether the relationship will be fruitful or fraught with fear and anxiety.

Some mentors give a gift (in the broadest meaning) to signal a level field, such as, "How about a cup of coffee?" But think how much more powerful is a statement such as, "Here's an article I thought you'd find useful." That signals an equal, helping relationship.

Foster Acceptance and Safety

Great mentors don't speak as if they're testing a protégé, being judgmental, or acting as a parent. Great mentors show their acceptance through attentive, dramatic listening. When listening is their goal, they make it the priority; they don't let anything distract.

Protégés feel a mentoring relationship is safe when the mentor is receptive and validates their feelings. The goal is empathetic identification. An "I am the same as you" attitude promotes the kinship and closeness vital to trust.

Give Learning Gifts

Leveling the learning field and fostering acceptance are the stages that lay the groundwork for the main event: giving the learning gifts of advice and feedback. Great mentors give many gifts, such as support, focus, and courage.

Resistance and even resentment from protégés to advice and feedback can hinder the teaching of lessons that stay taught. Frame your advice giving by letting a protégé know the intent of your mentoring. In addition, make certain the protégé is as eager to learn and improve as you are to see him or her learn and improve. Ask permission to give advice. That's the most important step. Your goal is twofold: 1) to communicate advice without eliciting resistance; and 2) to retain ownership of the challenge in giving advice and feedback.

Bolster Independence

All mentoring relationships must come to an end. How do we manage *farewell* with a focus on *well*?

Effective mentoring relationships are rich, engaging, and intimate. As such, ending them isn't without emotion. No matter how hard we try, there's a bittersweet aspect. A healthy mentoring relationship involves separation as a tool for growth. An effective adjournment of a mentoring relationship paves the way for the successful inauguration of the next mentoring relationship.

Creating Development Programs

Instructors will perform with excellence if they are developed to perform with excellence, according to Bob Powers' book, *Instructor Excellence: Mastering the Delivery of Training*. While a great deal of variation exists in professional development programs, in addition to mentoring and certification, consider the following elements in designing and deploying an effective professional development program:

Training evaluation data from written rating forms in the absence of other feedback is of limited usefulness. Gather data using various methods and then analyze the trends in the data for commonality.

Collect training evaluation data over time so as to form a motion picture, rather than just a snapshot. This is critical in determining the baseline skills of the trainer.

Document training development in a written plan with appropriate formal and informal developmental activities identified (articles, books, websites, trainer networking, observing exemplary trainers); regularly scheduled feedback sessions; and progress assessment on an ongoing basis.

The effective trainer is a change agent. Training is but one means of enabling superior performance. As W. Edwards Deming, quality guru and one of the major thinkers behind continuous improvement, pointed out, about 6 percent of the variation in human performance is due to the individual, while the remaining 94 percent is due to the organization and its processes. Therefore, how instructors perform in the class and the impact they will have on their trainees is largely a function of what the trainee will be able to do when he or she returns to the job.

To the extent possible, the trainer should consider ways in which the transfer of newly acquired knowledge and skill to the job can be facilitated. Specific methods include developing learning contracts between the employee and manager before the training; developing action plans to follow up the training; and conducting a force-field analysis of the factors that will facilitate and hinder applying skills on the job and then addressing the hindering factors and incorporating the solutions (see *Infoline* No. 8812, "Principles of Organization Development," for further information on this subject).

Actions to Begin to Improve Your Craft

On a scale of 1 to 10, with 10 being the highest, rate your credibility with learners in the classroom.

Not Credible	→	Somewhat Credible	→	Very Credible

1   **2**   **3**   **4**   **5**   **6**   **7**   **8**   **9**   **10**

1. If you scored 7 or below, begin to think about what you need to change to alter the learners' perceptions of your credibility. What immediate actions can you take to begin this process?

☐ *Action* _____
☐ *Action* _____
☐ *Action* _____

2. What do you do to put the learners' needs first? How effective are you in doing this? What actions can you take to ensure that the learners' needs are paramount?

☐ *Action* _____
☐ *Action* _____
☐ *Action* _____

3. What do you do to prepare for each program you conduct? What areas do you need to focus more on in your preparation? What immediate actions can you take to start this process?

☐ *Action* _____
☐ *Action* _____
☐ *Action* _____

4. How do you define respect in the classroom? What do you do to ensure that mutual respect is always present? What actions can you take to start this process?

☐ *Action* _____
☐ *Action* _____
☐ *Action* _____

5. What makes training and learning fun and enjoyable for you? Are these things compatible with being learner-centered? What do you try to incorporate into your programs to ensure an enjoyable atmosphere for everyone? What immediate actions can you take to start this process?

☐ *Action* _____
☐ *Action* _____
☐ *Action* _____

Used with permission from *The Credible Trainer*, by Robert J. Rosania. © ASTD 2000.

Training managers have a key role and shared responsibility with the trainer in the trainer development process. As noted above, some managers may have a content background and not a training background. Therefore, if necessary, managers also must be trained in the non-content aspects of training, including design, delivery, administration, and professional development.

Trainers only can be as effective as the content they are instructing. In addition to knowing how to design training, trainers' input should be an integral part of the instructional improvement process. Trainers can make invaluable suggestions about both the training content and the process.

Improving Trainers' Credibility

As Robert J. Rosania notes in his book, *The Credible Trainer*, successful trainers incorporate both the physical aspects of training—knowledge, training skills, and techniques—and the emotional aspects—how trainers approach their job and their students. Traditionally, trainers have focused their efforts on the physical parts of training. Unfortunately, that only encompasses 50 percent of what it takes to be an effective trainer. While skills and techniques are essential elements, overemphasis on that portion of training could have an adverse effect. What a trainer needs is to be honest and respectful of his or her students and to always be prepared. Enthusiasm for the subject matter also has been a positive impact on trainees' evaluations. In one study conducted at AT&T for example, enthusiasm was demonstrated to be a key dimension of instructor presentation skills, and, in turn, overall satisfaction with the instructor.

Honesty Is Key

A trainers' credibility is constantly tested by the learners. To gain their trust, trainers must start with a self-evaluation. This means they must reconcile any differences they may have with the material they are about to present. Rosania emphasizes that if trainers feel strongly about a specific part of the lesson, they should try to persuade and educate those with authority to make changes. This allows for an open and honest delivery of the lesson.

Be Prepared

How trainers prepare their program also affects how the learner views his or her credibility. Rosania notes that it is important that the trainer prepare for not only the expected, but also the unexpected. The trainer should think of questions, situations, issues, and problems that may come up during the program.

Show Respect

Credible trainers understand the value of establishing an environment of mutual respect. Rosania suggests one way to create this atmosphere is to greet each individual as he or she enters the room, shake hands, and offer a personal greeting. Be cautious, though; this credibility can quickly deteriorate if the trainer is not paying attention to the changing environment within the room. Therefore, it is important that a trainer quickly deal with situations that demonstrate a lack of respect for others. These situations include carrying on side conversations, interrupting class discussions, or returning late from breaks.

Make Learning Fun

Learners will retain more information in an enjoyable atmosphere. Rosania cautions that this is challenging to do while still keeping your credibility. The key is always to be yourself, develop an individual yet audience-centered style, and take your role as a trainer seriously, while not taking yourself too seriously.

The sidebar found on the previous page titled *Actions to Begin to Improve Your Craft* can help you focus on both the mental and emotional aspects of training and suggest ways to improve your training skills.

Recruiting and Selecting Instructors

A variety of sources exist for the training manager or project manager to identify, recruit, and select qualified candidates for instructional positions. Your own organization is a good starting point. This is particularly true if you have a specific career path for professional instructors, and instruction is viewed by management as a positive career path. Instructors need not progress into higher positions; many choose to remain as instructors and become exemplary performers in this role. This is an important development principle, a topic that we will discuss later in this *Infoline*.

Some organizations prefer to rotate trainers through training positions for a few years and then have them move back to non-training positions to refresh their subject matter expertise.

In addition to in-house resources, some other helpful resources to use to recruit and select trainers are as follows:

■ *ASTD, ISPI, and SHRM*

Professional associations like ASTD, the International Society for Performance Improvement (ISPI), and the Society for Human Resource Management (SHRM) are a good resource. Websites for these organizations are in the references and resources section at the end of this *Infoline*. These and other associations often have job-hunting services where interested employers can place training position vacancy announcements.

■ *Universities*

Many universities have formal education degree programs. A growing trend is the establishment of undergraduate and graduate-level degree programs in training and development. Marymount University, in the Washington D.C. area, for example, has developed an integrated Human Performance Systems (HPS) program to develop skills and competencies related to performance analysis, instructional design, facilitation, and evaluation. Check either the Peterson's or Riley Guides to determine which institutions offer degree programs in education or education and training; then contact the institution directly to obtain information about how to identify possible employment candidates who have completed their programs.

Assessing Candidates

Because selecting trainers involves many factors and the process for selecting trainers should conform to the legal guidelines for selecting any employee, you should follow a systematic process that focuses on the factors most important for your situation. For example, if your instructors are going to be delivering training via distance education, then it is important to include specific skills in using this technology among the criteria you assess.

Several major factors are important in selecting instructors:

Content knowledge. This consists of the instructor's subject matter expertise. You can assess it in various ways. One is via a review of the educational background and job history contained on the résumé. You also can verify this information via transcripts and by talking with the candidate's references.

Instructional experience. You also can assess subject matter knowledge from observation, if feasible, or from video or audiotapes supplied by the candidate. Having a candidate provide tapes as part of his or her portfolio has become increasingly common in training and is a useful way of confirming content skills covered on the résumé and in the interview.

Delivery skills. Platform skills are the communications skills possessed by the candidate. Examples are speech volume, clarity, conciseness, and pace. You can best assess these skills via direct observation or by audio or videotapes.

It is essential to specify the relative importance of the rating criteria before assessing the candidate. The following steps are useful for this purpose:

1. Determine job-rating criteria, and define them specifically.

2. Assign relative weights to each criterion.

3. Validate the weights with current instructors (SMEs).

4. Develop a standard process for assessing the candidates using a criterion rating form and subjective impressions from interview notes.

5. Make sure the process is consistent with your company's HR policies by having it reviewed by a representative from your HR department.

6. Orient the interviewers to the structure, content, and use of the forms.

7. Collect the data.

8. Review the data and rank order the candidates.

9. Select the candidate who fits best.

10. Document the process and offer the position.

Big Payoff for Your Business

Evaluation is an inherently complex endeavor, more so when the question is not *what* is being evaluated, but *who* is being evaluated. This *Infoline* has argued for the importance of evaluating trainer effectiveness, presented competency models, and described tactics for using those competencies in a systematic and systemic evaluation plan. If it's worth evaluating trainer effectiveness, it's worth doing it well. The potential consequences of doing it poorly should be measured not only in money and time, but in the human impact as well.

References & Resources

Articles

Bell, Chip R. "The Mentor As Partner." *Training & Development*, February 2000, pp. 52-56.

Cashin, W. "Student Ratings of Teaching: The Research Revisited." Center for Faculty Evaluation and Development, Idea Paper No. 32, 1995.

Cassidy, Michael F., et al. "Identifying Expectations for Service Quality in Training and Education Through Process Needs Assessment." *Performance Improvement Quarterly*, vol. 6, no. 2 (1993), pp. 3-16.

Foxon, Marguerite. "Evaluation of Training and Development Programs: A Review of the Literature." *Australian Journal of Educational Technology*, vol. 5, no. 2 (1989).

Holmes, Todd. "Developing Effective Training Programs." *The Armed Forces Comptroller*, Fall 1999.

Joly, Robert J., et al. "Evaluation of Teaching in the Department of Horticulture and Landscape Architecture." Report of the Purdue University HLA Teaching Evaluation Committee, March 1999.

Lee, Chris. "Certified to Train." *Training*, September 1998, pp. 32-40.

Kopinski, M. "NIH's Instructor Certification Program." *Public Roads*, July/August 1999.

McClelland, David C. "Testing for Competence Rather than for Intelligence." *American Psychologist*, vol. 28, pp. 1-14.

Trepper, Charles. "Evaluating Vendors and Courseware." *Informationweek*, June 14, 1999.

Books

Braskamp, Larry A., et al. *Evaluating Teaching Effectiveness: A Practitioner's Guide.* Newbury Park, CA: Sage, 1984.

Dixon, Nancy M. *Evaluation: A Tool for Improving HRD Quality.* San Diego: University Associates, 1990.

International Board of Standards for Training, Performance, and Instruction. *Instructor Competencies: The Standards.* Evergreen, CO: IBSTPI, 1988.

Kossek, E., and R. Block. *Managing Human Resources in the 21st Century.* Cincinnati: South-Western College Publishing, 1999.

May, Leslie S., et al., eds. *Evaluating Business and Industry Training.* Boston: Kluwer, 1987.

McLagan, Patricia A., ed. *Models for Excellence: The Conclusions and Recommendations of the ASTD Training and Development Competency Study.* Alexandria, VA: ASTD, 1983.

Powers, Bob. *Instructor Excellence: Mastering the Delivery of Training.* San Francisco: Jossey-Bass, 1992.

Rae, Leslie. *How to Measure Training Effectiveness.* New York: Nichols, 1986.

Rosania, Robert J. *The Credible Trainer.* Alexandria, VA: ASTD, 2000.

Spencer, Lyle M., and Signe Spencer. *Competence at Work: Models for Superior Performance.* New York: John Wiley & Sons, 1993.

Infolines

Callahan, Madelyn R., ed. "Be a Better Needs Analyst." No. 8502 (revised 1998).

Conway, Malcolm J., and Michael F. Cassidy. "How to Measure Customer Satisfaction." No. 0001.

Kaye, Beverly, and Devon Scheef. "Mentoring." No 0004.

Internet Sites

ASTD:
http://www.astd.org

Chauncey Group:
http://www.chauncey.com

International Society for Performance Improvement:
http://www.ispi.org

Peterson's Guides:
http://www.petersons.com

The Riley Guide:
http://www.rileyguide.com

Society for Human Resource Management:
http://www.shrm.org

Training Evaluations

Here are examples of a selection criterion rating form and a form for summarizing the impressions of the candidate captured during the interview.

Trainer Selection Criterion Rating Form: The first column represents the job rating criteria. The second column represents consensus on the weighting of the importance of each. The last row labeled "weighted average" represents the weight of each criterion multiplied by the rating given by the interviewer, averaged for each candidate.

TRAINER SELECTION CRITERION RATING FORM

Criterion	Weight (1-5)	Candidate A	Candidate B	Candidate C	Candidate D
Training experience—depth	3	5(15)	3(9)	4(12)	3(9)
Training experience—breadth	5	5(25)	3(15)	3(15)	3(15)
Fit with training team	5	5(25)	3(15)	2(10)	4(20)
Industry experience	4	1(4)	4(16)	1(4)	4(16)
Influencing skills	4	3(12)	3(12)	4(16)	3(12)
Flexibility	5	4(20)	3(12)	3(15)	4(20)
Self-motivation	4	3(12)	3(12)	4(16)	4(16)
Growth potential	4	4(16)	2(8)	3(12)	5(20)
Facilitation skills	5	5(25)	3(15)	3(15)	3(15)
Training content knowledge	3	2(6)	2(6)	4(12)	2(15)
Weighted Average		**4.32**	**4.24**	**4.10**	**4.25**

Trainer Interview Notes Summary Form: Impressions of the major strengths and growth areas for each candidate are captured on this form via handwritten notes taken with the candidate's consent during the interview.

TRAINER INTERVIEW NOTES SUMMARY FORM

Candidate	Strengths	Growth Areas/Issues
Candidate A	People orientation Pleasantly assertive HR generalist Developed training material Taught extensively Facilitation skills Broad training experience Writing/editing/media experience Some evaluation work with ASTD chapter Managed the interview well Asked insightful questions Interview lasted longest of four candidates due to her incisive questions	More front-end and back-end training experience needed Plan to complete graduate degree in instructional design

(continued on next page)

 INFO LINE

Job Aid

TRAINER INTERVIEW NOTES SUMMARY FORM *(continued)*

Candidate	Strengths	Growth Areas/Issues
Candidate A *(continued)*	Psychology degree Computer literate	
Candidate B	Industry experience Soft skills experience College teaching experience (adult learners) Proficiency with PowerPoint Mentoring /coaching experience Radio, TV experience	Somewhat mechanical in answers More front-end and back-end training experience needed
Candidate C	Broad business and consulting education experience Owns own business Proficient in many software packages Help desk experience Research skills Train-the-trainer experience Soft skills—teams—experience International training experience High energy and enthusiasm Likes "needs assessment" best of training processes	No industry experience More back-end training experience needed
Candidate D	Writing/editing experience Extensive training materials development experience Facility with technical content, for example, math background/interest Research skills Company employee referral Desktop package proficiency Industry experience Associate degree and BS in Business Growth potential high	More front-end and back-end training experience needed Front-end work done by others 1 year in 3 prior jobs

In this case, candidate A has the highest weighted average of the four candidates on the criteria that were assessed by the interviewer. The order of candidates from highest to lowest weighted average is A, D, B, and C. If more than one person interviewed the candidates, which is desirable from a legal and measurement perspective, then the ratings from each interviewer should be summarized and averaged across the raters. Make sure to capture the individual rater's ratings, if a discussion is needed to reach consensus on a particular trainer candidate.

A spreadsheet program was used for these calculations. Most spreadsheet programs have built-in functions for computing weighted averages.

Note that the spread or range of the weighted averages (4.10 to 4.32) is very small. Therefore, no conclusion about the statistical significance of the differences should be drawn. Furthermore, the fact that there were only four candidates is too small a sample to generalize from to the entire population of training candidates of interest. Finally the intrinsic value in an approach such as this is that it helps make the process explicit. It doesn't blindly or objectively provide the "correct choice," but it does provide a structure that can be systematically applied and that can be audited.